MILES OF DESTRUCTION

A TRUE STORY OF OIL, GREED, LUST AND MURDER

C.J. WYNN

MILES OF DESTRUCTION

A TRUE STORY OF OIL, GREED, LUST AND MURDER

C.J. WYNN

BLACK LYON PUBLISHING, LLC

PRAISE FOR THIS BOOK

"In MILES OF DESTRUCTION, C.J. Wynn provides a detailed and thought-provoking look into the darker side of the oil boom, how money and greed impacted lives across the country, and the tireless efforts of law enforcement to bring justice. It's a must-read for those who love the true crime genre."
       —Joe Skurzewski, News Director & Anchor, KMOT-TV

"MILES OF DESTRUCTION is an exhilarating ride laying bare one of the most gut-wrenching, gruesome tales spurned by the modern oil boom. C.J. Wynn has taken a labyrinth of seemingly disconnected facts and circumstances—and two murders 800 miles apart—and woven together a heart-pounding page turner. Her brilliant storytelling will keep you on the edge of your seat until the very last page."
       —Steven B. Epstein, author of *Murder on Birchleaf Drive*, *Evil at Lake Seminole*, *Extreme Punishment*, and *Deadly Heist*

"NETFLIX, pay attention. Here's your next hit true-life crime drama mini-series. MILES OF DESTRUCTION is a gripping story that holds the reader from start to finish as C.J. Wynn reminds us that fact really is stranger than fiction. Early on you'll go from "really?" to "I want to know more" as you turn the pages and find yourself being pulled deeper and deeper into the harsh reality of a world C.J. has exposed. Each clue in the journey, seemingly unrelated to the one before or after, is carefully authenticated with astounding research and then presented for the reader's consideration. Engaging, superbly documented, and told with passion, this is one story you'll want to read. Good luck finding a place to pause and put it down."
       —Jim Huggins, New Shepherd Films award-winning filmmaker and screenwriter of *Footprints, Forgotten Heroes — The Robert Hartsock Story* and *The 211 Home;* and author of *Memoirs of an Angel*

MORE PRAISE FOR THIS BOOK

"C.J. Wynn has created a readable and captivating story about a complicated investigation into a twisted criminal enterprise. Miles of Destruction details how a team of investigators in the States of Washington and North Dakota brought down James Henrikson, a greedy, murderous conman, who had no loyalty to anyone—not to his best friend, his business associates, not even to his wife—his partner in crime, murdering two and plotting to kill the other. Henrikson's only loyalty was to money. This book reveals the skill, patience, and grit required to capture and convict a dangerous man. Kudos to that team of investigators, and to C.J. Wynn for telling their story."

—Beth Karas, former prosecutor and
Legal Analyst on Investigation Discovery's series
Curious Case Of … and *Curious Case of Natalia Grace*

"An exceptionally well-crafted and riveting true crime story—full of shady criminals, astonishing greed, and the uncompromising efforts of investigators and citizens who refused to let justice slip away. C.J. Wynn masterfully untangles a web of complicated elements, delivering a gripping, tragic narrative with clarity and compassion."

—Jonah Lantto, host of *Midwest Murder*

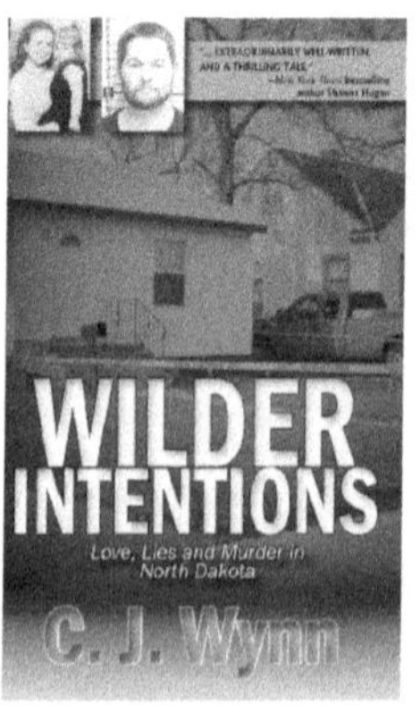

ALSO FROM THIS AUTHOR

"…EXTRAORDINARILY
WELL-WRITTEN,
AND A THRILLING TALE."

—*New York Times* bestselling
author Shanna Hogan

ANGILA WAS
STABBED 44 TIMES.
THIS WAS PERSONAL.

*For
Aine Ahmed,
Darrik Trudell, and
Mark Burbridge*

FOREWORD

Mark Burbridge
Spokane Detective (Ret.)

I've lived in Spokane, Washington, for nearly my entire life. With a population of roughly 250,000, one would probably tend to think it's generally a quiet and peaceful place to live. But I suspect most people would be stunned to learn just how much serious violence occurs in a given year.

I began my career with the Spokane Police Department in 1988, spending the first six years as a patrol officer. In 1994, I was promoted to Detective in the narcotics division—a very rewarding yet high-risk role that lasted over the next eight years. Each day brought the potential for danger, from high-speed chases to drug busts gone wrong.

Ready to face new challenges, I transitioned to the Robbery/Homicide Unit in 2002. Fourteen years earlier, as a young patrol officer, I had dealt with assaults and an occasional murder, but nothing could have prepared me for the level of devastation I encountered while investigating my first solo homicide case.

I still remember the scene in the apartment I was called to that morning. A small, 18-inch-high Christmas tree, its lights silently twinkling, sat on a coffee table. Joyful holiday music drifted softly from a nearby radio. And there, on the floor, lay two-year-old Victoria Ramon with injuries too unimaginable to describe. Standing with me in that tiny apartment, surveying the horror in front of us, were seasoned, hardened patrol officers. None of them even tried to hide their sobs.

Victoria's mother, Joan, was in the hallway outside the apartment, completely broken and emotionally destroyed. I introduced myself, then hugged the grieving mother for several minutes, until she gained some control of her emotions and was able to tell me what happened.

Joan said she and her boyfriend, Robert, had got into a violent fight. It wasn't the first time it had happened, but this time, he crossed a line that could never be undone. In some sick and twisted drug-and-alcohol fueled attempt to teach Joan a lesson, Robert had grabbed little Victoria by the ankles and beat her against the wall until she was dead.

That afternoon, I attended my first child autopsy. When a child dies from suspected violence, their autopsy is different from an adult's. During a child's autopsy, the medical examiner removes the child's eyes to check for signs of shaken baby syndrome. No one warned me about that. It took my breath away to witness this.

Like most detectives' spouses, my wife, Sue, loved hearing about my adventures and the cases I was working on. A fan of true crime novels, especially those by author Ann Rule, Sue often enjoyed offering tips and suggestions. But the one thing my wife never wanted to hear about—and what I never wanted to share with her—were cases involving dead children. Our own kids were only eight, ten and 11.

I finally drove home late that night, knowing that Sue would not be able to offer solace. Halfway up our long driveway, I stopped. The emotions were overwhelming, and I needed a moment to release them. I walked into the woods to a spot where I could see the top of the mountain from where I lived. There, I sat down and had a quiet conversation with Victoria and cried for her.

I placed a small stone next to a tree to remember her. Little did I know that stone would mark the beginning of a ritual. Eventually, there would be 24 stones under that tree, one for each child death I investigated. Seven of those deaths would be children who were murdered.

The cry of a mother who has just lost a child is something I have heard two dozen times. The deep, soul wrenching emotion in that cry is something you can never forget. To Victoria Ramon's mother, Joan: I think of you often, I hope you have found peace and are living a great life.

I left the Robbery/Homicide unit in 2016 after 14 years, having served as the lead investigator in over 40 murders, as well as hundreds of robberies and serious assaults. I also solved three cold case murders. The first time I met a family after solving a cold case, I was caught off guard by their emotional response.

The depth of their gratitude and the significance of finally having closure after so many years of unanswered questions made a lasting impression on me. It reminded me that a murder investigation is never just about the victim—it's also about the family members left behind, whose lives are forever impacted by the loss.

Before I retired for good in 2020, I frequently heard from some of those families. They would call simply to talk about their loved ones and share how much they missed them. They'd thank me for the role I played in their journey. This was the most fulfilling part of my career—knowing I had truly made a difference.

Aine Ahmed
Former Criminal Chief, Eastern District
United States Attorney's Office

I became a lawyer by accident. It wasn't something I ever planned on, but I wouldn't trade my experiences getting there for anything.

I was born in Sialkot, Pakistan, in 1971. It's a place known for two things—surgical instruments and World Cup soccer balls. My family moved to the United States when I was two, settling on the South Side of Chicago in university housing while my father pursued a Ph.D. Gunshots and sirens were just part of the background noise, and having your bike stolen or dealing with attempted break-ins was just a fact of life.

When I was nine, we moved to Greensboro, North Carolina. It was quieter and safer, but life wasn't easy. We didn't even have a hot water heater until I was 14—my mother warmed our bathwater on the stove. We were broke, but none of us really knew it. My older sister, younger brother, and I had a great childhood. My parents insisted we speak Urdu at home—the native language of Pakistan—and we all became fluent.

Education was everything in our family. My dad always said, "It's the one thing they can't take away from you." We all took that message to heart. My sister became a nationally recognized pediatric infectious disease specialist, my brother earned an MBA, and I—after a long and unexpected odyssey—became a lawyer.

I joined the Army and served in Iraq. I lived with fellow grunts—"Joes," as we called ourselves—crammed four to a tent that smelled like ass and feet. I had heated arguments with a CIA operative. A fellow captain and I snuck out of the wire to dine with Iraqi contractors. We'd return to the base late at night, our hands raised, rifles pointed at us, making excuses for where we'd been.

One time, my convoy was sent to a safe house where Uday and Qusay Hussein had been hiding. We found millions of dollars in three massive safes. Sitting in our armored Humvee afterward, my sergeant turned to me and asked, "When we found that money, did you think about killing me?"

I said, "Yes. But I would have had to kill everyone else, too, and getting it over the border would've been a pain."

He laughed. "Did all of that really go through your mind?"

"Yes."

"Me, too," he admitted.

I went to Wake Forest and worked constantly to pay for school—mornings at a golf course, evenings at a department store. I considered joining the CIA, which recruited me for the Clandestine Division, but my parents shut that down. Instead, I pursued a master's and was later accepted into George Washington's Ph.D. program—but I couldn't afford it.

My dad said, "I want you to be comfortable in life, and following my path won't get you there." So, I applied to law school instead.

I was lucky to get into the U.S. Attorney's Office in 2001. Hiring was all about who you knew, and I didn't know anyone. I had more jury trial experience than most of my colleagues, but connections always trumped merit. When I became Criminal Chief, I tried to change that culture, but higher-ups always quashed my hiring decisions. Favors had to be paid, and I had no control over that.

Then came the Carlile case.

I practically had to beg people in my office to take it. The only person who agreed was Scott Jones—a U.S. Attorney recently transferred from California. Truth be told, I think he took it because he had nothing better to do. He wasn't married and had no real ties in Spokane yet. But he was the perfect addition—brazen, smart, and relentless.

I felt terrible that Doug Carlile was murdered. He had a beautiful family and a devoted wife who loved and adored him. But what really shook me to the core was Kristopher "K.C." Clarke. I kept a photo of him in my desk drawer, and I must have looked at it a thousand times. A kid who hadn't even lived yet—his whole future snuffed out in the blink of an eye for no good reason. That stayed with me.

I trusted our team—FBI Agent Eric Barker, Detective Mark Burbridge, and DHS Agent Darrik Trudell. We gelled, and we were relentless. They never said no. Barker handled forensics. Burbridge and Trudell worked with the witnesses. Without them, this case would have never moved forward.

Justice was served. But the journey there? Well, that road was paved with hard-earned lessons and defining moments—each one shaping me into the lawyer I never planned to be.

Darrik Trudell
Homeland Security Investigations Special Agent

Growing up, I never aspired for a career in law enforcement.

I really didn't know much about being a cop other than what was portrayed in movies and what I saw in the news. From the skewed perspective I had, it wasn't a life that interested me. I'm not a very adventurous person, nor have I ever wished for a life fueled by adrenaline. Frankly, I prefer a very risk-averse existence—perhaps one might even consider me to be boring and pragmatic—but I am most comfortable and happy when spending time with my friends and family.

No one was more surprised than I that I ended up in law enforcement. Oftentimes, the job is rather boring. The amount of adventure is usually determined by where you work and what your assignment is. There is plenty of opportunity for door-kickers to find their adrenaline rush, but a career as an investigator is mostly done in an interview room, behind a computer screen, or sitting in a car.

More often than not, we're just waiting for something to happen. The excitement of chasing bad guys is what draws many people to the job, but I believe it's the people you work with who keep you in it.

I still remember the day before graduating from the North Dakota Police Academy. A retired officer addressed our class and our families, speaking at length about the hardships of the job and the profound mental toll this career can take—not only on the officer but also on their loved ones.

He explained that most law enforcement marriages end in divorce, and that at some point our kids would hate us. Furthermore, he warned that half of us would likely become alcoholics (the other half already were) and cautioned our families about the significantly increased risk of suicide that comes with a career in law enforcement. He ended his "encouraging" remarks with some profound advice: "Don't become bitter."

I remember thinking, *This is the worst motivational speaker ever, and what terrible advice!* He made the job sound miserable. How could anyone not be bitter?

Twenty years later, I understand and appreciate his honesty. He wasn't wrong about the challenges that come with this career. Telling people the truth, not what they want to hear, is hard for most, and the truth is, this job isn't for everyone. But challenges exist in every profession and aspect of life. Focusing on the negatives will grind you down and make you miserable. I've consciously chosen not to do that.

I am thankful every day for the people I get to work with and the work we get to do. Throughout my career, I have been surrounded by good people who dedicate their lives to making others' lives better and ensuring the worst among us are brought to justice.

I've never viewed investigating crimes committed against victims as a burden or something traumatic for me or the other investigators. To think of it that way would be selfish. It's impossible not to feel empathy and sadness for the victims and their families. Seeing people endure the pain and loss of their loved ones is emotional. But during those times of insufferable hurt, I've also seen the incredible resolve and strength human beings are capable of.

The commitment to justice for K.C. Clarke, Doug Carlile, and their families displayed by everyone involved in this investigation reflects what extraordinary people all of you are. The culture of law enforcement and our justice system is built on the foundations of loyalty, duty, honor, integrity, and courage. These core values are in direct contrast to the way the cowards who committed these crimes lived their lives.

If I am ever honored with the opportunity to stand before a Police Academy class and speak about this job, I will share the good things I've had the privilege of witnessing: the compassion of Mark Burbridge, the incredible judgement of Eric Barker, Tom Irvin's unrelenting determination, Randy Helderop's loyalty, the discipline of Brian Cestnik, the selflessness of Steve Gutknecht, the wisdom of Gary Delorme, the brilliant legal mind of Scott Jones, and the resolve and dedication of Aine Ahmed.

Because of what these men—and many others—stand for and are willing to do, miserable, lesser men are in prison. This job is about having the opportunity to help and serve others. I can't imagine finding the same satisfaction or fulfillment doing anything else with my life.

I've been blessed to do this work surrounded by the best

people—servant leaders and peacemakers.

PART I

CHAPTER 1

The White Van

Rockwood is one of the oldest neighborhoods in all of Spokane, Washington. Perched on a winding hillside and encapsulated by majestic evergreens, it is conveniently located within a few blocks of the bustling Interstate 90—the longest highway in the United States, stretching approximately 3,000 miles from Seattle to Boston. Rockwood's street names, such as Overbluff, Upper Terrace, Highland, and Woodcliff, are constant reminders of the area's hilly terrain.

The charming enclave boasts a diverse array of homes, ranging from million-dollar Queen Anne mansions to cozy bungalows and cottages. The central boulevards that divide the neighborhood's meandering street design are lined with towering maple, oak, and ash trees. In fall and winter, brilliantly red, yellow, and orange leaves pile up in muddy yards and stick to the roads in the region's notoriously damp climate. Come summer, brown, brittle grass gives way to vibrantly green, lush lawns. The sounds of family barbecues and children splashing in in-ground pools echo through the community on steamy afternoons.

It is hard to fathom that the darkest and seediest underbelly of Spokane is not far away from Rockwood's quaint and serene atmosphere. But just a few miles down I-90 is downtown Spokane, where the homeless roam the sidewalks, gather in gas station parking lots, sleep on grassy boulevards by day, and eventually find a pillow to lay their head at one of the several available homeless shelters at night.

Sacred Heart Medical Center sits atop another hillside, casting an almost ominous gaze over the city below. The bustling hospital is a constant destination for first responders, who race day and night with screaming sirens and flashing lights to its emergency room, transporting victims of drug overdoses, domestic violence, and street crimes in urgent need of care.

The jolting sounds of the police and emergency vehicles rarely reach the streets of Rockwood, but on the night of December 15, 2013, residents on the normally tranquil South Garfield Road would be plunged into a chaos that no one could have imagined.

• • •

Jamie Roberts, petite with shoulder-length strawberry blonde hair, had just moved to Rockwood in April of 2013, when she and her husband Brett purchased their charming three-bedroom, three-bath brick Tudor home on South Garfield Road. Brett and Jamie each had demanding jobs that intersected with Spokane's dark side on a near-daily basis—she as an emergency-room nurse, he as a fireman and first responder with Fire Station #3. They were raising a 20-month-old son and would soon be expecting a second child.

On their side of Garfield, it was mostly young families living in bungalows and ranch style homes with one-and-a-half-car garages. The architectural juxtaposition across the street, however, was stark. It was where larger homes were situated several yards back from the road, often inhabited by what Jamie thought of as the "snooty," older residents of the neighborhood. Those properties were 5,000-square-foot mansions with wrought-iron gated driveways, four-car garages, arched entryways, wine cellars, and professionally manicured yards.

For the most part, the seemingly mismatched sets of neighbors on each side of the street kept to themselves. They would exchange pleasantries with one another as appropriate, while still maintaining a level of privacy. There were rarely any spats or disagreements between households, and in general, everyone felt safe and secure in their surroundings. Crime, especially those of a violent nature, was almost non-existent in this part of Spokane. So rare, in fact, that it was not uncommon for residents to leave their doors and windows unlocked at night.

Just a few weeks shy of Christmas that year, it did not matter which side of Garfield Road one lived, as the excitement of the holiday season was ubiquitous. Bright lights and festive decorations adorned houses of all shapes and sizes, and elegantly trimmed Christmas trees beckoned from picture windows up and down the road.

On Sunday, December 15, Jamie Roberts and her toddler spent the latter part of their afternoon shopping for toys at the local ShopKo in preparation for an upcoming Toys for Tots event. Her husband Brett was in the middle of a shift at the fire station and was not expected back home until the next day.

The sky was already dark at 5:45 p.m. when Jamie's SUV turned onto Garfield Road, then headed north toward her house. The late afternoon had brought with it a steady rain shower, and the wet streets now glistened under the glow of moonlight and dim streetlamps. Tired from a long afternoon of shopping, Jamie was looking forward to fixing dinner and getting her son to bed early.

As she approached her driveway, Jamie noticed a long, white work van parked on the curb directly in front of her house. Although she would later find it hard to explain, the sight of the van made her instantly uneasy; an instinctive shiver crept up her spine, alerting her that something was amiss. The van did not belong there, she knew that for certain. In Rockwood—and particularly on Garfield Road—people parked their vehicles in their driveways or garages. The streets were too narrow to accommodate parked vehicles.

Why on earth would a work van be parked on the street, in front of my house, on a Sunday evening?

Jamie continued driving north and pulled into a neighbor's driveway a few houses down. Her focus remained on the van, silently willing it to just drive away. When it stayed put for several additional minutes, Jamie fished her cell phone out of her purse and called her husband. Since Brett was just a few blocks away at Fire Station #3, Jamie asked if he would mind terribly coming home to check things out.

Brett knew that Jamie would be the last person to make such a request based on an irrational fear or reaction. His wife was tough. She worked in a highly trafficked emergency room and had dealt with plenty of dangerous people and situations. If something spooked Jamie, it was worth the two-minute drive to check it out for himself.

While on his way home, Brett notified Crime Check—a local call center that partners with 911 dispatch to support emergency calls—that something might be going on at his residence and requested the operator to be on standby if needed. At 5:55 p.m., the headlights on the van switched on and it slowly pulled away from the curb, heading south on Garfield. Impulsively, the young mother decided to follow it.

"I just knew something was wrong," Jamie would later explain. "When I first saw it, I don't think it was even running. Then, all of a sudden, it started moving, and I guess I needed to figure out where it was going. I was hoping it was just someone who had gotten lost and would leave the area once it found its way."

As she drove, Jamie took mental notes of as many details as she could make out, though the dimly lit streets offered little assistance. Most notably was the absence of a rear license plate. Instead, a piece of paper adorned one of the rear windows, resembling the temporary "plates" that newly purchased vehicles must display until the arrival of official state-issued plates. She continued to follow from a distance as the van turned onto 27th Avenue, drove a few blocks, and turned north onto Hatch.

"When it got back to 25th Avenue, it stopped and sat there for several seconds. I doubt whomever it was even realized I was following them. But then it turned back east on 25th Avenue and then back south on Garfield. As it went by my house again, it drove very slowly. But then it left, and I didn't see it again."

As soon as she felt reasonably confident that the van was gone, Jamie finally pulled into her own driveway. Still uneasy, she inspected all of her doors and windows from the outside, looking for signs of a possible break-in. Her husband arrived a few moments later, and the two checked every room inside the house to ease Jamie's concern of a possible intruder. Finding the house empty, Brett kissed his wife before leaving to return to the firehouse and told her to immediately call 911 if anything else startled her.

At 6:46 p.m., as Jamie was clearing away dinner dishes, she peered outside her dining room window and gasped when she saw the van was back. Only this time, it was parked on the opposite side of Garfield. She scrambled to get her son out of his highchair and away from the window. Then, just as her husband had instructed, she called 911.

Her voice trembled as she spoke to the dispatcher. "Hi, um, I called because there was a suspicious vehicle in front of my house about 30 minutes ago. And now they just came back, and it's just sitting there, and I'm really freaked out. Maybe I'm just being paranoid, but it's really bizarre that a van like that would be in this neighborhood."

To Jamie's chagrin, however, the dispatcher didn't seem to share her concern, making it clear to her he wasn't in any hurry to send someone to check it out. Frustrated, she hung up and called her husband.

"I told him I wanted him to come home and help me get the shotgun out of the safe," she would later recall. "I was so scared at that point, and I could not remember the damn combination to the lock."

Brett recruited two fellow firemen, Dan Wilson and Steve McMullen, and the three men jumped in one of the firetrucks and headed toward the Robertses' house with lights flashing and siren blaring. Hopefully, they reasoned, if the person driving the van was up to something nefarious, the siren would deter him. Perhaps the tactic had worked, because by the time they got to Garfield Road, the white van had once again vanished.

Brett, Jamie, Steve, and Dan stood outside in the front

yard, bewildered. It was strange that the van was in the neighborhood in the first place, to be sure, but it was even more disconcerting that it kept coming back and parking in front of Brett and Jamie's house.

Although the description of the van was straightforward enough—a long white work van, no license plates—Jamie had never gotten a glimpse of the driver, nor did she have any idea if there were passengers. There was nothing that could calm her nerves at that point, and Brett made the decision to stay with his wife and son for the remainder of the evening.

At 7:00 p.m., as Brett thanked his co-workers for their help and understanding, Jamie turned to go back inside the house. Just as she reached the front door, six loud pops rippled through the cold night air, one right after the other.

In that instant, a silently shared realization swept over all four individuals—although it was not clear from what direction the ear-piercing bangs had come from, there was no doubt that what they had just heard was the unmistakable sound of gunshots. Jamie, Brett, Steve, and Dan stood frozen in place, not sure where to move, scared that more shots would follow. But instead of the anticipated cacophony, an unsettling stillness settled over Garfield Road.

The silence and tension were broken when, at 7:06 p.m., the radio in Dan Wilson's hand chirped, relaying a call for emergency responders to attend to a possible gunshot victim at 2505 South Garfield Road.

A mere 200 feet across the street from where three first responders and one terrified wife stood.

CHAPTER 2

We Were All Going To Be Rich

Elberta Carlile scrambled around her house, calling for her husband Douglas to get ready. They were going to be late. It was not unusual for the Carliles to be running behind, everyone knew, but tonight, December 15, 2013, was special—they were attending an early Christmas celebration at their church. The party was scheduled to begin promptly at 5:00 p.m. and it was already 4:45 p.m. They had at least a 15-minute drive ahead of them, which could be extended depending on late Sunday afternoon traffic.

The Carliles had lost track of time, Doug absorbed in business paperwork as he prepared for a meeting the next day, while Elberta listened to Christmas music and studied Bible passages from the morning's church service.

The 63-year-old husband, pleasantly plump with wavy blonde hair and bright blue eyes, and his bride, with a full figure and flowing dark hair, had already powered through a busy weekend. Friends and family had organized a party for Elberta's 61st birthday the night before, which had lasted until the late evening hours. They had then risen early Sunday morning to attend church, something they never missed, rain or shine. Though their devout faith had kept their marriage strong for decades, it had not always been that way.

Doug and Elberta had been teenage sweethearts, marrying in 1971 when he was 21 and she 19, settling at first in a small town in Oregon. They welcomed their first child, a daughter they named MeLainee, about a year later. MeLainee was soon followed by brothers Seth, Shane, Skyler, Shad, and then finally the baby of the family, another daughter named MeLody.

Early on in their marriage, Elberta had begun exploring a deeper understanding of religion, and gradually forged a powerful connection with God. It was a faith that she would rely on and cling to in every aspect of her life, even much later on, during unforeseen moments of profound despair.

But while Elberta's convictions only grew stronger, Doug's religious views became more ambivalent. It was a bridge that continued to divide them until the fissures in their marriage became too much for Elberta to bear.

"The closer I got to the Lord, the further we came apart," Elberta reflected years later. "So, I did something extreme. We had four kids at the time, and I packed all of them up and left Doug without him even knowing."

With no money or job, Elberta loaded up her young brood and headed for Seattle. Doug, meanwhile, was grief-stricken. As the weeks passed with no sign of Bertie—his affectionate nickname for his wife—returning with their children, Doug fell into a deep hole of unbearable depression. It was during this time that Doug, an avid collector of rifles, found himself contemplating a dire choice, and one evening, he resolved to turn one of those guns on himself. However, what transpired instead was later recounted by Doug as nothing short of extraordinary.

"Doug told me he was sitting on the floor of our bedroom with a shotgun in his hand. He was ready to kill himself," Elberta said. "Doug said he heard two bellowing voices over him. The first one was a horrid voice, that yelled, 'He's mine!' And then a second voice, this one thunderous and authoritative, saying, 'No, he's not! He belongs to me!'"

Doug described feeling the enormous strength of two arms lifting him off of the floor and laying him down on the bed. To him, there existed no plausible explanation other than the undeniable intervention of a higher power, and it was evident to Doug that God's own hands had rescued him.

It was the precise moment that the lovingly devoted husband vowed to begin his own journey discovering faith, and the catalyst for he and Elberta reuniting.

•••

With an official end to their brief separation, the Carliles embarked on a new life in Seattle. While Elberta raised their children, Doug focused on his long-time goal of becoming a successful entrepreneur. The couple also became deeply involved with the Prosperity Gospel—a branch of Christianity that believes God rewards true belief with financial success.

Doug dreamed of owning his own business and had grandiose visions of turning it into a multi-million-dollar empire. One he could someday pass onto his children and grandchildren and retire to a life of luxury with his beloved Bertie.

With urban development ramping up in the northwestern corner of the country, Doug's specific focus was on construction and excavation. In 1983, he incorporated his first company and for almost a decade the business thrived, making Doug and Elberta very wealthy. They purchased a large family home in Seattle and also acquired farmland in Moses Lake, Washington—where they planned to eventually build a dream house to accommodate large family gatherings with their adult children and what they hoped would be dozens of grandchildren.

Over the years, Doug cultivated relationships with several professionals in Oregon and Washington. Initially, he earned a reputation as an honest and hardworking entrepreneur—someone people could trust and prefer to do business with. Doug always talked a good game and had fantastical ideas that made green dollar signs dance around in the eyes of anyone willing to listen.

"My dad could sell anything to anyone," boasted MeLainee, Doug's eldest daughter.

While that sentiment may have been true, Doug's reputation soon devolved into that of a snake oil salesman. Although he could supposedly "sell anything to anyone," it seemed

Doug had a consistent inability to follow through on much of what he promised. Contracts were broken. Money was lost. Trust was destroyed. Disagreements between business owners and contractors occurred over the years, and word spread that it was not a smart move to get involved in any financial dealings or projects with Doug Carlile. Along the west coastline of Washington anyway, Doug became a pariah in the business world.

Before long, Doug and Elberta received notice from the Internal Revenue Service that their business was in some fairly big trouble—the company owed almost a million dollars in back taxes. In an instant, the Carliles's upper-middle class lifestyle came to a screeching halt. The couple was forced to sell their big house in the city, and moved to their property in Moses Lake where they lived in a double-wide trailer until they were able to stabilize their financial situation. It was a far cry from the glorious mansion they had once envisioned being their family's oasis.

"It took us years to pay that off," Elberta later noted, despondently. "We went back and forth with the IRS and were able to come to a settlement. But we paid off the amount. Every penny."

Over the next several years, Doug would start and eventually dissolve a handful of new excavation and construction ventures. Because of their financial woes and problems with the IRS, all of the businesses were listed under someone else's name—in most cases, one of their adult children.

"Doug still completely operated all of the business negotiations and things," Elberta would later explain. "But we just couldn't put any of the businesses in our names because of the IRS."

Ever her husband's champion, Elberta clung to the conviction that her beloved was a skilled entrepreneur who always conducted himself with honesty and integrity. Despite their serious financial problems and unfavorable murmurs circulating within the business community, she remained steadfast in her belief that true success would eventually find its way to them.

"Everyone loved Doug," she recalled lovingly. "People always wanted to be in business with him. Doug loved people. He was a mentor. He believed in giving people a second chance."

Perhaps that was because of his own desire to continue giving himself multiple chances. But it seemed that each time he did, nothing ever reached the level that he hoped for, and eventually, he picked up and moved on to the next thing.

•••

In 2011, Doug and Elberta discovered an incredible deal on a 5,200-square-foot, six-bedroom mansion at 2505 South Garfield Road in the Rockwood neighborhood of Spokane. At one time, the home had been valued at almost a million dollars. But in the aftermath of the 2008 housing market bust, the value had fallen to a mere $257,000.

The couple managed to scrape together financial backing to purchase the home, believing that even if they were not quite able to build the dream home they had once imagined, this would do in the meantime. It had plenty of space to welcome what would eventually be more than two dozen grandchildren.

By this time, the Carlile children were well into their adulthood, and a few of them were launching their own ventures in the excavation industry across Washington state. With Doug's guidance, his sons' and daughters' new businesses were achieving moderate financial success.

Doug and Elberta also became active members in a church, where they would make many new friends. Despite a focus on their new community, they had maintained contact with a former employee named Tim Scott.

Several months earlier, Scott had been communicating that he was currently working for a trucking company in North Dakota. According to Scott, there was a significant "oil boom" happening and he was making a lot of money.

"There's a potential to make millions of dollars," Scott assured the Carliles. "It will take some time, a significant investment, and the right people, but it can be done."

It was a dangling carrot that Doug Carlile simply could not resist. Without much forethought, he poured every last remaining ounce of hopeful energy, and money, into this new venture. This, he believed, was finally going to be *it*.

"My dad said we were all going to be rich!" MeLainee recalled later of the excitement her father displayed when he began talking about his new opportunity.

And so it was, on the night of December 15, 2013, that Doug had become so engrossed in reading dozens of pages of business proposal materials, he had completely lost track of time, and now Bertie was annoyed that he was not ready to go to the church celebration.

Always making it his mission to stay in his wife's good graces, Doug adjusted his wire-rimmed glasses and left all of the paperwork lying haphazardly on his desk and across his laptop. He hurried outside to the driveway to open the passenger side door of his new Ford pickup truck for his Bertie, then rounded the front of the truck to climb behind the steering wheel.

Doug backed down the long driveway, but abruptly tapped on the brake pedal, realizing he had forgotten to close and lock the wrought-iron gate at the side entrance. Because they were in a rush, Elberta told him not to bother. They would be sure to lock it when they returned home and retired for the night.

As they sped south on Garfield Road, Elberta glanced out the window to her right and silently noted to herself how very odd it was to see a long, white work van parked against the curb in front of the house owned by their new neighbors, Brett and Jamie Roberts. Still nervous they would be late for the party, Elberta pushed the van right back out of her thoughts.

CHAPTER 3

He Just Came Out Of Nowhere

Though the Christmas celebration at All Nations Christian Center had been joyous, Doug and Elberta Carlile were thoroughly exhausted as they drove across Spokane's rain-soaked streets on their way back home. Doug still planned to finish reviewing paperwork to prepare for an important business meeting the next day, but Elberta was looking forward to a long, hot soak in the tub, and more Bible reading before bed.

As they approached their house on Garfield Road shortly before 7:00 p.m., Elberta sighed heavily as she realized that in their haste while leaving earlier, she and Doug had left virtually every light on inside. They burned yellow through numerous windows on both the first and second levels, illuminating the front yard. Tall trees barren of their leaves surrounding the yard cast eerie shadow patterns across the wintered brown grass.

Doug slowly maneuvered his blue Ford F-250 up the narrow driveway into a circular parking area in front of the detached four-car garage. He parked alongside Elberta's new white Lexus SUV. The couple exited the vehicle, breathing in the fresh smell of rain and falling leaves. While Elberta made her way to the back door of the house, Doug descended down the driveway to close and lock the wrought-iron entrance gate he had forgotten to close hours earlier. Because Elberta didn't feel like digging through her purse for her keys, she reached for the spare key hidden atop the ledge of the door.

When she walked inside the house, she realized that not only were the lights on, but she had also left their Bose stereo playing. Propped on top of a counter in the corner of the kitchen, it was tuned to a Christian music station. During the month of December, the station exclusively played traditional and modern holiday themed music.

The Carliles loved Christmas. Their youngest daughter, MeLody, was born on December 24—a child Elberta considered a precious Christmas gift. Elberta had decorated the interior of the house with strings of colorful lights. A fat evergreen tree adorned with golden doves and snowflakes stood in the front solarium for the neighborhood to admire from the street. Soon, there would be mounds of presents underneath the tree and the aroma of baked Christmas goodies would filter into each room. Doug and Elberta's grandchildren would wake on Christmas morning and there would eventually be piles of wrapping paper and bows strewn across the hardwood floors.

Instead of turning off the radio, Elberta pivoted to her right and ascended the back stairway leading to the second-floor master bedroom suite. Before she could reach the top of the staircase, however, she heard the murmuring of voices coming from the kitchen below.

"Doug?" she called out. "Is someone here?" At first, she thought perhaps one of their four sons had come to pay a visit.

"Elberta, don't come down here!" Doug shouted back. There was a fear in his voice she had never heard before. Then, seemingly to someone else, Doug said softly, "Hey, it's okay. It's okay."

"Back off!" came the booming voice of another male. A voice Elberta did not recognize.

Ignoring her husband's warning, Elberta slowly inched her way back down the stairs toward the kitchen.

"You don't have to do this!" Doug pleaded, his voice quavering.

When Elberta reached the bottom of the staircase, she carefully peered around the corner and saw a man standing next to the breakfast nook just a few feet inside the back entryway. He was wearing all black including a black ski mask that covered his face. To her chagrin, Doug had retreated deeper into the kitchen, making it so Elberta could no longer see him from her vantage point.

To her horror, Elberta then noticed that the man in black was holding a gun pointed in the direction of where she knew her husband was standing. She froze in fear, her heart thumping loudly in her chest. Who was this person? Why was he inside her home, with a gun?

"It was like he just came from out of nowhere," Elberta recalled.

The unknown intruder turned his head toward Elberta in a deliberate motion, meeting her gaze momentarily before then swiftly redirecting his attention toward Doug.

"Please don't do this," Elberta heard Doug whimper.

Elberta's breath caught in her throat as she felt her entire body go numb. She desperately tried to scamper backward up the stairs, gripping the railing to assist in pulling herself along.

As she reached the landing atop the staircase, six gunshots rang out in quick succession. The loud bangs ricocheted off the walls throughout the house, piercing like a hot knife through her eardrums.

Her head throbbing from the ringing in her ears, Elberta hoisted herself off the floor and sprinted down the hallway to an open bedroom. She ducked into a closet and quietly closed the door. Miraculously, her cellphone was still in her pocket. At 7:02 p.m., her trembling hands fumbled to retrieve it and dial 911 for help.

"Quick!" Elberta whispered loudly into the phone before the 911 operator could even finish her opening salutations. "2505 South Garfield. A man just came into our house and shot my husband, I think. Oh my God!"

"Slower," the 911 operator robotically instructed. "What are the numbers?"

"2-5-0-5 South Garfield," Elberta hissed. "If he hears me, he's going to shoot me too!"

Though the operator was just doing her job by asking clarifying questions, to Elberta, each passing second felt like a maddening delay, preventing help from reaching her in time.

"Oh my God!" Elberta shrieked again, talking over the 911 operator's questions. "Someone just shot my husband, I think. I worry he is going to find me. I'm hiding in an upstairs closet!"

"Okay, just stay on the line for me, okay?"

"Nooooo!" Elberta wailed. "Please, oh please, please just hurry! He fired shots. Six shots. He had a gun and was dressed in all black!"

Even in her panic, Elberta was trying to make sure she offered a description of the man who had shot her husband—ostensibly in the event that the masked man found and shot her too before police could arrive.

"Just stay on the line," the operator repeated.

"I can't keep talking. He'll hear me and find me. Just get here. Please!"

The police arrived at 2505 South Garfield Road at 7:10 p.m.—almost eight minutes after Elberta first connected with the 911 operator. Fortunately, during those excruciating minutes that felt more like hours, the man in black had not ventured upstairs to find her.

But neither had Doug.

CHAPTER 4

You Never Know When The Call Might Come In

Spokane Detective Mark Burbridge woke before the sun came up on the morning of Sunday, December 15, 2013. His beloved football team, the Seattle Seahawks, were scheduled to play against the New York Giants that day. Because the game was being played 2,568 miles away in the Giants' home stadium in New Jersey at 1:00 p.m. Eastern Time, Seahawks fans in Washington would be tuning in to catch pre-game coverage and predictions from professional sportscasters well before 10:00 a.m.

It was week 15 of the NFL season. With just two weeks to go until the playoffs began, the Seahawks were sitting atop the NFC Conference with a record of 11 wins and two losses, while the New York Giants were struggling with only five wins and eight losses. For Seahawks fans, this week's game had all the makings of a blowout, enhancing the team's chances of being the number one seed in the playoffs.

For Mark, every Sunday the Seahawks played was cause for celebration. It was tradition for him and his wife, Sue, to host friends and family members at their home to watch the action on the gridiron. Far from the bustle of city life, the Burbridge's quaint bungalow was nestled among towering rows of evergreen trees, concealed in the shadows of Mica Peak—the southernmost tip of the Selkirk Mountain Range, cresting a breathtaking 5,205 feet above sea level.

It was customary, in fact required on these football get-together occasions, for guests to arrive at the Burbridge's home sporting their favorite Seahawks jerseys. On this morning, Mark's jersey bore the name "Dangeruss"—the nickname the team's quarterback at the time, Russell Wilson, had bestowed on himself. During the playoffs the prior year, the Seahawks had lost a nail-biting divisional game against the Atlanta Falcons, abruptly dashing hometown fans' hopes for a Super Bowl. But Mark had been a Seahawks fan since the team's very first game in 1976—when he was just 14—and was supremely confident that 2013 was their year.

• • •

Mark was born in 1962 in the small town of Great Falls, Montana—a state he loved, and would still travel to decades later for hunting in the winter and golf in the summer. His upbringing had not been without its challenges. His father had numerous brushes with the law; his mother struggled with addiction. His parents' relationship could not withstand the ups and downs and they eventually separated, with Mark becoming estranged from his father, and helplessly watching as his mother's addictions soon grew more severe.

While two of his siblings eventually succumbed to the same cycles of addiction and law-breaking as their parents, for Mark, the experiences of his childhood and teen years fostered a steely resolve within himself to be on the opposite end of the spectrum. He pursued what would eventually turn into a lifelong career in law enforcement. But some of his difficult childhood memories would haunt him well into his adult life.

In 1974, Mark's family relocated to Wenatchee, Washington, a three-hour drive from Spokane. In high school, Mark met Sue, a pretty redhead with a warm and bubbly personality that would rival Mark's own stoic disposition. The couple married in 1984 and both graduated from Eastern Washington University in the spring of 1985. Over the next few years, Mark and Sue would expand their family by welcoming three children—a son and two daughters.

In 1988, Mark was hired by the City of Spokane as an entry level police officer. Though he loved being out in his cruiser, interacting with the community, he craved the potential for in-depth investigative work. Putting the pieces of complex puzzles together, solving mysteries, and catching the bad guys was what made him jump in feet first every time a new case came his way.

His superiors in law enforcement recognized his potential early on and promoted him to detective in 1994. Over the next three decades, he would become one of the most revered detectives in Spokane Police Department history.

Mark spent his first seven years as a detective with the Special Investigations Unit and SWAT, largely focusing on drug-related crimes. Spokane had become increasingly infiltrated with gang activity, and illegal drug smuggling and distribution had surged.

Years later, Mark was still proud to share photos he had kept of the large piles of both real and counterfeit cash, as well as containers and bundles of illegal substances he and his team had seized in their many sting operations.

"Working in narcotics was definitely the most rewarding time in my career, but it was also the most dangerous," he reflected.

When the opportunity to transition to the homicide division presented itself, Mark found himself in a conflicting state. While it made logical sense, he wasn't necessarily brimming with joy about the change. Mark had found genuine fulfillment in his work within the narcotics division, but with a wife and three young children at home, he had to weigh the impact on his family.

What he may not have anticipated, however, was that despite the comparatively lower danger level to his physical well-being in this new role, the emotional weight of being a homicide detective had the capacity to inflict equally devastating consequences.

Above all, and what would become the dominant, driving force behind every homicide case Mark worked on, was the burning desire to find answers, justice, and a level of solace for crime victims. With his kind green eyes, boyish smirk, and sincere empathy, Mark was someone people trusted.

As much as he was a friend—and sometimes counselor—to victims and their families, Mark was extremely private with his own personal life. He let very few people into his realm. When his retirement came almost 30 years after his initial promotion to detective, it would become office fodder to discuss how no one was ever allowed to "hug" Mark Burbridge.

When it came to handling suspects, Mark was a force to be reckoned with. Some even used the term "pit bull" to describe his steely persona, but there were never any complaints from Mark if others viewed him as tough as nails. His patience for timewasters was scant, driven by an intense determination and a deeply personal investment in his cases.

Mark had a healthy level of skepticism about every person he spoke with—both in his personal life, and during his investigations. He never took anyone's word at initial face value and was quick to discern sincerity from deception. Though his lack of trust in others contributed to a limited social circle, this characteristic made him a skillful interrogator, with a unique ability to leverage varying approaches to garner confessions and admissions.

Having once been a passionate weightlifter, Mark was a big guy with broad shoulders and a barrel chest, which was intimidating enough on its own. When he positioned himself in a way that would bring him up close and personal to his subjects, they had nowhere else to look but dead-straight into Mark's eyes.

Conversely, as soon as suspects would start to show cracks in their initial stories or denials—which he was most often able to get them to do—Mark could instantly shift gears and become a sympathetic and understanding listener even to those who may have committed the most heinous of crimes.

But no matter how strong-willed Mark's outward demeanor appeared, even he couldn't always ignore or conceal the personal toll inflicted by certain cases.

The one person Mark depended on to share the details of some of his most horrific cases and frightening experiences was his wife, Sue. She was the calming presence that offered balance in his otherwise stressful work life. She would listen patiently and with empathy and even offer helpful thoughts and guidance.

But the subject that Mark never discussed with Sue—with anyone, for that matter—were cases involving the death of children. For those, no one could ease the deep pain and burning anger Mark grappled with. He found them agonizing to the point of being debilitating.

"I never wanted to talk about those cases with Sue," the detective recalled. "I didn't want her to have to think about them. So, whenever they happened, I would drive home from work, and I'd stop at an area of forest a few yards off of the winding gravel road that leads to our house.

"One day, I decided to start compiling rocks and branches, and put together a makeshift memorial. I would add a rock to it each time I worked on another case with a child death, whether it was a murder or an accident. I've never been a religious man, but I would sit down by that rock pile and I'd talk everything out. I don't know who was listening, but I'd just talk until I felt good enough to go home."

●●●

By the time the Seattle Seahawks trounced the New York Giants 23-0 that Sunday morning, Mark was in his twelfth year as a homicide detective with the SPD. The family and friends celebrating at the Burbridge house cheered loudly while scarfing down the pancakes, bacon, and eggs their hosts had prepared. As the on-call detective that weekend, Mark declined an invitation for extended afternoon celebrations, opting instead to settle into his favorite recliner for the Sunday night football game.

"During an on-call weekend, I try to get to bed early," Mark explained. "You never know when the call will come, and then you're gone from home for two or three days."

That call came shortly before 8:00 p.m. from Sgt. Mark Griffiths. The sergeant relayed that there had been a shooting in Spokane's South Hill, the ritzy part of town. Police officers were already on the scene. The details were scant at that point, but what they knew so far was the following:

There was one victim—a male, age 63. Shot multiple times.

The only known witness was the victim's wife who had been the one to call 911.

The witness was distraught to the point of inconsolable.

There were immediate red flags raised about her demeanor.

The witness was being transported to the Spokane Police Department for questioning.

Mark would be assigned and immediately assume the role of lead detective on the case.

He would be the one to meet Elberta Carlile firsthand.

As straightforward as it may have seemed at first, Mark Burbridge would soon find that this was going to be far from an open-and-shut case.

"The murder of Doug Carlile was the most unique homicide case I ever investigated," he later remarked.

But he would solve it, as he always did.

In the midst of it all, the Seattle Seahawks would go on to win the Super Bowl that season—a long-awaited championship that the team's biggest fan would have no time to celebrate.

CHAPTER 5

His Skin Was Ashen Gray

By 7:15 p.m. on Sunday, December 15, 2013, the Rockwood neighborhood in Spokane was swarming with police cars and emergency vehicles. What was once a peaceful evening soon turned into a scene of chaos with bright flashing lights illuminating yards and the scream of loud sirens reverberating off of living room windows. More than a dozen police officers descended onto the 25th block of South Garfield Road, many of them positioning their cruisers to block off access to side streets. Eventually, almost the entire street would be cordoned off with yellow crime scene tape.

The first officers to arrive at 2505 South Garfield Road entered through the same back door that Doug and Elberta Carlie had walked through 15 minutes prior, which was still standing wide open. The door did not appear to be damaged in any way, which was a sign for the officers that the intruder had not used force to enter the home. Inside, 63-year-old Doug was on his back, completely still on the kitchen floor, approximately ten feet from the open back entryway.

"He was lying on the floor in a pool of blood," Sgt. Rob Boothe, the first officer to enter the home, observed. "His skin was ashen gray, his pupils were unresponsive, and I did not feel a pulse."

With his gun drawn, Boothe took the lead in the group of officers as they worked quickly to secure the first and second levels of the home. When he was confident the scene was contained and there was no longer an imminent risk, he waved in the paramedics, who had been waiting for the green light to assess Doug's condition.

It was immediately clear that Doug was not breathing, and the paramedics began frantic life-saving measures. They used trauma shears to slice through Doug's blood-soaked jeans and sweater and undershirt, removing the articles of clothing and discarding them in a pile on the floor. One of the medics removed Doug's cell phone from the back pocket of his jeans and handed it to one of the officers who then placed it securely in a plastic evidence baggie.

A bag valve mask was placed over Doug's mouth and nose, and one of the medics rigorously squeezed it to pump ventilation into his lungs. Dozens of packages of medical materials were ripped open and haphazardly strewn across the kitchen floor.

Nervous that the frenzied activity might disturb crucial elements of what was now an active crime scene, Officer Shane Oien rushed out to his patrol car to retrieve his digital camera. Once back inside, he began clicking photos one after the other, capturing and preserving the scene as best he could to help aid detectives in their subsequent investigation of what had occurred in the Carlile home that night.

●●●

While paramedics continued to work on Doug in the kitchen, Officer Aaron Kirby and Sgt. Rob Boothe located Elberta Carlile in a second-floor bedroom still hiding in a closet behind a rack of clothing. Although she appeared to be unharmed, she was visibly distraught and demanded that she be allowed to go to her husband. When told she could not go downstairs at the time because medics were tending to Doug, Elberta became hysterical.

"She was crying and yelling, and very upset with me when I told her she could not see her husband," Kirby wrote in his report later. "She was worried about calling family and could not stay focused to answer my questions at first."

Kirby could certainly understand that Elberta had just been through a tremendously traumatic situation, but he remained mindful that her presence near Doug at that moment could risk disturbing evidence or medical intervention. Elberta's belligerence also caught Kirby's attention. Initially, her insistence on calling family members and rushing to her husband's side came across as an effort to avoid answering the officer's questions. At that moment, the officer had no way of knowing whether Elberta was responsible or involved in the shooting of her husband, but Kirby's focus shifted to calming his only current witness and urging her to recount the evening's events while they were still fresh in her mind.

From Elberta's perspective, she had already explained to the emergency dispatch center what had just transpired and could not understand why she needed to do it again. She did not know if her husband was alive, harmed, or dead, and felt helpless as no one was giving her any information. The officers on scene also did not know Elberta's deep religious conviction, and the desperation she displayed was a guttural plea to go to her husband and pray—whether it was with him if there was hope he would be okay, or over him if he was not.

Officer Kirby was patient, and eventually Elberta began to answer his inquiries. In spite of the shock and despair she felt, it was remarkable how vividly she remembered some of the details. Elberta noted that the man was holding what looked like a large semi-automatic pistol. She described that the man was likely around 6' tall, and in the brief moment she had locked eyes with him, she was reasonably confident he was Caucasian. He was wearing black from head to toe, including what looked like a turtleneck style shirt to cover his neck, gloves, boots, and a stocking cap with two eye holes.

But there was more. It seemed like the garments the man was wearing were somehow professional. As she spoke, Elberta studied Officer Kirby intently. Suddenly, it dawned on her.

"It was like what you are wearing!" Elberta pointed to the police officer's uniform. "All black and almost like tactical gear."

Officer Kirby looked up from his notepad. Why would someone wearing a police officer's uniform, or something similar, be wandering around an upscale neighborhood, shooting elderly homeowners on a Sunday night?

"Do you have any idea who could have done this, Mrs. Carlile?" he asked.

"No," Elberta wailed.

"Does your husband have any enemies that you know of?" Kirby asked a different way.

"He did have a business deal go bad recently. We were getting into the trucking business in North Dakota. It was with a man named James."

Their conversation abruptly ended there, as Kirby was given the green light to escort Elberta from the house. Additional police officers assisted with carefully navigating Elberta downstairs and through a side entrance door to avoid the medics who were still working on Doug in the kitchen. She sank down into the backseat of Kirby's police cruiser as they began their drive to the Spokane Police Department.

● ● ●

By 7:32 p.m., several police officers had already begun a canvass of the immediate neighborhood while even more guarded the perimeter of the surrounding streets. At the intersection of Garfield and 24th Avenue, one block down from the Carliles's house, Officer Dustin Howe was startled when he saw a light-colored SUV barreling down the street toward him. The vehicle barely came to a full stop before a hysterical man emerged from the passenger-side door and charged toward the officer, his arms waving in the air, pointing further down Garfield Road.

"That's my dad in that house! He's the one who just got shot!" The man screamed at Officer Howe.

"Okay, calm down, sir. Just calm down for me, please." Howe spoke slowly, trying to diffuse the situation. "Can you please tell me who you are?"

The man sobbing in front of him was Shad Carlile, the 29-year-old, and youngest, son of Doug and Elberta Carlile. Standing at 5'11" and weighing 280 pounds, Shad was formidable in his own right, but especially in the state of emotional despair he was in. He demanded that Howe let him go to his parent's home.

"What is going on? Is he dead? My mom is in there! I need to get to my dad. Please!" Shad wailed.

"Sir, I cannot discuss what is going on with an active investigation, and I cannot let you go to the scene," Howe explained. This only agitated Shad further.

Howe would document later in his report that at the time, his knowledge of the details of the situation was scant. He had simply been asked to help set up a perimeter to secure the scene of a shooting incident. The officer had no idea who had been shot or what condition that person or persons were in.

"He kept asking details about the status of his father," Howe wrote. "I did not know, so I attempted to take his mind off of the event and began asking him questions about any possible suspects that may have had an issue with his father."

According to Shad, his father had been involved in what seemed like a promising business partnership pertaining to oil drilling and trucking in North Dakota. In recent weeks, however, it appeared as though that partnership had hit a rocky point and there was some fallout happening between those involved. Shad said someone by the name of James had been threatening his father.

"Just a few days ago, my dad told me that if he winds up dead, I am supposed to tell police that it was James Henrikson who did it," Shad revealed.

The details of who James was or the extent of the relationship he had with Doug Carlile were scarce, but Shad did know at least one thing: "I've heard that James might also be involved in a murder up in North Dakota."

• • •

Back in the kitchen at 2505 South Garfield Road, all nine medical emergency personnel who had responded to the shooting, including Brett Roberts, Steve McMullen, and Dan Wilson, stared quietly at each other in defeat. Despite their best efforts, there had been nothing they could do to save Doug Carlile's life, and he was officially pronounced dead at 7:39 p.m. on Sunday, December 15, 2013.

Within seconds of the pronouncement, the cell phone medics had removed earlier from Doug's pants pocket began to ring from the plastic baggie it had been placed in. One of the officers peered through the plastic to see the name appearing on the screen was Shane Carlile, the 33-year-old second oldest Carlile son, who had just then learned his father had been shot.

CHAPTER 6

A Single Glove

Doug Carlile was a 63-year-old grandfather who had been murdered in his home, a mansion located in one of Spokane's most affluent neighborhoods, on a Sunday night just weeks before Christmas.

The Spokane Police Department had deployed no less than a dozen officers to respond to the initial 911 call, all of whom were eventually mobilized in one capacity or another until well into the next day. Several remained positioned guarding the exterior perimeter of the Carlile home as well as ensuring the extended area surrounding that section of South Garfield Road remained cordoned off with parked and running police cars and fire trucks. A handful more were charged with canvassing the neighborhood to find out who may have seen or heard something in the hours leading up to the shooting, or the minutes immediately following it.

Of the homes they approached, it was surprising to find that most of the residents had not been home at the time of the shooting, and of the ones who were home that night, the only people who had seen or heard anything were Brett and Jamie Roberts, and Brett's two co-workers. And between the four of them, only Jamie had seen a strange white van creeping throughout the neighborhood.

Given the fact that the foursome had not seen anyone running in front of the Carlile home or anywhere along Garfield

Road after the gun shots were fired, police had to operate under the assumption that whoever had killed Doug must have quickly fled from the home on foot through the backyard. Based on the information provided by Elberta Carlile, the person they were looking for was a man dressed in all black, who was also armed. Which meant that anyone who crossed paths with this man could also possibly be in danger. The police had to act quickly.

Master K9 trainer and officer Craig Hamilton arrived alongside his seasoned partner, Leonidas (Leo)–a handsome brown Belgian Malinois. Hamilton had been with the Spokane Police K9 Unit for almost ten years, and he and Leo had been an impressive duo for five of them. Leo was just 18 months old when he joined the unit, and as it would seem to all who knew him, he never quite got over being a fun-loving puppy—even when he was capturing the "bad guys."

It was still chaotic on Garfield Road, with media personnel and curious neighbors now clogging the sidewalks and street in front of the Carlile home. The commotion did not faze Leo as Hamilton placed him on a long line and cast him toward the driveway. Hamilton and Leo were not able to enter the home, as medical personnel were still milling about near the backdoor and porch area, but they were soon made aware that it was assumed the person who shot Doug had both arrived and left on foot through the backdoor. All of the other entrances to the home had been closed and locked when police came on the scene.

A fair amount of hope was placed in Leo to be able to sniff out a possible trail of where the suspect had gone, and he and Hamilton joined Officers Paul Buchmann and Shane Oien to begin a cursory search of the Carliles's expansive backyard.

A tall and rickety wood-planked privacy fence separated the Carliles from the property to the north, and a narrow road behind their house to the east. Rows of bushes and magnificently tall trees shrouded most of the east side of the yard. The forest-like wall of vegetation might have been the perfect hiding place for someone had it not been the time of year when most of their leaves had dispersed, leaving wide gaps of bare branches.

As they continued navigating, the ground below them became more saturated because of the rain that had come earlier that day. Shallow, muddy puddles dotted along the property line. The Carliles's wooden fence ended in the southeast corner of the backyard and transitioned to a 4' tall chain-link that separated their property from the neighbors to the south at 2515 South Garfield.

The gate to the fence was standing slightly ajar, and there, in the middle of what seemed like a makeshift grassy trail between the two estates, was a large welding glove. It was clean, but a few leaves lay over top of it, so it was initially difficult to discern how long it had been there. Leo's behavior changed then, indicating to Hamilton that he had picked up on something.

"Just inside the gated area was a mudpuddle with standing water in it. This puddle was right next to a solid wood fence," Officer Paul Buchmann wrote in his report. "There was water and mud splashed up on that fence. I then noticed what appeared to be the impression of a footprint in the mud puddle, which had been filled in with water."

Buchmann also noted that the water and the mud that had been sprayed on the fence was fresh, and still wet. In addition, he speculated that based on the direction the shoeprint was pointing, and the trajectory of the splash marks, that whoever had caused them had been running away from the houses.

Carefully avoiding the shoeprint and the glove, Leo led the gang of officers another 15 feet into the neighbor's yard and came upon yet another fence—this time a white picket—with its gate also standing wide open. Leo continued through the gate, and across an empty lot toward East Plateau Road. On the other side of the road sat Hutton Elementary School. At the time, the school consisted of two separate buildings with a wide swath of parking lot in between them. Because the property was not gated or otherwise secured, anyone could leverage the gap as a potential walkway to get from one side to the other.

Leo tugged at his lead as he continued, making his way in

between the buildings to the other side of the school out onto East 24th Avenue, which subsequently dead-ended in a cul-de-sac at the school's basketball courts. At first, Leo paused—an indication he may have lost the scent he was following. Then, he abruptly crossed the cul-de-sac and led the officers to the entrance of a wide gravel pathway. On the west side of the pathway was a rehabilitation center; on the east were the driveways and fenced-in backyards of several homes.

Leo and the officers ascended the steep incline of the walkway while illuminating it with their flashlights as they progressed. It was a path that was widely used in the neighborhood for dog walkers and bikers alike, but the day's rain shower had made it muddy. Officers could plainly see one set of fresh shoeprints pointing north, heading away from the Carlile home—but there were no prints pointing back south.

The path continued on for another half block and eventually ended in another steep embankment down onto East Rockwood Boulevard. It was where the shoeprints ended, and also where Leo indicated he could no longer pick up the scent he had been trailing for almost two full blocks.

If the scent he had picked up on and followed thus far was correct, it indicated that Doug's killer had exited the backdoor of the Carlile house, walked to the southeast corner of the yard, opened the gate to the chain-link fence, continued through the gate of the white-picket fence in the next-door neighbor's yard, walked through an empty lot to cross East Plateau Road, cut through the Hutton Elementary school parking lot to reach the south end of a long pathway, then taken the path an additional half-block to Rockwood Boulevard. Since this was also where Leo lost the scent, it was possible that the killer had gotten inside a vehicle and driven away.

There was a sense of relief, at least for the time being, that he was likely no longer in the neighborhood. However, this also meant they were still no closer to finding him.

CHAPTER 7

Where Is Rockwood?

Detective Brian Cestnik was in the process of tucking his two young children into bed when he received a call from the Spokane Major Crimes Unit (SMCU) on-duty supervisor, Sgt. Chuck Reisenauer, relaying to him the current details of what was now being officially considered a homicide case in the Rockwood neighborhood of Spokane.

Reisenauer advised that Detective Mark Burbridge was taking on the role of overall lead investigator on the case, and that he was already enroute to meet the victim's wife, Elberta Carlile, at the police station. Reisenauer requested that Brian assume the role of the lead investigator at the actual crime scene and suggested that he get there as soon as possible.

Rockwood? Brian thought, perplexed. Although the 37-year-old detective had only been with the SMCU since January of 2013, he had never responded to any calls in that neighborhood. Truth be told, he would sheepishly admit later, he had no idea how to even get there.

Brian Cestnik was born in the fall of 1976 in Billings, Montana and spent most of his childhood there before he and his only sibling, a brother three years younger, were uprooted to Spokane when his stepfather was offered a new job. At first, it was not an easy transition to make for the middle-schooler. Even though his parents had divorced years earlier, he had remained close with his father and paternal grandparents, and the move brought them over 500 miles away from the only family and friends he had known at a time when things like cellular phones and the internet did not yet widely exist.

But Brian was a bright and determined young man, not about to let anything stand in the way of paving a promising future for himself. He immersed himself in his studies, consistently being recognized with honors for his grades, and even though he was not as tall as some of the other young men in his class, he was a stand-out star on his high school baseball and basketball teams.

In his sophomore year, Brian turned his attention to preparing for what would come next and began working as many hours as he could at multiple jobs to save up money for college. When he graduated high school in 1994 with honors, he was ecstatic to learn he had been accepted to the prestigious Gonzaga University, a private Jesuit college that had first opened its doors in Spokane in 1887.

"I had no idea what I wanted to do with my life as far as a career," Brian shrugged. "But a friend talked me into volunteering with the Spokane Police Department during my freshman year at Gonzaga. He said the experience would look good on a resume someday."

The SPD had partnered with the college to offer a "Cooperative Education Program," whereby students could earn additional credits by volunteering with the police department. While the students were not technically card-carrying law enforcement personnel and certainly did not don a firearm, they were permitted to respond to non-emergency calls such as car accidents, cold burglaries, and property collections, and also went on ride-a-longs with other sworn officers. It was not long before the young Brian determined this was his calling.

"I eventually decided that this was something I wanted to do for a living," Brian recalled. "I was 20 and in my junior year at Gonzaga when I took the Spokane Police Department Civil Service Test. I went through the process and was placed in the first academy after I turned 21 in September of 1997."

The SPD wanted him to join immediately, which meant that Brian was faced with making the choice to leave Gonzaga before his senior year had begun. For him, it was a pretty clear-cut decision: A formal degree could wait. He was ready to start working, and for the next 16 years, an impressive career Brian would make.

"I spent 11 years on patrol, almost all of which were the graveyard shift," Brian proudly described the beginning of a long tenure with the department. "During that time, I also spent seven years as a field training officer for new recruits and was also an instructor at the police academy, an advisor in a program for high school volunteers interested in law enforcement, and one of the first members of our department's Critical Incident Team."

He was promoted to Detective in 2008 and was assigned to the Property Crimes unit. Just a few months later, he was moved to the Sexual Assault Unit, and then to a position working Crimes Against Children. He also eventually finished the degree he had started and graduated with a double major in Criminal Justice and Sociology—a degree he would later argue was worthless but necessary to keep advancing his career.

Along the way, Brian met and married Katie, a pretty blonde who worked as a social worker for the state of Washington, and the two soon welcomed daughter Elizabeth followed closely by son Mason. The couple settled into a modest home in a neighborhood in North Spokane, and Brian eventually leveraged his own past athletic experience while coaching his daughter and son in their youth basketball and baseball leagues. Between the kids' sports schedules and Brian's demanding job, there were only small pockets of leftover free time, which was often spent camping or taking short trips to visit extended family in Montana.

In January of 2013, Brian shifted his focus again, this time moving to the Major Crimes Unit where he would spend the next eight years as a brilliant homicide detective. He was meticulous and methodical, never missing a detail, often seeing things even the most seasoned detectives unwittingly overlooked. His outward personality was quiet and careful. He took no issue being in a position of command or authority, but even then, it was more common for Brian to be on his own, subdued in serious contemplation, rather than barking out orders. In the spotlight was never his favorite place to be, and he did not waste a lot of time with personal formalities, preferring instead to be laser focused on moving his investigations along.

But during happy hour after a long day, or on any given Sunday on the golf course with his buddies, Brian shrugged off the cloak of seriousness of his work. His dark hair had begun thinning as he was inching closer to his 40th birthday, but where he may have lacked in locks, his razor-sharp wit made up for it. His sarcastic one-liners and quips came so fast and furious during conversations that a person would sometimes miss half of the (mostly!) good-natured jokes and jibes he rattled out.

He had a hilarious retort for virtually everything anyone said. It was impossible to best him in a war of trading barbs, and it was futile to even try.

He was 11 months into the job as a homicide detective when he received the call that Douglas Carlile had been shot to death in his home. Brian changed out of the gym shorts and T-shirt he had been wearing that Sunday evening into a pair of jeans, polo shirt, and dress shoes. He kissed his wife and children, knowing full well that it might be a few days before he would see them again. That was the life of a detective that he had signed up for.

As he climbed into the driver's seat of his unmarked Ford Crown Victoria, Brian took a deep breath of anticipation, feeling the adrenaline begin to pulse through his veins. He was determined to put the pieces together. This was also what he had signed up for.

He just needed to find 2505 South Garfield Road first.

• • •

With the assistance of Siri from his iPhone, Brian arrived to the Carlile home at 8:23 p.m. and was met by Sgt. Boothe who gave him a brief rundown of the situation. By this time, the paramedics had left, but Doug's body remained on the kitchen floor until the coroner could arrive to transport him to the medical examiner's office for a full autopsy.

Brian was also approached by Officers Art Dollard and Darrell Quarles. Quarles had been inside the house with paramedics and had noted several spent bullets and shell casings scattered throughout the kitchen and dining room areas. He wanted Brian to be aware of their existence and positioning, as there was concern that some of the paramedics may have inadvertently moved them while they had feverishly worked to try to save Doug's life.

Dollard had accompanied Officer Craig Hamilton and K9 Leo as they followed the possible track of the suspect. Dollard led Brian into the backyard, where additional crime scene tape had recently been set up to preserve the muddy area near the wooden and chain link fences where the footprint and single glove had been found. What had stood out most, Dollard explained, was that the glove itself was dry while everything else around it was wet.

Brian's own initial observations were insightful. "I noted that it was very dark in the backyard. The gate was at the back of the property and not visible from either Garfield or the street behind the Carliles's, East Plateau Road. A person would have to be pretty familiar with the area to even know where this gate and path were."

This raised questions on the possibility the killer was someone Doug knew or at least someone who had spent time at the Carlile home.

Before he could conduct a thorough search of the crime scene inside the house, Brian needed to obtain a proper search warrant. He instructed the remaining officers to continue monitoring all three entryways into the house, the perimeter of the yard, and the dirt path that stretched between East 24th Avenue and East Rockwood Boulevard.

He sped to the SPD, and worked with Detective Mark Burbridge on drafting the affidavit, which included requests to collect all phones, computers, firearms, ammunition, spent casings, bullets, fingerprints, fibers, biological samples for DNA testing, and shoe impressions from the Carlile home and corresponding scene. The detective then drove to the home of Spokane Superior Court Judge Tari S. Eitzen, who reviewed and signed the warrant at 11:26 p.m.

When he returned to Garfield Road a short time later, three forensic specialists from the Spokane County Forensic Unit—Jodie Dewey, Tracye Boniecki, and Charles Hause—arrived and were ready to assist with a thorough search of the yard and house.

Before they even started to collect any evidence or anything was touched or moved in any way, however, Brian instructed Dewey to videotape the entire interior and perimeter of the house, and the killer's presumed escape route. It was not until 1:52 a.m. that Brian stepped foot into the Carlile house for the first time.

CHAPTER 8

The Music Played On

What Detective Brian Cestnik and his team of forensic specialists would remember most about first walking into the Carliles's house was the Bose stereo that was sitting atop a counter in one corner of the kitchen—the one Doug and Elberta had accidentally left on when they hurriedly left the house for their church party, now almost nine hours earlier. Of all the paramedics and police officers who had been in the home since then, no one had bothered to turn it off.

"This was actually one of the first things I noticed when we entered the home," Brian recounted later. "We made numerous comments about it as we worked the scene. It was a Christian radio station, and it was playing all Christmas music. We would find ourselves singing along to the songs while working, only to quickly realize how strange the whole situation was. We were standing over a man's dead body while listening to happy Christmas music during what is normally a family time of the year. The entire scene was very surreal and weird."

It was also not hard to discern that the Carliles were very religious people. Several stencil-lettered Bible verses adorned the walls while more scripture was scribbled onto loose pieces of paper, randomly placed on desks and end tables. The verse that was printed in block letters and adhered to the wall above the doorway leading into the dining room, seemingly overlooking Doug Carlile's lifeless body as it lay on the kitchen floor, read:

FOR WITH GOD NOTHING SHALL BE IMPOSSIBLE
(Luke 1:37)

•••

Doug was wearing only a pair of black boxer briefs, olive green dress socks, and black Nike tennis shoes. His blue jeans and a white short-sleeved undershirt and black sweater, which the paramedics had cut off with trauma shears and removed earlier, lay in a heap a few inches away from Doug's head. A blood-soaked medical cloth had been tossed on top of the pile. Along both sides of his body, several blue latex gloves that had been removed by medical personnel lay amongst dozens of open and discarded plastic packages and various tubes strewn across the kitchen floor.

All of the medical equipment that had been used to try to save Doug's life remained on his face and chest, including the bag valve mask that had been placed over his mouth and nose in an effort to pump air back into his lungs. Dried blood covered his face and saturated the top part of his hair, making it appear significantly darker than the light blonde it had once been. A sterile white pillow had been nestled underneath his head to aid in his comfort, even though no amount of comfort would have saved him.

A red circle of blood soaked through thick sheets of gauze draped over his chest. Once detectives carefully removed the dressing, they could now see that Doug's upper torso was riddled with bullet wounds.

"I observed what appeared to be several bullet holes in his arms and chest," Brian recorded in his report. "There were three bullet holes on his left upper chest and one in the center, just above his stomach, another in his right armpit and two more in his right forearm. There was another hole in his right upper arm and shoulder area and one in his left upper arm."

What Brian did not realize at the time was that Doug

had also been shot once in the mouth. The impact had caused Doug's glasses to fly off his face, skitter across the kitchen floor and land near a baseboard, one of its bows folded inward. Tiny droplets of blood speckled the lenses. Some of his dentures had shattered and fallen out of his mouth in small pieces onto the floor next to his head. The blow had also caused one tooth to become fully dislodged at the root and was found several inches away from his body—likely kicked away by one of the first responders on the scene. Later, medical examiners would find additional fragments of teeth and dentures inside his mouth.

The wounds across his upper body were wide in diameter, indicating a large caliber of gun was likely used. The injuries to his stomach, right armpit and forearm had all created narrow rivers of tacky red blood that had snaked across the hardwood floors of the kitchen, inching toward an antique popcorn machine that stood in the corner of the room. He still wore his gold wedding band on his left ring finger.

During his autopsy, which was performed early the next morning, it was determined that Doug had been shot a total of six times. There were 12 total bullet holes across his upper body, however—a combination of entry and exit wounds. Of the six bullets that had entered Doug's body, only two bullets stayed there—one in his left chest and the other in his abdomen. The other four had exited somewhere in the Carlile home.

There were no visible bruises or defensive wounds on Doug's arms or hands. He had barely had a chance to put his arms up to protect himself, let alone advance on the perpetrator for any kind of altercation. He had only been able to do what Elberta heard from him, which was vocally beg for his life. His killer had not even considered the pleas, because if what Elberta had reported was true, the whole encounter was over in less than two minutes.

Notably, this did not appear to be the work of a professional. The entry wounds were erratic, suggesting a sloppy "point and shoot anywhere" approach rather than a calculated shot to the head or heart. Nevertheless, the shooter's indiscriminate barrage of bullets had fulfilled the grim task of ending Doug's life.

•••

Detective Brian Cestnik began walking through and documenting the yellow placards the forensics team had placed near spent bullets and shell casings scattered throughout the kitchen and dining room areas. In total, he was able to locate seven .45 caliber shell casings and 5 bullets. This meant that with the two bullets found in Doug's body, along with the four additional original entry wounds, the shooter had actually fired his weapon a total of seven times. One bullet had seemingly managed to miss Doug altogether.

Brian carefully measured the entirety of the kitchen, then spent time meticulously documenting the actual coordinates of where each shell casing and bullet were found.

One bullet and shell casing were located in the breakfast nook, the furthest most point of the kitchen away from Doug's body. This was potentially the bullet that had not reached Doug—instead possibly ricocheting off of an object and ending up in an area that would have actually been behind the shooter.

"Almost all of the shell casings were near the base of the walls," Brian documented. "I later learned that there had been numerous paramedics and officers in the home, and many of these items had most likely been inadvertently kicked as they tried to save Doug Carlile."

The second bullet was found amongst leftover fluffy popcorn pieces and un-popped kernels in the popcorn machine, having blown through the front metal enclosure. A toaster in the southwest corner of the kitchen had also been struck by a bullet, which had then bounced down onto the floor. Another bullet had cut through a large bread maker, then lodged into the wall behind it, and was later cut out of the framework by officers. In the dining room, another bullet had exploded through and wedged itself inside the heavy oak dining table. Shards and fragments of wood from the damage to the table lay on the floor below.

Beyond the grim scene of the alley-shaped kitchen and dining room areas, the living room boasted a sense of classy elegance. Refurbished hardwood floors supported cozy brown leather furniture, complemented by a stunning grandfather clock that ticked loudly beside a Replogle floor globe and large flat-screen television. The TV was on, set to a program on the *Animal Channel.*

As Brian would later explain, "At first, the family was confident that the television had been turned off when they left for their church celebration, so we thought this might mean that the killer had been lying in wait for the Carliles to return home that night. Because of this initial theory, we spent an extraordinary amount of time in the house looking for evidence of items the suspect may have touched or places he might have been while waiting for Doug and Elberta to arrive."

Three sets of French doors were opened wide on the west side of the living room, leading into a large glass-enclosed sunroom that showcased a polished black baby grand piano, several large plants and small potted succulents, and an armoire holding dozens of classic board games.

The main floor was where the charm of the mansion ended. The remaining areas of the 5,000 square foot home that was built in 1923 were in near shambles. There were exposed electrical wires throughout the house, hanging loosely from holes in the ceilings and walls. The insulation in the walls had never been updated since it was erected 90 years before, and the furnace could no longer keep up with heating the home. To compensate, the Carliles had set up several electric heaters and fireplaces in various rooms in order to keep the home at a livable temperature during the frigid winter nights.

None of the rooms across the two upper floors had received a fresh coat of paint. The old paint and decades-old wallpaper had long since begun peeling away, revealing yellowed walls beneath. The carpets had never been replaced and were permanently flattened and soiled from years of family traffic. The same thing was true for the unfinished basement, with obvious signs of erosion and water damage on its burgundy-painted cement floors, and black mold beginning to creep along rotting baseboards and rickety old door frames.

It appeared that the Carliles were pack rats. Spare bedrooms and offices were crammed with dozens of plastic containers and boxes holding decades worth of paperwork, photographs, records, trinkets, heirlooms, and more. Nearly every available space in the Carlile home—whether closet, built-in shelf, or floor—was occupied. Even the four-car garage was filled to the brim with pieces of damaged furniture and years of collected junk.

In Doug's third floor office were three laptops that Brian had already listed as some of the items his team would collect and analyze later. Dozens of loose papers were neatly stacked on Doug's desk, including what appeared to be recent bank statements. Based on what those pages detailed—and later confirmed by the banks themselves—there was a reason that repairs had never been done to fix the water damage in the basement, or to repaint the patchy walls. The Carliles were flat broke.

Brian also noticed several papers that looked like legal documents and contract agreements. His forehead wrinkled in confusion when he saw that some of them were written in Arabic.

Scanning the documents that were written in English, Brian's attention was caught by a handful of words and phrases that were repeated throughout: oil, leases, mineral rights, North Dakota, trucks, and drilling. Doug's childlike cursive signature was on most of the pages.

● ● ●

At 5:40 a.m. on December 16, Rayna Orgill and Randy Shaber from the Spokane Medical Examiner's Office arrived to do a final examination of Doug's body before he was removed from the house. The only additional action they took was to place brown paper bags over his hands in order to preserve any potential evidence.

At 6:26 a.m., Doug's corpse was finally placed into a black body bag and hoisted onto a stretcher. He was then carefully wheeled out the same back door he had used to enter what he believed was the safety of his own home almost 12 hours before.

• • •

At 11:30 a.m., after almost ten hours of scouring the Carlile home for every piece of evidence they could find, snapping over 600 photographs, and videotaping every inch of land between the Carliles's backdoor and the end of the walking path on Rockwood Boulevard, Detective Brian Cestnik and his team gathered to exit the home together.

As he turned off the last light and pulled the back door closed behind him, Brian realized that once again, no one had turned off the Bose radio. The lively sounds of Christmas tunes would now eerily echo throughout an empty house.

CHAPTER 9

Hell Happened

Detective Mark Burbridge raced toward 1427 West Gardner, where the Spokane Police Department Homicide Unit was housed. The building, a blend of gray stucco and red brick, stood just down the road from the county courthouse and jail, and was separate from the more expansive main police station several blocks away on Mallon Avenue.

Aside from the American flag flying high on a flagpole in front, the one-story building tried its best to remain a non-descript structure—a place few in a neighborhood mostly populated with college students and young families would recognize as the headquarters for homicide and narcotics detectives when they weren't actively in the field.

Late on a Sunday evening in December, a mere handful were still working quietly inside darkened cubicle spaces lit only by the harsh blue glow of computer monitors. Framed pictures of children and spouses collected dust on desktops, while loose pages featuring printed mug shots of frequent offenders, various newspaper clippings, and recognition certificates were pinned up on the cloth walls with multi-colored thumbtacks.

It was true that Mark wasn't the cubicle-decorating type, but it was only partially true when he claimed he was not particularly fond of being formally recognized for his work. The fact was that he did enjoy being recognized—just not out loud, not in public, and most certainly not with a generic certificate printed on thick cardstock paper.

For Mark, recognition of a job well done was demonstrated by his superiors trusting him to make the right decisions, providing all the resources he needed, allowing him to work autonomously, and very seldom ever asking questions.

After using his keycard to enter the building, Mark stopped by his desk to grab a fresh notebook and ballpoint pen, then made an immediate beeline for the interrogation rooms. He did not even bother to take off his winter jacket.

The detective's attention was fixated solely on meeting with the newly widowed Elberta Carlile. Based on years of experience investigating similar cases, Mark already harbored deep suspicions that she was somehow involved.

"I knew that Mrs. Carlile was telling officers that a masked man had come into her house and shot her husband," he later explained, "but if she wasn't involved, it made no sense why the killer would leave her alive to be a witness."

Given those initial assumptions, Elberta was going to have to work hard to convince him otherwise.

•••

She was still dressed in a black and white floral blouse, black slacks, gold ballet flats, and a black button-up peacoat that she had worn to the church Christmas celebration. Her shiny black hair cascaded over her shoulders in soft waves all the way down to the small of her back. Any makeup she may have worn earlier in the evening had long since been washed away by an endless stream of tears.

Elberta still clutched the cell phone that she had held on to the entire time she was hiding in a closet to save her own life, desperately pleading with a 911 operator to send her help.

Her eyes were red and swollen, but they were now dry as she sat facing a young police officer who had been tasked with keeping her company until Mark arrived. The officer's chair was positioned in the furthest corner of the interrogation room away from Elberta, almost as if he was afraid of getting too close.

Although by this time Elberta was calm, she was an animated storyteller, and her arms waved around in the air as she described for the officer what she had just experienced. The young man was not there to get her statement, nor was he there to ask her any questions, and so he nodded along, providing an appropriately timed "uh-huh" each time Elberta paused for his acknowledgement. He appeared relieved when Mark finally burst through the door.

"Hi!" Mark said cheerily. The young officer took that as his cue and quickly ducked out of the room.

"What's your first name?" Mark asked Elberta.

Elberta's calm and leveled voice from just seconds before turned into a whine, and her chest heaved as she gulped in several breaths of air between words.

"I'm not very happy," she huffed. "I wanted to see my husband and they wouldn't let me see him!"

"Well," Mark said carefully. "The evidence is what we have right now—"

"I don't care about the evidence!" Elberta interrupted by slamming her hand on the table, breaking down into tears again. "I want my husband! Who cares about stupid evidence?"

Mark set his notebook on the table and finally unzipped and removed his jacket, draping it on the back of a chair directly across from Elberta. He'd dressed casually in a red polo and dark blue jeans.

"You don't understand!" Elberta continued her rant. "You want to watch someone you love die, and you can't get near them because someone says evidence? Who cares about evidence?"

"Do you want me to catch the person who did this?" Mark sighed as he lowered himself into the chair, adjusting his notebook and pen in front of him.

"I want my husband!" Elberta slammed her hand on the table again.

Mark had encountered his fair share of grieving family members. He fully understood the despair and anguish people exhibited after losing a loved one in such an abrupt and horrific manner. But there was just something off about this woman's behavior. It seemed contrived.

"Elberta is … well, let's just say that Elberta is very different," Mark acknowledged later of her eccentric personality.

Perhaps it was how calm and at ease she had appeared when he first walked into the room, and how quickly she devolved into an emotional wreck, demanding things that were just not feasible. It came across as bizarre that she was so entrenched in wanting to see and touch her husband's dead body.

"There's nothing we can do for your husband right now," Mark said softly, trying to help her understand that seeing Doug's body would help neither her nor the investigation at that point.

"Well, I could have held him. I could have told him I loved him. I could have prayed for him!"

"What happened tonight?" Mark tried to divert her focus.

"We went to church!" Elberta said, her arms raised in the air. "I don't know what happened. Hell happened! A nightmare happened. That's what happened."

"What time did you get home?"

Elberta slowed down and tried to regain her composure.

"We left at a quarter to five," she said in between shallow breaths. "We got home at … well, I don't know. Right before I called the police. Whatever time that was."

"How long had you been home?" Mark asked as he jotted down notes.

Elberta reiterated the same thing she had told officers when they had first found her hiding in an upstairs closet. "It happened instantly. It was like somebody ambushed him!"

She described how they had arrived home that evening, and then followed their typical routine of Doug making sure the driveway gate was shut while she went to unlock the back-door to get inside. She hadn't wanted to dig into her filled-to-the-brim purse to find her set of house keys, so she had instead grabbed the hidden key sitting atop the door frame. Once inside, Elberta realized the lights were on, and could not remember if she had left them on, or if one of their sons had been by to visit or was still there somewhere else in the house.

"I noticed all the lights were on in the kitchen. I didn't remember doing that, but you never know when you're in a hurry and are going to be late. I was telling Doug to hurry and that I didn't want to be late."

As she ascended the stairs to put away her personal belongings and get ready for bed, she heard male voices coming from the kitchen downstairs.

"When I heard the voices, I thought maybe I was right," Elberta said. "I thought that must be why the lights were on — because someone was there to visit."

When she walked back down the stairs and peered around the corner into the kitchen, that is when she saw a man dressed in all black, pointing a gun at Doug. Realizing the person talking to her husband was not one of their sons, Elberta recounted how her legs had gone numb, but she had managed to pull herself up the stairs and run to hide in the closet and call 911.

While Mark started on the second page of scribbling notes, Elberta continued, telling the detective how she had heard five or six gunshots, and that she had "freaked out" in the closet believing that the man was coming for her next. The man had never come, and she had stayed on the line with 911 until police arrived at her house.

"What kind of gun was it, do you know?" Mark looked up from his notes.

"It was a black gun," Elberta said confidently, also stating she knew it was a semi-automatic handgun and not a revolver. "A big one. Like a .44 or a .357."

"Did you notice if he had gloves on or not?"

It was the only question that made Elberta pause for longer than a few seconds. Her hands in the air, looking directly in Mark's eyes she finally said, "I think so. Yes, I think so."

"Did you guys have any disputes with anybody?" Mark tried a different angle.

Elberta nodded, then launched into a lengthy and confusing story. "His name is James Henrikson. We started a business with him, but he can't have any businesses in his name. We didn't know any of this. He gave us all sorts of reasons for why he couldn't have any business in his name. He said some guy from the Bureau of Indian Affairs [BIA] had a lawsuit against him, and he couldn't do business in the oilfields up in North Dakota because of that.

"So, we started this trucking business. It was hell. Sheer hell. Then we went to the BIA offices to get approval for our oil. We have an oil lease. And we saw this poster with his name on it. Him and his wife both. And it freaked us out. So, we just handed the business over to him. We have no intention of being in business with someone with no integrity. And they had some issues. All I know is I've never seen manipulation like this in my whole life. This guy was so manipulative, and his wife was just as bad. Just horrible. It was like there was a drama every day. I finally told my husband to do whatever it takes to get away from him."

Mark paused for a few moments to process Elberta's dizzying tale of oil leases, Indian Affairs, trucking businesses, and bad guys in North Dakota—a state almost 800 miles away.

"Where does James live in North Dakota?" Mark asked.

"He lives in Watford City," she answered.

"Was James angry, then?" the detective posed.

"Angry? I don't know." Elberta shrugged then added, "Well, he has threatened my husband."

Mark's head snapped up from his notes. "Threatened him how? When?"

Elberta's response did nothing but add more to the confusion. "I don't know. Probably two months ago. I wasn't there. Doug just told me James had grabbed him really hard. He didn't want to talk to me about it. But we handed over the business to James. Well, he does the business with John Wark of Eagle River Development and his partner Richard. They have the trucking business with James now."

Who the fuck are all of these people? Mark thought.

Elberta's phone buzzed then, an incoming call from her pastor. The soothing sound of his voice was enough to make Elberta break down into sobs once again.

"I'm at the police station. Pastor, they wouldn't let me see him!" she wailed. "They just made me leave my house!"

The pastor encouraged the new widow to be patient and told her that it was important to let the police do their job so that they could figure out who had done this to Doug, but Elberta was having none of it.

"I don't care! It's not fair!"

The clergyman communicated he was on his way to offer any support she might need. This, thankfully, calmed Elberta down again.

Mark resumed his questioning. "Can you think of anyone else who would want to hurt you or your husband?"

"No," Elberta's voice trembled in between sniffles. "We're just ordinary, everyday people with a dream. We had a dream to have an oil well. That's how this whole thing started. We got an oil lease. We are 51% owners of Kingdom Dynamics Enterprises. John and Richard are 49%."

"Does James own any part of the oil lease?"

"No," Elberta said, but then corrected herself. "Well, he invested money, but we were going to buy him out. We don't want a part of him in anything because he is obviously a terrible person."

The detective set down his pen with a deep sigh and looked up from his notes to study Elberta's face and eyes. Admittedly, the information she had shared thus far had thrown him for quite a loop.

Mark later discussed his initial doubts. "When Elberta first described a man in all black with a black mask, I was thinking she must be making it up. It was too much like a Hollywood movie. I was very concerned she had something to do with it."

But now, he wasn't so sure. Even if what Elberta was saying was true, it still seemed a stretch to link the brutal murder of a grandfather in Spokane to a seemingly minor business dispute with someone four states away.

Sensing the detective's skepticism, Elberta shifted her tone to a desperate pleading.

"Listen," she breathed, her hand outstretched across the table to him, "we saw a paper, a poster, when we were at the Bureau of Indian Affairs in North Dakota. You can look on the internet. It's a huge page with all of James's felonies."

"Okay, okay," Mark acknowledged. "I'm definitely going to research the heck out of this guy. So, when—"

"Wait!" Elberta shouted, her hands gripping both sides of the table as if she was trying to keep herself from falling out of her chair. "A guy disappeared after he had an argument with James Henrikson. They've never found him. He's probably dead! His name is K.C. Clarke."

PART II

CHAPTER 10

The Oil Boom

It is believed that the Williston Basin, a vast geological feature spanning nearly two million square miles of western North America, was formed almost two billion years ago. It was not until the early 1950s, however, that the Bakken Formation was discovered—a subterranean rock formation beneath a sub-section of the Basin, occupying roughly 200,000 square miles across parts of Canada, Montana, and North Dakota.

Named after farmer Henry O. Bakken—whose land in Tioga, North Dakota, became famous for significant oil discovery with the drilling of the Clarence Iverson No. 1 well in 1951—the Formation is said to extend nearly 16,000 feet deep into the earth.

The massive rock unit is made up of three distinct members—lower shale, middle dolomite, and upper shale. Throughout the 1980s, renowned geochemist Leigh Price dedicated his career to unraveling the scientific mysteries of the Bakken. By the end of his research, Price had concluded that the dolomite member of the formation was a source of infinite amounts of sweet crude oil and natural gas. If the scientist's early assertions were correct, up to 500 billion barrels (approximately 21 trillion gallons) of oil could be recoverable from the Bakken shales, potentially making it one of the largest oil reserves in the world.

For a layman, that was a lot of scientific mumbo jumbo at

the time. But for big oil companies and their tycoons around the country, it meant massive dollar signs. There was just one major caveat: unlike other rock formations, the Bakken shale doesn't allow oil to flow easily, making it much more difficult to extract using traditional vertical drilling methods. Adding to the complexity, the richest part of the formation—the dolomite layer—sits between 8,500 and 10,000 feet underground.

At the time of Leigh Price's discovery, drilling to such depths was feasible, but technology and extraction methods weren't advanced enough to make it economically viable. It would still be well over a decade before practical and cost-effective ways to tap into the Bakken's extensive oil reserves were introduced.

•••

In the 1990s, geologists attempted to use horizontal drilling—technology that drills non-vertical bores—as a means of extracting oil from a portion of the Bakken located in Richland County, Montana. Variations of horizontal drilling had been used since the 1890s, but never before in the type of shale formation. The initial trials were unsuccessful, and any further exploration with the use of horizontal drilling was abandoned until the year 2000.

Undaunted by the failures of his predecessors, geologist Richard Findley was determined to find a way to make horizontal drilling work. After thorough analysis, he opined that those who had tried and failed before him simply had not drilled deeply enough into the dolomitic layer. His hypothesis proved ingenious, and oil recovery soon surged.

By 2007, the Elm Coulee Oil Field in Montana became the highest-producing onshore oil field in the United States. But the Field—and the state of Montana—would not hold that title for long.

•••

On a parcel of land on the Bakken located near rural Parshall,

North Dakota—420 miles east of the Elm Coulee Field—several oil companies had drilled a number of "dry holes" in the early 1980s. Those exploratory drills failed to yield oil, and the holes had remained dormant for many years. In 2006, a petroleum geologist from Denver, Colorado named Mike Johnson began analyzing the well log of one of the decades-old dry holes. It didn't take long for him to recognize a similarity with Richard Findley's discoveries on the Bakken in Montana: the original attempts had not drilled down far enough.

Johnson and a partner leased a large position on the land, but because they did not have the resources needed to begin a major exploration of their own, they successfully petitioned a prominent energy company based in Texas—EOG Resources. That same year, EOG drilled a discovery well, named Parshall #1-36H, next to one of the dry holes that had been dormant for 25 years.

Leveraging the technology used on the Elm Coulee Oil Field, the well was horizontally drilled thousands of feet into the dolomite. For everyone with a stake in the early stages of the game, it was like Christmas morning when oil literally began bubbling to the surface. It was astonishing to realize that the pot of black gold at the end of the rainbow had been there for thousands of years, just waiting patiently for humans to figure out how to get to it.

Before long, EOG expanded by drilling multiple development wells on leased land along the eastern edge of Parshall, and soon spread to the north, south and west. By then, it was no secret that there was a lot of oil to be found on the Bakken. Unsurprisingly, additional energy companies began swooping into northwestern North Dakota, trying to stake their claim.

Soon, hydraulic fracturing—also called fracking—was introduced to extract oil even more expediently and less expensively. Fracking is a process that involves breaking up, or "fracturing," bedrock formations with the use of pressurized fluid—most often water combined with sand particles and other chemicals—which facilitates the release of the embedded oil and natural gas within the rock. The process of fracking requires lots and lots of water, which in turn necessitates tanker trucks making round-the-clock trips between water supplies and fracking sites.

••••

By 2008, prominent oil companies had descended upon North Dakota, feverishly negotiating leases and mineral rights contracts with landowners. The vast expanse of Bakken oil land stretched across small towns such as Williston, Watford City, Dickinson, and Tioga. A significant portion also rested within the Fort Berthold Indian Reservation encompassing the quiet communities of New Town and Mandaree. Much of this land belonged to members of the Three Affiliated Tribes: Mandan, Hidatsa and Arikara, also known as the MHA Nation. Eventually, at least a third of the total oil production in North Dakota came from the reservation.

As production ramped up, landowners with mineral lease contracts across the western part of the state began raking in between $60,000 and $100,000 a month in royalties—unprecedented sums that instantly transformed lives.

The fracking process made it possible to extract oil safely and effectively, but it also fueled the drive to extract as much as possible, as quickly as possible. With the potential of recovering billions of barrels of oil, there was no time to slow down. Naturally, the rapid growth opened up incredible opportunities for countless new jobs, stretching the gamut from roustabout to executive. Not only did men in North Dakota leave their jobs in droves to find work in the oilfields, but eventually, workers from all across the country came.

Thousands of men flocked to the state, quickly filling hotels and apartment complexes to capacity. As housing became scarce, "man-camps"—sites that accommodated portable trailers and cabins for out-of-town workers—began popping up everywhere.

The highways and city streets were congested with tankers and heavy diesel trucks, morning and night. For rural residents unaccustomed to heavy traffic—let alone gridlock—everyday tasks like making a left turn onto a highway could mean enduring long, frustrating delays.

The oil companies leased out countless white Ford and Chevy 4x4 trucks to their workers, and it was hard to miss them as they clogged gas station lines, filled hotel parking lots, and spilled into overflow lots at airports when workers had time off to visit their families.

Seemingly overnight, these sleepy bedroom communities became an indistinguishable mix of exciting economic growth and overcrowded chaos. Small businesses struggled to find employees, as everyone preferred the higher wages in the oilfields. State and local governments struggled to keep up with the increased infrastructure and housing demands.

Frequent automobile accidents, often involving fatalities, plagued streets and highways that were not designed to handle the increased traffic. Oilfield workers who could not find a hotel, apartment, or man camp began sleeping in their cars or pitching tents in people's backyards.

Drunken men and nightly barroom brawls replaced bingo and weekend meat raffles at neighborhood haunts. Violence, prostitution, and drug activity rose dramatically with law enforcement agencies overwhelmed and severely understaffed. It was difficult to identify and prosecute perpetrators because people working in the oilfields could easily disappear just as quickly as they had arrived.

The crime problem was even further exacerbated by the blurred jurisdictional authority lines between state, local and tribal police forces. Many of the crimes, including rape and murder, went unsolved and some were not even investigated at all. Friendly and trusting rural North Dakotans, particularly women, who had never had to lock their doors, grew fearful of going to the hometown supermarket in broad daylight without their husbands along.

"It was like the Wild, Wild West up here," many residents lamented years later.

But alas, the frenzy finally began to stabilize in 2010. Several new hotels and multi-unit apartment buildings were erected, although the nightly rates and monthly rental prices were astronomical. At the time, even a small one-bedroom apartment could run up to $3,000 a month, more than what it would have cost in New York City at the time. It became common practice for oilfield workers to pool together and share an apartment to save on costs, staggering their work schedules so that only one or two men at a time would need a space to sleep.

Police forces had ramped up hiring and training, and along with the assistance of federal authorities, were much better equipped to address and tamp down the elevated crime levels. Minimum wages had risen exponentially to increase the attractiveness of working at newly built fast-food restaurants, fine dining, swanky clubs, hotels, and retail stores. Business was so good that even the small mom-and-pop shops that still lined Main Streets were able to compete with the massive employee wage growth.

Improvements were made to roads and highways that greatly decreased traffic disruptions and incidents. Additional transportation options had also become available. Codeshare jet services from both United Airlines and Delta Air Lines began offering daily connections out of regional airports to major hubs in Denver and Minneapolis, making it easier for out-of-state oilfield workers and executives to get to and from their jobs and families.

The Amtrak station in Williston had been there decades before the oil boom came to town. Located in the historic downtown district, the entire station underwent a two-million-dollar restoration project in 2010 to accommodate the increased demand for travel in and out of The Bakken. That year, roughly 20,000 passengers took advantage of its once daily train that crossed in both directions from Portland, Oregon, all the way to Chicago, Illinois, with multiple stops along the way. By 2012, that number had swelled to nearly 55,000.

That same year, when most areas of the country were experiencing a severe economic downturn, North Dakota was producing up to one million barrels of oil a day, boasted the lowest unemployment rate in the nation, and recorded a billion-dollar budget surplus, with no signs of the economic tsunami slowing down any time soon.

It was also the year that an outsider, a man with a lengthy criminal record, set out on a dangerous rampage across the oil fields of North Dakota. His name was James Henrikson, and he was eager to find his fair share of the wealth on the Bakken. He was also determined to destroy anyone who dared to stand in his way.

CHAPTER 11

James Henrikson

Born in 1979, James Terry Henrikson spent his early childhood in the comfort of an upper middle-class neighborhood in Kennewick, Washington. The middle child of the Henrikson family, he had an older brother, Randy, and a younger sister, Kahli. On the surface, the Henriksons appeared to embody the quintessential American ideals of hard work and strong family values.

But that illusion was shattered when James's parents unexpectedly announced their divorce. Relocating to Oregon with his father, James soon began to exhibit a darker side—one that would prove impossible to suppress.

It was early on when educators recognized that James struggled with a learning disorder that significantly hampered his academic ability. It was a defining moment for the person he would become. Being labeled a "slow learner" was something that deeply embarrassed the young boy and generated devastating feelings of inadequacy that he would desperately try to mask.

As a way to compensate for his shortcomings, beginning in his teens, James immersed himself—not in academic studies or programs that would assist in his intellectual development—but in weightlifting and prolific steroid use. In his mind, if he was bigger and stronger than everyone else, no one would notice that he wasn't very smart. But bulging biceps and beefed-up pectoral muscles couldn't mask his struggles in the classroom.

There was one thing James had going for him: his boyish good looks. His smile and charm were enough to win over a wide-eyed teenage girl named Cassie, who soon found herself pregnant with James's child. After high school, the young couple hastily married and the newlyweds welcomed a baby girl not long after.

Over the next few years, James would at least attempt to find his niche in the world. For a time, he was a racer for the Oregon Motorcycle Road Racing Association. Unfortunately, he wasn't very good at it, and he did not receive the more lucrative endorsements or sponsorships that some of his fellow racers did.

The years he had spent feeling inferior to his peers in school only intensified, and James was determined to one day be richer and more successful than anyone whom he believed had ever doubted his abilities. But since he had limited education and no skills to qualify for a high-salaried job, he began seeking out other ways to make money. By the age of 20, James began a nearly 15-year run of increasingly dangerous criminal behaviors.

He first engaged in petty theft but eventually graduated to burglary. His feelings of inadequacy combined with steroid use also put him in a near constant state of rage, resulting in multiple instances of him assaulting others. When theft didn't yield the financial return he hoped for, James—now father to an infant daughter—teamed up with members of a local gang and shifted to growing marijuana. That venture quickly escalated into manufacturing and selling oxycodone pills.

As it turned out, James made a good drug dealer—insofar as his personality, anyway. He was cunning, manipulative, controlling, and violent. No one would get the best of James Henrikson, and he made sure that everyone knew it.

"He always bragged that he once had a couple of business partners killed," one source later described. At the time he made such a boastful claim, it was a lie, but it still made those in his inner circle wary of what he might do if provoked.

The part James wasn't very good at, however, was staying under law enforcement's radar, and he soon racked up several charges related to drug trafficking and manufacturing. A jail cell in Deschutes County, Oregon, became like a second home for the rough-and-tumble blonde muscle man.

When he wasn't dealing drugs or in jail, James was busy at home, physically and sexually assaulting his wife, Cassie. In June 2000, he was arrested and charged with rape in the first degree, sexual assault in the first degree, and multiple counts of sexual abuse. He was immediately released on bond but rearrested in July for trying to intimidate Cassie into not testifying against him in court. Cassie filed for divorce and was granted an expedient judgment to dissolve the marriage.

Still, James refused to leave his ex-wife alone and was arrested for a third time in September for violating the restraining order she had against him. Two months later, while out on bond, James attacked Cassie and was arrested and charged with assault and rape. Yet again, he was released on bond and continued to terrorize his ex-wife and their young daughter. Over the next eight months, well into the summer of 2001, Cassie called the police no fewer than ten times with complaints of James intimidating and/or assaulting her.

Eventually, Cassie asked the authorities to drop the rape charges, saying she would not testify in court against her ex-husband. She could no longer emotionally or physically endure the abuse and constant harassment—especially since the legal system kept inexplicably letting him out of jail to do so.

James was able to plead to much lesser charges and spent less than six months in prison for his crimes. While he was incarcerated, Cassie took their daughter and went into hiding. James would never again see his first-born child, but he didn't care. Once Cassie's serious allegations against him were dropped, he no longer had any use for her or a child he would have to support financially.

•••

In March 2002, James was released from jail but wouldn't

stay out for long. A few days later, a call came into the Bend, Oregon police department, reporting an attempted burglary in progress. Upon arriving at the scene, police officers could barely contain their snickers when they saw it was none other than the notorious testosterone bandit attempting to duck and weave through the beams of their flashlights.

Realizing he would be going straight back to jail, James refused to go easily. Before they could stop him, he managed to run to his nearby car, squealing the tires as he sped away. With flashing red and blue lights of the police cars following hot on his tail, James led the convoy on a high-speed chase throughout the city, crashing into parked cars and other stationary objects, causing thousands of dollars of property damage along the way. Eventually, the criminal mastermind gave up and surrendered.

"Henrikson just recently got out of jail and appears to have returned to his criminal behavior," the police report included in a tongue-in-cheek observation. "It would seem Mr. Henrikson has made the decision to return to jail."

In 2004, 25-year-old James was given a chance for a fresh start. According to sources, James's family loaned him funds to start a masonry business in nearby Benton County, Washington. Having spent time working in the industry alongside multiple generations of family members, the intricate craft of masonry was one of the few things at which James was actually skilled.

It was a crucial life moment for the young man—an opportunity served on a platter to straighten out his path. The potential to build an honest business entirely his own and cultivate a pathway into entrepreneurial success. The other option, of course, was to continue further down the road of criminal mischief and behavior. It should have come as no surprise to anyone, least of all his family, that James would choose the latter.

•••

Somewhere along the way, James met and married his second

wife, a woman named Stacey Firth. While the new bride wanted to believe in the happily ever after that James was promising, it didn't take her long to realize she was just a pawn in her husband's financial schemes. But even after that revelation, Mrs. Henrikson chose to board the train that was hurtling down the tracks at a breakneck speed.

James had reservations about using his name on any of the legal documents needed to incorporate his company. He also feared that anyone he tried to do business with would conduct research on his qualifications and quickly ascertain that he was a criminal with a lengthy rap sheet. As such, Accent Masonry, LLC was established in Stacey Henrikson's name.

Even though his name wasn't on the company's paperwork, James still needed to deal with other businessmen, employees, and customers who would certainly become aware of his full name. To combat that, James began using what became a lengthy list of aliases, starting with simple variations of his last name, including Henrickson, Henderson, Hendriksen, Hendrikson, Henricksen, and Henriksen.

James and Stacey also set up multiple shell companies, including Greystone Masonry, LLC in 2005, Greystone Development Group, LLC in 2006; and West Coast Cranes, LLC, Extreme Speed Race Team, LLC, Greystone Granite & Marble, LLC, and GH Builders, LLC, all in 2007. A shell corporation is a company that exists only on paper and has no actual employees or physical office locations. While shell companies sometimes do have legitimate business purposes, it isn't uncommon that they might be used for tax evasion and money laundering.

For James and Stacey Henrikson—or whichever variation of that last name they chose to use on any given day—these shell companies were used to launder money away from employee union dues, hide money and assets that they owed to vendors, and to take out massive loans that they never intended to pay back. But it didn't take terribly long for their schemes to catch up with them.

"There were always payroll problems," recalled one manager of a bricklayers union. "It was always a chase with this guy. He smiles while lying to your face, and people believe him."

In 2006, Masonry Industry Trust Administration filed a civil lawsuit against Accent Masonry, LCC, and Stacey (Firth) Henrikson, citing their failure to make contributions to Masonry Industry Fund. The Fund manages contributions from employers for health and welfare benefits as well as pension trust funds for union members. The lawsuit took over two years to reach a courtroom, and both James and Stacey—by then divorced—were ordered to pay back the money they had taken. In January 2008, however, James and his second ex-wife filed for bankruptcy. The civil case against them, including the judgment, was stayed by the court pending further review.

A bankruptcy judge listened to their woes of not being able to pay their debts before appointing a trustee to review all of the information. In the final report, the trustee documented that the couple had operated businesses through LLCs listed solely in Stacey's name but asserted that the assets acquired in the businesses were used by both James and Stacey.

As for James, the trustee listed a plethora of accusations, including that he had failed to disclose assets, testified falsely under oath, transferred assets without court authority, transferred assets through the use of several shell companies, failed to list loans made to the shell companies and all debts owed by those shells, and commingled assets personally and among the various business entities.

Based on the trustee's finding, the judge dismissed their bankruptcy claims and ordered James and Stacey to pay their obligations. But rather than pay his share, James took off, leaving the bulk of the debt owed in Stacey's lap. There wasn't much she could do about it, given that the companies had all been in her name, and any additional legal proceedings on her part would have cost money she didn't have. Eventually, like most people who were finally able to escape further damage inflicted by James, the former Mrs. Henrikson was relieved when it seemed he was gone for good.

● ● ●

Throughout 2009 and 2010, the criminal charges against James piled up, including breaking and entering, driving without a license, unlawful delivery of marijuana, unlawful manufacture of marijuana, criminal conspiracy, and theft.

In October of 2010, he was arrested for a violation of his probation and thrown back in jail where he would spend the next four months.

Shortly after this latest stint in the slammer, James started another new relationship. This time, with a blonde bombshell seven years his junior named Sarah Marie Creveling. Sarah was petite, pretty, smart, and sweet. At least, that's how she pretended to be.

James and Sarah had taken a liking to one another several years earlier when she was still in high school, working as a barista at a local coffee shop he frequented when he wasn't busy breaking into homes and businesses, assaulting his two ex-wives, or selling drugs. Though they lost touch for a few years—Sarah attending college while James was in and out of jail—they never forgot each other.

By the time they reunited, James was 32 and Sarah was just shy of turning 25. James's lengthy criminal history was of little concern to the young vixen. Having grown up sheltered and pampered by father, Charles, a physician, and mother, Jennifer, in the affluent Seattle suburb of Issaquah, the "bad boy" persona of her new beau was exciting.

"He's very cool, calm, collected," Sarah later gushed to NBC *Dateline's* Keith Morrison. "He was an older man, good-looking. It was fun. We would always go out and he was nice. It was easy."

As it seemed, the two also shared a similar craving for deviance. For James, it was the only way he knew how to live, the only way he felt he could appear smarter than he was and stay several steps ahead of everyone around him. For Sarah, it was simply a way to rebel against the facade of perfection and privilege that she'd resented having to portray for most of her life.

Just a few months into their budding new courtship, James convinced Sarah to run away with him to Texas, where he hoped his name wouldn't be known and his criminal past wouldn't catch up with him. Even though she would be leaving her friends and family and the only home she had ever known, Sarah couldn't pack her bags fast enough to join her new love on a thrilling adventure.

Of all the things that would eventually be said about Sarah Marie Creveling, the one thing no one ever described the blonde beauty as, was naïve. Sarah, many would say, knew exactly what she was getting herself into when she followed James Henrikson down to Texas in February 2011.

CHAPTER 12

Joint Ventures

James Henrikson and Sarah Creveling coasted into Austin, Texas in early 2011 with the same roadmap that he had tried once before: establishing a masonry business as a launching pad for shell businesses to launder money slowly and systematically back to himself. This time, it would be Sarah who would willingly sign her name on the dotted lines. As such, Blackstone LLC was incorporated on February 23, with Sarah listed as the sole shareholder and registered agent. Shortly after, she established the shell company Blackstone Building Group LLC, doing business as Blackstone LLC.

In 2011, the economy in most parts of the country was still struggling and Texas was no exception. Unfortunately for James and Sarah, they quickly realized that trying to get a new construction business off the ground during a time of stagnant residential and commercial growth was going to be a significant challenge. One that neither of them had the patience—or financial backing—to take on.

To sustain themselves in the short term, James resorted to his reliable but illegal approach of generating quick cash through drug production and distribution. He acquired a pill-making machine and chemicals from an online supplier and started manufacturing oxycodone pills. At the time, the cost of producing one pill was relatively low yet the street price was high, often selling for $50 or more per pill.

Drug-dealing was a lucrative business indeed, but the problem for James was that the market for distribution was already heavily saturated by several local dealers—none of whom appreciated an outsider trying to infiltrate their turf. For once in his life, James accepted that he was out of his league and eventually abandoned the endeavor.

Perhaps it was a greater blessing in disguise, because as it would turn out, his time in Austin, Texas happened to be the only period in James's life where he would never have any encounters with law enforcement or spend any time in jail.

•••

Before he and Sarah had even left for Texas, James had been paying close attention to current news and began fixating on the oil boom in North Dakota. Through his research, he learned there was the potential for a lot of money to be made in a relatively short amount of time—a prospect that sparked a burning desire he needed to pursue. It was true that he had little experience or knowledge of the industry, but James wasn't interested in actually working in the oilfields, anyway. There was no way he would be getting his hands dirty as a roustabout or a truck driver. No, James' ambition was to dominate the oilfields. Anything less was unacceptable.

Prior to making the trek to Texas, James had put out a feeler to a man named Steve Kelly who owned Trustland Oilfield Services in New Town, North Dakota. Promising that he had trucks to haul north if Kelly had work, Kelly had invited him and Sarah to North Dakota for a meet-and-greet; an occasion that had gone exceptionally well given James's ability to talk a big game and Sarah's knack for batting her eyelashes. Of course, Kelly hadn't known at the time that James and Sarah had neither a truck, nor a business under which to operate it.

For the next few months, James scrambled to procure a truck, and someone who was willing to front the money for it. Enter self-proclaimed entrepreneur extraordinaire Jedediah "Jed" McClure. Through a mutual friend named Ron O'Neil, McClure and James were introduced by phone.

McClure was from Indiana and had graduated from De-Pauw University with a degree in political science and economics. He had begun his career as a real estate acquisition specialist, and according to his published autobiography, was successful in amassing more than ten million dollars in assets for his firm before he had even turned 25. He then moved on and started his own manufacturing and distribution business. Although it is not clear exactly what products or goods were being manufactured or distributed, according to his own reflections, McClure's start-up business was prominent across the country with several locations and dozens of employees.

He was also a family man with a wife and three young children. Despite his early success and a seemingly promising future on his own, McClure couldn't help but be interested when his friend O'Neil called wanting to connect him with someone who was looking for a partner to launch a business in the oilfields in North Dakota.

"I was close friends with Ron and we had done quite a bit of business together," McClure recounted. "To me, Ron's words were golden. James had worked for him in the past, and Ron was quick to vouch for him."

For the next six weeks, McClure and James spoke by phone on multiple occasions, with James explaining his idea for a new subcontractor trucking business to operate in the oilfields. The business would entail trucks being used to haul water to and from oil fracking sites with the hope that there would eventually be an opportunity to expand those services.

What James needed most was upfront money from investors to purchase the trucks. James posited that he would be the owner and operator, living in North Dakota to oversee and manage everyday operations, while the investors would receive a percentage of the monthly profits. James's business model also guaranteed that the investors would receive 100% of their initial investments back in the first month.

James exuded an air of confidence and enthusiasm that played right into McClure's own greedy ambitions. With the potential of earning hundreds of thousands of dollars from an initial investment of just a few thousand, McClure couldn't see any downside to the venture.

Before he officially signed on, however, McClure wanted to do a background check on James to ensure that he was doing business with someone who had an untarnished past. Had McClure searched for James Terry Henrikson, he would have found the lengthy criminal history James had piled up. But since James was using one of his aliases, McClure's search for James Henricksen yielded nothing of concern. All James and McClure needed now was one or two additional investors, and they would be off to the races.

"In July of 2011, I agreed to invest in Henrikson's trucking company," McClure recalled. "I brought in one of my childhood friends, Brian Ford, who eventually introduced me to Ryan Olness."

•••

The story of the relationship between Jed McClure and Ryan Olness depends on who is telling it. While McClure contended it was a casual acquaintance through a mutual friend, Olness claimed that the two had worked together in a drug manufacturing business.

"I met (Jed) McClure through cold calling for my spice business," Olness later relayed to authorities. "I initially only knew him over the phone, but we gained trust with each other by wiring large sums of money between us."

The "spice" business to which Olness referred was merely a euphemism for the illegal manufacturing of synthetic marijuana. At the time, before states began legalizing weed, the spice business was quite profitable. And much like McClure, when an offer to make even more money was presented to Olness, he had a hard time letting it pass by.

"Jed shared the new business proposal with me," Olness later recounted. "I thought it sounded like a great idea."

McClure, Olness, and Brian Ford pooled together the initial $100,000 to purchase the first truck. Soon, McClure recruited several of his family members to invest an additional $100,000 to procure a second truck. Two months later, Mc-

Clure lured in yet one more friend, who ponied up the money for a third and fourth truck.

When Ford was unceremoniously ousted from the plans after a concerning run-in with law enforcement, it was only McClure and Olness who inked a joint venture with Blackstone Trucking in September 2011, granting them each a 12.5% share of the monthly gross profits. Under his signature line, James again misspelled his name as Henricksen. The contract further established that all parties retained the right to engage in other business ventures or financial interests, but with one specific caveat.

"I made sure the contract stated that I would have an ownership interest in any business James started in the oil industry," McClure later explained. "We had discussed additional potential businesses including renting lights and electrical equipment that are used on the oil rigs."

A few weeks after the contracts were signed, unbeknownst to McClure, James and Sarah set up the shell companies Blackwell Services LLC, Blackstone Crude LLC, Blackstone Oilfield Services LLC, and Blackstone Electric. On paper, each of these new entities was owned and operated solely by Sarah Creveling.

•••

When the agreement between Blackstone and Steve Kelly's Trustland Oilfield Services was finalized in October of 2011, the newly acquired trucks were put into immediate action, transporting water to and from oil fracking sites around the clock. As expected, the operation was a massive success, with the trucks filling up as quickly as they could be emptied, resulting in a steady stream of thousands of dollars in monthly revenue for Blackstone Trucking and its investors.

It appeared that Blackstone was well on its way to evolving into a very lucrative enterprise that could generate a continuous stream of income for the foreseeable future. All it required was its owners to exercise patience and hard work.

Sadly, these basic principles of successful entrepreneurship were dismissed by both James Henrikson and Sarah Creveling. At no time did either of them have any intention of applying ethical or lawful practices in their business dealings, and it wouldn't take long for their house of cards to begin tumbling down.

CHAPTER 13

Turds In A Punch Bowl

James and Sarah married in late summer of 2011, before any of the contracts had been signed for Blackstone Trucking, or work had begun in the oilfields. Their ceremony, if it could be described as such, was held in a small ballroom at a local hotel in Minot, North Dakota, in front of a sparse audience. The reason for the hasty nuptials wasn't so much because the couple was madly in love; after all, their relationship was barely a year old.

Sarah herself even eventually admitted that she had never envisioned marrying the ex-convict. Instead, the union was a calculated move. "It was easier to convince his probation officers to transfer James's residence to North Dakota if he had relatives—or a wife—there."

More importantly, the marriage gave James a convenient front for his business dealings. Still unwilling to use his own name for fear his checkered past would come to light, it was Sarah who readily affixed her signature to checks and contracts.

But even though he shied away from using his real name, James hardly tried to lay low. Rather, he stuck out like a sore thumb, primarily due to his penchant for wearing tight T-shirts to show off his sculpted physique and donning bedazzled jeans and leather vests in an environment where most men wore coveralls and steel-toed boots.

"It would be 20 degrees outside and he'd be wearing a T-shirt," one oil field worker remarked. "He is standing there shivering, but he's making sure his arms are pumped up and people see his 'guns.'"

His choice of outerwear aside, James's personal interactions also raised eyebrows. Although there was no doubt James was a "schmoozer," his persistent desire to project an image of authority and affluence manifested as tall tales of grandiosity, such as falsely claiming that his business endeavors were supported by a billion-dollar trust fund.

While many were repelled by James's flamboyant personality and dismissed him as an overbearing braggart, there were just as many who seemed to be enamored by him. Having a beautiful young bride on his arm didn't hurt, either. When James and Sarah went out on the town together, it was impossible not to notice them.

"With their perfectly white teeth and fake tans, they stuck out like two turds in a punch bowl," recalled one Blackstone employee. "They were like Ken and Barbie."

James drove a shiny new truck, and Sarah was always dressed to the nines in designer clothing. Because of the oil boom in North Dakota, the male population in small towns had surged, resulting in a staggeringly disproportionate ratio of men to women. Although James relished being the object of envy for single men who ogled his wife, Sarah claimed to despise the attention.

"It was rough," Sarah complained through giggles during an interview with *Dateline NBC*'s Keith Morrison. "I totally hated it. It was miserable. Every day was a plan on how to get out of there."

Even worse for Sarah was the nickname bestowed on her. Dabbing at her eyes during the interview with Morrison, Sarah decried the label. "I feel like I have somewhat of a brain. I don't want to be called just a Barbie."

A brain Sarah did indeed have. Disregarding the idle social gossip surrounding her and her husband, Sarah immersed herself in overseeing Blackstone's accounting and financial matters. Within a few months of launching their new company and signing contracts, the newlyweds were enjoying an endless flow of thousands of dollars into their bank accounts.

James and Sarah didn't hold back indulging themselves with extravagant gifts of clothing, jewelry, tropical vacations, and even paid almost $60,000 cash for a Bentley. Sarah snapped dozens of photos of herself smiling and posing in front of a full-length mirror, proudly showcasing her new handbags, lavish gowns, and countless pairs of designer shoes.

James also began collecting a cache of firearms—something he wasn't lawfully allowed to do because he was a convicted felon. No matter, because James always had a workaround.

"James and Sarah would go to a store," one detective later described. "James would point out which guns he wanted, and Sarah would buy them."

James also used plenty of the money to purchase steroids and other drugs for himself—habits he was unwilling to give up, and for which Sarah was either oblivious or willfully turned a blind eye.

•••

The joint venture agreement between investors and Blackstone Trucking required that Sarah hire an independent accountant to assist with managing and monitoring the company's finances. Each of the trucks that had been purchased or leased—which eventually reached a total of nine with more than $500,000 in investor's money—were to operate independently, and the accountant was expected to prepare separate detailed monthly profit and loss statements for the investors and be readily available to answer any questions they may have. Sarah hired a woman named Renee Johnson, a CPA from a local accounting firm in Watford City.

It soon became evident that Sarah had made a fortuitous choice in involving Johnson, for when Sarah began manipulating numbers and diverting significant chunks of Blackstone's profits into the shell companies she had set up, Johnson either didn't notice or didn't question the obvious accounting discrepancies.

Even though it was Sarah's name on all of the documents, checks, and bank accounts, she would later claim that it was James who made all of the decisions for the business. She was simply a passive participant, just doing what she was told.

"It was a James show for sure," she told *Dateline*.

When their checks began to dwindle and the financial reports looked fishy, Jed McClure started asking questions, and Ryan Olness decided to temporarily relocate to North Dakota so that he could see for himself what was going on. But as Olness would later explain, despite asking numerous times, he was never given the opportunity to study the financial documentation. Even more concerning, it appeared that there was a collective effort to cover something up.

"At first, the girls in the office were nice and willing to talk to me," Olness recalled. "Eventually, they began acting shady, and it seemed like maybe James and Sarah were paying them off to lie."

It did not take long for Olness to surmise what was going on.

As revenue had begun to flow in, James secretly leased additional trucks. These newly acquired trucks were strategically prioritized for work over those initially leased by investors. Consequently, the trucks that had been generating monthly revenue for McClure, Olness, and the other investors, were now often sitting idly in a field collecting dust.

Instead of being transparent with McClure and Olness about his decision to establish an additional entity of his own for subcontracting trucks, James resorted to repeated lies and gaslighting. James asserted that the original trucks were plagued with various mechanical issues, and that there wasn't enough money to get them fixed.

"When I started asking questions, James told me that Blackstone didn't have any money," Olness revealed later. "But I saw a lot of invoices passing through indicating that Blackstone was actually making plenty of money." Just not with the trucks that Olness and others had a financial stake in.

Jed McClure, still hundreds of miles away, sent a daily

barrage of text messages to James, demanding an explanation for why his trucks were no longer generating the profits they had been. Soon out of excuses, James eventually stopped responding to McClure altogether.

What McClure and Olness didn't know was that James and Sarah had much bigger fish to fry at the moment. Amid the financial wranglings with their investors, the couple had also somehow managed to begin a war with the very person who had opened the door to them for business in the oilfields in the first place—Steve Kelly.

CHAPTER 14

We Should Run, Not Walk

Steve Kelly was, first and foremost, a devoted family man. He was born and raised in Sidney, Montana, where he met and eventually married his lovely bride, Sandy. Both Steve and Sandy were members of the Mandan Hidatsa Arikara Tribe and were deeply proud of their cultural heritage. Sandy bore him three children—son Matt in 1985, daughter Amanda in 1987, and the baby of the family, Melissa, in 1990.

From a very young age, Steve knew he wanted to be a lawyer. His hard work and determination earned him a law degree in 1994 from the University of Colorado Boulder. He began his legal career by moving his family to Billings, Montana, where he became an associate with Fredericks, Pelcyger, Hester & White Law, which specialized in Tribal Law across several states. While Steve honed his skills as a lawyer, Sandy worked as a dental hygienist and raised their children.

In 2006, Steve was recruited by then MHA chairman Tex Hall to be the new tribal counsel for the Three Affiliated Tribes. While it was no doubt an honor and a tremendous recognition from the tribal community, the new position required the Kellys to leave Montana and move almost nine hours away, to the Fort Berthold Indian Reservation in New Town, North Dakota.

•••

By the time he arrived in New Town to assume his new position as tribal counsel Steve was in his mid-40s and had racked up over ten years of legal experience. He had barely settled in before being plunged into the new world of "oil," especially the ongoing wrangling between state and tribal leaders over how to divide the newly expected wealth and which side would bear the bigger brunt of inevitable taxes and regulation costs. It was a debate that would continue to be discussed, resolved, and then redebated anew many times, even 15 years after Steve Kelly was no longer the tribe's legal counsel.

In early 2008, Sandy Kelly began working part-time as a "landman" for Playa and Blackrock Resources. Landowners typically own not only their individual parcel, but also the mineral rights for any subterranean resources that might lie beneath the surface. Since the oil and gas companies hold no claim to those mineral rights, the only way they can begin exploring and drilling for oil is if the landowner agrees to it. A landman serves as the representative for the energy company, tasked with coordinating legal negotiations to lease mineral rights from the landowner. In most circumstances it is the oil company that retains the lion's share of profits, and the landowner agrees to a meager percentage.

As straightforward as it may seem, these negotiations can be difficult and messy. Oftentimes, it is not just one person who owns a particular plot of land—in many cases, it can be dozens or even hundreds of listed owners—which meant that the need for landmen, and experienced ones at that, was in high demand. A good landman had to be able to relate and listen to the legitimate concerns coming from landowners and the community as a whole. Even though the smallest percentage of profit could yield a windfall of money—the likes of which precious few had ever seen before—many tribal members on the reservation still felt they were making deals with the devil.

But that was why Sandy was so good at her job. She was able to balance the interests of her employer with the needs and concerns of her community. She was so skillful, in fact, that a few other landmen on the reservation became envious of her success and began attempts to sabotage not only her, but her husband. There were concerns that Sandy's partnerships directly with the oil companies might impact Steve's ability to remain neutral in his work as the tribal attorney. Pressure and public scrutiny soon began to mount against the Kellys.

Largely as a result of that pressure, in August 2008 Steve agreed to be bought out of his contract. In September, he and his wife formed Trustland Consultants, working together as landmen. In early 2009, they pivoted from consulting to trucking, bought a building they converted into a shop, and established Trustland Oilfield Services.

"It was small at first," Steve later reflected. "We had just a few roustabouts and one or two trucks. The trucks began hauling loads of water to and from drilling rigs and oil well locations, and we were running about 50 loads a day."

The oil work in and around New Town quickly ballooned to an almost impossible level to manage. Steve and Sandy were running Trustland by themselves, with Steve at the helm of field operations, and Sandy managing human resources and payroll. They had moved to Minot, which was over an hour away, and when the day-to-day roundtrips became too much, Steve would often spend the night in his office at the shop, while Sandy drove back to Minot to care for their two teenage daughters. Before long, important aspects of the business began to fall through the cracks.

"We were hiring people and contracting with truck drivers as fast as we could, and sometimes that meant not conducting extensive background checks," Sandy admitted later.

It was no sooner that Steve and Sandy recognized they were close to drowning that they received a call from a man named James Henrikson, who claimed to be a successful businessman from Texas with at least ten trucks he was willing to bring up to North Dakota to begin subcontracting out for Trustland. The name of Henrikson's company, he told the Kellys, was Blackstone Trucking.

Though Steve's initial instinct was to leap at the possibility of expanding his company's fleet, he first wanted to meet James. He invited James and his then-girlfriend, Sarah Creveling, to join himself and Sandy at a professional MMA fight at the 4 Bears Casino in New Town.

James and Sarah were both young, gregarious, and gorgeous: he, well-built with a flashing white smile, she with a stunning physique and equally blinding grin. They wore designer clothes and impressed Steve with their energy and what seemed like prudent business speak. To Steve, it was an easy answer. Yet something about the couple made the hairs on Sandy's neck stand up.

"I told Steve at the time that we should run, not walk, away from these people," Sandy recalled. "I didn't know what it was. I just knew something was off about them."

"You worry too much," Steve chided her at the time. "Besides, what could they possibly do?"

Had either Steve or Sandy been aware that the charismatic James already had a rap sheet multiple felonies long and had recently finished up his latest stint in jail, running away might have been precisely the thing they had done.

•••

Perhaps the first red flag for Steve and Sandy had come when James arrived in North Dakota a few months later–with only one truck. Not the ten he had originally promised. But even one truck was one truck more than he had running, and Steve was willing to take anything he could. Any initial hesitancy the Kellys felt was tamped down when in the fall of 2011, Blackstone Trucking made partial good on their initial promise with a handful of additional trucks.

As they expanded their payroll, Steve and Sandy purchased several trailer houses for truckers and employees to stay since housing was so scarce. They also ramped up hiring for the administrative side of their business, which began easing the burden resting on their shoulders.

This also meant that Sandy had more time to effectively scrutinize the work contracts and receipts that were coming in and going out. She began noticing that the invoices coming in from Blackstone Trucking did not seem to match her own records. Although it would take her some time to reconcile the information, it appeared that Blackstone had been overcharging them for weeks.

Sandy's intuition told her that James and Sarah were up to something. She also started to observe Sarah acting strangely whenever she visited Trustland's offices. Sandy would often catch Sarah trying to look through the paperwork sitting on her desk. The more Sandy watched, the more her concerns grew. Finally, after several weeks, one day everything came to a head.

"Steve's office was always locked when he wasn't there. But one day I walked into the main office and saw Sarah coming out of Steve's office. I have no idea how she would have gotten in there, but I had enough by that point," Sandy relayed later. "I told her, 'You two are up to no good. I know it and you know it. What I need from you right now is to get up and get the fuck out of here!'"

Sandy recalled how Sarah had given her a deer-in-the-headlights gaze and fled the office in tears. It was the last time Sandy would talk to Sarah, and the last official day that Blackstone Trucking did any contract work for Trustland Oilfield Services. But it would not be the last time the Kellys crossed paths with James Henrikson.

•••

After the Kellys abruptly terminated their contract, James and Sarah found themselves navigating an unfriendly business environment. Though they had not understood it at the time, the opportunity to partner with Steve and Sandy the moment they stepped foot onto the reservation had opened up a pathway for infinite possibilities. By burning that bridge, however, James and Sarah had effectively slammed the door in their own faces.

The couple had to quickly educate themselves on the way things worked when conducting business on a Native American reservation, particularly as it related to the oilfields. The Tribal Employment Rights Office (TERO) had long since established the precedent that tribal members would always have Tier 1 status priority for all oil contracts on any part of the Bakken oilfields located on the Fort Berthold Reservation.

While he could still bid for jobs in the oilfields not located on the reservation, as a white man, James and Blackstone Trucking were the last in line for anything in New Town and Mandaree, where a significant portion of the work was being done. TERO was the governing body making decisions on who won highly coveted contract bids, and in almost all circumstances, tribal members submitting bids were awarded the jobs. Not to be outdone, James would soon find a way around the red tape.

In November 2011, Steve Kelly learned that Trustland had been awarded the bid for a lucrative contract with the oil and gas company Petro Hunt. It was a cause for celebration, and as such, he and his wife scheduled a vacation to Mexico. Their excitement would be short-lived, however, as while lounging on the beach they received a call from the TERO offices, informing them that the contract had instead been awarded to a company called Blackstone Oilfield Services. Its owner, they were told, was Stephanie Wellmaker, a Navajo woman from Texas. While she would not be running day-to-day operations in North Dakota, her business partners would. The "business partners" were of course none other than James and Sarah.

Steve immediately cried foul and returned to the States to launch an appeal. After further review, TERO ultimately determined that while Wellmaker was indeed Native American, she was not a member of the Three Affiliated Tribes and therefore did not enjoy the same preferred status on the Fort Berthold reservation. Consequently, Blackstone Oilfield Services' contract was revoked and was instead returned to Trustland.

For the Kellys, that was the conclusion of the situation. For James, however, it was the gasoline needed to fuel an already burning flame.

CHAPTER 15

I Probably Should Have Checked Up On Him

In December of 2011, James Henrikson instructed one of his truck drivers to purposely stall his rig on a highway in the middle of the Fort Berthold Indian Reservation in Mandaree, North Dakota—directly in front of the sprawling ranch owned by then tribal chairman Tex Hall.

Hall, in his 50s, was raised on the cattle and buffalo ranch and had always been told by his ancestors that he would one day be the leader of the Three Affiliated Tribes. It was a pre-ordained destiny that he took very seriously.

"I knew I would grow up to lead my tribe," Hall later reflected. "My grandfather told me I bore the weight of the tribe on my shoulders."

With his lean 6' frame, Tex Hall towered over most and greeted people with a penetrating stare and a firm handshake. He wore his long salt and pepper hair in a ponytail that was always topped with his signature black cowboy hat. His brown skin was deeply weathered from years of working outdoors on his ranch, and his dark eyes lit up with pride when talking about his heritage and culture. Hall was not shy to voice his deeply rooted mistrust in government, but he was a fierce Democrat who played a prominent role in the national political discourse regarding tribal interests.

He was a highly revered leader, seen by many as a strong champion in fighting for the sovereign rights of his tribe. Having served two consecutive four-year terms, Hall had recently been reelected for an unprecedented third term in 2010, just as the peak of the oil boom had begun to take hold in the region. Soon, his priorities as tribal leader shifted nearly exclusively to oil production on the reservation.

"Sovereignty by the barrel," Hall's signature tagline boasted at the annual Bakken Oil and Gas Expo seminars held at the 4 Bears Casino and Lodge in New Town. The conference was coyly nicknamed the "TexPo" as it was Hall's opportunity to speak to a wide array of political and industry leaders to emphasize the benefits of continued collaboration amongst them in the ongoing oil-drilling frenzy.

"Tex Hall was a very good advocate," Steve Kelly later recognized. "I could never take that away from him."

But as Hall's enthusiasm for oil grew, his focus on the betterment of the tribe as a whole waned significantly. The community became impatient when the tribal government began raking in tens of millions of dollars with very little of the royalties being distributed amongst the roughly 14,000 members of the tribe. Worse still, only a small percentage of the oil revenues were being allocated to important social programs and badly needed infrastructure improvements to roads and housing.

"I have no problem with the government making profit," tribal elder Marilyn Hudson said later in an interview. "But when they make a profit for themselves and not for the people, that's another story."

At one point, the decision to purchase a $2.5 million dollar 96-foot yacht for the 4 Bears Casino, charmingly named "Island Girl," was heavily criticized as a waste of money. The original purpose of the yacht was to conduct cruises across the lake from the casino, but the massive boat sat as an unused eyesore on cement blocks for years.

Not only was the general tide shifting toward disapproval of tribal government priorities, but the chairman was also raising eyebrows with a perceived conflict of interest. Before being reelected to his third term, Hall had begun his own oil field services company named Maheshu Energy. His longtime girlfriend, Tiffiany Johnson, acted as the chief operating officer while also managing a popular clothing boutique called the Sparkling Spur.

While the tribal ethics ordinance forbade leaders from leveraging their positions in office for personal gain, there was nothing that prohibited them from operating oil-related businesses. Once Hall won his reelection bid, it was no secret that Maheshu Energy began winning the lion's share of new oil contracts. Not only did the tribe's legal counsel take notice, but so too did other business owners.

"It was a good-old-boys club," a former supervising attorney for the tribe lamented in an interview. "If you are going to do business on the reservation, obviously it's best to do it with the chief."

"Trustland's prices were better, and we had the same qualified workforce," Steve Kelly later told a reporter. "It was pretty clear why Maheshu got the contracts. I wanted to make it an issue of ethics, and so I did."

Unfortunately, the concerns fell upon deaf ears, as a seven-member tribal council, including Tex Hall, nixed the discussion outright, ostensibly because the tribe did not have a committee to conduct any oversight or inquiry into possible ethics violations. There was nothing Steve, or any other businessman on the reservation, could do.

Hall was riding on a wave of triumphs, completely unaware of the sharks circling below.

• • •

The highways sandwiching Hall's ranch in Mandaree, North Dakota are desolate—no service stations in sight, no other houses for miles, and cellphone and internet service spotty at best. If James Henrikson's driver had actually broken down right in front of Hall's property, it would have been difficult for him to communicate with someone that he needed help.

For anyone who was unaware that the whole thing had been orchestrated, it seemed sheer luck that James pulled up in his own truck just as the rig broke down. Noticing the commotion, Hall walked out to greet his unexpected visitors. Unbeknownst to Hall, James had been asking around town for weeks about how he could connect with the chairman and where he lived.

"My driver just ran out of gas," James explained. "Do you have any gas cans I could borrow?"

An odd request, perhaps. If James had his own vehicle, there was no reason he could not drive the 20 or so miles to the nearest gas station and get a few gas cans for himself. But this was North Dakota, where neighborly goodwill was still a prided hallmark of culture. Hall invited the stranded stranger onto the ranch property, where the newly built office building and shop for Maheshu Energy were also located.

James wasted no time in getting down to business. "Is that your shop? I run my own subcontracting trucking business, and we have been looking for a new space to operate from."

Whatever it was James said that day to convince him, Hall soon agreed to a subcontracting agreement with Blackstone Trucking, signing on the dotted line in January 2012. Just as Henrikson had planned, Blackstone set up operations in Maheshu Energy's shop in Mandaree, leasing the space for a reported $5,000 a month.

It did not take long for James and Sarah to become close with Hall, his girlfriend Tiffiany Johnson, and her teenage daughter Peyton. The families spent Christmas together and embarked on an exotic vacation to Hawaii to escape North Dakota's brutal winter climate.

Back in the oilfields, James touted his connection to the chairman and was soon enjoying privileged access to contracts, including a $570,000 road watering job that was never put out to bid. Hall even encouraged his tribal council to vote in favor of the contract award, neglecting to reveal he had a personal connection to James or Blackstone Trucking.

In late January 2012, Hall faced a serious health scare when his gallbladder burst, which led to even more complications. While he spent weeks in hospitals across North Dakota, South Dakota, and Minnesota, with his family fearing they would lose him, James and Sarah viewed his compromised state—and his prolonged absence from Maheshu—as a golden opportunity.

Sarah did her best to feign concern and empathy during her hospital visits. Nurses craned their necks to catch a glimpse of the rail-thin blonde in designer heels, her footsteps click-clacking down the corridors. One hospital employee later claimed Sarah had carried a fifth of whiskey in one hand for the ailing chairman, and contracts for him to sign in the other. Hall would later vacillate on whether the whiskey-and-contracts story was indeed factual.

Before long, James and Sarah were the ones running Maheshu under the guise they were stepping in during Hall's time of need. In reality, they were taking him to the cleaners.

Upon his return, Hall discovered invoices totaling hundreds of thousands of dollars from a company called Geneva Investments, a name he didn't recognize. When he asked about it, James and Sarah claimed Geneva was an entity they had established to loan money to Maheshu's employees in advance of their paychecks. The invoices reflected the amount Maheshu now owed for those loans. It didn't take a rocket scientist to figure out there were never any "loans" handed out to employees. But because they were the ones controlling operations for Maheshu, James and Sarah had gone ahead and written themselves the checks for the fictional "loans."

"James and Sarah became very defensive and eventually refused to answer any further questions," Hall recalled. "I found $540,000 worth of checks written out to Blackstone Crude, which is James's company. I was suspicious and told my accountant not to disperse those checks. I received a call from my bank asking me about several large checks that were in the process of clearing. The bank was able to stop payment on only about half of the checks."

But money wasn't the only thing James and Sarah would take from him. The full extent of their treachery would not be known for many months. By the time Tex Hall did understand, it was already too late to do anything about it, and the chief's once untarnished reputation within his own tribe would eventually be destroyed.

"I probably should have checked up on him," Hall reluctantly admitted later.

•••

After the fallout with Trustland, James had masterfully managed to redeem himself. Blackstone Trucking was once again making money hand over fist, and James and Sarah had almost reached the pinnacle of oilfield royalty by partnering with the once-admired tribal chairman. But it still wasn't enough.

It was not enough to make them stop stealing money from Tex Hall and Maheshu Energy. It wasn't enough for them to discontinue defrauding their Blackstone Trucking investors. And it most certainly was not enough for James to leave the dust-up with the Kellys far behind in the rearview mirror.

The fact that Steve and Sandy had triumphed and wrestled back a lucrative contract from his grip was humiliating and unforgiveable. Rage simmered within James before he reached a disturbing conclusion: the only way the score could be settled was if Steve Kelly was dead.

CHAPTER 16

The Plan To Get Rid Of Steve Kelly

In February 2012, James Henrikson was a very busy man. While continuing to scam his investors, and actively working to sabotage Tex Hall and Maheshu Energy, James was simultaneously trying to recruit someone to murder Steve Kelly. As an ex-convict who had spent his fair share of time in prison in both Oregon and Washington, it was no surprise that James had made a few friends while behind bars.

One of them, a man named Robert DeLao, was a former member of a violent Hispanic street gang and was currently living in Spokane, Washington. Short in stature with jet black hair and eyes as dark as night, DeLao had a reputation for being extremely manipulative and dangerous, but he masterfully disguised his violent tendencies with a distinctly charming and goofy personality.

DeLao was out on parole, having most recently served time for burglary. Before that, he'd done a stretch for manslaughter, after stabbing a rival gang member to death. DeLao wore his crime like a badge of honor, even getting a large tattoo of himself urinating on the man's grave. His lenient sentences were the result of deals he struck with law enforcement, agreeing to become a confidential informant in exchange for early release.

Just days after walking out of the iron prison gates, DeLao received a call from his old friend James, offering what seemed like a legitimate opportunity to work in the oilfields. Before DeLao could travel to North Dakota and begin working for Blackstone Trucking, James had a pre-employment test for him to complete—procure a hitman.

•••

As it turned out, Robert DeLao's candidate pool for hitmen wasn't very deep. Near the bottom of the barrel was a man named Timothy Suckow, another former convict living in Spokane.

At 48 years of age, Suckow had spent almost half of his life in and out of prison for a variety of crimes ranging in severity from bike theft to armed robbery. In his last stint in an Arizona prison, Suckow promised himself that "this time was the last time," and he had been out of prison since 2004, spending the last eight years trying to rebuild his life.

He married an outspoken woman named JoAnne DesJarlais, and they had built a somewhat modest life for themselves, renting one side of a duplex in a quaint northeast neighborhood of Spokane, an industrial community just over a dozen miles west of the Idaho border. While his wife worked various administrative jobs, Suckow had maintained steady employment at IRS Environmental (IRSE).

IRSE, a full-service industrial asbestos and lead removal company, was well-known for its openness to hiring ex-convicts, providing steady blue-collar work in an industry that few chose to enter. Suckow had done well during his employment with IRSE and had become a rather trusted member of its workforce. As the years wore on, he was given additional responsibilities, including keys to supervise the secured backyard lot where IRSE's white work vans were parked and stored.

In his younger years, Suckow described himself as a scrawny weakling. And while he had engaged in petty theft during that time, he went out of his way to avoid physical confrontations of any kind. In fact, he made it a point to avoid most human contact as much as he could, period. He would later claim his reluctance to develop relationships with others was because he did not trust most people. But he also struggled with bipolar disorder—a diagnosis that came much too late in life, and for which he blamed the penal system.

"They don't care about mental disorders or making sure inmates have the treatment they need," he complained of prison institutions. "If someone had taken the time to figure out what was wrong with me, maybe some of these other things would not have happened."

By the time he left prison in 2004, the once scrawny teenager had transformed himself into a beefcake of a man, standing over 6' tall and weighing 250 pounds. Suckow had used much of his time on the "inside" in the weight room, developing bulging biceps and perfectly sculpted abdominal and pectoral muscles.

"Lifting weights was a good way to bide my time. But weights aren't allowed in prisons anymore," he later complained.

Along his lengthy institutionalized journey, he also acquired dozens of tattoos to accentuate his physique, including—in what would seem ironic years later—a huge phoenix that spanned his entire back. When the ink of some of his older tattoos faded, Suckow would simply get a new one to go over top of the old one, creating a haunting shadow effect across most of his body.

But even the total transformation in body composition didn't boost his self-confidence. Suckow was still a loner and did not go out of his way to make new friends. That is, until 2006, when IRSE hired two new employees, Lazaro "Laz" Pesina and Robert "Mugsy" DeLao. In Pesina and DeLao, Suckow found common ground given that all three had similar backgrounds and experiences.

"I was always very standoffish because I never trusted people," Suckow explained. "I had more trust with the criminal element than for 'regular' people, and even that was minimal. But Laz and Robert and I got to be good friends."

Even though Pesina and DeLao were only with IRSE for a short time, the trio stayed in contact for several years.

In late 2011, things began to unravel for Tim Suckow. He had become obsessed with end-of-the-world conspiracy theories, and in turn, had made a hobby out of purchasing and trading illegal firearms, ammunition, and military tactical gear. He paid a hefty monthly sum to store his accumulated prized possessions in a large space at a nearby storage facility. But in his preparation for the impending apocalypse, Suckow had squandered away most of his savings.

In early February 2012, things went from bad to worse when he was temporarily laid off from IRSE. But just in the nick of time, he received a call from his old pal Laz Pesina. Pesina relayed that he had spoken with the recently paroled "Mugsy," who was actively looking for candidates to fill an urgent job opportunity in North Dakota.

"Did you hear Mugsy got out? He called me the other day. He's over in North Dakota, trying to get into the oil drilling business," Pesina reported. "Sounds like there might be drama up there. He asked if I knew of someone who might be willing to help with some affairs he's dealing with."

"What kind of help?" Suckow asked, intrigued.

"You know, like a hired muscle. Someone to rough somebody up a bit. Nothing too major. Just enough to scare them. I'd guess it pays pretty well. Give Mugsy a call," Pesina urged.

In the hours that followed this phone conversation, Suckow pondered the proposal— vague as it was at the time—that had been presented. The bottom line was that he was desperate and looking for any means to make some money, which meant calling "Mugsy" wasn't a choice—it was a necessity.

Over the next few days, Suckow and DeLao exchanged a flurry of phone calls and text messages, with DeLao outlining the situation:

DeLao worked for a man named James Henrikson. James operated a trucking company just outside of Watford City, North Dakota, on Native American land. In recent weeks, James had become embroiled in a contractual snafu with another business owner named Steve Kelly. At present, Kelly was threatening to "run James out of town." Something needed to be done quickly to stop it. The question was, could Suckow come to North Dakota to take care of this Kelly guy, get him off of James's back?

"How much is he going to pay?" Suckow inquired.

DeLao wasn't sure. "I don't know the exact amount, but I would guess a couple thousand dollars."

A couple thousand dollars to Suckow meant catching up on rent payments, getting some much-needed repairs done on his vehicle, and perhaps buying something pretty for his wife if there was enough left over. Without further hesitation, he purchased a $240 round-trip train ticket from Spokane to Williston, North Dakota, where James planned to meet him.

●●●

By the time Suckow's train rolled into the newly remodeled Amtrak station in Williston late on the night of Tuesday, February 21, 2012, the plans had changed. It took a minute to register when James explained that he didn't want Suckow to just "rough up" Steve Kelly.

"I want him dead," James said point blank. "And I want it done tomorrow."

At first, Suckow tried to reason with his new friend. "Hey man, have you tried hashing it out with him? You're both grown men. I'm sure you can work it out."

But James wouldn't budge. And Suckow didn't refuse the new assignment.

Suckow was dropped off at one of the trailers that James and his wife Sarah Creveling had rented out for their truckers in Watford City. Despite knowing he was expected to commit a murder the next day, Suckow fell into a deep sleep the minute his head hit the pillow.

He was still half-asleep when James barged into the trailer before 7:00 a.m. the next morning, announcing that the plan to murder Steve Kelly had to be put on hold.

Suckow was irked that he had purchased a train ticket to North Dakota for a wasted trip. When he asked if he would be reimbursed for his time and trouble, James reassured him that there was still work to be done, for which a handsome payment would indeed be provided.

"I need you to kill someone else," James stated. "His name is K.C. Clarke."

CHAPTER 17

Timing Is Everything

Handsome and charismatic Washington native Kristopher Clarke had nearly died once before. After a horrific accident on a motocross circuit, Kristopher found himself in a hospital bed, his body badly mangled. Motocross racing is often described as being one of the most skilled and energetic motor sports around, but it can also be very dangerous.

Kristopher was obsessed with the sport, spending most of his teen years and every free moment of his time developing his skills for the trails and showboating his prized dirt bikes. There was very little else he cared about.

The accident had occurred in the blink of an eye, no one really knowing exactly how it had happened. In dire straits, Kristopher was rushed to the nearest hospital, where doctors and nurses frantically worked to stabilize him. At first, his doctors did not think he would survive the damage his head, neck and body had sustained. Then, once it seemed that he would pull through, there was fear that he would never walk again.

But after weeks in the hospital and multiple surgeries—which included placing dozens of plates and pins and screws throughout his body—Kristopher Clarke was miraculously put back together again. The lingering scars were there to remind him every day. Most notably was the marked limp he would always walk with—a noticeable gait that earned him the moniker of "Gimp Daddy" from his many friends. To most, though, he was affectionately known as "K.C."

While many of his supporters felt that the whole experience would end his motocross career, it served to only further K.C.'s desire to participate in risky sports—but this time on a more stable racing surface, and with a much faster machine.

In 2006, K.C. traded in his dirt bike for a bright green Kawasaki motorcycle and became a Team Racer with the Eternal Professional Motorcycle Road Race Team in Tacoma, Washington.

Soon thereafter, he met and competed against another young man who raced for the Oregon Motorcycle Road Racing Association. His name was James Henrikson.

•••

Born in 1983, K.C. was the third child for Jill Williams, a petite brunette who would eventually have five children with multiple fathers. Outwardly, it seemed as though Jill fiercely loved her children, but she struggled to care for them. It was something that K.C. would grow to resent the older he got, and it was his grandfather, Robert Clarke, who had taken on the lion's share of raising the young boy.

The bond with his grandfather was one that K.C. cherished and viewed as one of the most important relationships of his life. The strong foundation and moral values the elder Clarke instilled in his grandson were always evident in the way K.C. conducted himself. When he was finally old enough to be out on his own, K.C. still made sure to call his grandfather at least once a week.

The relationship with his mother, however, never completely healed, and the two would often find themselves estranged, not speaking to each other for years at a time. She would never know that to his dying day, K.C. carried in his wallet a tender photo of his young mother holding her infant son close to her face, planting a soft kiss on his forehead.

By 2008, K.C. Clarke was 25 years old and well into his career as a motorcycle racer. While he still bore some of the lingering pain and physical limitations due to his accident years before, he still felt the familiar adrenaline rush of firing up his bike, pulling on his helmet, and pushing the limits of speed around the racetrack.

K.C. immersed himself in the life, building a close-knit circle of fellow racers. He had prominent sponsors embellishing his bike with their logos and was revered within the community. With thick brown hair and puppy dog brown eyes, K.C. was a very attractive young man, and there was no shortage of female admirers who vied for his attention. It was his boyish charm and dimpled grin that allowed him to get away with enjoying a woman's company for an evening without the promise of a long-term commitment. For a time, he had no interest in settling down.

But a last-minute vacation to Texas quickly changed that. There, he met a beautiful young woman named Josephine Paulino, and he was instantly smitten.

"I met the one," K.C. revealed to several friends.

And he meant it. To everyone's surprise, K.C. dropped everything he had worked for in an instant and moved from Washington to the small town of Brownwood, Texas to be with Josephine.

The couple rented a house together for the next three years while K.C. earned a modest salary working at a local car dealership. His days of racing were stalled, but he still enjoyed admiring souped-up motorcycles, and planned to eventually purchase more for himself.

In September of 2011, K.C. was blindsided when Josephine announced that she wanted to end their relationship. He was heartbroken and had no idea what his next move would be. He did not want to remain in Brownwood, where it was likely he would run into Josephine, but he also dreaded the thought of picking up and starting over somewhere new yet again. He was at a crossroads, unsure of where to turn.

No sooner had K.C. and Josephine cut the cord on their courtship did an old friend reappear in K.C.'s life. None other than James Henrikson.

"No one even knows how James found K.C.," a friend close to K.C. would later explain, "but he just showed up at the car dealership one day with quite a sales pitch ready."

James told his old friend that he and his wife Sarah Creveling had moved to Texas a few years before with the hopes of starting a masonry business. When that had not worked out as planned, the couple set their sights on the massive crude oil production boom happening in North Dakota. With nothing to lose, they had picked up stakes and headed north, hoping for success. After only six months, the gamble paid off. He boasted to K.C. that he and Sarah had made nearly half a million dollars operating a subcontracting trucking company they named Blackstone Trucking.

"If you're interested in checking things out up there, I'll have a job waiting for you," James promised. "There is a lot of money to be made."

"But I don't know anything about working in an oil field," K.C. remarked.

"You'll figure it out," James assured him.

If it had been several months earlier, K.C. would have never even fathomed the thought of leaving Texas or Josephine to follow James anywhere, least of all North Dakota. But now it seemed like the perfect opportunity, and he became increasingly enthusiastic about a potential fresh start.

Within a few weeks, K.C.'s bags were packed, and he headed north on US Highway 183 out of Brownwood. Not quite ready to permanently sever ties to the small town, he left the bulk of his personal belongings behind in the house he had shared with Josephine and paid the rent for several months in advance.

CHAPTER 18

I'm Going To Kill Him

K.C. Clarke embarked on an epic solo adventure, traveling roughly 1,400 miles from Brownwood, Texas to Watford City, North Dakota, chronicling his journey through dozens of photographs. He felt especially exhilarated each time he crossed into a new state, ensuring that he captured the standard "Welcome To" signs along the highways of Oklahoma, Kansas, Nebraska, and South Dakota.

Many of the photos he snapped were from his vantage point behind the steering wheel, featuring long stretches of highway, oftentimes with no other vehicles in sight. He quickly realized that the scenery across much of the plains is quite different than that of his home state of Washington, but nevertheless appreciated the tranquility of sprawling farmlands, deep blue skies, and magnificent sunsets.

Upon entering North Dakota, K.C. marveled as he drove by massive oil wells that were seemingly everywhere, their horseheads and counterweights slowly bobbing up and down, mimicking the seesawing motion of a teeter-totter. Giant wind turbines pumped through crisp November air while gusty breezes rippled across harvested sunflower and wheat fields. Dozens of mud-caked Ford and Chevrolet pickup trucks raced to pass him on narrow and winding two-lane highways while more than once he found himself stuck behind a sluggish procession of tanker trucks.

It was an exhilarating time for K.C. He was starting a whole new chapter in his life, moving to a place where he had never been, and where he knew virtually no one. For a moment, anyway, it seemed that nothing could go wrong.

James Henrikson and Sarah Creveling had been renting a trailer and offered K.C. a room until they could all find more permanent accommodations. K.C. was barely able to get his bags unpacked before James was ready to put him to work. Although he was never assigned an official title or provided a specific list of job duties to fulfill, K.C. was a determined employee and it did not take long for him to learn the ropes.

Blackstone Trucking had subcontracted out a fleet of a dozen trucks to a handful of oilfield services companies. Since K.C. did not have the proper license to operate one of the trucks, James and Sarah instead put him in charge of overseeing the coordination of truck schedules and supervision of the contracted drivers at their assigned sites.

"K.C. basically did everything but drive the trucks," Sarah explained later. "He was a truck pusher and an operations manager."

Before long K.C. was working well over 60 hours a week, putting on hundreds of miles each day driving to and from various frac sites. He was also settling in and moved into an apartment in New Town with another oil field worker named Judd Parker, while James and Sarah purchased a sprawling ranch-style home 50 miles away on the outskirts of Watford City.

K.C. had even leased a white Chevy pickup truck for himself. He quickly became a familiar face in the oil fields and loved to shoot the breeze with the many contractors, roustabouts, and oil company representatives he came into contact with each day.

"He was just a really nice guy," one oil worker recalled. "That kid always had a huge smile on his face."

K.C. enjoyed whiskey and frequented the local bars whenever he had a night off, which was becoming increasingly rare. It was on one of those occasions that he met a bleached blonde Native American woman named Tesha Jo Fredericks, who was a manager at the 4 Bears Casino in New Town. Rumors swirled that the two had embarked on a casual intimate relationship, although both denied it. K.C. also met and befriended a burly blue-eyed oilfield worker from Indiana named Rick Arey. The three of them, Tesha, Rick, and K.C., were often spotted huddled in a corner of the bar, talking quietly amongst themselves.

It turned out that K.C. was really good at his new job. Perhaps too good. Even though Sarah was in charge of record keeping and payroll, K.C. kept copious logs for himself of Blackstone's fleet schedule, as well as the hours of the contracted truckers who drove the rigs. Within a few months, many of the drivers had developed a trust in K.C. and began to approach him with concerns that Sarah was underpaying them for the hours they had put in. When compared to his own records, he could see their concerns were legitimate.

In truth, K.C. had not paid much attention to his own paychecks, but soon realized that his rate of pay also did not seem to match the hours he was working. There were days he worked 24 hours, went back to his apartment to shower, then went right back out to the grind again.

"He was working his ass off and not getting paid for it," one of K.C.'s friends later lamented.

On top of that, there were whispers starting to swirl around the oil fields that James and his wife were engaging in dishonest business dealings with some of Blackstone Trucking's investors. There was also talk that James was back to dabbling in illegal drug manufacturing. K.C. not only became increasingly exhausted and frustrated, but he also grew more and more uneasy working for the likes of James and Sarah. If they were up to something nefarious, he wanted absolutely no part of it.

K.C. shared these concerns with his new friends Tesha and Rick, revealing that he was ready to get out. Arey was also frustrated with his pay and eager to find a new job.

"I have an idea," Fredericks said one night. "Maybe I should start my own trucking company, and you can work for me."

Both K.C. and Rick Arey jumped at the opportunity, but there would be some logistics to work through before any transitions were made.

•••

Perhaps it could be argued that this trio of entrepreneurial novices did not go about planning for their new venture in the most responsible or professional way. But the reality was that no one did. As John D. Rockefeller—himself an oil magnate from the late 1800s through the 1930s—famously mused, "Competition is a sin." It was no different in the modern-day oilfields. Since the boom had begun around 2008, it was every company/man/machine for themselves, and it did not matter who got trampled along the way.

When Tesha Fredericks decided she wanted to start Running Horse Trucking, she recruited K.C. Clarke and Rick Arey to begin quietly poking around for potential customers, including those who were already doing business with other contractors. The customers and contractors working with James Henrikson and Blackstone Trucking were no exception. Given that K.C. had regular daily contact with many of them, there were abundant opportunities to put a bug in their ears. And as it turned out, quite a number of them were more than interested in jumping ship and signing on with Running Horse.

Although they did their best to keep conversations discreet, word gets around in a small town, and it only took a few weeks before James got wind that one of his main employees—someone he also considered a good friend—was actively trying to poach some of his customers and workers.

Enraged, James began telling close confidantes that he would "kick K.C.'s ass." He even told a few that he wanted to "kill" K.C. because he was "stealing contracts away from him," but few people took a threat of this magnitude too seriously. And as far as anyone knew, James had never even directly confronted K.C. about the situation.

Still, the people who were in K.C.'s corner cautioned him that James knew what was going on and wasn't happy about it. K.C. was uncomfortable appearing as though he was deliberately trying to undermine his friend. Indeed, he felt that both companies could be successful given there was more than plenty of work to go around.

His decision to sign on with Running Horse had more to do with him being tired and fed up. It had been several months since he ventured to North Dakota, and the exorbitant long hours, lagging pay, and shady business dealings made him want a clean break from Blackstone Trucking and those running its operation. He warned Fredericks and Arey that they needed to be more careful moving forward.

"K.C. told me that we needed to fly under the radar until he was sure there would be no problems with him leaving Blackstone," Fredericks recalled. "He wasn't ready to tell James he was leaving. He was very adamant that he did not want Blackstone to hurt me or this new business in any way."

Although James still had not confronted him on the matter, K.C. knew that things were reaching a fever pitch, and he soon grew concerned about his own safety. In January of 2012, he purchased a .45-caliber handgun, which he kept stowed in the center console of his truck wherever he went. Just in case.

CHAPTER 19

It Will Be A Quick Trip

In February 2012, James and Sarah surprised everyone and called for a mandatory, all-employee meeting to take place at Blackstone Trucking's main office located at Maheshu Energy in Mandaree, North Dakota. Such a meeting had never taken place before, but everyone, including K.C. Clarke, dutifully arrived on time, eager to hear what the topics of discussion would be.

Following some brief morning pleasantries, James and Sarah joyfully revealed the primary purpose of the gathering. They shared with the employees that the organization was formally acknowledging K.C.'s tireless efforts and commitment in the preceding months by awarding him a two-week paid vacation to recuperate and unwind.

"Right before he left, he was just not doing anything," Sarah would say later. "A lot of the guys thought he was depressed."

No one was more shocked to hear this announcement than K.C. himself. He had not mentioned to anyone that he wished for, or was planning, any type of vacation. He had also not requested any time off from either James or Sarah.

For several weeks, he'd been most worried about being fired, beaten up, or maybe even worse, because he was looking to leave the company for a new venture. Instead, he was now being rewarded. In fact, James and Sarah insisted that he take the vacation immediately.

Rather than dwell on the reasoning, K.C. jumped at the chance. He could use the two weeks to continue scouting new customers and mapping out his final exit strategy from Blackstone Trucking. Deal accepted.

On February 21, a week into his vacation, K.C. received a call from Sarah, asking him to come to the office to turn in his company-issued gas card. Details vary on the reasoning why, but one report suggested it was because Blackstone Trucking forbade employees to hold onto their company gas cards while on leave. Another was that the company had just received brand new cards with individual employee names printed on them to replace the old ones. As it would turn out, though, the actual reason was much more sinister.

Oblivious to possible nefarious motives for the request, K.C. agreed to come in the next morning, Wednesday, February 22, to turn over his gas card as Sarah had requested.

K.C. relayed the information to Tesha Fredericks and Rick Arey, who both issued dire warnings urging K.C. not to be alone with James Henrikson at any time, for any reason. The trio planned to meet right after K.C. was finished turning in his card.

"Don't worry," K.C. assured them. "It will just be a quick trip."

• • •

K.C. awoke on the morning of February 22, 2012, never knowing it would be for the last time. He dressed himself in a cozy gray sweatsuit and climbed into his cold truck to drive the 37 miles from his apartment in New Town south on Highway 22 toward the Blackstone Trucking shop in Mandaree.

It was just after 10:00 a.m. when he pulled into the gravel parking lot. On this chilly winter day, there was a flurry of activity as men milled about in tan coveralls, thick gloves, and stocking caps, waiting on their assigned truck routes for the day. Their rigs pulsed with diesel fuel, thick fogs of white billowing into the frigid air as they struggled to pump heat through the vents and make sure the water in their 4,000-gallon tanks didn't freeze.

K.C. turned off his ignition and reached into the center console to retrieve his wallet. As he exited his truck, he exchanged greetings with a handful of truckers in the yard before making his way to the shop's main office door. Inside, he greeted the all-female administrative staff with his usual charm and smile. Sarah was waiting with a wide smile of her own, and thanked K.C. as he handed over his gas card.

Grateful that the encounter was as seamless as he hoped it would be, K.C. made a beeline for his truck just outside the door, hoping for a quick getaway. By turning in his gas card, in his own mind, he had informally severed ties with Blackstone Trucking for good. When his second week of vacation was over, he planned to make it official. But there was no reason to announce it now when he was still getting paid to enjoy another several days off.

But before K.C. could pull his driver's side door shut, James appeared seemingly out of nowhere.

"Hey!" James's tone was playful. "Thanks for coming in. Before you go, you have to come and see the new bike I just got."

K.C. hesitated. He was supposed to meet Tesha Fredericks and Rick Arey right after his visit to the shop. They would be waiting for him. But in that moment, K.C. harbored hope of resolving his uncomfortable situation with James. His one-time friend's seemingly jovial disposition made him believe such a goal was not entirely unrealistic. If he and James could bond one more time over their love of motorcycles, maybe all the brewing animosity that had bubbled to the surface in the preceding weeks could be diffused and their friendship salvaged.

Perhaps it was the dozens of people milling about, in broad daylight, that made K.C. believe he was enveloped by an invisible shield that protected him against anything nefarious James might attempt. Surely, he wouldn't try to harm K.C. with that many witnesses around. Whatever his reasoning, and despite his friends cautioning him to be careful, K.C. swallowed back the sharp taste of knowing better and agreed to accompany James into the shop.

He didn't notice when James locked the shop door behind them after they were both inside. He was startled when a large, baldheaded man with menacing tattoos covering his arms suddenly emerged from the shadows of the poorly lit garage—a man whom K.C. had never seen before.

"Oh, hey there," James cheerily greeted the man. "K.C., this is my friend Tim."

Timothy Suckow let out an incoherent grunt, his eyes darting toward the cement floor.

James and K.C. walked past Suckow toward the back of the shop where the new motorcycle was parked. As he stood admiring the bike and listening to James brag, K.C. did not notice the hulking Suckow quietly removing the four-foot-long aluminum handle from a three-ton floor jack resting in the middle of the shop floor.

With his back turned, K.C. Clarke never saw what was coming next.

CHAPTER 20

No One Noticed

Four. That is how many blows to the head with an aluminum floor jack handle that it took to kill 29-year-old Kristopher David Clarke.

Suckow's first strike knocked K.C. to his knees. As he struggled to pick himself up, a second blow came down harder than the first, further disorienting him. A thin stream of blood emerged from his hairline and slowly trickled down his forehead, nose, and chin.

K.C. glanced up just long enough to see James Henrikson witnessing the attack unfold. Instead of helping, a sickening smile spread across James's face.

The third hit completely incapacitated K.C. His body crumpled face-forward to the ground. Unable to brace his fall, his head landed with a hideous thud directly on the concrete floor.

The fourth and final strike crushed the back of K.C.'s skull. His body convulsed for several seconds before becoming still. The brutal attack was over in less than two minutes.

Blood gushed from the mortally wounded man's head, rapidly forming a crimson river across the shop floor, quickly soaking into natural cracks in the concrete and pooling in between the joints. Panic set in for James and his hired hitman. In their hasty plan to kill a man, neither one of them had considered the aftermath.

"You need to clean this up!" James screamed at Suckow, who was still holding the bloody jack handle.

Suckow rushed into the shop's restroom looking around for anything that would help curb the flow of blood and brain matter from K.C.'s mangled head. The only thing he could find was a black garbage bag lining a nearby trash can. Suckow flipped the can upside down, dumping piles of wadded up used tissues and other garbage onto the floor, and removed the plastic liner.

He hustled back into the shop, carefully avoiding the pool of blood now surrounding K.C.'s upper body. Suckow lifted his victim's head from the ground by the hair, pulled the used trash bag over it, and haphazardly tied the open end into a knot around K.C.'s neck. He then dragged the lifeless corpse into the restroom and grotesquely propped it up against the wall.

• • •

While he was being savagely beaten by a man he had never met, the gun that K.C. purchased to protect himself was still hidden in the console of his truck. The cellphone he might have used to call for help buzzed on the empty driver's side seat with a call coming in from Rick Arey, who was wondering what was taking his friend so long.

As the late morning turned into early afternoon, Arey and Tesha Fredericks grew more and more concerned. K.C. had promised he would turn in his gas card and then immediately leave the shop, but it had been several hours since they had heard from him. All of their calls and text messages went unanswered.

Arey began making calls to other Blackstone workers, asking if they had seen K.C. at the shop that morning. A few of them informed James that Arey was poking around, asking questions, and was on his way out to the shop to locate K.C. himself.

Inside the shop, Suckow was still desperately trying to clean up a gruesome scene. He had found towels and rags to sop up most of the thickening puddles from the concrete floor, but that had not prevented the blood from soaking in, creating dark red stains on the surface. If anyone had entered the shop at that moment, the entire jig would have been up. But James had made sure that wouldn't happen—he'd sent one of his other employees on a mission to collect all the shop keys from people in the yard. Not wanting to get his own hands dirty, he had also left Suckow to clean up the mess on his own.

Suckow began pouring industrial solvent over the blood stains, vigorously trying to scrub them out. When that didn't work, he resorted to using motor oil, which he surmised would cover up the red stains with inky black ones.

Throughout Suckow's frantic clean-up process, James appeared sporadically to check on his progress, ridiculing him for not working faster. Before long, he came in to let Suckow know that they needed to get rid of K.C.'s truck, which was still parked outside in the yard.

"Some of K.C.'s friends are asking around about him, and are on their way out here," James urgently relayed. "We have to move his truck."

Suckow hesitated, worried about leaving K.C.'s dead body and the lingering mess without anyone there to ensure no one came inside the shop. Not only that, but Suckow himself was now covered in K.C.'s blood—an unavoidable circumstance given the situation. It was still daylight outside with several people around. Someone would surely see him, notice the crimson stains on his jeans and boots, and wonder what the hell was going on.

However, to his good fortune, no one did. Not one person noticed when the bloodied Suckow drove away in K.C.'s truck with James following closely behind in another truck. Remarkably, even the workers Rick Arey had already spoken with, the ones who had confirmed that K.C. and his truck were there at the shop, didn't notice when his truck left the yard without him in it.

•••

James knew of very few options for where to ditch K.C.'s truck but settled on temporarily hiding it in a random neighborhood in the town of Watford City, 30 miles east of the shop on Highway 73. With Watford no more than an hour away roundtrip, leaving the truck there would buy some time to clean up the rest of the mess at the shop before they decided on a more permanent plan.

When they returned to the shop, James was relieved to learn that Rick Arey had already come and gone, evidently satisfied that K.C.'s truck was not there. George Dennis and Justin Beeson, two of James's reliable lackeys, also ensured that no one had gone into the shop while they were off ditching K.C.'s truck.

While he was finally making headway on masking the blood stains with motor oil, Timothy Suckow fretted about K.C.'s body sitting in the shop's bathroom, his head still wrapped in a black plastic trash bag. Not only would they need to quickly come up with an idea for how to dispose of his corpse, but also a better way to hide it until they did.

The shop's bathroom was brand new, the toilet and sink having just been installed a few days before. The large box in which the toilet bowl had been delivered sat empty in the corner of the shop. It was the perfect temporary coffin. With James on one end and Suckow on the other, together they hoisted K.C.'s stiffening body and clumsily deposited him head-first into the cardboard box.

It was nightfall by the time Suckow felt satisfied that there was no lingering evidence of his crime. In the midst of his panic, he couldn't have known there was no rush to clean up. No one would be coming to the shop to look for K.C.—let alone inspecting for blood stains and brain matter—anytime soon.

Out of over 30 people who were wandering about the yard on a cold sunny day in February, not a single one reported anything suspicious. Somehow, no one other than James Henrikson, Timothy Suckow, George Dennis, and Justin Beeson knew that K.C. walked into the shop that morning and never came back out again. No one had seen a bald, hulking man walking around in blood-soaked clothing. Nobody had noticed that it wasn't K.C. who was behind the wheel when his truck left the yard that afternoon.

When they did not hear from K.C. ever again after February 22, 2012, neither Rick Arey nor Tesha Fredericks reported him missing. When he did not return to his apartment, his roommate Judd Parker did not call the authorities, but instead eventually turned over all of K.C.'s personal belongings to their landlord.

When K.C. did not return to work after his mandatory two-week vacation, though people wondered where he was, no one seemed concerned enough to report him missing. Especially not his bosses, James and Sarah.

K.C. had always kept in regular contact with his grandfather, Robert Clarke. The elder Clarke did initially wonder why he had not heard from his grandson in several weeks. A few months after the murder, however, he received a phone call from an unknown male who identified himself simply as "Joe."

Joe told Clarke that K.C. was fine, and that he had purposely chosen to take himself off the grid and was working in a remote mountain area somewhere near Auburn, Washington. Joe further communicated that K.C. wished to be left alone, and also instructed Clarke to "not speak to authorities."

Although he had no idea who the caller was, Grandpa Clarke opted to respect his grandson's so-called wishes, even though it greatly concerned him.

"What was I supposed to do?" Robert Clarke later lamented.

Nick Meyer, K.C.'s closest childhood friend with whom he had regular weekly communication, had last spoken with him the morning of February 22. During their conversation, K.C. mentioned that he was pulling into a gas station and promised to call Meyer back later on that day. However, K.C. never made that call, or any other calls afterward.

Because K.C. and his mother Jill were estranged at the time, she had no idea that her son had not been seen or heard from.

It was not until several weeks later that someone finally realized that something could be amiss. But by the time authorities in North Dakota finally took a serious look at the case, what remained of Kristopher David Clarke was long gone.

CHAPTER 21

I Think I Found His Truck

On March 23, 2012, Gloria Paulino dialed the Montrail County Sheriff's office in Stanley, North Dakota, to file a report about the possible disappearance of her daughter's former boyfriend, Kristopher (K.C.) Clarke. Calling from Brownwood, Texas, Paulino revealed that neither K.C.'s friends nor family members had heard from the 29-year-old for several weeks.

As K.C.'s once potential mother-in-law explained, several attempts had been made to contact him by phone, but in most instances, his voicemail picked up on the first ring. He had also not responded to any text messages or emails in that same timeframe.

Most importantly, though, was that Paulino was informed that K.C. had missed the last month's payment on a property he was still renting in Brownwood. That, above all else, had been the biggest cause for concern. While it was fair if K.C. wasn't answering his phone because he didn't want to talk to anyone, it was extremely out of the ordinary for him to miss or fall behind on his financial obligations.

"This isn't like him at all," a worried Paulino said.

While she couldn't provide the exact address for where K.C. currently resided in North Dakota, she did know he worked for Blackstone Trucking and that his boss was a man named James. The spelling she provided for his last name was Henricksen.

Although the Mountrail County Sheriff's office documented her report and initiated a preliminary investigation, the reality was that it was pretty common for out-of-state oilfield workers to come and go just as quickly as a tanker truck could be filled with water and emptied at a fracking site. Keeping track of every drifter who came, worked for a few weeks, then departed again was an arduous task that bordered on the impossible.

Investigators surmised it probable that the young and single K.C. Clarke had simply chosen to move on and did not feel an obligation to let anyone know, least of all the mother of his ex-girlfriend. And even if it was odd that K.C. was delinquent in his rent payments for a residence in Texas, that wasn't a problem that authorities in North Dakota could do anything about.

Since he was estranged from his mother, Jill Williams, the only real family connection K.C. had was with his grandfather, Robert Clarke. But by that time, Clarke had already received a call from the mysterious "Joe" and believed his story that K.C. was working in a remote area of Washington and wished to be left alone.

While losing touch with K.C. was undeniably painful and bewildering, the elder Clarke found himself grappling with serious health issues that left him gravely ill. Consequently, he had no capacity to focus on the situation or entertain the possibility that something sinister could have befallen his grandson.

Operating on the information from Robert Clarke that K.C. was alive and well, the Mountrail County Sheriff's department closed the investigation just a few days after Gloria Paulino's phone call.

• • •

Two months later, at 1:41 p.m. on May 11, a woman named Carol Porterfield walked into the Brownwood Police Department (BPD) in Texas, stating she wished to file a missing person's report on a tenant of hers named K.C. Clarke.

"K.C. has been renting a house from me for several months," Porterfield explained to Officer Danny Hutchins. "But I have not seen or heard from him since October or November of last year when he left to work in the oilfields in North Dakota."

According to Porterfield, K.C. had sent her a cashier's check in December, which covered his rent payments through February 2012. Since then, she had not received any additional payments, and she had been unable to reach him by phone or text message. She had attempted to connect with him via his mother, Jill Williams, and his grandfather, but neither of them had heard from K.C. either.

At this juncture, Porterfield found herself struggling with a mixture of deep concern and mounting frustration. Having known K.C. for a significant period of time, his sudden abandonment of financial obligations struck her as highly uncharacteristic. Moreover, the inability to establish any form of contact with him was completely unprecedented, further intensifying her unease.

"I have become so worried that I finally opened a letter that came for him from Mid Tex Federal Credit Union," Porterfield admitted. "The statement showed no recent activity, and there was only a small amount of funds in the account."

When Detective Larry Owings later took over the case, he was able to confirm that K.C. had paid off a loan with the bank a year prior, in 2011, and currently only had a $25.00 balance in a savings account. K.C. had never had a checking account or debit card with the bank and there had been no activity with his savings account in the past 12 months.

Three days after Porterfield filed her report, and after multiple failed attempts, Owings finally connected with Jill Williams, who was currently living in Washington state. Williams confessed to the detective that she and her son were no longer on speaking terms.

"We had a falling out," Williams said. "I knew he was working in North Dakota on an Indian reservation near New Town, but I have not spoken with him for a long time."

By this time, Williams had received multiple calls from

K.C.'s concerned friends in Oregon, Washington, North Dakota, and Texas. While she at first ignored most of them because of the estrangement with her son, uneasiness settled in when she finally understood the gravity of the situation.

Within a few weeks of Carol Porterfield filing the missing person's report, Williams enlisted the help of a friend to start a Facebook page called "Find K.C. Gimp Daddy." Several people joined the group, but their contributions offered little helpful insight into K.C.'s possible whereabouts. Most of the posts consisted of heartfelt hopes and prayers for his swift and safe return.

On May 18, Detective Owings issued a subpoena to AT&T, requesting the data records for K.C.'s cell phone. Days later, he spoke with an AT&T representative, who confirmed K.C.'s cell phone had zero user activity over the prior several months.

"The account is active and paid up," representative Lynette Grilo noted. "But the phone has not transmitted a signal or registered with a tower since February 22, 2012."

Perusing the report AT&T provided, Owings was able to ascertain that the last time K.C.'s phone had connected with a tower was at 11:37 p.m. near Williston, North Dakota on the 22nd, but the last actual activity was a call K.C. made at 9:48 that morning to a man named Steve Agre.

"We talked about a bid to haul water to a few different oil well sites," Agre recalled for Owings. "I don't remember anything out of the ordinary in our conversation, and he seemed fine to me."

Owings then himself dialed K.C.'s phone number, but much like both Gloria Paulino and Carol Porterfield had experienced, the call rolled straight to voicemail.

The case stalled almost as soon as it had started, as virtually no one had any helpful information as to the whereabouts of K.C. Clarke. It appeared he had vanished without a trace, and the fact that no one had reported it for nearly three months only added to the challenge. It was almost impossible to determine the exact date that he had disappeared—if that was even what had actually happened.

Then, seemingly out of the blue and by sheer coincidence,

late on a Friday night in June, the BPD received the most peculiar of calls.

"Hello, um, my name is Joe Uzdavinis," the young man stammered. "I was wondering if you by chance have a missing person's report for a Kristopher Clarke?"

"Are you a family member?" the dispatcher asked.

"No," Uzdavinis responded.

"I unfortunately can't give out any information if you aren't a family member, but I can have one of the detectives call you back."

"Okay, yes, please have someone call me back as soon as possible," Uzdavinis pleaded. "Because I think I found Kristopher's truck. It's a 2007 Chevy Silverado with Texas license plates AC6 3117. It's been parked on a curb outside my friend's house in Williston, North Dakota for the last four months."

CHAPTER 22

The Name On It Was Kristopher Clarke

Much like hundreds of other young men at the time, Joe Uzdavinis and his childhood friend Tyler Krone were ambitious 24-year-olds hailing from Kalispell, Montana, who had ventured to North Dakota with aspirations of finding their own success in the oilfields. Both were good-looking with athletic builds, dark hair, and charismatic personalities. While Krone was working to support his wife and infant daughter back in Montana, Uzdavinis was happy being single with no attachments—something he would boast of even years later.

"Forever single," Uzdavinis said with a laugh. "Maybe it will happen, but it just hasn't yet."

Throughout 2011 and 2012, housing options were extremely limited across North Dakota, and the few properties available for rent came with exorbitant monthly price tags. Given the circumstances, sharing a living space with several roommates became a practical and financial necessity for many. Uzdavinis moved into a cramped trailer on the outskirts of Williston. Krone was fortunate enough to bunk in a home owned by a generous co-worker, who extended the same hospitality to a few other men in need of a place to stay.

The one-story rambler was located on 4th Avenue West, a quiet residential road which intersected with the busier stretch of Broadway Street. The roommates worked varying schedules, coming and going throughout all hours of the day. Between work and sleep, there was little time to notice or become preoccupied with the goings-on in the neighborhood.

But early on the morning of February 23, 2012, Krone and a few of his housemates ventured out into the cold, frigid air and spotted an unfamiliar white Chevy truck with Texas plates parked alongside the curb a few yards down the street from their residence.

Initially, the sight of the truck didn't raise alarm or prompt any of the roommates to question it being there. In an industrial town like Williston, where white Chevys were as common as a cold beer on a Friday night, there was nothing remarkable or unusual about this specific truck that would have immediately caught their attention. While it might have been as innocuous as a visitor in the neighborhood, it was also just as likely that the vehicle had been abandoned. Even the out-of-state license plates weren't that surprising.

"People left their property behind all the time during the oil boom," Krone said later. "It could be that the equipment broke down and someone didn't have the money to fix it and decided to just leave it somewhere, or they had skipped town altogether."

By the end of March, the truck hadn't budged an inch and had since weathered a few late-winter snow and ice storms, withstood the onset of the spring thaw, and was now covered in a thick layer of dirt with a flat rear passenger side tire.

The filthy vehicle had become such an eyesore that the residents on 4th Avenue decided to do something about it. Though the doors were unlocked, no one was brave enough to open up the cab and begin rifling through the contents left inside. At the time, it wasn't important to figure out to whom the truck had belonged. The roommates just wanted to know if they could somehow acquire the vehicle since it was now obvious someone had intentionally left it behind.

"We started to wonder how long it needed to be abandoned before we could maybe file for a title," Krone explained.

To find out, he enlisted the help of his friend Joe Uzda-vinis, who had once worked at the law offices of a criminal defense attorney and was able to research legal means through which ownership of the vehicle could be transferred.

"I was aware the vehicle had been sitting there for a few months," Uzdavinis later documented in a written statement. "Tyler asked me to see if we could file for a title, but I didn't get a chance to look into it until Friday, June 1. I first tried to do a reverse license plate search, but Texas didn't offer a lot of free public records regarding vehicle registration."

Unlike Krone and his roommates, Uzdavinis had little reservation about entering the vehicle to search around.

"I found that the truck was unlocked and opened the glove box," he wrote. "On the registration, the address was listed for Brownwood, Texas, and the name on it was Kristopher Clarke."

•••

Before calling any authorities about the white Chevy, Uzdavinis spent several hours conducting Google searches to gather whatever information he could about the truck—which he discovered was still worth a substantial amount of money—as well as details about its owner.

"It seemed odd that a $20,000 truck was just sitting there abandoned," Uzdavinis mused.

He quickly became immersed in an endless maze of online information. Through North Dakota court record searches, he found that K.C. had been cited for a few traffic violations over the previous year, and that he had also been arrested on a DUI charge in nearby Minot.

A court date had been set for some time in April, but the records showed the defendant had not shown up for the hearing. A few days after that, the case against K.C. was dropped altogether with the court citing a "lack of evidence" as its basis for the decision.

"I then called the Minot Police Department," Uzdavinis documented. "They told me that K.C. was in their system, but that the information was not related to a missing persons case."

Uzdavinis also called the Williston Police Department

(WPD), which checked and confirmed that there was nothing in their records pertaining to a Kristopher or K.C. Clarke.

Digging deeper into his online searches, Uzdavinis soon discovered a link to the "Find K.C. Gimp Daddy" Facebook page that Jill Williams had set up to collect tips and information about her missing son.

Amongst the posts on the page was an entry that included a description of K.C.'s truck, as well as the license plate number registered to the vehicle.

"I uploaded a picture of the truck to the page and posted, 'I'm staring at his truck right now,'" Uzdavinis recalled.

He then sent a private message to Jill Williams and impatiently counted the seconds until he received a response back from her.

While he waited to hear from Williams, Uzdavinis forged ahead and phoned the Brownwood Police Department—twice in two hours—pleading with the clerk he spoke with to have a detective call him back as soon as possible.

After what felt like an eternity, Sgt. Mike Sheedy from the BPD finally called back. Uzdavinis was so excited he could barely organize his thoughts into a coherent message but did his best to convey how K.C.'s truck had been found, and where it was currently located.

"His pickup is parked right outside my friend's house on 4th Avenue West in Williston, North Dakota," Uzdavinis relayed to the seasoned sergeant. "It's been there for probably close to three or four months."

After several minutes, Sheedy begrudgingly let the young man from Montana know that the BPD was indeed working on a missing person's report. The revelation that K.C.'s truck had been located over 1,350 miles away from Brownwood was a huge development, and one Sheedy immediately acted on.

•••

Shortly after midnight on June 2, 2012, Sgt. Sheedy called the WPD and asked that an officer be sent over to the area of 4th Avenue West and Broadway to check on a possible abandoned white Chevy truck with Texas license plates AC6 3117.

It wasn't until three hours later that Lt. David Belisle called back, informing him that a patrol officer had been out to locate and perform a cursory inspection of the truck.

"My patrol units checked the vehicle and there does not seem to be any sign of foul play," Lt. Belisle told Sgt. Sheedy. "It's possible that Clarke just went to visit the Indian reservation about 80 miles away. We'll try to track down some contacts on the reservation and get back to you."

It is unclear how the determination was made that there were no signs of foul play, because it was not until several days later that the WPD actually impounded the vehicle, where it then sat for several more days before a proper warrant was obtained to search and analyze the interior.

Nevertheless, at 3:30 a.m. on June 6, Sgt. Michael Wilson sent an email to Detective Larry Owings in Brownwood:

> *On Wednesday, June 6th at about 0230 hours our agency impounded the white 2007 Chevrolet pick-up registered to the listed missing person, Kristopher Clarke. The vehicle is currently impounded in our municipal lot.*
>
> *During an impound inventory, suspicious substances and vehicle alterations were noted. Our regional narcotics task force has been notified and will inspect the vehicle later today.*
>
> *Due to running the plate for impound an administrative message was sent to notify your agency of the vehicle's disposition.*

Given that it was now assumed K.C. Clarke's last known whereabouts had been in North Dakota, and that his truck was also located there, the Brownwood Police Department promptly ended its missing person's investigation, thus leaving Gloria Paulino, Carol Porterfield, and Jill Williams no closer to finding answers than when it first started.

CHAPTER 23

You're Just Going To Leave It Here Like That?

What Sgt. Sheedy didn't know during their late-night phone conversation on June 1 was that Joe Uzdavinis was parked in his own car directly behind K.C. Clarke's white Chevy with Jill Williams patiently waiting on the other end of the line. When his short call with Sheedy ended, Uzdavinis returned to K.C.'s mom, who asked him to go back into her son's truck to gather additional information.

"She didn't believe me at first," Uzdavinis later recounted. "She asked me to send her a picture to verify that I was for sure looking at K.C.'s truck."

Although she may not have trusted him right away, once she figured out that Uzdavinis wasn't lying, Williams soon began sharing intimate details of K.C.'s life with him. The fact that K.C.'s truck had been found gave the worried mother a glimmer of hope.

"Jill became emotional on the phone because she was hoping this would solve where K.C. was," Uzdavinis recalled.

While he could certainly empathize with Williams's plight, the 24-year-old bachelor realized there was a chance he was getting in over his head and was hesitant to go back inside the truck for fear he might disturb possible evidentiary materials.

"I told her that I could open the doors, but that I didn't want to go digging through everything or leave my fingerprints on anything important."

With Williams still on the line, Uzdavinis reluctantly got out of his car and approached the white Chevy. When he'd first entered the vehicle hours before, the only thing he had searched was the glove compartment to find the registration information. Now, looking around more thoroughly, he could see that the inside of the missing K.C. Clarke's truck was an absolute pigsty. Dozens of articles of clothing were piled in the back cab. Either K.C. typically lived out of his truck, or he hadn't made a trip to the laundromat in quite some time. Stacks of paperwork, an mp3 player, and a GPS device were just some of the items that caught Uzdavinis's attention.

Curiously enough, amid all of the clutter was a box of latex gloves. Realizing that he now had a means to prevent his fingerprints from transferring onto anything, Uzdavinis eagerly pulled on a pair of the gloves, and began fervently sifting through the truck's contents. As he worked, he continuously relayed what he was finding to K.C.'s anxious mother.

"I know he had a gun," she told Uzdavinis. "Can you look for that, along with his wallet and phone?"

"I looked under the seats, in the glove box and the center console the best that I could without disturbing too many things, but I did not find the items she was asking for," Uzdavinis later documented.

Though he did not locate a gun, he did find a box of .45 caliber bullets and plenty else.

"There was a lot of paperwork for a trucking company called Blackstone," Uzdavinis reported. "I saw invoice books, water tickets, and company information. Besides that, there was food remnants, several small knives encased in sheaths, random license plates, and needles and syringes."

As Uzdavinis continued sorting through the contents of the truck, four Williston police cars arrived on the scene. Naturally, the officers were concerned about why someone was rifling through the interior of the vehicle, and asked Uzdavinis to provide his identification and an explanation for what he was doing there.

Uzdavinis nervously provided a brief summary of his

amateur investigation, outlining his initial identification of the truck as belonging to K.C. Clarke, his recent contact with the detective in Brownwood to discover K.C.'s status as a missing person, and his current conversation with the concerned mother of the missing man. Searching the vehicle at the moment, he explained, was at the behest of Jill Williams.

"I didn't feel comfortable leaving the truck sitting here unattended after I spoke with the detective in Texas," Uzdavinis told the officers. "I am on the phone with K.C.'s mom right now."

Seemingly disinterested in the information Uzdavinis was sharing, the officers cautiously walked around the perimeter of the truck, their flashlights illuminating the inside of the cab. None of them entered the truck to look around further, and no measures were taken to secure anything in or around the vehicle. Before leaving, they warned Uzdavinis against any additional exploration of his own.

"But it's still unlocked, and all of his things are just sitting in there. You're just going to leave it here like that?" Uzdavinis asked them incredulously.

"It's already been out here for a long time, and so far no one else has disturbed it," one of the officers shrugged. "We'll investigate it, but for now just leave it alone."

Uzdavinis heeded the officer's warnings and did not reenter the truck after that night, but it made him extremely uneasy knowing it was still sitting out there unlocked and unprotected from anyone else who came upon it.

His work hadn't all been for naught, however. In the time he did have to search, Uzdavinis had mentally scanned several names while perusing the trove of Blackstone Trucking receipts and records strewn about the vehicle.

"I have a pretty good photographic memory," he later boasted.

Before hanging up with Jill Williams that night, Uzdavinis promised her that he would begin researching Blackstone, starting with the listed owner—Sarah Marie Creveling.

•••

From the time that Uzdavinis opened the passenger side door to inspect the contents of the white Chevy's glove compartment and reached out to authorities on June 1, to the time the WPD finally impounded it on June 6, the truck had remained unlocked and unattended for anyone and everyone who still had interest to go through it.

While Uzdavinis obeyed the police officers and never re-entered the vehicle, his curiosity had gotten the best of him, and he returned to peer inside through a window.

"I know things were moved around," Uzdavinis said later. "There was a GPS device that was no longer in there. Who knows what kind of information could have been gleaned from that? That still keeps me awake at night. I should have done more to try to get that preserved."

But it wasn't Uzdavinis' responsibility to preserve evidence in an ongoing investigation. It would have been easy for him, or anyone living on or near 4th Avenue West in Williston to seize the opportunity to take any items left behind inside the unlocked Chevy truck during its three-month presence.

It would have been equally feasible for someone to steal the truck altogether. In leaving it parked unattended for an additional five days after it was reported as belonging to a missing person, perhaps that is exactly what the WPD was hoping would happen.

"It wasn't uncommon for people to just take abandoned property at the time," Tyler Krone later said. "But we were all pretty honest, hard-working guys and didn't feel comfortable doing something like that."

Joe Uzdavinis and Tyler Krone could have easily opted to ignore the presence of the mysterious truck, mind their own business, and carry on with life. It is difficult to know where the missing person investigation surrounding K.C. Clarke would have ended up if that had been their choice. Thanks to Krone's curiosity and Uzdavinis's persistence, however, several dots related to K.C.'s disappearance were now coming into focus, waiting for someone to finally connect them—even if it would take nearly two more years.

CHAPTER 24

They Were Very Dodgy

At 8:10 a.m. on Sunday, June 3, 2012, Sarah Marie Creveling called the Williston Police Department in tears.

"Someone by the name of Joe is calling me asking about K.C. Clarke," Sarah sobbed into the phone. "He's asking all of these questions and will only give me his first name. It's really freaking me out."

Sarah explained to the dispatcher that K.C. had once worked for her at Blackstone Trucking, but that he had not worked there for several months. The dispatcher assured the distraught young woman that a detective would soon be in touch with her regarding the matter.

•••

At 1:45 a.m. on Tuesday, June 6, Jill Williams phoned the WPD to inquire about the investigation into her son's disappearance. She had not heard a word from them since the police had been out to briefly look at K.C.'s truck in the early morning hours of June 2.

"Sgt. Wilson sent Officer Dickerson to check on the vehicle, which was still at 4th and Broadway," a police report later documented. "Sgt. Wilson ordered the truck be impounded."

An orange sticker was placed on the driver's side window of K.C.'s truck, warning that if the truck was not moved within

24 hours that it would be impounded.

On Wednesday, June 7, Officer Ryan Zimmerman was officially assigned to the case. After reviewing all of the information gathered thus far, Zimmerman invited Joe Uzdavinis to meet with him at the police department to discuss any helpful insight he could provide.

• • •

A few days later, a very nervous Uzdavinis arrived at the police department wearing a navy-blue suit with a crisp, pale yellow button-down shirt and color-coordinated tie. As he was led into a cramped room, Zimmerman assured the 24-year-old that he wasn't in any trouble.

"I hope not," Uzdavinis said with a jittery laugh.

Zimmerman asked for his identification, and while the young man fished in his wallet to find it, he chattered on about why he had decided to rummage through the truck's contents.

"Had I not gone in there, you guys probably still wouldn't have any idea what was going on, or where the truck was," Uzdavinis said.

Although it came across as an arrogant statement, it was far from it. It was evident Uzdavinis still felt edgy about being inside an interrogation room and wanted to further rationalize his actions. But even if he had intended to be haughty, one could have argued that his observation wasn't entirely unfounded.

Zimmerman, with a cleanly shaven bald head, wearing a striped polo shirt and khakis, barely registered a response to the comment.

"So, you were telling me a lot of this over the phone," the officer said as he scribbled some notes on a manila folder. "Can you just start from the beginning?"

Uzdavinis leaned back in his chair and stretched his arms over his head. He then shifted his weight forward and launched into a lengthy narrative of the research he had done in the previous days. After several minutes, Zimmerman finally interrupted to ask another question.

"So, um, since you obviously know a helluva lot more about this than I do," he said somewhat sarcastically, "was the truck left in a condition where someone was planning on returning to it, or was planning on leaving it?"

"Planning on returning," Uzdavinis answered confidently, even though there was no way he could have known. "There were tons of clothes, food, soda, beer … he even had a protein shake that ended up getting moldy."

Zimmerman nodded along as Uzdavinis explained that he had spoken to several of K.C.'s friends and acquaintances. What he had been told was that K.C. had abruptly left Washington state to move to Texas without telling many people, so there was a collective belief that it was within the realm of possibility he had done the same thing by leaving North Dakota.

Uzdavinis reported to Zimmerman that while most people he talked to were very open to providing information about K.C., he had received a markedly different reception from the folks at Blackstone Trucking.

"The weirdest thing about it," Uzdavinis offered, adjusting the position of his chair, "the people I talked to at Blackstone …they were very, um, dodgy."

The first person he had spoken with at Blackstone was Sarah Creveling. Uzdavinis had concocted a ruse to get her talking, telling her he had received a business card from K.C. Clarke some time ago, and was wondering if Blackstone was currently hiring any truck drivers.

"K.C. doesn't work here anymore," Sarah told him flatly. "Call our Operations Manager, Elliott, and he can give you more information about open jobs."

Sarah provided a number for Uzdavinis to call, but when he tried it, he received an automated message saying the phone number was no longer in service.

Undeterred, he had called Sarah back. This time, however, a man by the name of "Kelly" answered the phone.

"Hey there," Uzdavinis had said cheerfully. "I called earlier and spoke with Sarah regarding a possible open position. She gave me a phone number to call Elliott, but the number is disconnected."

"Sarah is in a meeting," Kelly responded tersely. "We aren't hiring. Even if we were, I have 60 applicants ahead of you, so we already have plenty of drivers."

With that, Kelly promptly ended the call. Still unfazed, Uzdavinis then found a third number to try, and reached a man named "Arden," who was considerably more helpful.

"I have heard of K.C., but he quit before I was hired," Arden had volunteered.

Uzdavinis asked for a phone number for "Elliott," and Arden happily supplied a number that was just one digit off from the one Sarah had provided. Perhaps it had been an honest mistake on Sarah's part, but it seemed peculiar enough at the time to question the small discrepancy. Now skeptical of what was going on, Uzdavinis came up with a different approach. This time, the phone number provided for Elliott worked.

"I called Elliott and told him that I had a couple of boxes that belonged to K.C.," Uzdavinis recounted to Zimmerman. "I said that the boxes contained some Blackstone hats, shirts, license plates, business cards, invoice books, and water tickets, and I asked if there was an address that I could send them to. "Elliott" started to give me an address, but then began saying, 'Hello? Hello? Hello?' like he couldn't hear me. Then the call ended."

A few minutes later, the person supposedly named Elliott called back, asking how Uzdavinis had found all of these items. He had been quick on his toes with an explanation.

"I made up a story about them being dropped off at my house by K.C. Clarke a long time ago," Uzdavinis continued his fascinating tale. "I didn't want to tip them off that I was looking for a physical address, so I just asked again if there was an address I could ship them to."

"How do you know K.C.?" Elliott, who had a Hispanic accent, had asked.

"I told him that I didn't really know K.C. at all but tried to bring the focus back to the boxes and where I could send them," Uzdavinis explained.

"We aren't missing any apparel or license plates, and we don't want them," Elliott told him. "K.C worked here long before I started, and he is now working for Running Horse Trucking."

Uzdavinis then heard the unmistakable click of being hung up on for a second time.

At the mention of Running Horse Trucking, Uzdavinis typed the company name into a Google search and found both a phone number and an address listed in New Town. When he dialed the number, a woman named Tesha Fredericks answered the phone.

"I told Tesha that I was a friend of K.C.'s and was trying to find him."

It was almost as if Fredericks had been waiting for someone like him to call, because she did not hold back when sharing all of the information she knew about K.C. He had been her friend, Fredericks confirmed, and it had been an agonizing three months wondering what had happened to him.

"Tesha told me how her and K.C. met, and that they had become good friends," Uzdavinis relayed for Zimmerman. "She said K.C. was working for a man named James at Blackstone, and that K.C. was being worked to the bone. She said that James was a liar and could talk his way out of anything. By coming to work with her at Running Horse, Tesha had promised to take good care of K.C."

"I thought we would make a good team," Fredericks's voice had cracked with emotion during her conversation with Uzdavinis. "The last time I talked to him in February, he was going to turn his gas card into James at the Blackstone shop, and he was going to meet me afterwards. I waited for hours, and called and texted him several times. He never responded, and I haven't heard from him since."

Uzdavinis relayed for Zimmerman how Tesha Fredericks had spoken of her surprised reaction when she had received a phone call from K.C.'s grandfather, Robert Clarke, a few weeks later. The grandfather had let her know that K.C. had been found, and was working in Auburn, Washington. The fact that K.C.'s grandfather had also received a call from someone named Joe was purely coincidental and had no connection to Uzdavinis.

"I was pretty angry when I heard that," Fredericks told Uzdavinis. "I didn't understand why he would just cut off contact with me like that. But now that you're calling and telling me his truck has been abandoned, I'm really worried that something happened to him."

• • •

Despite the significant revelations Uzdavinis was sharing with him, Zimmerman sat through the interview stone-faced, barely taking any notes. He didn't follow up with any questions; instead, he turned to scold Uzdavinis for presumably upsetting Sarah Creveling.

"I know I talked to one of the owners, or the wife of the owner of Blackstone, Sarah I think is her name," Zimmerman stammered. "She was pretty freaked out about you calling and asking questions. Which, you know, I can see. She's really upset. I could hear her bawling on the phone."

"Really?" Uzdavinis asked, confused.

"Well, you know, I can kind of understand ..." Zimmerman trailed off.

Uzdavinis nodded his head as if he also understood, but then furrowed his brow, expressing surprise over such an extreme reaction. While it was true that he had indeed unnerved both Sarah and James Henrikson by poking around and asking questions about K.C., at the time, it made no sense as to why. Why would the mention of a former employee's name be enough to elicit tears? Apparently, though, this potential question was lost upon Ryan Zimmerman, who after less than 30 minutes, had heard enough from Joe Uzdavinis.

"Yeah, I wouldn't keep calling people, because they start getting pissy," Zimmerman warned, before handing Uzdavinis a document to complete a formal police report. "But if I could just send this with you, I need the information and copies of all you have as soon as possible."

Uzdavinis tried to keep talking about additional information he had uncovered, but Zimmerman wasn't in the least bit interested. All he wanted was for Uzdavinis to take the form home and complete it.

"Could you get this done by tomorrow?" Zimmerman asked, rubbing his bald head.

As Uzdavinis perused the form, Zimmerman pondered aloud if K.C. was simply doing a "piss on you thing"—suggesting that he had intentionally left as a way to spite his friends and family and make them worry.

Zimmerman also admitted he hadn't spoken with anyone from the Brownwood Police Department and had no idea what information their investigation had accumulated. Surprisingly, he hadn't even bothered to go look at K.C.'s truck for himself yet and questioned if the windows had been left down.

Uzdavinis confirmed that the truck was unlocked, but that the windows had been rolled up.

"Okay, well, if you could get this done for me by tomorrow," Zimmerman repeated, "then I'm not having to play a whole lot of catch-up."

Joe Uzdavinis was nothing if not diligent. As soon as he returned home that afternoon, he typed out a five-page single-spaced document, supplemented by an additional ten pages of the chicken-scratched notes he had kept while doing his research. Once he submitted the report the next day as Officer Ryan Zimmerman had requested, Uzdavinis never heard another word from anyone at the Williston Police Department.

CHAPTER 25

It's Spelled H-E-N-R-I-C-K-S-E-N

Officer Ryan Zimmerman was tongue-tied when the beautiful Sarah Creveling waltzed through the front doors of the Williston Police Department. She wore a pink tank top covered up by a white linen jacket, and denim capris on this hot June day. Her long blonde hair flowed freely down her back, and her toenails showcased a bright pink shade, evidence of a recent pedicure. The petite and sweet-voiced young woman hoisted a turquoise-colored designer tote bag over her bony shoulder as she followed Zimmerman down a narrow corridor to a small interview room.

When she had received the invitation to come to Williston to meet with Zimmerman, Sarah had immediately jumped in her $60,000 Bentley and driven the 70 miles west from her office just outside of New Town. Much like he had done with Joe Uzdavinis a few hours before, Zimmerman assured Sarah that she was not in any trouble and was free to leave any time she wanted.

"So, when did K.C. start working for ya?" Zimmerman began in his low, garbled voice.

"Probably October or November-ish?" Sarah responded.

"What did he do?"

"He sort of did everything. We started him out as a truck pusher, and then we had him as operations manager. He kind of did whatever needed to be done."

"Did you ever have any problems with K.C.?"

"No, not at first," Sarah hunched over in her chair. "But right before he quit working for us, he just wasn't really doing anything at all. Like, people thought he was really depressed. A lot of the workers would call me and say they were trying to get a hold of K.C. but couldn't find him because he was out drinking."

K.C.'s purported drinking problem, she said, was a recent development, as he had never had issues with substance abuse in the past. She blamed the drinking on Rick Arey, who had become close friends with K.C. earlier in the year.

"Drivers were constantly telling us that Rick and K.C. were always at the bar, and that they could never remember anything," Sarah complained.

Though Sarah elaborated at length about the employment challenges she and Blackstone were having with K.C., she didn't suggest or imply that any corrective measures had been taken, or that there was a possibility of the newly identified alcoholic losing his job.

"So, what was Rick like?" Zimmerman changed the subject to K.C.'s supposed drinking buddy.

"Rick's really laid back. He doesn't really care about much," Sarah said. "I mean, don't get me wrong, he did his job and stuff. But I think he was a really bad influence on K.C."

"Did you notice a personality change in K.C. before he quit working for you?" Zimmerman asked, pivoting again.

Sarah recalled that it seemed like K.C. was pulling away, and that she asked him several times if he was missing Texas and wanted to go back.

"He always told me no, and that he was 'in the game' and wanted to be here," she said. "But he still had a house in Texas and had left most of his belongings there. We offered several times to have his stuff brought up here, but he didn't want that."

Zimmerman then asked her what had transpired between K.C. and his ex-girlfriend Josephine Paulino. Sarah seemed confused by the question, claiming she knew very little about the relationship, other than that K.C. had told her how much he wished it could have worked out.

"What do you know about his truck?"

"Oh, he loved it," Sarah smiled. "But he did get into an accident before he left. He had been trying to pass some semi-trucks on the highway and merged back into his lane too soon, and one of the semis clipped the rear panel of his truck. It ripped the panel off and he ended up in the ditch, but he wasn't hurt. My husband asked if he was going to file an insurance claim on it, and K.C. told him he was probably just going to ditch it on the side of the road and say it got stolen on the reservation."

Sarah's blue eyes filled with tears.

"I'm sorry," she sniffled. "I'm just really worried now."

"Aww," Zimmerman cooed. "You did a really good job hiding the tears on the phone, though." Perhaps the detective had forgotten that he had just scolded Joe Uzdavinis for supposedly causing Sarah to "bawl her eyes out."

The portly detective's coddling seemed to make Sarah uncomfortable, and she redirected the focus back to K.C.

"We had this big meeting," she recalled. "And we told K.C. to please go on vacation. We were politely telling him, 'You suck right now.' So when he left, everyone was taking bets on whether he would come back. When he didn't come back, I felt kind of bad that he didn't let me know, but I don't think he contacted anyone."

Sarah then burst into a new wave of tears when she told the detective that K.C.'s grandfather had called and assured her of K.C.'s well-being. Following that phone call, Sarah said that she hadn't dwelled on it any further.

"I hate to keep going back to Rick, but what kind of history do you know about him?" Zimmerman probed.

"I don't really know much about him, other than him talking about how crazy he used to be, and that he had once shit himself when he was high on drugs. But I don't think he does drugs anymore," Sarah laughed.

"Do you happen to have his birthdate?"

"Yeah, it would be in his employment records. I could text the girls in the office to see if they can get it for me."

"You have an office, too?" Zimmerman marveled. "Wow, you guys are really moving up, aren't you?"

"We're trying to get there," Sarah giggled.

•••

When they finished discussing Rick Arey's sordid history—which included Sarah divulging private information about Arey's child support obligations—Zimmerman finally turned the conversation back to K.C., asking Sarah if there had been any love interests in his life.

"Well, there was a girl named Tara that he used to hang out with," Sarah shared. "I would consider myself close with K.C. but he was really secretive about girls. I don't know if it was because he had talked to me about his previous relationship, and he didn't want me to know about anyone else, but Rick always told me when K.C. was on a date with a new girl. But K.C. would not introduce me to that Tara girl. I bumped into her one time at the shop because K.C. was changing her oil. I mean, she was nice and polite but K.C. was like mortified that I met her, and I don't know why."

"White girl?" Zimmerman asked. "Native?"

"She was native, but I would say maybe a 'white' native?" Sarah posited. "I mean, I don't want to be rude, but she was very, like, put together. Her makeup was nice, her hair was nice, her clothes were nice ... she wasn't, kind of, you know…"

Zimmerman latched onto the subtly biased remarks, letting Sarah know she could talk freely with him about her views of the native population.

"Born and raised in Wolf Point, Montana," he revealed. "Right next to the Fort Peck Indian Reservation. I was a deputy stationed in Parshall for a year, so you don't have to pull any punches with me."

"You know what I'm talking about, right?" Sarah flashed her bright white smile, then thought of something else to add. "I know he was sort of hanging out with this other trucking company, Running Horse, that K.C. and Rick went to work for. When K.C. was on vacation and Rick was still here, Rick came in and said he was going to quit. We were like, 'Why?'"

Sarah said that Arey then supposedly divulged his belief that K.C. would also be quitting as soon as he returned from his two-week vacation.

"Oh, so K.C. was sort of moonlighting on the side type thing?" Zimmerman asked, his eyes widening. "How would you even have time to do that?"

"Well, we thought maybe that would explain why K.C. was so tired all the time," Sarah said. "And Rick didn't even like K.C. when they first met. Rick said he got annoyed because K.C. talked all the time, which was true. K.C. loved to talk, but it was weird that they became so close. But I suppose if they are both working for the same company, that's going to help them."

Zimmerman asked if Sarah believed K.C. was bipolar or schizophrenic or suffered from any other sort of mental illness.

"No, no, I don't think anything like that," Sarah said, shaking her head. "I would just say kind of a hot head. He would get worked up. But I would have never even said he was depressed until right before he left. He was not the same person."

When Sarah was asked what bank K.C. used for his direct deposit checks from Blackstone, she said she would need to check her records, but did volunteer that K.C. made upwards of $6,800 a month. Zimmerman let out a distinguished huff and lamented how he was clearly in the wrong line of work.

Even though Sarah knew what K.C.'s total monthly compensation was, she was not asked, and did not offer, what the date of his last paycheck had been, or if he had actually been paid for the two-week vacation she had sent him on. She and Zimmerman also did not discuss the last known date that Sarah had seen K.C. The suggestion from others that the Blackstone Trucking shop was the last place K.C. visited before he seemingly vanished—presumably to drop off a gas card—seemed like it would have been important to discuss, but Zimmerman never brought it up.

"So, do you think he would just disappear and not tell anyone?" Zimmerman asked instead.

Sarah pondered the question, then said that she did not

believe K.C. would leave without letting anyone know. Zimmerman then asked her to consider the possibility that K.C. could have stolen money from someone, or another business, and was on the run.

"No, he wouldn't do that," Sarah said, dismissing any such notion. "But a lot of his friends are saying that he will probably reappear in six months to a year. My husband even said that he didn't know where K.C. was for a year when he moved to Texas."

"What's your husband's name?" the detective asked.

"James," Sarah answered, and then corrected Zimmerman when he jotted down James's last name as Creveling. "It's actually Henrikson. Spelled H-e-n-r-i-c-k-s-e-n."

"So, is your husband concerned at all?" Zimmerman inquired, unaware that Sarah had just lied to him about the spelling of her husband's last name.

"Yeah, but like I said, all of his Washington friends think he's just going to reappear at some point."

Sarah followed up with a question about where K.C.'s truck had been found. Zimmerman described the location as 3rd and Broadway, even though it was actually still sitting at 4th and Broadway.

"It wouldn't be out of the ordinary if he'd left it there and then jumped on a train," Zimmerman hypothesized, noting that the Amtrak station was only a few blocks away from where the truck had been abandoned.

Bizarrely, the WPD officer continued speculating about a few additional scenarios to explain K.C.'s disappearance—all of them centering around some sort of romantic rendezvous with a mysterious woman of the night. Perhaps he had met someone, left the pickup behind, then gone on a road trip and decided to stay wherever. Or, that K.C. and that same "someone" could have met up and driven to Minot and hopped a plane to Vegas. He perhaps even could have taken off somewhere with a stripper from the local club "Heartbreakers."

"If he was smart with his money, three months-time, who knows?" Zimmerman theorized.

After 37 minutes of conversation, Zimmerman clicked his

tongue and tapped the tip of his pen, struggling to think of more questions for Sarah. When none came to mind, he shifted to assessing her well-being, his approach awkwardly straddling the line between professional and inappropriate.

"Well, do you feel a little bit better now that you got to talk to me?" Zimmerman asked hopefully. "I know you've been feeling kind of helpless."

Though Sarah acknowledged that talking with the detective had provided her a level of comfort, there was still something nagging at her. Expressing her unease about living amongst so many "scary" men who now worked in the oilfields, she told him how her family back in Washington was really worried about her, given "everything that was going on."

Zimmerman assured Sarah that as long as she was smart and used common sense, it was unlikely anything bad would happen to her. He shared some helpful tips for staying safe and encouraged her not to become a hermit, reminding her to go out and have fun from time to time.

In what seemed like an effort to impress the beautiful blonde, Zimmerman launched into a lengthy tale, describing his own youthful escapades of partying. He proudly reminisced about how he and his friends managed to evade trouble despite frequently flouting the law.

"Well, I appreciate you coming in," he finally said when Sarah appeared bored. "I'll try not to bug you again because I don't want to take you away from making money. Are there any more questions you have for me?"

"Yeah, I've been meaning to ask you," Sarah said as she gathered up her belongings. "Who is this Joe guy that's been calling me?"

Zimmerman rolled his eyes and Sarah laughed. Rather than express curiosity over why those calls had caused Sarah so much angst, Zimmerman instead dismissed Joe Uzdavinis as just an overly curious kid and reassured her not to be concerned with him.

Whereas he had appeared disinterested and impatient with Uzdavinis, Zimmerman had hung on every bat of Sarah's eyelashes. He had avoided any probing questions that might have rattled the sexy blonde, and the interview ultimately provided minimal insight for unraveling the mystery of what had happened to K.C. Clarke.

• • •

The following day, Zimmerman leveraged the phone number list researched and compiled by Joe Uzdavinis to call Jill Williams, Robert Clarke, K.C.'s closest friend Nick Meyer, Tesha Fredericks, and Gloria Paulino.

The collective message the brief conversations conveyed to Zimmerman was that there was no chance K.C. would voluntarily disappear without informing at least one person—most likely his grandfather—and that he would never neglect his financial obligations.

More importantly, they all pointed to K.C.'s well-known reputation for being overly protective of his belongings and expressed grave doubts about him intentionally leaving anything unattended in an unlocked vehicle, let alone ditching the valuable truck itself.

Zimmerman then checked with the airline charter company in Williston, Great Lakes Airlines, and was told there was no record of a Kristopher or K.C. Clarke. The Amtrak Police provided him with the same discouraging response. These dead ends dashed each of Zimmerman's wild guesses as to where K.C. might have gone.

• • •

On June 13, 12 days after Joe Uzdavinis' initial call to the Brownwood Police Department, a warrant was obtained to search the interior of K.C.'s truck, which had been sitting in the Williston impound lot for almost seven days. Zimmerman called the North Dakota Bureau of Criminal Investigation (NDBCI) to assist with the search.

As NDBCI Special Agent Steve Gutknecht physically sifted through the contents of the vehicle, Zimmerman and another detective from Williston, Jameson Seim, took photographs and logged the evidence. A total of 14 items were taken into custody for further review. Amongst them was a half-empty water bottle, business cards, various receipts, notebooks, miscellaneous paperwork, an atlas, a Bible, multiple unused syringes and needles, several unopened clear and brown glass vials labeled *Testosterone Cypionate* and a box of .45 caliber bullets.

While many of those items were neither personal nor significant, even a novice detective would have recognized the importance of bullets to a gun owner and the cache of unused paraphernalia to a steroid user. Both items held monetary value and were much less likely to be deliberately abandoned. Even more importantly, several sources had reported that K.C. did in fact own a .45 caliber gun. While the case that held the gun was still in the truck, the gun itself was gone.

As the gravity of the situation started to mount, the Williston Police Department recognized it lacked sufficient resources to effectively manage the investigation, and formally requested NDBCI Special Agent Steve Gutknecht to assume control over the case.

CHAPTER 26

He Still Would Have Called His Grandfather

Amidst the COVID-19 pandemic in 2021, Steve Gutknecht was bestowed with the prestigious North Dakota Peace Officers Association Lone Eagle Award, in recognition of his distinguished 28-year tenure and multifaceted contributions to law enforcement throughout the state. Having begun his career as a drug enforcement officer in 1996 in Williston, Gutknecht had advanced through the ranks, spent time with the NDBCI, and was now back where he had first started, serving as Captain with the Williston Police Department.

Towering over everyone with his commanding height, the broad-shouldered veteran, notorious for his modest personality, posed for media photographs, flanked by Chief David Peterson and City Commissioner Tate Cymbaluk. He held up a wooden plaque adorned with the traditional sheriff's six-pointed gold star while wearing a black mask, both to follow city protocol at the time, and to disguise any emotion that might have been displayed on his face.

"It is an honor to have Captain Gutknecht as one of our own," Commissioner Cymbaluk spoke proudly to the small crowd gathered at the ceremony. "It is with great pride and respect that we present this award. We thank you. You've earned it. You've provided great wealth to our community."

Nine years earlier, in June of 2012, Gutknecht not only had quite a bit more hair on his head and a lot less gray, but he was also a skilled Special Agent with the NDBCI, immersing himself in one of the most perplexing cases of his career.

Having been initially called in to simply assist in the search through a missing man's abandoned vehicle, Gutknecht had now taken over the case, and spent the first few days familiarizing himself with the information that had already been accumulated.

Before he even began reaching out to potential witnesses, Gutknecht received a call from an individual identifying himself as a native from the Fort Berthold Indian Reservation. The caller expressed a desire to remain anonymous and be treated as a "confidential informant."

"I believe that it is possible someone at Blackstone Trucking ordered the killing of K.C. Clarke because he was attempting to take business away from Blackstone, and bring it over to Running Horse Trucking," the informant said bluntly.

The man also shared his knowledge that Blackstone was operating out of then-tribal chairman Tex Hall's oil services business, Maheshu Energy, which was located on Hall's sprawling ranch outside of Mandaree. It seemed the informant's suspicion lay more toward the chairman, and not the actual owners of Blackstone Trucking.

"If Tex Hall needed to get rid of a body, he could have it buried somewhere out on his ranch," the informant surmised. "Tex Hall loses a number of cattle every year throughout the winter because of his bad ranching practices, and he was burying up to 100 animal carcasses behind where he operates Maheshu Energy. But Tex is also currently excavating ground out there to put in housing for workers, and a body could easily be buried there as well."

Gutknecht was aware that rumors had begun swirling concerning Tex Hall and his associations in the oilfields, but the idea that the tribal chairman was killing and burying bodies alongside deceased cattle out on his ranch seemed a bit far-fetched. Nevertheless, he dutifully documented the information and set it aside for the time being.

On June 18, Gutknecht met with officials from the Mountrail County Sheriff's Office (MCSO) and Agent Sterling Mueller from the FBI. Chief Deputy Corey Bristol from MCSO confirmed there had been a missing person's inquiry made sometime in March, but then revealed that the case had been quickly closed when K.C. Clarke's grandfather let them know that the young man had been located and was working in a remote area of Washington state.

The next day, Gutknecht issued subpoenas to Dakota West Credit Union (DWCU) in Watford City, North Dakota, and to the Alaska USA Federal Credit Union (AUFCU). The DWCU responded immediately to let the special agent know that K.C. had only used their services one time, to cash a check, and that he had never held any accounts there.

The AUFCU, on the other hand, was the lien holder for K.C.'s truck and was much less cooperative. The bank demanded that the Williston Police Department release the vehicle at once, but Gutknecht refused. There would be no returning of the truck until he received information about the account. After some wrangling, the bank finally acknowledged that no payment had been made on the truck since February, and the bank had been trying to locate it to have it repossessed.

Gutknecht eventually hit paydirt when a subpoena answered by Bank of America revealed that it had been K.C.'s primary banking institution, and that the account currently held over $6,000. The bank reported K.C. had not made any transactions or accessed his account since February.

After almost two weeks of trying to track down a paper trail that might lead to K.C.'s whereabouts, the fact that he hadn't accessed his only source of money in more than four months made it less likely that K.C. was just another oilfield worker who had voluntarily moved on for a change of scenery.

While Gutknecht wasn't yet ready to concede that this information confirmed foul play, the signs were there that something was most certainly amiss. The investigator's next step was to find answers from the people who had been closest to K.C. during his brief tenure in North Dakota.

• • •

Judd Parker was about as unassuming a person you could find, describing himself as very laid back and unfazed by most things. But he admitted to Gutknecht that when his roommate of only a few short months left to run errands one morning and never returned, it had bothered him. K.C. had left behind all of his belongings, and when he failed to pay rent for two months in a row, Parker and the apartment landlord made the decision to clear out K.C.'s space to make room for a new tenant.

It wasn't intended to be a callous move by either party, but if K.C. truly had left with no intention of returning, Parker urgently needed a second renter to share the burden of the expensive monthly costs, and there were plenty of prospects waiting in line.

"K.C. was a great roommate," Parker shared. "He kept to himself, he was clean, and he never brought any parties back to our place or anything like that."

While the roommates were not particularly close, Parker relayed that he was well aware of the fact that K.C. was planning to leave Blackstone Trucking in favor of going to work for Running Horse Trucking. He also knew of K.C.'s boss, James Henrikson, because James had been embroiled in a few tussles with Parker's own employer, Steve Kelly of Trustland Oilfield Services. Both situations were messy, with a lot of he-said, he-said back-and-forth floating through the rumor mills, and Parker had done his best to stay out of the fray.

But he had since surmised that James was not a nice man—someone not to mess with—a sentiment echoed amongst many at the time. It was Parker's impression that James and K.C. had been close friends before arriving in North Dakota, but that the relationship between them was beginning to sour because of the business wranglings.

"I knew they had been best friends," Parker told Gutknecht. "Which is why I found it very strange that James never called me or came looking for K.C., and didn't seem to be concerned about his whereabouts at all."

But it wasn't just James who didn't appear to be bothered. Parker was dumbfounded that after four months, only a few people had contacted him to ask what he knew about K.C. or where he was, and none of them included his family members.

"I just couldn't believe it," Parker stated. "How could none of his family be worried? Even people at my work, Trustland, started calling around to hospitals and police departments to see if they had any information. My boss, Steve Kelly, told me to report K.C. missing."

Although Kelly hadn't known K.C., even he thought the situation was strange. "How could it have taken so long for anyone to worry that he's gone?" Kelly had asked Parker.

Yet, perhaps feeling he did not have the grounds since he wasn't a family member or that K.C.'s personal affairs were his own business, Parker had forgone filing a police report. But he added one last tidbit for Gutknecht to consider.

"Rick Arey told me that K.C. compiled a list of information and gave it to Rick, asking him to contact his grandfather in the event that anything happened to him," Parker said quietly. "I don't think anything good is going to come of this. I mean, maybe he really did just say, 'Screw everybody, I'm out of here,' but he still would have called his grandfather."

CHAPTER 27

I Honestly Believe He Is Alright

On June 26, Gutknecht located the pudgy, icy-blue-eyed Rick Arey just as he was preparing to embark on a fishing trip at the Van Hook boat landing on Lake Sakakawea in New Town.

When Gutknecht introduced himself and revealed he was there to talk about the disappearance of K.C. Clarke, Arey set down his angling equipment and let out an audible sigh. His shoulders slumped, as if an invisible weight had been lifted.

Arey told Gutknecht that he had been in a serious car accident in March, having hit a giant pothole while traveling at high speeds. The impact had caused him to lose control, and his unbelted body was subsequently ejected from the vehicle. Had he not been wearing a hardhat, Arey said, he likely would not have survived when his head smashed into a set of nearby railroad tracks. He hadn't escaped the accident totally unscathed, however. One of his femurs had been shattered and, as a result, he now walked with a surgically placed titanium rod stretching from his hip to his knee.

"So, what can you tell me about this whole deal?" Gutknecht asked.

Much like Judd Parker before him, Arey had been waiting to talk to someone about this for quite some time, and his words came out in a steady stream. He began by describing his and K.C.'s experiences working tirelessly for Blackstone Trucking under James Henrikson's thumb and shared how both men were feeling they were grossly underpaid and actively looking for a way out.

Arey then marveled over K.C.'s ability to forge friendships with just about anyone and recounted how the two disgruntled employees had met Tesha Fredericks during a rare evening out at the 4 Bears Casino in New Town. This chance encounter laid the groundwork for Fredericks to eventually propose that Arey and K.C. consider working at her new business venture, which was called Running Horse Trucking. Both K.C. and Arey were enthusiastically on board but harbored concerns about the potential blowback from James and Blackstone.

"K.C. was really worried about James finding out," Arey recalled.

"I know it's not going to be good," K.C. had confided in Arey. "I just don't know what to do."

A few weeks after both men agreed to join Fredericks in her quest to establish Running Horse Trucking, K.C. sent an ominous text message to Arey: *Hey Rick. Can I give your contact information to my grandpa, in case something happens to me?*

Arey felt the request was strange, but assured K.C. it was perfectly fine to share his contact information with anyone he wanted.

"I didn't question it, and I didn't ask what was wrong," Arey confessed. "I didn't think anything of it, but I shit you not, four days later, K.C. vanished."

Gutknecht furiously jotted down notes as Arey continued.

"I talked to K.C. on the morning of February 22, and he was on his way to return his gas card to Sarah Creveling at Blackstone," he said.

Arey shared how the plan was for K.C. to meet with himself and Tesha Fredericks after he turned in his card and admitted he was at first more annoyed than concerned when K.C. never showed up.

"Nighttime rolls around, and Tesha and I start calling and calling his phone, and it rolls over to voicemail right away," Arey explained. "And then his voicemail filled up, and we were like, 'What the fuck is going on?'"

Arey said he had then reached out to his boss, James, to voice his concern for the sudden disappearance of his co-worker.

"K.C. does this shit all the time," James had said, brushing off Arey's anxiety.

But the attempt to pacify him hadn't worked, and both Arey and Tesha Fredericks agreed that something didn't seem right.

"Tesha suggested we go to his apartment and look around," Arey recalled. "So, we drove over there and we met with his roommate, Judd Parker, who gave us the okay to search through K.C.'s room."

Arey and Fredericks were alarmed to find that virtually all of K.C.'s belongings were there, including his work boots, clothes, tools, vitamins, jackets, and a brand-new camera. If K.C. had been preparing to leave for a while, it didn't look like he'd taken anything with him.

"Before we walked out the door, I asked if K.C.'s toothbrush was there," Arey told Gutknecht. "Judd went to check and came back and told us that yes, even K.C.'s toothbrush was still there."

Arey continued. "Around the beginning of March, his grandpa called me and said they were starting a missing person's report for K.C. Then, like a week later, his grandpa called again to say that K.C. had been located, and that he was working in Auburn, Washington. His grandpa was actually really rude about it and warned me not to even bother trying to contact K.C. He also told me not to talk to any private investigators."

The tone and message conveyed by the elder Clarke had left Arey confused and frustrated, but also at a loss for what he was supposed to do about it. Arey relayed to Gutknecht that K.C. came across as a very private person, and that he had not shared a whole lot of intimate personal details about himself. In fact, the two men had really just begun forging a close friendship not long before K.C. disappeared. If K.C.'s family members were reaching out to assure his well-being and were urging others to respect his privacy, Arey concluded that it was no longer his place to intervene.

Even so, the slight had stung, and Arey described how he had tried to forget about it and move on. Still, every once in a while, curiosity got the best of him, and he would call or text K.C.'s phone, but it always rolled straight to voicemail, and he never received any response to his messages.

"He never called me back, so I thought, whatever, he obviously doesn't want to talk to me," Arey told Gutknecht. "I honestly believe he is all right. I don't think he's dead. I just don't know because his family all say he's done this before. I think he just kind of said 'screw it' and went on a walkabout."

The burly oilfield worker ran a hand through his dark hair, then sat back and waited for Gutknecht to catch up on his notes. It was clear the past few months had taken a mighty toll, and he hadn't quite determined if he should be angry that his friend left with no word, or worried that something bad had happened.

"I don't know," Arey sighed. "I don't get it. I've never dealt with anything like this before."

Gutknecht asked if Arey could think of any reason that K.C. might have gone to Williston, given that the town was 70 miles away from where he lived and worked. Arey acknowledged that trips to Williston were fairly regular, as they conducted a lot of business for Blackstone there. But the fact that K.C.'s truck had been abandoned there did not make much sense, he said, because even if K.C. had gone there for a meeting or a job, he would have driven his truck back home again.

Gutknecht listened patiently as Arey then pondered aloud the possibility that K.C. could have run off somewhere with a woman.

"He had girlfriends in several different states and towns. Like I said, he could just make friends anywhere. He showed me a few pictures of a girlfriend in Arizona, and she was pretty hot—I mean, I probably would have left North Dakota for her, too." Arey shrugged.

And though he had harbored concerns about the situation since the day K.C. went missing, he admitted he'd spent a fair amount of time convincing himself that his friend was alive and well, just enjoying life somewhere with a new love interest.

•••

Later in the interview, Gutknecht shifted Arey's attention toward the relationship between K.C. and James Henrikson.

"Both of them were really into fitness," Arey shared. "Protein shakes, working out, eating healthy, that kind of stuff."

When Gutknecht asked, Arey said he did not think either K.C. or James used steroids as he had never witnessed it, or come across any evidence, like pills or syringes. Arey did concede, however, that if James and K.C. were steroid users, it was possible it was a habit they had chosen to hide from people. Curiously, he also mentioned that K.C. did not like to drink very much because of a splenectomy procedure several years prior.

"He said he just got drunk too fast, and kind of stayed away from it," Arey explained. "James didn't drink much either because I think it made him sick. Neither of them was much into partying."

Even though many people had characterized James and K.C. as being close, longstanding friends, that dynamic wasn't at all what Arey had observed.

"They were fucking mean to him, man," Arey said, referring to both James and Sarah. "Especially Sarah. She was just awful. They didn't really treat me badly, because they knew I wouldn't take their shit. They kind of had K.C. by the balls, though, because they knew he would take it and he had nowhere else to go.

"That was the thing about K.C.—he was really loyal," Arey added. "He didn't particularly want to go over to Running Horse Trucking, because he wanted to be positive that everything would work out with James and Blackstone Trucking. We'd talk ourselves into being positive for a week, but then something would happen, like a driver would spill water or something, and James and Sarah would just unleash on K.C.

in front of everyone, in meetings … they just shit-talked him."

These open displays of abusive ridicule toward his friend enraged Arey, and he confessed to Gutknecht that during his efforts to procure business for Running Horse Trucking, he unapologetically criticized James, Sarah, and Blackstone, going to great lengths to tarnish their reputations across the oilfields.

"We tried to bring Blackstone down to its knees," Arey admitted. "I'm not going to lie. I talked all kinds of shit."

Most of their trash talking related to how Blackstone Trucking was cheating truck drivers and oil companies out of money. Arey encouraged the drivers to file complaints against Blackstone with the Tribal Employment Rights Office (TERO), and several of them did.

Arey told Gutknecht that he knew that James had become aware of the complaints being made, and the things being said. James had started getting questions from employees and various business contacts, as well as inquiries from TERO, and was scrambling to pacify their concerns and clear his name.

But what Arey didn't know was that James blamed K.C. for the mounting scrutiny bearing down on him. And Arey had no idea what James was capable of if he felt that someone had betrayed him.

Gutknecht signaled he was ready to bring the interview to a close.

"Well," he said, sighing heavily while riffling through his notes, "you have my card. If you hear anything else, give me a call. Or, when I get this thing resolved, I'll give you a call. If he shows up somewhere, make sure you give me a call, and we'll grab him and punch him in the nose and figure out what the hell he's been doing."

"Yeah, because I just want to know if he is alive," Arey said.

"Well, everybody does," Gutknecht agreed.

"Because if there is some sort of frickin' foul play …" Arey trailed off. "I don't know, man. Everybody's pointing their finger at James, and I don't know James that well outside of working for him for six months at Blackstone. But I've just heard things come down the pipeline, some bad things, and I just don't know."

The anguish in Arey's words was palpable, and Gutknecht saw no need for further questions. Instead, the men shook hands, and Gutknecht drove away from the dock while Arey continued preparation for his fishing venture.

The next person Gutknecht had on his list was none other than James Henrikson himself.

CHAPTER 28

Benzos And Crotch Rockets

Merely weeks after recruiting someone to murder K.C. Clarke and then standing by to watch as he was brutally bludgeoned to death on February 22, 2012, James Terry Henrikson nearly died himself.

While traveling at dangerously high speeds on his sports bike—sometimes mockingly referred to as a "crotch rocket"—on a rural road near his home in Watford City, North Dakota, the 33-year-old lost control and rammed into the side of a steep embankment.

Upon impact, both James' body and the motorcycle had been launched several feet. Somehow, the bike and its scorching hot tailpipe had then landed on James's face and upper torso and seared through several layers of his skin until a Good Samaritan came upon the wreckage and peeled the pipe away.

James suffered horrific burns across his face, chest, and arms, and had spent several weeks in the hospital undergoing multiple surgeries and skin grafts to repair severely damaged skin, nerves, and muscle tissue. The surgery on a once-flawless face that many said resembled that of famous actor Matt Damon had taken more than six hours alone.

When James agreed to sit down for an interview with Steve Gutknecht on August 1 of 2012, his injuries were still in various stages of healing. The large scabs, scrapes, and bruises scattered across his face and arms didn't deter James from his well-known attraction to tight shirts that accentuated his bulging muscles, however. On this day, James even voluntarily rolled up the short sleeves of his navy-blue T-shirt to proudly show Gutknecht his battle wounds.

James also wore his signature designer jeans, but the tight pants put pressure on his right thigh where skin had been grafted to repair the burns on his face. As a result, fluids from the open wound oozed through a layer of gauze wrapped around James's leg and grotesquely soaked through the denim.

Gutknecht tried to avoid fixating on James's visible injuries but was interested to hear more about the ordeal. "Wow! So, where did this accident happen?"

James described the terrifying experience as best he could, noting how most of the details had been conveyed to him through doctors and eyewitness accounts because he could not recall any events from the week leading up to the accident or the two weeks that followed.

What James did remember, but conveniently neglected to share with Gutknecht, was that he had been higher than a kite after snorting an obscene amount of powdered benzodiazepines right before he impulsively decided to take a late-night joyride on his cherished bike. It was probably a miracle that he was still alive to talk about it.

As he wrapped up his story for Gutknecht, James tenderly rubbed the scabs near his right eye. "Shit, they say I need to stay out of the sun for like a year and a half. I guess I better get used to putting on sunscreen."

• • •

It had been over five long months since the day K.C. vanished, but a hot sheet bulletin and a flyer had finally been produced and distributed to all law enforcement agencies and businesses across the state of North Dakota, listing him as a missing person. K.C.'s mother had provided three older photos of him for the bulletin, and Gutknecht had printed out a copy of the document and placed it atop a thick case file situated on the table in front of him.

"I am with the North Dakota Bureau of Criminal Investigation," Gutknecht—wearing a maroon Polo, blue jeans, and tennis shoes—formally introduced himself to James. "We handle major crimes that are way more in depth than some investigations, and this one is turning out to be that way. So, um, we're looking for this guy."

Gutknecht slapped his palm down on K.C.'s flyer as he said this. The detective then helpfully slid the paper closer to James so that he could get a closer look at the pictures of a beaming K.C. staring back at him.

To this point, James had been quite cheerful and talkative while recounting his frightening accident. Upon seeing the photographs of K.C., however, James froze as if he had seen a ghost.

"You and Sarah know K.C. as well as anyone, probably even better than anyone," Gutknecht said. "So, tell me about him."

"Uh … he's just … uh … fun, I guess," James stammered quietly, his gaze still transfixed on the flyer. "I mean, he's always happy. He worked pretty hard. He … uh … he … uh … he was working really hard for us."

His focus then snapped back, remembering that the narrative he needed to convey was that of K.C. inexplicably turning into an alcoholic mess who refused to show up for work. If James told the truth that K.C. was a valued employee who worked hard, it would be difficult to justify the hurried need for he and Sarah to put him on a paid leave.

"We made him go on vacation," James said. "We told him to take at least a two-week vacation. We didn't know what was really going on with him, but he was tired all the time, and he just looked like shit, to be honest."

The reasoning behind why the directive was specifically for a two-week vacation—rather than just a few days off to decompress and catch up on rest—was unclear, and Gutknecht didn't ask. However, James admitted that K.C. initially displayed reluctance toward the idea of going on such a prolonged break.

K.C. had complained that he didn't want to spend money on a vacation, and even if he did, there wasn't really anywhere he wanted to go. But it didn't matter because, as James explained to Gutknecht, K.C. didn't have a choice—his employers at Blackstone were demanding he leave on vacation immediately.

James then oddly shifted back to praising K.C. "But, like, he did awesome with all of our company guys. All of our employees loved him. I loved him."

"But he was looking to leave you guys, wasn't he?" Gutknecht asked, referring to the information he had received about K.C. going to work for another company.

"I found that out after," James answered. "But he never said anything to me at all. Like, nothing."

James recounted that when K.C. did not return to work from his two-week leave, and no one had heard from him, Rick Arey paid a visit to the Blackstone offices to share the news that he and K.C. were planning to go to work for Running Horse Trucking. James told Gutknecht he hadn't believed the news.

"We've been friends forever, so I don't really see K.C. doing that to me," he said. "There's no way."

●●●

Following the momentary jolt he experienced when confronted with the photographs of a smiling K.C. on a missing persons flyer, James had maintained the same posture—perched at the edge of his chair, legs spread apart, one leg straddling the table's edge, and elbows casually propped atop the table. Occasionally, his knee would rhythmically bob up and down, and he would pause momentarily to gently tend to the annoying itching caused by the healing injuries on his face. He came across as charming and amiable, and he projected an air of confidence.

But when Gutknecht asked him to share the last time he had seen K.C., James visibly winced. It was a reaction so fleeting that Gutknecht, who was peering down at his notes, didn't even see it happen.

James cleverly avoided providing a specific date for when he had last seen K.C. by turning the question back to Gutknecht. "Gosh, I have no idea. Months ago. How long has it been since he went missing?"

"February 22 is the last time that I can track him anywhere."

James feigned surprise. "Really?"

"Throughout this entire investigation," Gutknecht said, "a lot of people told me that he was coming to meet with you guys to turn in his fuel card, because he was getting ready to leave the company."

Gutknecht embellished the point just a bit. Though several people had mentioned to the detective that K.C. was going to return his gas card to Blackstone on the day he disappeared, none of them had said it was because of his plans to leave the company. Rather, what he had learned was that K.C. turning in the gas card was based solely on Sarah Creveling's demand that he do so.

"Nope, he never turned it into me," James said quickly.

When Gutknecht asked if K.C had perhaps brought his card to Sarah, James acknowledged that he knew of Sarah's plans to get new gas cards for all Blackstone Trucking employees but could not confirm whether or not K.C. had ever turned his card into his wife.

Gutknecht then cleverly caught James off-guard. "See, he kept a log of what he was doing daily. And on there, it mentions meeting with you guys, on that day, to turn in a fuel card."

The contents of the journal discovered in K.C.'s truck was a meticulously kept record of his activities for a period of several months leading up to the day he disappeared. Each entry was accompanied by a brief note to describe the reason or purpose for every meeting and appointment. Unless K.C. had been in the habit of documenting fake events, his plan to turn the gas card over to Sarah Creveling at Blackstone Trucking on the morning of February 22 was memorialized in black ink.

"You don't know anything about the meeting that day?"

Gutknecht pressed.

"Well, I know he was supposed to," James conceded.

"But you don't know if he ever made that meeting or not?"

"No," James said. "I don't know. I'm just not sure. And honestly, my memory is a little bit—like I said, when I got out of the hospital, I didn't even remember for about a week that K.C. didn't still work for us."

Before Gutknecht could ask another question about the scheduled meeting with K.C., James deftly steered their conversation in an altogether different direction, telling a fanciful story to demonstrate that his memory struggles were legit.

James recounted how he and his wife had recently taken a trip to Seattle. While Sarah attended a hair appointment at an upscale salon in the city, James offered to go on a shopping spree to find her some new clothes—as so many husbands often do.

"I told her I was going shopping for her," he said, "and, uh, you know, I see this shirt, and I like this shirt. So, I buy the shirt, you know, for her. Well actually I buy two of them because you know, everything I buy, I buy two of because I'll probably never find them again."

James shared that much to his chagrin, once Sarah saw the new blouses, she reminded her memory-impaired husband that the couple had purchased the exact same blouse a few weeks before while they were on another vacation in Las Vegas.

"She still hasn't proven it to me, but she says it's in our closet," James laughed, flashing his bright white teeth for Gutknecht.

He then became wistful. "But, I mean, it's weird, and, like, when I saw the photos of my burns and stuff, I just kind of like teared up. Not for me, of course. I don't care about me. But for her. What she went through was pretty emotional. And I got a little emotional about K.C. I don't know. I guess it's just, like, changed me a little bit."

If the accident had indeed changed James, it wasn't clear in what way. Throughout his life, any time he had managed to escape real consequences for his actions—even in a near-death experience of his own making—it had not motivated him to reevaluate and take steps to course correct for the better. Instead, it seemed to grant him a newfound sense of invincibility and grandiosity, emboldening him to push the limits further each time.

He certainly wasn't about to admit that he had orchestrated the murder of his best friend five months prior and, for the time being, had managed to slither his way out of a potentially difficult line of questioning. But he wasn't out of the woods yet, as Gutknecht still had plenty more to go.

CHAPTER 29

The James Henrikson Show

Special Agent Steve Gutknecht was well aware that hundreds of men voluntarily came and went from the oilfields on a regular basis—some vanishing into the ether nearly as quickly as they arrived—but there was something about the circumstances surrounding K.C. Clarke's disappearance that did not seem to fit that same pattern.

By all accounts, K.C. was a single, gregarious young man who had frequently maintained contact with numerous friends in both North Dakota and elsewhere. It wasn't just that K.C. had not reached out to any of them—or, for that matter, the grandfather he reportedly cherished more than anyone else in his life—for several months, it was also that Gutknecht could not find *anyone* who had seen or heard from him.

K.C.'s roommate, Judd Parker, hadn't even been that close to him, and he harbored a sickening sense that something was wrong. Rick Arey and Tesha Fredericks had both displayed almost a guttural plea for some sort of answer as to what had happened to their friend.

Gutknecht was now seated in a cramped interrogation room, across the table from one of K.C.'s purported "best" friends, and former employer, James Henrikson—one of only a few people reportedly known to have physically seen and interacted with K.C. almost every single day in the weeks leading up to him suddenly vanishing into thin air. Yet, James was the only one within K.C.'s inner circle who seemed unfazed by his friend's disappearance.

James had avoided confirming if K.C. had turned in a fuel card on the day he disappeared, and he had also denied knowing about K.C. leaving Blackstone to work for another company. But if it were true—as had been confirmed by several people—that K.C. was planning to leave Blackstone, it made sense that there might be some bad blood between the friends. "I felt like James was making stuff up as he went along," Gutknecht later recalled. "He was the only one I could find with a motive. In my career, as soon as you see a guy with a motive, that's usually who it turns out to be."

So, he pressed on.

"What do you think happened to K.C., James?" Gutknecht asked.

"I thought maybe he shacked up with a girl and just took off, to be honest," James quickly answered, shrugging his shoulders. "I'm a little bit worried about him now, you know, after this long. I mean, it is something he would do, but to not be in contact with his grandpa … I can't see that."

James also conceded that it was very out of character that K.C. had not contacted any of his close friends, either. These acknowledgments placated Gutknecht for the time being, and he shifted to his next area of concern.

"He's got money in the bank, and he hasn't touched any of it," the agent stated.

"Oh, so he did save some of the money I paid him." James let out a hearty laugh.

Gutknecht also revealed that K.C.'s truck had been found in Williston, and that it was in the process of being repossessed by the bank because a payment hadn't been made for several months. The fact that K.C. had not accessed a single penny of the several thousand dollars he had sitting in the bank didn't jibe with the notion of a voluntary exit.

"He's just gone," Gutknecht said, raising his arms into the air. "You don't just disappear and not use any of your money. I think something bad happened to K.C."

Left with little choice, James agreed with the investigator's obvious logic. "Yeah, that's what I think, too."

Gutknecht carried on. "How about K.C.'s handgun? What do you know about that?"

"Oh," James began, then paused to buy himself time to formulate a response. "Huh. I remember he had something. He always carried that thing with him. Like, real close to him. I don't know what that was about … if he didn't feel safe or something. I don't know what it was."

"His gun is missing as well," Gutknecht revealed. "So, that's why I am asking you … if we could find that … or if that turns up as well …" He trailed off.

James offered no further response about the gun and appeared pleased when Gutknecht gave up and moved away from the subject.

Unbeknownst to Gutknecht, James knew exactly where K.C.'s .45 caliber pistol was. Even though it was far, far away from where they were sitting in North Dakota, it rattled him to know authorities were looking for it. Later, James would make a call to a friend in Washington, ordering him to immediately destroy all traces of the weapon.

• • •

The detective finally returned to an earlier point—pressing James a little harder this time. "Everything points to the fact that K.C. was going to see you guys as one of the last things he did. So, you don't have anything to do with his disappearance?"

"Nah," James scoffed, acting as if Gutknecht was raising a farcical possibility.

"Did you guys have a physical altercation, at all?"

"No, never."

"You've never fought?"

"Not ever once have we fought," James reiterated.

"Because I've heard everything from you guys having a fight, to him pulling a gun on you." Gutknecht said.

"Holy shit!" James laughed, conveying amusement over the notion.

"Has he been in any physical altercations with anyone else, or pulled a gun on anyone else?" Gutknecht asked.

"I wouldn't think he would," James said. "That just doesn't seem like him, to pull a gun on someone. That would be really weird. I mean, K.C. would do, like, anything to help—I mean, he's helped me a ton. And that's why I've helped him a ton, you know?"

"So, he doesn't have any enemies up here that you know of?" Gutknecht asked.

James acknowledged he didn't know of any enemies that K.C. had. Period.

Toward the end of the hour-long interview, Gutknecht invited James to take a polygraph as a simple matter of procedure.

"It's something that we would just set up a date with you, you know, later this week or next week, and run a polygraph, or a lie detector test. You could do it right here. I'm just wondering if you'd be willing to do that for us?"

As a career criminal who had participated in a few polygraphs himself, James expressed his reluctance. "Hmm. I've had a couple buddies go away for those things because they're not very accurate."

"Well, just the results of that wouldn't get you prosecuted for anything, obviously," Gutknecht tried to reassure James. "But it would give me peace of mind that you're telling the truth, and everything you're telling me is accurate. And then we can put you off to the side, you know what I'm saying?"

"Right, right," James replied, his voice dripping with sarcasm.

"I'm going to offer the same thing to Sarah as well," the detective revealed. "It's just another tool that I use, but if you fail the polygraph, it's not gonna put you from here right into jail or anything like that."

"I mean, maybe," James said, trying to appease Gutknecht. "Let me think about it."

Gutknecht kept pushing. "It would just tell me if you're lying or telling the truth. If you're telling the truth about everything, then I could consider you out, and continue on in my investigation. But obviously, if you were lying, then I would know. And then it would be the James Henrikson show."

James, desperate to move on from the polygraph discussion, turned the tables, interrogating his interrogator. "So, from your end, honestly, like, from your investigation on this side of things, what do you think happened?"

The detective took the bait, providing a rambling answer: "You know, I don't know him even remotely as good as you do, but when you're gone, and you're not accessing your accounts, and you're not using your cell phone anymore—because people can't do things without cell phones and money anymore—I think something bad happened to him. It's just a matter of finding out what, and it will come out eventually. He'll be found, or someone who knows will share that information. I just want to find out as soon as possible. His family wants to know. His mom, his grandpa. They all want to know."

"Me too," James said. "I loved that kid to death."

Unfortunately for the detective, he had no clue that those words were tantamount to a confession.

●●●

A few hours after her husband's session with Steve Gutknecht, Sarah Creveling arrived for her turn. Stylishly dressed in denim capris and a white polyester zip-up jacket—her blonde hair perfectly coiffed with a high-end straightener—Sarah appeared comfortable and expressed eagerness to provide any help she could offer.

But if Gutknecht had hoped for any fresh insights, he would leave the interview sorely disappointed. Sarah merely rehashed the same information she provided Officer Ryan Zimmerman in early June.

Just as she had done with Zimmerman, Sarah batted her eyelashes and conjured up tears to garner sympathy over her "fear" of having to exist amongst very scary and dangerous people in North Dakota. She attempted to convince the detective of her sincere concern over K.C. Clarke's disappearance.

Sarah reiterated the same uncorroborated stories of K.C. being a raging alcoholic who wasn't performing well in his job, yet she still was not asked to explain why such a terrible employee was granted a two-week paid vacation instead of corrective action, or even a termination letter. Nor was she—or James for that matter—ever asked if K.C. had indeed been paid for those two weeks.

Sarah did finally put the questions surrounding the fuel card to rest, however, by admitting that K.C. had indeed turned his in. Although she was unable to recall the specific date for which he had done so, Sarah was particularly insistent that it had absolutely not been on February 22. Gutknecht accepted this explanation and moved on.

"In doing this investigation, I wouldn't be doing this whole thing justice if I didn't offer people polygraphs." Gutknecht told her. "I want you to, and I've offered this to James as well, and we've already done polygraphs on some of the other close people. We're almost done investigating every piece that we can on this, so I'm just going to offer people polygraphs and see if everybody's telling the truth. Would you be willing to take a polygraph?"

"Probably," Sarah said slowly. "I mean, I'd probably have to think about it. I've never been asked that question before."

"What I want to find out is if you had anything to do with K.C.'s disappearance."

"Of course."

"Well, did you?" Gutknecht prodded.

"No." Sarah declared.

"Right now, everybody's a suspect," Gutknecht said. "This would just help me to put Sarah aside. To put James aside. Because, right now, the investigation and what people say is that K.C. was coming to see you and James, to give you his fuel card. According to Rick [Arey], K.C. was saying, 'Screw you guys, I'm going over here, I'm taking all your business with me.' To me as an investigator, that shows me that you guys would have a beef with him. But sitting here talking to you, I can see that it didn't take place that way."

It wasn't terribly clear if the detective had truly accepted

Sarah's version of the events over everything else he'd heard, but Gutknecht shifted his focus and tried to appeal to Sarah's vanity and self-absorption instead.

He reminded her that local gossip was rampant with loud voices saying that both she and James likely had something to do with whatever happened to K.C. Sarah was all too aware her perfectly crafted image was being publicly tarnished, and she wasn't happy.

Gutknecht promised that the whole idea behind the polygraph was to be able to assure K.C.'s family and the public that Sarah and her husband had demonstrated their honesty and cooperation throughout the investigation, and that they were entirely uninvolved with K.C.'s disappearance.

Sarah nodded along and agreed to think about it more, but the 30-minute conversation had clearly taken an uncomfortable turn for her. She began collecting her belongings, eager to leave as quickly as possible. Gutknecht did not attempt to impede her exit with any further questions.

The following day, both James and Sarah informed Gutknecht that they would not consent to a polygraph exam after all and declined any further communication with him or any other investigators.

With no additional information to proceed with, the investigation surrounding the vanishing of K.C. Clarke stalled for several more months.

• • •

Free from the scrutinizing eyes of law enforcement for the time being, James and Sarah did their best to ignore the whispers and went straight back to their extravagant lifestyle. It was the fall of 2012, and they were at the zenith of their success in the oilfields, rolling in the dough. Partnering with the tribal chairman, Tex Hall, had been a lucrative move.

Putting aside the fact that James and Sarah were secretly siphoning money away from the chairman's own business, Maheshu Energy—pouring it into shell accounts for Blackstone—there was a mutual admiration that had developed between Hall and James. Whenever anyone tried to warn Hall that he was dealing with a potentially dangerous man—and there were several who did—the chairman dismissed the concerns outright.

But there were a few people who felt so wronged by James and Sarah that they weren't quite willing to let things go as easily. At the top of the list was Jill Williams, who firmly believed that James and Sarah had something to do with the disappearance of her son. Another was Jedidiah McClure, the once-enthusiastic businessman whom James and Sarah had unashamedly screwed out of tens of thousands of dollars.

In addition, there were some members of the Three Affiliated Tribes who were curious about the peculiar case of a missing white man that seemed to have at least an indirect link to the tribal chairman. One of them was an Arikara woman named Lissa Yellowbird.

Despite having no prior connections to one another, and very different motivations, K.C.'s mom, McClure, and Yellowbird would soon team up, devising a wicked plan to ruin James and Sarah and scatter the ashes of their reputations all across the oilfields.

CHAPTER 30

An Unlikely Friendship

Lissa Yellowbird was 43 years old when K.C. Clarke went missing from the Fort Berthold Indian Reservation in February of 2012. At the time, she had been out of prison for almost four years, living in Fargo, North Dakota, existing on little more than tuna fish sandwiches, nicotine, and regret.

In her nearly four and a half decades of life, Lissa had amassed a catalog of trial and triumph that could rival even the most fascinating of autobiographical tales. Although she was a member of the Three Affiliated Tribes (Mandan, Hidatsa, Arikara) of Fort Berthold, she'd never spent much time living on the reservation.

Her early life had been a nomadic journey across the country alongside her mother, the pair never staying in the same place for very long. When she was old enough to be on her own, Lissa frequently succumbed to the familiar pattern of restlessness, and didn't hesitate to leave people—even her own children—and possessions behind when it was time to move on.

The short and stout Arikara woman with jet black hair and penetrating dark eyes was skilled in a variety of trades and had earned a degree in criminal justice at the University of North Dakota in Grand Forks. She had also worked as a prostitute, been addicted to crack, given birth to five children with five different men, and in 2006, was given a 15-year prison sentence after multiple arrests for possession of methamphetamine.

When she was released early from the Dakota Women's Correctional Unit in 2008, having served only two years of her sentence, she was finally ready to fully embrace sobriety and turn her life around.

She'd heard about K.C. Clarke through a family member who still lived on the reservation, but the details were relatively scant: K.C., a white man, had been working for James Henrikson and Sarah Creveling at Blackstone Trucking when he suddenly vanished. It had now been several months since anyone had seen or heard from him.

Typically, a white man missing from the oilfields would not garner the attention of most tribal members, but by the time Lissa heard about it, most everyone was aware that Blackstone was operating out of Maheshu Energy's shop in Mandaree, which was owned by the tribal chairman, Tex Hall. The possibility of a link—even if remote—between the chairman and the mysterious disappearance of a man was far too intriguing for Lissa to ignore.

Lissa soon learned that the NDBCI had opened an investigation, but K.C.'s whereabouts remained a mystery. Even though K.C. had supposedly gone missing on the reservation, the tribal police had not initiated an investigation of their own because of complex jurisdictional boundaries that hindered both state and tribal authorities.

But crimes left unsolved on the reservation—especially those that involved a missing or murdered indigenous person—frustrated and disturbed Lissa to no end, and she would even later publicly crusade for the cause.

If there was one thing Lissa could proudly boast of, it was her unwavering determination. When she set her mind to something, very little could deter her. Now free from the clutches of drug addiction, but in need of another vice to replace it, Lissa was resolute in her decision to pursue the truth about K.C.

And so it was that in the summer of 2012, Lissa officially embarked on an independent investigation of her own, vowing to herself that she would be the person to find K.C.—dead or alive.

•••

Lissa began her quest by first perusing the "Find K.C." Facebook page for hours upon hours, marveling at the content of the posts from friends and family, as well as from strangers far and wide. The page had amassed several thousand followers, yet none of them had provided a single helpful piece of information to bring clarity to what had happened to K.C.

She scrolled through the dozens of posts from K.C.'s mother, Jill Williams. At first, Jill had seemed hopeful, asking for people to reach out if they had seen her son. As the weeks and months had passed, however, Jill had become distraught, with some of her posts amounting to rambling expressions of desperation.

Jill's deeply personal and agonizing words grated on Lissa's nerves. She believed such profound anguish should be kept private and not aired in a public forum. In fact, although she would keep this opinion to herself for quite some time, Lissa felt that Jill was making a mockery of K.C.'s page with her histrionics.

Still, Lissa knew that if she had any hope of solving K.C.'s case, she would need insight from those who knew him best. Eventually, Lissa typed out a private message to Jill. In this message and several more that would follow, Lissa emphasized her ties to the reservation and subtly hinted that she had access to areas, people, and information far beyond what Jill could obtain on her own.

Up to this juncture, Jill felt strongly that K.C.'s case wasn't receiving the attention it deserved from the authorities. In certain respects, she was correct. It seemed no one was listening to her claims that James and Sarah were involved and was frustrated that they were still walking free while her son was nowhere to be found. When Lissa started messaging her, Jill was not only desperate for answers—she was also longing for a friend.

Within just a few weeks, the two women became extremely close. That is, as far as Jill was concerned. Once K.C.'s mother felt comfortable, she opened up like a fire hydrant, sharing absolutely every intimate detail of her life with Lissa. But Jill's incessant storytelling and especially her syrupy voice bored and annoyed Lissa.

Before either of them realized it, Jill and Lissa formed an unhealthy dependency on one another. While Jill leaned far too heavily on her new friend for emotional support, Lissa clung to the relationship solely to stay intimately involved in the investigation of K.C.'s disappearance. But Lissa's good-natured façade could only be maintained for so long, and soon, she would no longer have any use for Jill.

CHAPTER 31

Tear Everything Down

By early autumn of 2012, Lissa Yellowbird and Jill Williams were working in tandem to solve K.C.'s case. Jill spent most of her time sifting through public posts and private messages sent to her via the "Find K.C." Facebook page. She was also calling Special Agent Steve Gutknecht on a nearly daily basis. Gutknecht never seemed to get annoyed with Jill's inquiries, but his answer was always the same:

"I don't have anything new."

Meanwhile, Lissa had begun compiling as much information as she could, oftentimes spending every free moment she had conducting online research. What she knew so far was merely a thread, but enough to keep pulling at the tapestry.

The prevailing theory suggested that on the morning K.C. disappeared, he had a meeting scheduled with his employers at Blackstone Trucking. According to several people, K.C. was supposed to turn in a fuel card to Sarah Creveling at the shop in Mandaree, which was located on Tex Hall's sprawling ranch. So far, however, there wasn't any concrete evidence to prove that.

No one had come forward to confirm they had seen K.C. at the shop that day. Additionally, both James and Sarah had denied the meeting took place on that date, and authorities hadn't pressed them any further on the matter.

Several people had tried to engage Hall to get his perspective on K.C.'s disappearance and to understand his relationship with James and Sarah, but the chairman would become angry and adamantly refuse to discuss either subject.

While Lissa felt reasonably certain that Hall didn't have anything to do with K.C.'s disappearance or possible murder, the fact that one or both of those things might have happened on his land made it seem awfully strange that the chairman resisted acknowledging it. It was also odd that Hall didn't appear to be interested in distancing himself from the two individuals who were rumored to be involved.

In the absence of Hall himself providing any additional explanation, Lissa pursued answers on her own. Specifically, she wanted to better understand how the tribal chairman got tangled up in doing business with a white man in the first place. It was virtually unheard of for such a thing to happen on the reservation. Following a request for paperwork from the TERO office in New Town, Lissa ascertained that Blackstone was a subcontractor for Maheshu.

The business agreement seemed fairly straightforward at face value, but Lissa was taken aback when she discovered that the partnership had also somehow afforded Blackstone a Tier 1 status on the reservation. What that meant was that Blackstone was enjoying advantages that were typically reserved only for tribal-owned businesses. This type of preference given to a non-tribal, white-owned company made Lissa's blood boil. She couldn't understand why on earth the chairman would have facilitated it.

But efforts to communicate with Hall were fruitless, and any attempts to continue urging the chairman to respond would have been foolish. Lissa was warned by several family members to avoid such an endeavor.

Instead, it was James and Sarah who Lissa decided to place in her crosshairs for the time being, primarily because of her ire toward them for reaping a huge profit on Indian land. In no uncertain terms, Lissa told Jill that the only way to get to the husband and wife was to covertly work on tearing down everything they had built.

If Tex Hall's own reputation was inadvertently tarnished

along the way, well, that would just be icing on the cake and a deserved comeuppance for him refusing to publicly address the community's concerns.

•••

More information had surfaced on the Facebook page, suggesting that Blackstone was really a front for drug running, and that K.C. had been roughed up on the day he went missing. However, it turned out that all of it was based on hearsay and no one had provided any direct firsthand knowledge to support either claim.

Unfortunately, Jill ate up all of it no matter how outlandish while Lissa displayed greater discernment in differentiating fact from rumor and conjecture. Each time another tip proved to be untrue and a waste of time, Jill crumpled, and Lissa would have to pull her back up by the bootstraps encouraging her to press on.

Lissa proposed that she and Jill meet in person in New Town, North Dakota, and that they could recreate the path that K.C. had supposedly taken on the day he disappeared, visit the site in Williston where his truck had been abandoned, and search parts of the vast countryside of the reservation where someone might possibly dump a dead body.

It was a cruel experiment. Outwardly, Jill was clinging to the possibility that K.C. was alive, but that hope—and her well-being—was hanging on by a very thin thread. Being in places her son had once been and trudging through desolate fields with the thought that they might just happen to stumble upon K.C.'s remains only served to haunt Jill further.

Ultimately, the trip to North Dakota was what finally broke Jill. Her patience and hope had run out. She fully believed that James and Sarah had done something to her son. If the authorities were reluctant to keep pushing for answers, then she would do it for them using the only tool she had at her disposal.

Upon returning to Washington, Jill reignited her efforts on the "Find K.C." Facebook page, determined to keep up the public pressure campaign against James and Sarah.

James and Sarah, What's up? I don't get it. As friends of K.C.'s don't you want to help? Please take the polygraph test and clear yourselves so we can move on. I'm trying to understand what's going on, but you don't seem to come to the page anymore, you don't donate to the reward/find K.C. fund, you don't write to me, won't take the poly and from what I've heard, you don't spread the word about K.C. or display or post elsewhere K.C.'s missing posters. I'm confused, it's not making sense to me. James, didn't you know K.C. for years? I thought you guys had known each other from here or Texas for some years—don't you want to help find your friend?

The revelation that law enforcement had asked the pair to sit for polygraph exams and their refusal to do so was a bombshell that no one else had known up until that point, and it triggered a firestorm of angry comments directed at James and Sarah. James did not have a social media account, but Sarah did, and she had been quietly following the page for some time. When she saw her and her husband's names splashed across dozens of posts and the rage in the public comments, Sarah was mortified and soon deleted her personal account.

Although Lissa remained mostly in the background, she spurred Jill on, even helping her compose some of the posts. One of them urged people to write to the tribal council to request that Blackstone be called upon to explain why it was not cooperating with investigators.

In a post marked as being sent "via mobile near Fargo, ND," Lissa wrote:

I think everyone should flood Tex's office with letters that he needs to conduct a hearing on Blackstone for their refusal to cooperate with police AND for all the money they've ripped off from good honest people! Could someone please post that for me?

Another post took square aim at the chairman, accusing him of doing business with a conman who had a rap sheet longer than the contract that Maheshu Energy and Blackstone Trucking had signed with each other.

... Time to blacklist Blackstone and bring the truth out here. I wonder what Tex would think of all this—I hear that it's an election year. I'm sure that Tex, being a tribal big wig would certainly want to use his power to do good and wouldn't want to dirty his good name covering for a piece of crap like James ... wouldn't look good to those doing the voting.

But the Facebook crusade aside, the more Jill leaned on Lissa for support, the more she pulled away. Jill's neediness was off-putting, and Lissa no longer had a tolerance for it. The final straw for Lissa came when Jill responded to a woman on the page who claimed to have seen K.C. partying on a beach somewhere abroad. Jill replied, pleading for K.C. to call her. The original post with K.C. on a beach was silly and clearly a red herring, and everyone seemed to know it but Jill.

This made Lissa furious. But rather than address her friend privately, Lissa wrote a scathing reply for all to see, admonishing Jill for making the page look like a soap opera. Jill followed up with a direct message to Lissa, asking why she had chosen to publicly humiliate her in such a way. Lissa responded callously, telling Jill she could understand why K.C. had chosen to remain estranged from her.

The disagreement between the two was too much to overcome, with neither woman interested in repairing the relationship. Jill ultimately blocked Lissa from the Facebook page, but it didn't matter. By then, Lissa wanted nothing more to do with either Jill or the page. Her primary focus had long since shifted from finding out what happened to K.C., and on to doing whatever it would take to ruin James and Sarah.

Luckily, there was someone else who had the same aspirations as Lissa and was eager to join forces.

CHAPTER 32

The Beware Flyer

Jedediah McClure was a desperate man. When he'd invested thousands of dollars of his own money—signing a business contract with James Henrikson in September of 2011—he believed he would not only recoup his initial investment but also reap hefty monthly revenues for years to come.

Much to McClure's dismay, however, neither of those outcomes had materialized.

Rather, James and his wife had masterfully pilfered tens of thousands of dollars away from the joint venture and into their own network of shell companies. To add insult to injury, McClure's lawyers were telling him that battling the couple in court to reclaim the money would be an exercise in futility.

Although losing such a large sum of money was devastating, it was also the damage done to McClure's self-image that he couldn't move past. As someone who fancied himself to be a sophisticated and shrewd businessman, the fact that he had been so easily swindled by a muscled-up career criminal and a ditzy blonde was a bitter pill to swallow. He later documented his experiences in a brief tell-all, including this poignant excerpt from his personal website, jedediahmcclure.com:

For James Henrikson, it was easy to steal, so easy to lie, so easy to feign ignorance and pass the blame on to someone else, and so incredibly easy, in the dust and rumble of heavy machinery, to mask that something evil had come to town with gilded promises and fingers cold as death.

But even if those words poetically conveyed an accurate portrait of who James was, McClure unfortunately had missed it entirely. Not only had he placed an enormous amount of blind faith in James—a man he had never even met—but he had also willingly abandoned any pretense of discernment in exchange for grandiose promises of financial windfalls.

To make matters worse, McClure now believed his life was in grave danger—a mantra he dramatically emphasized later in the writings on his website:

… with a bounty on his head for more than a year, Jedediah and his young family lived in constant fear that a hitman would show up at their home, gun in hand, ready to exact Henrikson's revenge.

Despite his fear, McClure wasn't quite ready to wave the white flag just yet. The embattled entrepreneur wanted retribution, and the only way he knew how was to strike where it would hurt the most, and in the exact same way it had been done to him—by targeting James's own bloated ego and financial status.

McClure ultimately hoped to tarnish his reputation to an extent that would scare off contractors, employees, and potential business partners. If that worked, then perhaps Blackstone would eventually collapse. An even better outcome would be if James was left with no choice but to totally abandon the oilfields in complete humiliation.

But there was also an ulterior motivation, as McClure was still largely driven more by greed than revenge. If he could remove James from the equation, McClure had visions of rebuilding a version of Blackstone that would solely be under his direction and control. He could recruit additional investors and work on mending the relationships with other oilfield business partners.

The challenge McClure faced was devising an approach

in which there would be no way for James, or anyone, to trace anything back to him. In February 2013—a full year after K.C. Clarke had gone missing—much to McClure's delight, and perhaps his good fortune, a call came in from the most unlikely and unexpected of allies: Lissa Yellowbird.

Although their underlying reasons differed, McClure and Lissa shared the same goal: destroying James and Sarah and any enterprise with which they were associated. While Lissa was disgusted by the advantages James had been given to the detriment of other tribal business owners, McClure mostly just wanted another chance at a piece of the pie.

Lissa had some ideas for how to accomplish their parallel missions, but they were much smaller in scope than McClure had in mind.

"I wanted to expose James Henrikson and Sarah Creveling to everyone for the criminals and frauds that they were." McClure later explained. "The only way I knew how to do that was to share information about their backgrounds as far and wide as possible. Hopefully after seeing it, no one would ever want to do business with them again."

Disseminating that information would be no easy feat. Phone calls could easily be traced back, so that idea was a quick non-starter. Face-to-face conversations would not only be tedious and time-consuming, but Lissa and McClure both had to consider the fact that the last time a couple of people went around publicly denigrating James, one of them ended up missing. The only alternative the duo could come up with that would take fairly little time and had a low risk of being traced back to them, involved distributing something by mail. In what would later be referred to in multiple publications and police reports as the "Beware Flyer," McClure developed a one-page mailer that crammed in as much information as possible about the alleged misdeeds of James and Sarah.

The headline in boldface read:

BEWARE
JAMES T. HENRICKSEN
SARAH M. CREVELING

CON-ARTISTS AND THIEVES

McClure positioned individual color photos of James and Sarah below the headlines, as well as a picture of the two of them snuggled up close together, beaming for a selfie. A list of their distinctive features appeared beneath their photographs, including that James was missing an eyebrow and had "major burns" on his arms and chest from a motorcycle accident that occurred months prior. The flyer also noted that "James may wear a baseball cap to cover the burn scars over his eye and on his forehead."

James's known aliases were listed as well including both spellings of the name Henrikson, with the incorrect spelling inadvertently receiving top billing.

Below the descriptors, McClure recorded a list of the companies and shells registered to James and Sarah:

> *They own Blackstone LLC, Blackstone Trucking, Black-*
> *stone Crude, Blackstone Electric, Blackstone Building*
> *Group, Blackstone Construction and Blackwell.*
> *They work on the Fort Berthold Reservation.*

McClure also chronicled a snippet of James's arrest history:

RAPE 1/SEXUAL ABUSE 1 2000
AGGRAVATED THEFT/1ST DEGREE 2001
ELUDE POLICE ATTEMPT 2001
THEFT 2001
BURGLARY 2001
FRAUD-OBTAIN SIGNATURE 2001
ASSAULT IV 2001
TAMPER WITH PHY. EVIDENCE 2001
DELIVER MARIJUANA 2009
MANUFACTURE MARIJUANA 2009
ASSAULT 2 2009
THEFT I 2009
ASSAULT II ATTEMPT 2009

THEFT I ATTEMPT 2009

The flyer closed with a stark warning:

CAUTION

> *James is very charismatic and charming. He may claim to have money in order to build confidence with vendors or companies to steal from them. He owes thousands to vendors and investors. James has a history of filing for bankruptcy and running off with people's money.*
>
> *James and Sarah may also have been involved in the disappearance of a former Blackstone employee Kristopher D. Clarke (K.C.) but have refused to cooperate with the BCI. Consider them dangerous!*

The messy flyer harkened back to early 20th century "Wanted" posters from the wild west, but it was nevertheless quite damning. McClure had several thousand copies printed, and shipped them to Lissa's apartment in Fargo, North Dakota. Lissa went to great lengths to avoid any possible link back to herself: wearing gloves while she stuffed all of the flyers into envelopes and driving nearly five hours away from her apartment to mail them out.

Once the envelopes were deposited into a postal drop box, there was no turning back. Lissa and McClure sat on pins and needles, anxiously awaiting the volcano they hoped would erupt. But even they could never have imagined the fallout the "Beware Flyer" would cause.

It wasn't until years later that either of them would disclose that they had been the unseen architects behind the single piece of paper that brought James Henrikson and Sarah Creveling to their knees. Nor would Lissa or McClure ever take responsibility for the cascade of consequences that followed.

CHAPTER 33

The Fast Fallout

It didn't take long for the "Beware Flyer" to bear fruit. It was mailed to thousands of homes, government officials, oil contractors, restaurants, bars, grocery stores, and more. Just as Lissa and McClure had hoped, those receiving the mailers took heed of their warnings—and then some. Almost overnight, the flyers were plastered on windows and noticeboards throughout the oilfields.

McClure was cunning—he had instructed Lissa to list James and Sarah's names and their Watford City home as the return address. The couple was none too pleased to find clusters of the beaten-up envelopes marked "undeliverable" in their mailbox nearly every day. Not only was the content of the flyer a stinging rebuke, but the sheer volume of the undelivered mailers left little doubt that the western part of North Dakota had been blanketed with the ones that could be delivered.

Sarah was in unfamiliar territory, unsure of how to handle the smear campaign lobbied against her. She'd never faced a situation in her life where not everyone adored her. In the summer of 2012, she had cried to North Dakota authorities that it was "scary" living in the oilfields. But this was a whole different ballgame.

By March of 2013, virtually everyone within a 100-mile radius now recognized her face and was also aware of her husband's criminal past—something both she and James had worked assiduously to hide from their customers and business partners. They'd concealed their dark secrets for nearly two years, but the ruse was now over. The denials and gaslighting James and Sarah had deployed in the past could no longer deflect the onslaught of questions and accusations coming at them from every direction—even from some of their longtime customers.

The pressure of the intense public reaction was also bearing down heavily on Tex Hall, making it impossible for him to continue avoiding questions and warnings regarding his association with James and Sarah. Left with no other choice but to try to salvage his own legacy, the chairman soon dumped the couple like hot potatoes—dissolving the partnership between Maheshu Energy and Blackstone Trucking with a short email sent from his iPhone.

In a matter of weeks, James, Sarah, and Blackstone had become pariahs, with no obvious path to redemption. Once Tex Hall officially cut them off, their business in the oilfields came to a sudden halt. The far-fetched plan concocted by Lissa Yellowbird and Jedediah McClure had—rather remarkably—unfolded almost precisely as they had envisioned.

Unfortunately, James and Sarah falsely suspected it was K.C. Clarke's mother, Jill Williams, who was behind the flyers, and they filed a defamation lawsuit against her in the state of Washington in June 2013. The husband-and-wife plaintiffs claimed that Jill's public accusations—namely, the Facebook posts, the flyers, and some other letters—had caused them to lose a major contract, which had in turn essentially shut down their once-thriving business.

Part of the suit stated that "... as a result of defendant's actions, Blackstone LLC has been dissolved. The plaintiffs were grossing about two million a year with the contract with Maheshu Energy. Furthermore, the plaintiffs have been effectively 'blackballed' from doing business in the area due to the flyers posted and the unfounded allegations against them."

In one excerpt of her lengthy affidavit, Sarah wrote:

I believe the defendant also started to post "Beware" of my husband and I all around town and on the internet. My bank received this poster and Tex Hall received this poster as well. It states that we are con-artists and thieves. These allegations on the poster are untrue. Tex Hall gave me the envelope address (sic) to him with this flyer.

People in town are constantly asking us if we are involved in Mr. Clarke's disappearance. Many businesses have stated that they don't want to do business with us because of these rumors. We are the center [of] the town's gossip and live under a constant cloud.

As a result of these posters and false allegations, our contract between Maheshu Energy was terminated on March 16, 2013, which was also around the same time the flyer was sent to Tex Hall. We were forced to dissolve the LLC.

I do not know where Mr. Clarke is. My husband and I have nothing to do with Mr. Clarke's disappearance and are not suspects. I have never threatened physical harm against Ms. Williams.

The defendant has ruined our name. Just type Sarah Creveling and Blackstone into Google, and there are thousands of hits stating that I am involved with a crime and that I have physically threatened Ms. Williams.

Our names are ruined and the defendant has stated she will not stop until we tell her where her son is. I do not know what happened to her son. She needs to be stopped. I have experienced emotional stress because of this and have lost money.

The defendant has recruited a vast following and has encouraged others to defame and harass us. She won't be stopped. We all want to find K.C., but blaming everything on us is wrong. I do not know what happened to K.C.

Not only did the lawsuit claim that James and Sarah were being harassed, but evidently, Sarah's parents, Charles and Jennifer, had also received a strange, anonymous letter at their home in Issaquah, Washington. The return address on the envelope was oddly listed as "Blackstone LLC," using Mr. and Mrs. Creveling's own address—strikingly similar to the devious way Lissa Yellowbird had used James and Sarah's address as the return address for the Beware Flyer.

Inside the envelope were two pieces of paper. The first was a photocopy of a lengthy statement Jill had originally posted to the "Find K.C." Facebook page in the early days after her son went missing. The statement mentioned James and Sarah as the last two people to see K.C. Clarke alive. The second piece of paper was a letter typed in tiny, almost unreadable font, and riddled with poor grammar and spelling.

Dear Charles and Jennifer

you are receiving this letter the concerns for Sarah, unfortunately she is involved in a missings person case involving an employee, which you may or may not have heard about. At any rate james is the prime suspect many of us watching are sure sarah knows more than she should and knows what happened and rumor has it her life has been threatened with her life. The evedence is stacking up fast the young man missing is thought of as dead dumped in a field many people are searching for him the area they feel the body is located is under constant watch. I personally feel if protection can be provided sarah may come clean with info. We don't want to see sarah go down for something james is involved in there has already been one misshap (James's burns were no accident many people watch James and Sarah daily. Please we want Sarah safe we need to get her away from james and come clean for confirmation for what I am telling you you can contact special agent SteveGutknecht on the Williston police department.

thank you for your time please keep sarah safe

Naturally, Sarah's parents were extremely upset. Charles Creveling penned a statement in an affidavit for James and Sarah's lawsuit against Jill.

It is chilling for parents to receive a letter like this. Not only is it accusatory, but it feels threatening especially in reference to James' accident in June and the statement that they are watching our daughter daily. It is our understanding that James and Sarah have spoken with the authorities and are concerned about their friend K.C. I feel empathy for anyone who has to deal with the uncertainty of what happened to their child. I am concerned that this letter appears to have been written by someone making accusations and seemingly trying to address the matter outside of the legal system. I am concerned for my daughter's safety due to the hostile tone of these documents. Both my wife and I have spoken with both Sarah and James about precautionary measures to make sure they both remain safe.

Sarah had also received an anonymous letter addressed to her. Like the letter to her parents, the return address on the envelope was her own, but chillingly, it bore the name K.C. Clarke and was postmarked from Salt Lake City, Utah. The tiny font size and style matched exactly that of the letter her parents had received, and the spelling and grammar were equally atrocious.

Dear Dear Sarah

You are receiving this letter due to K.C.'s disapearence this has gone on long enough thee family is really hurting over this. Many of us who are watching you and James very closely feel you know more than your telling. We are not here to threaten you for we know your in a bad spot and can not speak of this how ever everyone knows james is the main suspect we also know a lot more than to police do. We are sorry you got mixed up in this. But you should know we want to help you we are around you all the time day and night we have pump gas by you stood behind you at stores and restraunts many of us have spoken to you many times. You should be aware the wall is falling down and fast. As for james that neck of his has got to be stiff from always watch-

ing his back. Dear it your call we are all growing inpatient we do not want to see you hurt or placed in prison over this and the drug running going on. As far as the family goes please help them put k c to rest and end there torment as well there is so much pain and unfortunately more to come bot not for them we know James burns were not an accident. Sarah we want you safe and to come forward with any info you have. If you want or need help many of us are here for you just ask go to kc s page and comment on a status(Kc the bomb) and we will know you want help. Please do what is right you would want us to do the same if it involved your family. From here it is all up to you

While the letters rattled Sarah and her family, Jill Williams was equally shaken. Not only was she absolutely not responsible for circulating the flyers or sending the letters—a glance at any of her online communications showed that K.C.'s mom was adept in spelling, grammar, and punctuation use—but she had absolutely no financial means to fight back against the accusations. As always, she turned to her audience on Facebook for support:

Someone wrote to me offering help and after composing this reply I realized that I need to post it on K.C.'s page for all to see. Here's what I wrote: I am so grateful to all of you. You keep me going, your help and support is priceless to me. My love goes out to all who care, who pray, write, offer advice and help and donate. I do need help and I am willing to take what you all are offering.

You know, there seems to be a lesson in every hardship that we endure and learning to accept help is one of them for me. I was always the one helping everyone else before. I'm not a proud person, I just had a bad childhood where I was abused by an alcoholic stepfather.

We were not allowed to have many needs or wants and were terrified to ask for anything. Because of that I have a heart for the needs of other people and have always wanted to help them—putting me last.

The abuse created a problem where I was not able to ask for help because of feelings of worthlessness and mental blocks due to the abuse. On a good note, we were also never allowed to give up or make excuses.

These are the types of things I need, if anyone can help with any of this I would appreciate it:

1. I need all of the info I can get on Sarah Creveling and James Terry Henrikson and Blackstone.

2. I need a couple of those flyers that had been seen for some time before I even "came on the scene" that tell people not to deal with Blackstone because they don't pay. (They are trying to sue me because they say I went to companies and badmouthed them, causing them to lose business — which I have not done.)

3. I need letters/statements from those companies stating that I have not contacted them and the reasons that they decline doing business with Blackstone.

4. I need brave people who realize if we band together we can fight back and do not have to be afraid anymore. NOTE: People aren't coming forward because they are afraid of someone and some have even been threatened.

5. I need people who will write letters about their experience with Blackstone and James, and if they have not been paid and how much is owing.

6. I need people who will tell me what happened to my son at Blackstone the day he went into the office and was never seen again outside of that office.

7. I need people to talk to their tribal councilmen and women, to talk to the police, FBI and the BCI to give them info and leads.

8. I need people to hang my press release and K.C.'s missing posters EVERYWHERE.

9. I need people to pass on to me the threats they have received.

10. I need Lawyer referrals.

11. I need donations to cover costs related to this entire ordeal; finding my son, dealing with the lawsuit, etc.

12. I need anything else that someone with more knowledge than I have thinks would be important or helpful in fighting this lawsuit and in filing a counter-suit to sue James and Sarah and Blackstone.

Jill's heartfelt post received an outpouring of support and encouragement from her many followers. Notably missing from that list was Lissa Yellowbird, which was as hurtful as it was perhaps telling. At the moment, however, Lissa was far too busy with her latest obsession: Sarah Creveling.

• • •

While the lawsuit played out, Sarah hoped she could turn things around, if only she could get some people back in her corner. What Sarah needed was a friend, an ally, and she soon found one in none other than the feisty Arikara woman from the reservation.

The relationship that developed between Sarah and Lissa would have been comical, if it weren't for the fact that both of them actually seemed to take it seriously.

Sarah was familiar with Lissa's name through the "Find K.C." Facebook page and had taken considerable offense to some of Lissa's prior writings. Nevertheless, Lissa portrayed herself as a woman with significant influence on the reservation, making her a valuable potential resource in Sarah's efforts to restore her now tarnished reputation.

Lissa reflexively assumed that Sarah was an easily manipulable, naïve white girl. Through her persistent prodding, Lissa believed she could coax the unsuspecting wife into coughing up a treasure trove of dirty details about James, and perhaps even further clues about what had happened to K.C. Clarke.

Their dynamic unfolded into an ongoing cat-and-mouse game. Lissa pretended to care that Sarah and her husband had literally been tried and convicted in the court of public opinion and were now outcasts in the community.

Unaware of Lissa's role in facilitating her downfall, Sarah

adeptly played the part of victim, claiming total innocence and ignorance regarding the accusations against her and James and lapping up Lissa's over-the-top sympathetic gestures.

On numerous occasions, Lissa tried to bait Sarah into turning on James by suggesting that Sarah was a victim of her husband's severe psychological abuse. She even posited that Sarah might be the next person to turn up missing. Similar sentiments had been included in the anonymous letters sent to both Sarah and her parents. Still, Sarah dismissed it all as nonsense.

Although Lissa harbored a healthy level of skepticism when it came to nearly everyone she encountered, she inexplicably never questioned or doubted Sarah's sincerity. Instead, she was willing to accept that Sarah's apathy toward the accusations against her husband was due to blind ignorance. Lissa may have even eventually felt a tinge of compassion for the gorgeous blonde whom she believed served no purpose other than being James' emotionally abused puppet.

It simply didn't occur to Lissa that Sarah possessed the same manipulative and controlling tendencies she believed to be James's signature trademarks. Or that between the two, it was actually Lissa who was falling into the role of gullible pawn.

Nevertheless, the day-and-night, back-and-forth between the two women kept Sarah distracted enough so that James could focus on a new relationship of his own.

CHAPTER 34

The Affair

Peyton Rose Martin was but a tiny thing, standing barely five feet tall. She was beautiful with apple cheeks and an incandescent smile accentuated by perfectly straight teeth. The color of her long, thick locks frequently changed with the seasons—dark chocolate brown for the summer months and honey blonde with chunky auburn lowlights for the winter.

The 19-year-old had a deep love for fashion and was excited about any opportunity to get dressed to the nines for special occasions. She delighted in sharing pictures on her Facebook page showcasing herself in sequined gowns and elegant dresses. The photographs were often captured in the company of her mother, Tiffiany Johnson, and Peyton's stepfather, tribal chairman Tex Hall, at the many galas and formal parties they attended together as a family.

But as much as she was someone who could don a designer outfit and heels like a pro, Peyton Rose—or "Pey," as many of her friends affectionately called her—was primarily a country girl at heart who loved watching bull riding and chasing after handsome cowboys. This deep-rooted attachment to the rugged lifestyle made it all the more perplexing when she soon found herself drawn to a pretty boy like James Henrikson—a married man nearly 15 years her senior—who could barely ride a motorcycle, let alone a bucking bronco.

The pair were introduced during the Christmas holiday

in 2011 while Peyton was home from college on break. It was right before Tex Hall agreed to enter into a business partnership with James and Blackstone Trucking.

After seeing James for the first time, the young Peyton was instantly smitten. She'd also been captivated by James's wife, Sarah, and eagerly wanted to befriend the blue-eyed bombshell. Blissfully unaware that Peyton had lovestruck eyes for her husband, Sarah was happy to oblige the sweet admirer's friendship.

Years later, Sarah would smirk when a photo resurfaced that featured her and Peyton wearing skimpy bikinis, balancing on paddleboards during one of their shared tropical vacations. Their sun-kissed skin and perfectly coiffed beach waves made the photo frame-worthy for both to keep. But Peyton's playful smile in the photo coyly hid the fact that she was sleeping with Sarah's husband while Sarah's toothy grin seemingly conveyed that she was none the wiser.

Then again, there was also a chance that Sarah was aware of far more than she let on.

•••

Though Peyton developed an instant crush, James didn't recognize her attraction immediately. But it was just a matter of time before he grew weak in the knees for the brown-eyed beauty, his penchant for younger women eventually getting the best of him.

Before their clandestine relationship could move forward, however, Peyton also had to confront a troubling fact: a Blackstone Trucking employee had gone missing from her stepfather's Mandaree shop in February 2012, just two months after she first met James and Sarah. The disappearance was initially dismissed as just another situation of a transient who had simply passed through, but soon there would be questions about James and Sarah's involvement.

But any concerns that may have stirred within Peyton were swiftly assuaged by James's persuasiveness, leaving her no reason to doubt his words.

"Do you know anything about the missing man?" Peyton had asked.

"Yeah, but he does this," James assured her. "He's pretty famous for running away."

Those initial hurdles aside—his marriage conveniently not being one of them—Peyton and James dove headfirst into a steamy affair. For James, Peyton was merely another conquest, yet another young woman willing to shower him with admiration and affection. Conversely, for the inexperienced Peyton, James represented her first serious love.

The unlikely pair were initially adept at being highly secretive, creating separate email accounts to communicate with one another, and carefully choosing where to meet up for their trysts. James had even taken Peyton along on a few work trips that required overnight travel. Outside of New Town and Mandaree and the nearby surrounding areas, very few people recognized them, and the lovers enjoyed being able to openly flaunt their relationship in public.

It wasn't until the late winter of 2012 that people started to suspect that something was going on. The couple had begun to get sloppy, and they'd been seen cozily dining alone at cafes in small neighboring towns and had even been spotted riding around together in James's truck. There was simply no reason at all why Peyton would ever need to be alone with one of her stepfather's business partners. Especially a married one.

By then, Peyton was deeply in love with her man and no longer cared if anyone found out. He offered her a luxurious lifestyle that would allow her to escape the claustrophobic confines of North Dakota, and she was ready and willing to go anywhere he wanted to take her.

She believed James loved her back, and his promises of a future together kept pulling her further into his web.

"We were going to move to Brazil," Peyton would later testify in court. "He had a friend who owned a yacht, and James wanted us to get married on it. He told me he had a job that would be paying him $170 million dollars a year."

Young and gullible, Peyton had no idea the lengths James would go to get what he wanted, or how little he cared about whom he hurt along the way.

CHAPTER 35

A Baby Named Bently

Amid the whirlwind of chaos and secrets surrounding all of the players working in some way either for or against each other—James, Sarah, Jedidiah, Lissa, Jill, Tex, Peyton—it should have come as no surprise to anyone that another explosive bombshell was about to detonate in their faces, casting shards of betrayal and revelation in all directions.

Maybe no one could have foreseen it—except, perhaps, Peyton Martin herself. Some may have even argued she'd wished for it, while it could also be speculated that her lover had wanted it just as much. Regardless of whether it was an intentional outcome or not, there was no turning back when in the spring of 2013, Peyton announced she was carrying James Henrikson's baby.

Tex Hall was devastated. Even though Peyton was not his biological daughter, Hall had always treated her as his own, and she'd been privileged as such amongst the tribe and across the reservation. There was no way for Hall to grasp how any of it could have happened literally right under his nose.

Knowing that his family would forever be entwined with James left a bitter, wretched ache in the weathered Native American's heart. But if there was one thing Hall could accept, it was that he was going to be a grandfather. Of that, there was no other joy that could top it or any type of controversy that could diminish it.

• • •

The news of the tribal chairman's stepdaughter getting knocked up by her married lover raced through the reservation like a prairie fire. Most were aghast by the situation, but Lissa Yellowbird couldn't help but feel downright giddy. She'd been trying for months to convince Sarah that her husband was an abusive, lying, cheating, no-good scoundrel, but nothing had worked. Lissa hoped his glaring infidelity—with a younger woman no less—would finally turn Sarah against him.

But that epiphany would not come to pass. Sarah refused to believe what was right in front of her face. At least, that's how she portrayed her position to Lissa. Much to Lissa's chagrin, no matter how much mud she slung at James, Sarah did not budge in her defense of—and praise for—her husband.

"Why would he have an affair with a 19-year-old?" Sarah scoffed at the thought.

Whether Sarah believed it or not really didn't matter, because in November 2013, Peyton gave birth to James's son, who she aptly named Bently—an ode to his father's favorite automobile, sans the second "e." The same make of car James had paid nearly $60,000 in cash to bestow on his beloved wife, Sarah, just two years before.

"Of course she named him Bently," Sarah said sourly, later chuckling at the irony.

• • •

Unsurprisingly, salacious rumors continued to swirl through the community long after baby Bently's birth. Some believed that Sarah had known about her husband's affair with Peyton all along, suggesting that it was Peyton who was being manipulated by the more cunning Sarah.

Many also speculated that the relationship and pregnancy had been carefully orchestrated by James. That theory posited that having a child together would secure James a stake in Tex Hall's estate and permanent priority in the oilfields. James's persuasive pillow talk had certainly ensnared Peyton's love and devotion enough for her to run away with him to Brazil—would it have been that difficult to also convince her to have his baby?

In addition, Sarah's response to the situation was strange. Despite the affair and birth of James's illegitimate son, she remained fiercely loyal to her husband. Sarah's steadfast commitment raised questions—did she perhaps know or even encourage the affair for her own financial benefit?

Whether or not any of the rumors were true was anyone's guess. However, given James and Sarah's history of exploiting others for financial gain, these wild speculations weren't entirely implausible.

● ● ●

With drama and gossip continuing to surround them, James and Sarah had no inclination that far greater concerns were awaiting right around the corner. In the midst of the investigation into K.C. Clarke's disappearance, in November 2012, federal authorities had quietly launched a separate probe into the couple's financial proclivities. Nearly a year later, that investigation had gathered enough evidence to possibly put Ken and Barbie behind bars for years.

CHAPTER 36

Darrik Trudell Can

On a bitter-cold day in November 2012, Homeland Security Investigations (HSI) Special Agent Darrik Trudell stumbled into one of the most significant cases he'd ever have. Truth be told, the 35-year-old Montana native had never imagined a career in law enforcement to begin with, let alone at a high-profile government agency.

Born and raised in Sidney, a town of 4,500 residents ten miles west of the North Dakota border, Darrik described his upbringing as idyllic. With supportive parents, close relationships with his three siblings, and relatives all within miles of one another, the small-town kid grew up surrounded by the staples of hard work and strong family values. And, of course, football.

Even though he was six-foot-one with a strong muscular frame built for the part, Darrik would later describe his ability as a football player as merely average. Yet this perceived limitation didn't deter his passion for the game, aspiring to both play and eventually coach college football. After graduating high school in 1997, he headed off to Montana State University in Bozeman and successfully walked on to the Bobcat football team—a journey that turned out to be short-lived.

"I wasn't a troublemaker by any means, but I definitely prioritized having fun with my friends rather than focusing on my studies," Darrik later reflected. "After two years of being irresponsible and immature, the powers that be at MSU 'invited' me to leave ... A good decision on their part."

Despite that setback, it did not take long for him to understand that, in the words of Dean Wormer from the legendary movie Animal House—one of Darrik's favorite films—"fat, drunk and stupid is no way to go through life." If he was going to amount to anything, there was no time to waste.

•••

In 1999, Darrik secured a scholarship to Minot State University in North Dakota, a three-hour jaunt from Sidney. While he pursued a degree in social work, Darrik played football as a Minot State Beaver. There he met his future wife, Betsy, a standout player for the university's women's basketball team. Between classes and football, Darrik worked part-time at the Dakota Boys & Girls Ranch, counseling juveniles convicted of sexual offenses—a job that was challenging just as much as it was humbling.

"Working at the Ranch was one of the most rewarding jobs I have ever had," he later recounted, "and I developed a lot of skills I would use later as an investigator."

After finishing his bachelor's degree, Darrik was offered the chance to be an assistant football coach for the Beavers— a position he gladly accepted. Yet much to his own surprise, after only one semester, he realized that coaching was not all it was cracked up to be. His career as a college football coach came to an abrupt end in December 2005.

Shortly thereafter, while on vacation to visit his sister and brother-in-law in Tacoma, Washington, Darrik had an opportunity to catch up with an old friend, who was now a Special Agent with the FBI.

"Everything my friend talked about piqued my interest," Darrik recalled. "When I got back from vacation, I applied with the North Dakota Department of Corrections Parole and Probation."

Darrik's time with the Dakota Boys Ranch impressed the recruiter, and he was soon offered a job. Over the next four years, he learned crucial skills to prepare him for his next leap, which was applying to work as a law enforcement officer in the federal sector.

"I did not care with what agency," he explained. "I applied with all of them. After four years with the state, my wife and I had been married for six months, and I got a call with a job offer from the United States Secret Service."

It was an incredible, once-in-a-lifetime opportunity, but it came with a significant caveat. If he accepted the position, Darrik and his new bride would need to relocate to one of five distant locations within 30 days. Darrik and Betsy were both from small towns, with very close-knit family ties. The decision to leave their families was not an easy one. But the offer was simply too big to pass up and the newlyweds settled for the Philadelphia Field Office.

The Trudells thoroughly enjoyed their time on the east coast, forging lifelong friendships and welcoming two of their four children. But no sooner had the growing family begun to plant permanent roots when they learned that Betsy's mother had been diagnosed with stage IV colon cancer. The prognosis was not good, and Darrik and Betsy knew they needed to be back in North Dakota.

"At the time, the Secret Service only had one agent in North Dakota, and he was not going anywhere," Darrik recalled. "I was fortunate to get hired by Homeland Security Investigations in Minot. My wife's parents lived 45 miles north, so this was great for us, as she was able to spend as much time as needed with her mom and be there to support her dad."

$$\bullet \; \bullet \; \bullet$$

By November of 2012, Darrik Trudell had been an investigator with HSI for a little more than a year. While many of his cases involved crimes against children, he was also assisting the North Dakota Bureau of Criminal Investigation (NDBCI) in its efforts to curb the explosion of illegal drugs being trafficked into the region—from both domestic and foreign sources—an ongoing consequence of the recent oil boom.

The NDBCI office was conveniently located in the same building as HSI, and Darrik worked alongside Agent Mike Marchus on many occasions. The two had established a strong rapport, sharing both the passion for their respective investigative roles, and a similar self-deprecating sense of humor. Even when they weren't actively working on a case together, they wore out the staircase between their respective offices to shoot the breeze. On a relatively quiet morning a week shy of Thanksgiving, that's exactly what Darrik had intended to do.

"I was just going downstairs to Mike's office to bullshit about life and figure out the most important decision of the day," Darrik joked later. "Where to have lunch."

After a few minutes of idle conversation he stood up to leave, but stopped when he noticed a pile of papers stacked on the corner of Marchus's desk.

"What the hell is this you're working on?" Darrik asked curiously.

"Oh yeah, I was actually gonna talk to you about this," Marchus said. "It's kind of a crazy thing that came to me through a confidential informant I used to work with."

According to Marchus, the former confidential informant was a Native American woman named Lissa Yellowbird. He had arrested her a number of times for various drug and prostitution charges, and she had at one point spent a short time in prison.

After her release, it seemed Yellowbird was trying to turn her life around. Even though she did not have an official position with a law enforcement agency, she had been acting in a personal capacity to investigate crimes on the reservation in New Town, located two hours southwest of Minot.

Yellowbird had tried to establish an informal working relationship with Marchus, occasionally providing him with tidbits of information she had uncovered with the hope that he would reciprocate with something that could help her out.

"Lissa was really a quid-pro-quo kind of informant, and most of the information she brought to me was 'dirt' on her drug-dealing competitor," Marchus recalled later. "Most of the time, the information she gave to me wasn't very credible."

Still, he couldn't deny that he had developed a certain level of respect for her over time, and eventually succumbed to listening to whatever story was her latest.

"She is very smart and cunning, I'll give her that," Marchus acknowledged. "When she reached out in early November, she sounded pretty adamant about talking to me, and I agreed to meet with her."

Yellowbird arrived with a stack of documents resulting from months of online research, printed photos, and hand-written scribbled notes. It was all about a man named James Henrikson and his wife, Sarah Creveling—an out-of-state couple who owned and operated a trucking company on the reservation.

"She told me that these two—a muscled-up young guy and his attractive wife—were known as the Ken and Barbie of the Oilfields," Marchus relayed to Darrik.

Yellowbird had an exhaustive amount of information to share, but the gist was that James and Sarah were supposedly causing quite a stir on the reservation with rumors of illegal drug manufacturing and swindling oil companies, investors, and workers out of money. Marchus could barely contain his bored yawns. That is, until Yellowbird explained that the drugs and money were just the tip of the proverbial iceberg.

According to Yellowbird, a longtime friend and employee of the couple named Kristopher (K.C.) Clarke, had been missing for nearly nine months. No one had seen or heard from him since February of 2012.

"I think he's dead," she told Marchus. "And I think James and Sarah had something to do with it."

The mention of a missing person and possible murder quickly snapped Marchus's attention back into place. He agreed to look into it but couldn't guarantee anything beyond that. After thoroughly studying the information Yellowbird had provided, the agent felt that the situation indeed warranted further investigation. Following through on his promise to a woman he had once arrested, Marchus tracked down every lead he could.

"I found out Steve Gutknecht from NDBCI did some investigating in June 2012," Marchus told Darrik. "Several of the people Gutknecht spoke with suggested that Clarke might have disappeared on his own volition."

Gutknecht's sources had also confirmed that Clarke had visited a shop in Mandaree, owned by tribal chairman Tex Hall, to turn in a fuel card to Sarah Creveling on the last day he was seen alive. But because the shop was located on the reservation, Gutknecht had no jurisdiction to investigate any further.

"If Gutknecht couldn't get any traction on it, I wasn't going to be able to do anything either," Marchus later explained. "If something happens on the reservation, local and state agencies have no authority to open or conduct investigations. But as a federal agent, Darrik Trudell can."

CHAPTER 37

A Cache Of Financial Crimes

As an investigator, Darrik Trudell exuded a sense of restless energy, brimming with an intensity that rarely allowed him to sit still. His office was a refuge of organized chaos, humming with a perpetual buzz of activity. Despite the frenzy, or perhaps because of it, Darrik thrived, fueled by a relentless pace only he set for himself.

When the curious case of the disappearance of K.C. Clarke inadvertently fell into his lap that cold day in November 2012, his own caseload was already severely backlogged, and he could have easily chosen to disregard it. No one was holding his feet to the fire to act. Yet the decision to take on the case was one thing. Figuring out where to begin was another entirely.

"When I first looked at this case, I knew right away that K.C. was most likely dead," Darrik later explained. "Obviously, no one had shown up to surrender or confess, but it was pretty clear that James Henrikson was at the center of it all. The only thing I could do was start pulling on strings, until eventually somebody had the information we were looking for."

As a first step, Darrik reached out to Steve Gutknecht, the NDBCI agent who had opened an investigation earlier that summer. Although Gutknecht had not been able to find the smoking gun related to K.C.'s disappearance, he had learned from several people that James and a group of associates were possibly importing illegal substances in order to produce and distribute oxycodone pills. Going after James for narcotics smuggling would have been precisely the low-hanging fruit Darrik needed to begin unraveling the rest.

"The possible drug offense angle fell apart almost immediately," he laughed later, "because as it turned out, these guys were all idiots. They had purchased a pill press, and they had received the imports, but they'd gotten the wrong bonding agent to make the pills. None of the street addicts would take the pills, so their drug business was a total bust."

With the drug angle an unfortunate dead end, Darrik moved on to the next option on the list: financial fraud. From Lissa Yellowbird's research came the name Jedediah McClure. By then, it was already the spring of 2013, and unbeknownst to Darrik, Yellowbird and McClure had begun their own crusade by circulating the "Beware Flyer" across most of the western half of the state of North Dakota. McClure was still more than willing to share his story of how he'd been duped and defrauded by James and Sarah.

"K.C.'s case was getting stagnant to be sure," Darrik noted. "But once we talked to Jed McClure, we finally had something to go on."

Along with McClure, several additional sources described a meticulously planned scheme by James and his wife to defraud investors and businesses all across the state. The string had indeed begun to unravel, but it soon became an avalanche. Admittedly, the vast realm of financial crimes and fraud lay outside Darrik's general expertise. As such, he called in United States Postal Inspector Tom Irvin and IRS Agent Nate Glur.

"This looked like it was going to be a really large and complicated investigation, and we were going to need additional manpower," Darrik later said. "I knew Tom and Nate were fantastic in dealing with financial crimes, so I called Tom and harassed him into taking the case."

"What the hell are you getting me into now?" Irvin had jokingly complained at the time.

•••

After several months of investigation, Darrik, Irvin, and Glur unearthed a cache of fraud orchestrated by both James and Sarah. Much to the investigators' delight, it became evident the couple were far from being brilliant masterminds. Though their schemes had fooled numerous blinded-by-greed investors, James and Sarah lacked the necessary foresight to cover their tracks.

For starters, between 2011 and 2013, the pair had used no less than ten different aliases to dupe gullible individuals in North Dakota, Texas, Florida, and elsewhere. Their premise was almost always the same: courting investors to launch a trucking business in the oilfields. James was adept at portraying himself to be skilled in oilfield work, conning investors into believing that his business, Blackstone, LLC, had already procured multiple lucrative oil contracts in North Dakota. All that was needed, he'd told them, was investor money to purchase the equipment.

While Blackstone was a legitimate company on paper, the couple told investors that James was the owner, but in reality, it was Sarah's name on the legal documents. The couple had also set up multiple shell companies, all of which listed Sarah as the owner. Falsely reporting that James was the owner was in itself a crime, albeit likely the least serious of the litany of them to be uncovered.

The claims to investors that Blackstone had already secured oil contracts, and that James had experience in the industry, were also false. Nevertheless, investor money poured in. Initially, James and Sarah did use some of the money to purchase the equipment Blackstone needed to begin operating.

Once operations were underway, Blackstone was almost immediately profitable, raking in hundreds of thousands of dollars. Investors surely were giddy as they received their monthly checks. But instead of focusing on building Blackstone into an even larger money-making empire, James and Sarah devised a plan to cut their investors off.

They began diverting Blackstone's equipment and assets to complete work for another one of their companies, Blackwell Services. When their monthly checks began to dwindle, investors started asking questions. James and Sarah concocted a myriad of lame excuses to explain why the profits had suddenly dried up.

In an extensive report, U.S. Postal Inspector Tom Irvin laid their scheme bare: "James directed work away from Blackstone to Blackwell Services, which caused increased profits for the side business entities, resulting in decreased profits for Blackstone and its individual investors."

Furthermore, Irvin wrote that the couple had "defrauded individual investors from future ROI from profits made by Blackstone LLC," and that James "repeatedly made excuses with investors and continually claimed something was impeding the ability to pay."

James and Sarah had also promised investors that Blackstone's financials would be managed by an independent accountant, who would provide monthly statements documenting the activity for each individual piece of equipment. Several of those monthly statements, however, turned out to be falsified. Because the manufactured financial statements had been delivered to investors via United States Postal mail, it was a serious felony.

Making matters even worse for the couple, investigators discovered that James and Sarah were also embezzling money from Blackstone accounts to fund their lavish vacations, designer clothing, luxury vehicles, and more.

Darrik Trudell, Tom Irvin, and Nate Glur had amassed a mountain of evidence to charge both James and Sarah with a laundry list of federal financial crimes, but it hadn't gotten them any closer to finding out what had happened to K.C. Clarke. And unbeknownst to the investigators, the clock was ticking before another tragedy would strike.

CHAPTER 38

He Did It Again

On the morning of December 13, 2013—a full year into their investigation—Darrik Trudell, Tom Irvin, Nate Glur, and Assistant United States Attorney (AUSA) Theresa Rassas conducted a formal proffer interview with a man named Ryan Olness, who was living in Arizona at the time. In simple terms, a proffer is a question-and-answer session between law enforcement officers and a witness, in which the witness agrees to share everything he knows in exchange for leniency or immunity from prosecution.

Olness, along with Jedediah McClure, had been one of the original investors in Blackstone. He had relocated to North Dakota in January of 2012, working alongside James Henrikson for several months. With an offer of immunity, investigators hoped Olness would be able to shed some light on the disappearance of K.C. Clarke.

But although Olness had plenty of information about how James was defrauding investors—including himself—he swore that he knew absolutely nothing about what had happened to K.C.

Still, just a few months after K.C. vanished, Olness abruptly picked up and left North Dakota, and had not looked back, even though he was now claiming James and Sarah still owed him north of $100,000. Perhaps something had rattled him, but Olness remained tight-lipped.

At the conclusion of their conversation, Darrik emphasized the importance of confidentiality to Olness, stressing that the details of the proffer discussion were not to be shared with anyone, especially not with James himself. Olness nodded in agreement.

Inexplicably, however, within minutes of the interview ending, Olness phoned James to alert him that federal investigators were hot on his trail for a slew of financial crimes and his possible involvement in K.C.'s Clarke's disappearance.

•••

Three days later, Darrik Trudell received a frantic call from Lissa Yellowbird, alerting him that a man named Douglas Carlile had been shot and killed in his Spokane, Washington home the night before. Through her connections, Yellowbird had learned of an ongoing business deal between Doug and James—a tidbit federal investigators also had on their radar. The persistent Yellowbird had even attempted to caution Doug to stay far away from James—warnings that Doug had unfortunately ignored.

"James did it again!" Yellowbird declared. "He killed another business partner. It's all over the news in Spokane. I've already called the police out there to tell them what I know, but you need to call them, too!"

"I said I would," Darrik recalled, "but I needed to gather more information first. Not that I didn't believe her, but it was almost unfathomable that James would do something so brazen as murder, given that Olness had literally just alerted him that we were coming after him. The news reports online weren't giving much information yet, so I waited for a few days before reaching out to the investigators in Spokane."

Getting them to return his calls would be another story.

# PART III

CHAPTER 39

The Dreamer

In the realm of aspirations, Douglas Carlile stood out as a perpetual dreamer, always nurturing visions of himself at or near the summit of large-scale business ventures, destined to emerge as a highly successful and extremely wealthy entrepreneur. These grandiose ambitions, however, often clashed with reality. For Doug, his journey through the entrepreneurial landscape consistently fell short of the savvy and acumen required, leaving him to frequently navigate through financial messes of his own making.

What Doug was shrewd enough to recognize early on was the potential in excavation and construction, and in 1983, he and his wife Elberta launched their first business near Seattle, Washington. For ten years, they worked alongside several larger corporations as subcontractors, and their business flourished enough to afford their family of eight a large house, luxury vehicles, and additional property investments in nearby Moses Lake.

But in 1993, the IRS delivered most unwelcome news: the couple owed nearly $900,000 in back taxes. It was enough to force their once-thriving business into Chapter 11 bankruptcy and to eventually close its doors for good.

Neither Doug nor Elberta ever publicly admitted any culpability as to how their tax debt had risen so exponentially. Perhaps they had just been thankful enough to avoid any kind of criminal proceedings. Even though the Carliles were eventually able to negotiate and whittle down their liability by several hundred thousand dollars, the situation put a severe burden on their future plans.

From that point forward, Doug—in almost desperate fashion—pursued virtually any and all options to discover his next big break. One major hurdle he faced was trying to maneuver under the radar of the federal government while he and Elberta still owed a significant amount of money. This included refraining from affixing their signatures to any agreements or contracts.

"My husband was such a good businessman," Elberta raved time and again. "Everyone wanted to be in business with him. But we had to deal with the IRS stuff. So, we had a lot of businesses, but none of them were in our name."

The confidence she had in her husband was something to behold, even though the truth was that many viewed Doug with suspicion and distrust. Throughout his pursuit of new opportunities, Doug had courted and made lofty promises to wealthy businessman and investors across the western part of Washington—promises he either couldn't or never intended to fulfill. His failure to follow through had put a lasting stain on his name and reputation. It was later even revealed that Doug had faced several lawsuits related to his financial mishandlings.

When all other doors had been closed to them, the Carliles turned to their adult children for help. First, they launched Oasis International, an excavation and land clearing company in Moses Lake. On paper, the company was owned by their eldest daughter, MeLainee, but according to the Carlile family, it was Doug who was in charge of most of its operations.

"My sister was Oasis's owner of record due to my parents having financial difficulties with the IRS," Skyler Carlile later explained.

When Oasis unsurprisingly began having financial difficulties in 2002, Doug jumped ship and went to work as an estimator for Advanced Excavation—a company owned by one of their four sons, Shane—some two hundred miles away in

Everett.

Doug oversaw operations for Advanced, but all the while was searching for other endeavors. He sought a patent related to bailing hay, fiddled with a blow-sand technique to purify crude oil, and explored oil field road construction and maintenance. Time and again, however, his ventures fizzled long before they got off the ground.

•••

With financial assistance from Shane, Doug and Elberta finally paid off the remainder of their IRS tab in 2008, nearly 15 years after that problem had reared its ugly head.

Shortly thereafter, the Carliles purchased a dilapidated mansion in the Rockwood neighborhood of Spokane. Virtually every inch of the 5,000 square-foot house demanded extensive repairs and updates, an endeavor that would have required hundreds of thousands of dollars—far surpassing the price the Carliles paid for it. Yet none of that mattered, as this was the house Doug envisioned to be part of his legacy, even as the paint chipped off the walls and black mold grew in the basement.

With the move to Spokane, Doug began working for Skyler Carlile at his company Alliance Excavation. For nearly two years, Doug devoted himself to his work at Alliance, earning a stable and sufficient income. But stable and sufficient had never been part of Doug's grander plans. The perpetual dreamer was still very much alive, yearning for something more.

CHAPTER 40

Dakota

Beginning in 2009, a man named Tim Scott would figure prominently in Doug Carlisle's life. Scott was a former employee at Oasis—the company owned by the Carliles' daughter, MeLainee. On numerous occasions, Scott had discussed various business ventures with the Carliles, none of which had come to fruition. Whereas Doug and Elberta trusted him, MeLainee found Scott to be rather "shady."

"Tim just didn't have a lot of money, and was always trying to find a deal," Elberta later explained. "Doug always just tried to be a friend to him."

Scott communicated to the Carliles that a businessman from Texas was trying to secure a lucrative contract with the Russian government to construct roads in preparation for the upcoming 2014 Sochi Olympics. Scott encouraged Doug to consider getting involved in the project.

"We were doing well with Alliance Excavation at the time," Elberta later recounted, "but my husband believed in multiple strings of income. If you're successful, that's a good idea."

For Doug, it seemed he wouldn't rest until that notion became his reality. The "businessman" to whom Scott was referring was none other than James Henrikson. While it was never made clear to the Carliles how James and Scott had become acquainted, the trust that Doug and Elberta extended to their long-time friend completely clouded their ability for discernment.

Within a matter of days, Doug and James were introduced via telephone. James assured Doug that he was backed by a tremendous amount of financial capital, while Doug boasted a net worth of at least 12 million dollars. Though each man's claim was utter fantasy, they had no reason—at that point—to doubt the other. More importantly, Doug hadn't even considered that the very idea of a road construction venture in Russia was totally disconnected from reality.

The notion that the Russian government would pursue a contract worth hundreds of millions—perhaps even billions—with an unestablished businessman in Texas was preposterous on its face. But the talk of money always had Doug and Elberta's ears standing at attention. Common sense be damned.

"James really sparked Doug's interest in this," Elberta recalled. "He said it's big money, and that if he secured the contracts with the Russian government, then we could be a part of it. We thought James was a good guy. A good businessman, very smart."

The Carliles threw caution to the wind and forged ahead. At James's request, they diligently prepared an extensive resume, detailing their nearly three-decade history and experience in the construction and excavation industry. After sending it on to James for review, they eagerly awaited a response that never came. Numerous calls and messages to James went unanswered.

"Doug sent over that resume, and then it was really strange," Elberta later explained. "We didn't hear from James… and that Russia thing never happened. So, we just went about our business here in Spokane."

The Carliles had dodged their first bullet, as the ruse James had concocted was likely just a ploy to get money from unsuspecting investors. Perhaps the situation should have served as a giant red flag to caution them about considering any further business ventures with James—or Tim Scott. As things turned out, however, this episode barely even registered on their radar screen.

•••

Nearly two years later, in late 2011, Scott again reached out to the Carliles. On this occasion, he explained that he and James had been working in the North Dakota oilfields. Scott informed them of James's ownership of Blackstone Trucking, a company that subcontracted for major oil and energy corporations across the western part of the state. Scott boasted that vast numbers of oilfield workers—himself included—were making thousands of dollars a month.

"It sparked Doug's interest a little," Elberta later said. "It wasn't like we wanted to go to Dakota. We didn't even know anything about Dakota or the oilfields."

Elberta's lack of geographical knowledge aside, Doug soon delved into researching North Dakota's "oil boom" and concluded Scott was telling the truth—the potential to amass a considerable fortune was evident. Like always, Doug was immediately drawn to the prospect.

But almost as quickly as Scott had shared his excitement about working with James and the financial success he was enjoying, he informed the Carliles of a falling out with his former friend. Apparently, James had stopped paying him. Unbeknownst to the Carliles, Scott was at the end of a long line of those James Henrikson had bilked throughout the years.

Doug's desire to feed at the generous trough of the North Dakota oilfields was simply too strong to be tempered by this second red flag. Instead, he decided to once again place his trust in James Henrikson rather than his long-time friend, having willfully forgotten how James had left him at the altar just a few years earlier.

"We weren't sure if Tim was really telling the truth or not," Elberta later noted. "You hear two sides to the story, and it's really hard to know the truth unless you really know the person. And so, they had their falling out, and in the process of that, James started talking to Doug again."

With Doug and James now fully intertwined in possible new business ventures, Tim Scott opted to remove himself completely—a decision that was not only smart, but likely life-saving as well.

● ● ●

James initially urged Doug to visit North Dakota and experience the oilfields firsthand. Highlighting his influential connection to the tribal chairman, Tex Hall, he assured Doug that he could leverage this relationship to create opportunities—and promised that Doug could make a lot of money.

"James had ties, he knew people," Elberta said. "We didn't know any of this stuff. We thought he could get us in and open up doors that we couldn't."

Though the Carliles had little experience in the oil industry itself, they did have a few alternative avenues to explore for themselves. They discussed several options, including working with the railroad, getting into the trucking business, the potential for excavation work, and even the idea of building additional housing for oilfield workers.

As Elberta would later recount, "We weren't even talking about the oil at that point. That was a dream. That wasn't a reality to us. We were thinking of what we had in hand and what we could do."

Doug planned a visit to North Dakota in February 2012, but his trip was postponed when a bizarre fall resulted in a significant injury to one of his hands. Though his injury and the attendant delay could have—and in retrospect should have—provided the Carliles an opportunity to reflect further on what they were about to get themselves into, it didn't.

As it turned out, James had no issue with Doug's mishap or travel delay as he was busy literally cleaning up some outstanding matters of his own.

● ● ●

After much thought and deliberation, Doug landed on the idea of establishing his own trucking business, aiming to subcontract in similar fashion to Blackstone Trucking. Although he and Elberta did have a small chunk of savings to put toward the upfront expenses, it was only a fraction of what they needed. Doug had to come up with additional financial backing, and there was no time to waste.

Skyler Carlile had made a good name for himself as the owner of Alliance Excavation within the expansive network of contractors throughout the Spokane area. Recognizing that seeking interest for his new project from former associates likely wouldn't yield fruitful results, Doug instead leveraged Skyler's reputation and professional connections to initiate outreach for new potential business partners to land the investments he required.

Enter John Wark and Richard Curtiss, owners of Eagle River Development. Although Eagle River had never collaborated with Alliance, Wark and Curtiss knew of the company's solid reputation and were familiar with Skyler Carlile's name. When introduced to each other through another mutual business contact, Doug immediately shared his plans to launch a trucking service in North Dakota. Wark and Curtiss were eager listeners.

By July of 2012, the trio had used the popular website Legal Zoom to establish Kingdom Dynamics Enterprises, Inc. Under their agreement, Doug retained 51% ownership of the new company—and thus, the controlling interest—with Wark and Curtiss each holding 24.5%.

The next step was to procure trucks, which required either a project financer or a lender. Despite Doug, Wark, and Curtiss collectively investing nearly $60,000 in financing origination fees, they were unable to find a financial institution willing to extend Kingdom Dynamics a significant line of credit.

Adding to the setbacks, in the spring of 2013, James reported to Doug that his relationship with Tex Hall had fizzled, resulting in James losing Tier 1 status to do work on the reservation. The bidding and contract work preference promised to Doug had also vanished, meaning that Kingdom Dynamics had been formed and partially capitalized for no reason at all.

Once again, James Henrikson had strung Doug down the primrose path that led to a dead end and not a single penny in return. Even worse, Doug and Elberta had flushed what little savings they had straight down the toilet.

Still, none of the players were ready to quit the game. In a matter of weeks, James presented an entirely new business proposal for Doug Carlile, John Wark, and Richard Curtiss to mull over. This time, it came with the allure of not merely thousands, but rather, millions of dollars.

Surely this time Doug would come to his senses and run from James Henrikson as far and as fast as he could. Or, perhaps not.

CHAPTER 41

Trouble Ahead

At first glance, the business proposal James Henrikson hatched in the spring of 2013 appeared relatively straightforward. He had recently learned that Canadian energy company, Enerplus Corporation, intended to sell oil leases on two parcels of land in North Dakota. Though the leases had been established for quite some time, Enerplus had never drilled on the sites due to their significant distance from the company's primary operational area. The company decided to shed the leases without having engaged in the first bit of exploration.

The potential profitability of drilling expeditions on the land was estimated to generate hundreds of millions of dollars over time, but the upfront cost required to do so was nothing short of astronomical. The initial expense to acquire the leases was $2.4 million, but that was merely just a start. From there, it would cost somewhere in the neighborhood of $120 million to have rigs drilled and operational for pumping oil.

The payment for the leases was due in August of 2013, so Enerplus needed to divest the property as soon as possible to avoid having to fork over the $2.4 million price tag. That meant any potential buyer who was interested would need to act quickly.

Despite their prior struggle to secure financial backing for a significantly lesser amount to start their trucking business, James, Doug, Wark, and Curtiss felt confident they could come up with the initial investment of $2.4 million in just four short months—a feat that came astonishingly close to realization.

Doug drafted contract terms for investors that promised them 100% return on investment within 90 days of signing. Beyond that clearly empty promise, the contract terms posed a potential legal liability for Kingdom Dynamics if it failed to deliver. Nevertheless, they had no shortage of interested investors willing to blindly take the gamble.

At the top of that list were the Carliles' own sons, who kicked in $100,000. Wark and Curtiss added another $100,000. James and his wife Sarah contributed $300,000 and solicited another $300,000 from a man named Doug Simpson—a person no one had ever heard of.

"I kind of assumed that Doug Simpson was a fictional person, since the company he worked for, Blackwell Services, was one of James and Sarah's shell companies," John Wark later admitted.

Wark was right, of course, but only about part of it. As it would later be determined, the full $600,000 James and Sarah contributed came from Maheshu Energy, which the couple had funneled into their own shell accounts while Tex Hall lay in a hospital bed.

By the same token, James and Sarah's good friend and accountant, Renee Johnson, tossed in another $400,000, but it was eventually discovered that she'd "borrowed" that money from some of her clients. She was later convicted of wire fraud, but to her great fortune, the conviction was subsequently overturned by a federal judge due to an obscure technicality.

A handful of additional investors Wark and Curtiss recruited threw another $600,000 onto the pile. Lo and behold, by April, the group had amassed $1.8 million and secured the lease on one of Enerplus's parcels. But they still needed another $640,000 to secure the second parcel.

•••

While they scrambled to secure money to pay for the leases, Doug, Wark and Curtiss decided to try their hand once again in the trucking business. They formed a subsidiary under Kingdom Dynamics called Bridgewater Energy, the name to be emblazoned on the sides of their trucks.

Rather quickly, Bridgewater amassed $1.3 million in financial backing and leased 13 tanker trucks. The monthly lease payments totaled $31,500, while the cost to insure them added an additional $12,000 to the monthly tab.

Since Doug, Wark, and Curtiss lived in Spokane, they relied on James to monitor the trucks' operations in North Dakota. In exchange for his commitment to manage deployment and cover all maintenance and fuel costs for the trucks, James was promised a substantial percentage of the profits from Kingdom Dynamics and Bridgewater.

Meanwhile, Doug was tasked with ensuring the timely payment of monthly lease and insurance fees for the trucks, a responsibility he lacked the financial means to sustain for very long. When the payments fell into arrears, Wark and Curtiss had to leverage their own company's assets to cover the $43,500 monthly price tag—eventually forking out almost $250,000.

James also soon claimed he was also no longer able to meet his obligations to cover maintenance and fuel costs.

"James told me that Tex Hall had frozen all of his accounts and that he needed $55,000 to meet expenses," Wark later said. "I wired that money to James, with an additional $10,000 in both November and December."

When it was all said and done, only a few of Bridgewater's trucks were ever put into circulation for contract jobs. Of the remaining trucks, several were sent to a storage facility in Montana when the lease and insurance payments eventually fell delinquent, and two were later found in a junkyard somewhere in Wyoming, having been stripped of most of their parts.

Much like Doug's and James's initial venture into the trucking business, the aspirations for Bridgewater Energy failed to materialize—but this attempt had come with a much heftier price tag, especially for John Wark and Richard Curtiss.

●●●

Amid the latest financial debacle, Doug was also still working to secure the $120 million needed to drill the oil wells once the parcel leases were acquired. One of the companies he researched was based in Dubai. Communication was a struggle at first, as most of the company's paperwork was delivered in Arabic. Once Doug had everything translated into English, he quickly executed the agreement.

Once again, Wark and Curtiss provided money—$89,500—to cover the financing origination fee. Doug assured his partners that he would eventually pay his rightful 51% of the fee at a later date, but he never did. It also wasn't long before the group figured out the Dubai company wasn't real, and the nearly $90,000 they'd sent to a foreign scam artist was unrecoverable.

The crew's next move was to cozy up to a variety of wealthy businessman, hoping one would bite. The first was a well-known millionaire in western Washington. Initially receptive to the venture, his enthusiasm dissipated the moment Doug Carlile's name was brought into the conversation. Another potential option in Montana strung them along for a few weeks before refusing to respond to any of their subsequent messages and phone calls. A third, and final, businessman from Texas scoffed at the idea outright.

It became increasingly clear that convincing a potential investor to commit $120 million to a venture that was being presented by a motley crew—who had virtually no financial clout of their own—was an insurmountable task.

Given the significant and very costly blunders committed by Doug and his inability to financially contribute any further, coupled with at least one of the investor's hesitance tied specifically to his name, it wasn't surprising that the rest of the group began to view Doug's involvement as a major obstacle to their potential success.

The problem they faced was that Doug had made himself a 51% owner and had always been clear that he had no intention of ever giving up that majority stake. To boot, he had begun avoiding calls and messages from the rest of the group, subtly signaling his own possible intention to move on without them.

Overt pettiness and unprofessionalism aside, the reality was that the walls were quickly closing in on two fronts: the remaining payment for the parcel leases was due in just a few weeks, and the 90-day promise to the initial investors of 100% return on their investments was imminently approaching. Kingdom Dynamics was woefully unable to cover either. Not only were they in danger of losing their claim to the parcels, but they were also potentially looking at legal ramifications that could snuff out any life the company ever had.

Something needed to be done, and fast. By this point, Wark and Curtiss were agonizing over their rapidly dwindling bank accounts and seriously questioning how they had become involved in this mess to begin with. It wasn't until years later that Doug's son, Skyler, came clean with Wark and Curtiss about the true nature of his father's tarnished reputation.

"I had numerous conversations with Skyler," Curtiss recalled. "He told me that Alliance Excavations had actually started in Seattle, but they had to move the operations to Moses Lake after Doug's unscrupulous business practices. He had burned all of their bridges there. But then the same thing happened in Moses Lake, and they had to move Alliance to Spokane. Skyler told me that he wouldn't allow his father anywhere near the company's checkbook or allow him to manage any part of the business. I got the impression that Doug defrauded quite a few people."

While Wark and Curtiss consulted with their attorneys—who vehemently advised them to immediately cut ties and walk away—James had an entirely different idea for how to take care of the "Doug" problem.

"You and Curtiss need to take over," James warned Wark in late September 2013, "or there is going to be trouble."

"I really didn't think he meant anything other than financial trouble," Wark would later say.

CHAPTER 42

Warning Signs

Doug Carlile had made a promise to his wife and adult children that the oil business in North Dakota was the ticket to millionaire status they had all been waiting for. That promise was now fading by the day. But instead of throwing in the towel, Doug held firm, and tried to shield Elberta from learning that what had begun as an exhilarating and potentially lucrative opportunity was quickly taking a very dramatic—and sinister—turn.

Over the course of a few months beginning in the summer of 2013, a series of ominous events unfolded that foreshadowed the tragedy to come. The first occurred when the Carliles traveled to North Dakota to visit the TERO office to obtain permits for their trucks to operate on the reservation.

While waiting in the office, Doug and Elberta happened to notice a bulletin board that included the "Beware Flyer" Jedidiah McClure and Lissa Yellowbird had circulated across the oilfields. The allegations against James Henrikson and his wife Sarah Creveling were eye-opening to say the least.

"It was a huge poster of criminal activity with a picture of James and Sarah," Elberta later said. "I about fell over. I was really freaking out. It even said that a man disappeared and was never found, after an argument with James over business and money."

Doug, on the other hand, expressed skepticism that James's criminal past could really be as prolific as the flyer outlined.

"Doug said he knew there were some things in James's past, but he was just wanting to give James a second chance at life," Elberta said. "He thought maybe that's why we were with him. We could be the ones to help him go straight and have a good chance in life."

When the Carliles confronted James and Sarah about the information contained in the flyer, the latter pair casually brushed it off as falsehoods concocted by Tim Scott.

"Part of it is because Tim Scott is mad at me," James had claimed. "He got an attorney and wrote a bunch of false stuff and had it printed out and sent all over to get me barred from the reservation."

His explanation quelled whatever concerns Doug and Elberta may have had. But Elberta later noted that even if they had believed all of the information on the poster to be true—which it was—Doug was too deeply entangled in the situation to consider backing out, anyway.

"We're pretty stuck in this thing by now," Elberta explained. "My husband owes him money, and my husband is integrous. It doesn't matter who the guy is. If we owe him money, we're going to pay him."

Soon, though, they'd be confronted on multiple fronts regarding James's sordid past.

"I found James's criminal history report online sometime during the summer of 2013," John Wark later revealed. "I tried to show it to Doug, but he refused to even look at it."

It was also revealed much later that Lissa Yellowbird had even reached out to Doug on several occasions to warn him that he was getting involved with a criminal and a possible murderer. Doug had outright dismissed her cautions as well.

"Everyone deserves a second chance," Doug repeated his favorite mantra, then stopped answering Yellowbird's calls altogether.

In the late fall of 2013, Doug ventured to North Dakota by himself to check on trucking operations. While there, James had reportedly threatened him both verbally and physically.

"Doug never talked about it," Elberta later said. "He didn't want me to know what had happened."

But Doug did confidentially admit to his sons that James had grabbed him by the neck and shoved him up against the side of a truck. According to Doug, several people had stood by to watch his happen and done nothing to intervene.

"I'm warning you now," James had said. "You need to get out."

The situation had humiliated and terrified Doug, and he had fled North Dakota in the middle of the night back home to Spokane. Afterward, Doug asked his sons to purchase a pistol for him, also advising them: "If I disappear or wake up with bullets in my back, promise me you will let everyone know that James Henrikson did it. "

Sadly, none of it was ever enough for Doug to walk away. He held steadfast to his 51% ownership stake in Kingdom Dynamics—with every last penny and ounce of dignity he had.

"We were doing this on a dream," Elberta later reasoned. "We didn't have all the money in our hands, but we believed in God. We believed God was going to do a miracle for us."

CHAPTER 43

Lingering Hopes

It is conceivable that, at some point, Doug had reluctantly admitted to himself that the prospect of the oil venture in North Dakota materializing was swiftly diminishing. Perhaps he even recognized that it had never been realistically attainable to begin with. One-hundred-twenty million dollars simply didn't fall off trees.

But even if he had acknowledged those things, there was no doubt that Doug was still internally struggling with the conflict between a fading reality and a lingering hope. After all, as Elberta had asserted many times, they both fully believed that God was going to make a way where there seemed to be no way.

Their belief and trust in God to bring them fortune was earnest, to be sure. Yet what neither Doug nor Elberta ever considered was that, instead of paving a golden path for their immediate material desires, God might have deliberately strewn multiple obstacles in their way to warn them of grave danger ahead.

• • •

Shortly after 7:00 p.m. on December 15, 2013, Doug maneuvered his truck through the open wrought-iron gate and into his driveway, pulling up to park beside Elberta's white Lexus

SUV. Even though it was still relatively early in the evening, the couple was exhausted after having spent the past few hours at their church.

While Doug lumbered down the lengthy driveway to secure the gate, Elberta made her way toward the back door of their house. She reached above the door sill to fetch the spare key that was hidden there. Once inside, Elberta made a beeline upstairs to change out of her Sunday clothes and draw herself a bath.

Doug locked the gate and turned back up the driveway. He hadn't noticed the neighbors across the street—Brett and Jamie Roberts—standing with friends Dan Wilson and Steve McMullen in their front yard, the four of them still perplexed about the strange white van that seemed to be stalking Garfield Road. It was much too dark outside for Doug to see the concerned expressions on their faces.

Far more significantly, Doug didn't detect someone approaching him from behind as he neared the back door of the house. As the 63-year-old crossed the threshold, a masked man clad in all black tersely ordered him further into the kitchen.

Terrified, Doug turned around and threw his hands up in the air, now seeing the barrel of a gun pointed at his chest.

"Please, no," Doug whimpered. "You don't have to do this."

Unfazed by Doug's pleas, the masked man pulled the trigger, firing over and over again at point-blank range until his magazine was emptied. As the bullets plunged into Doug's body, he fell backward onto the floor, his glasses flying off of his face, and a tooth skittering across the floor.

Six months shy of celebrating his and Elberta's 43rd wedding anniversary, Doug Carlile's larger-than-life ambitions came to a screeching halt—as did the heart that pumped blood and oxygen throughout his body.

CHAPTER 44

It Had To Have Been Planned

The morning after Doug Carlile was mercilessly killed in his kitchen by a masked assassin, lead detective Mark Burbridge arrived at the house on Garfield Road to assess the situation for himself. Aided in part by K-9 Leo the night before, officers first on the scene had theorized that the killer had escaped through the Carliles' backyard and then vanished into thin air at the end of a gravel trail, two blocks away on East Rockwood Boulevard.

This notion was further supported by the discovery of two potential key pieces of evidence: a fresh footprint in a muddy puddle in the far corner of the Carliles's backyard, and a lone welding glove lying nearby atop a pile of wet leaves and twigs—the glove being clean and dry a clue it had not been there for very long. Additionally, officers had identified and marked several widely spaced shoe impressions on the gravel trail, suggesting the person who left them had been running.

Mark retraced the presumed escape route himself, walking the length of the Carliles' backyard—passing the shoe print and glove—and proceeding through the opened gate into the neighbor's yard. Continuing on, he walked out to the paved throughway that separated the yards from the elementary school parking lot across the street. As he traversed the lot, he paused momentarily to attempt to locate the entrance to the trail that led to East Rockwood. Even in the light of day, it wasn't within the line of sight from Mark's standpoint.

Because of its obscurity, it occurred to the detective that this pathway wouldn't have been an instinctive choice for someone hastily escaping a crime scene in the dark of night.

The fact that the killer had ambushed a 63-year-old grandfather in an otherwise crime-free, affluent neighborhood and was then able to stealthily navigate his way through backyards cloaked in darkness and thick shrubbery, latched fences, dimly lit parking lots, and hidden trails suggested to Mark the real possibility that the entire incident had been carefully orchestrated. The realization came quickly that this case was going to be far more complex than he had first assumed, and at that moment, an unfamiliar feeling overwhelmed him.

"I stood on that trail filled with fear," he later revealed. "Fear that I would never be able to solve this. I was on the crest of the trail, looking back toward the Carlile home, and I just knew that this had to have been planned out. There was no way the killer could have known about this route without mapping it out ahead of time. I told my sergeant that I needed every hand on deck and no limits for this one. And I got every single thing I asked for."

• • •

Mark's 12-year history with homicide investigations told him that the most likely suspect would be someone close to Doug. His widow, Elberta, hadn't done herself any favors in her initial interview. Her eccentric personality and the description of a masked intruder dressed in tactical gear initially came across as far-fetched and manufactured.

But after several follow-up discussions with both Elberta and the Carliles's six adult children, it was apparent that the family harbored nothing but deep love and admiration for each other and the patriarch who had been the cornerstone of their lives.

"My father was the best guy in the world," Shad, the youngest Carlile son, gushed. "Everybody loved him. He went to church two or three times a week, and he was always all about our family."

Beyond that, it appeared there was absolutely nothing to gain for any of them in the event of Doug's untimely death. The Carlile family willingly allowed access to any and all documentation, including financial and banking records. The unfortunate truth was that Doug and Elberta were nearly flat broke and living in a dilapidated mansion. Their adult children provided financial assistance when needed. Further investigation revealed there also weren't any life insurance policies for Doug's widow or the children to cash in on. Another common motive—infidelity—was easily ruled out as well. It was evident that neither Doug nor Elberta were engaged in any extramarital affairs.

"I made a list of all the family members and a cross-check of possible motives," Mark later explained. "All of them were dead ends."

Moreover, Elberta and the kids felt certain they knew exactly who was responsible for Doug's murder: James Henrikson. They described how Doug's current oil leasing agreement with James and other associates had gone dangerously sideways in recent months.

Skyler Carlile informed Mark how he and his brothers had desperately tried to stop their father from continuing in a business relationship with James. "I met James in the summer of 2013, and told my father numerous times that I did not want him working with James anymore. I also told James to stay away from my dad and family."

Skyler disclosed that Doug had recently been courting a wealthy oil businessman in Texas to discuss options for buying out James and the other investors from the lease agreement.

"My dad was about three days away from getting money to buy Henrikson out of the lease," Skyler said. "He was dealing with a guy named Stan Dedmon in Texas. I know James somehow found out about it."

Doug had been eagerly anticipating the prospect of extricating himself from James and his shady business dealings. That excitement unfortunately gave him loose lips, and the information eventually made its way back to James. Skyler told detectives that upon discovering what Doug was secretly doing behind his back, James had become enraged and started issuing threats toward several members of the Carlile family.

"James came to my office in August," Skyler recounted, "and said that if I didn't come up with the $400,000 that was owed to him, he and his wife would start filing frivolous lawsuits against me. I told James that I did not want anything to do with him, and I did not want anything to do with my father's business, Kingdom Dynamics Enterprises. Then he tried to spread rumors about my wife having an affair. It was untrue, but it was James just trying to start trouble."

James's threats to Doug had been even more serious. But while James's actions had scared the Carlile family, none of them had reported anything to the police. Instead, it seemed as though Doug had accepted the possibility that James was going to kill him.

"About a week and a half ago, my dad asked if my company [Alliance Excavation] could foot the bill for 'one last' father and sons snowmobile trip," Skyler said of the ominous request. It was a trip that would never come to pass.

The oldest of the four Carlile sons, Seth, left detectives with a final chilling thought. "I believe James hired someone to kill my dad. James Henrikson is a coward. He would never have the nerve to do it himself."

• • •

The allegations against James were serious, to be sure, but Mark Burbridge still wasn't entirely convinced. Was Doug really murdered by a man who lived 790 miles away in North Dakota, simply because their business relationship went awry?

"I called James on the night of the homicide," Mark recalled. "He told me he already knew that Doug Carlile had been killed. When I asked him how he knew, he said Tim Scott had sent him a text message. Tim later confirmed that information."

James told the detective that he was currently at home in Watford City, but when asked to provide his home address,

James coyly danced around the question. It was a strange response, one that instantly made the hairs on the back of Mark's neck stand up.

While James freely acknowledged there was indeed a beef between himself and Doug, he downplayed its severity and denied any serious entanglements between them.

"We have an oil lease together, and right now, I'm pretty angry with Doug," James admitted. "The guy never pays people the money he owes, and it is really frustrating. But I've never threatened him, and I've never been in a physical altercation with him. I didn't kill him, and I have no idea why someone would want to hurt him."

When Mark asked if there were any problems going on with James's oil business on the reservation, James lied and said everything was fine. In reality, because of the "Beware Flyer" and his affair with Tex Hall's stepdaughter, both James and Blackstone Trucking had been essentially banished from doing business on the reservation, and across most of the western part of the state.

When the detective pressed for more answers, James clammed up, declaring he had nothing more to say until consulting with his attorney.

James's odd responses and reluctance to cooperate was the pivotal moment when the game changed. Any lingering doubt Mark Burbridge still harbored vanished, as James had effectively placed himself directly in the crosshairs of the investigation.

"Innocent guys don't act like that," Mark said later.

● ● ●

Now completely immersed in his case, Mark had disregarded several voicemail messages from Homeland Security Special Agent Darrik Trudell.

"I was focused on solving a murder in Spokane," he said later. "I couldn't figure out who the fuck this Darrik Trudell was or why someone from Homeland Security was calling me."

As it would soon turn out, the two seasoned investigators and their teams would come to rely on one other to solve not one, but two homicides.

CHAPTER 45

I Only Give One Chance

Spokane Detective Brian Cestnik was tasked with discovering everything there was to know about James Henrikson and his wife, Sarah Creveling. In his pursuit, Cestnik stumbled upon the "Beware Flyer," which had gained traction on YouTube and various other social media platforms. Additionally, he obtained records detailing James's extensive criminal history throughout Oregon and Washington, which provided valuable insight into his true character.

As Cestnik delved deeper, he uncovered troubling allegations suggesting the couple's involvement in the disappearance of local oilfield worker Kristopher (K.C.) Clarke in North Dakota. Following this lead, Cestnik ventured further into James's business affairs, where his investigation unexpectedly crossed paths with Tex Hall. The former tribal chairman had a lot to say.

According to Hall, James and Sarah's company, Blackstone Trucking, initially entered into a subcontracting agreement with his oilfield services company, Maheshu Energy, in early 2012. Though it was difficult to admit now, Hall confessed to being mesmerized by the young and attractive couple. He had placed trust in them—something he didn't often do—and believed that by partnering together, they could be extraordinarily successful.

When Hall unexpectedly fell seriously ill and spent several months hospitalized, James and Sarah assured him that they would step in to oversee operations for Maheshu. However, upon Hall's recovery and return home, he was greeted not with welcome arms, but by the revelation that James and Sarah had apparently defrauded him and Maheshu of nearly $600,000.

It soon also became apparent they hadn't acted alone. Lurking in James's criminal orbit was a man named Robert DeLao—another ex-con whom James had befriended during one of his many stints behind bars. On James's recommendation, Hall hired DeLao to work directly for Maheshu, unaware of the relationship between James and DeLao, or that the two conmen had orchestrated the arrangement all along. Once he realized what had happened, Hall chased James and Sarah and their Blackstone Trucking operations out of Maheshu and off the reservation altogether. He also fired Robert DeLao.

The realization that James, Sarah, and DeLao had conspired against him was devastating. Determined to seek further justice, Hall shared with the detectives that he was cooperating with a federal investigation into the matter.

•••

Mark Burbridge and Brian Cestnik also learned that the investigation into the disappearance of K.C. Clarke, spearheaded by NDBCI agent Steve Gutknecht, had come to a standstill in the summer of 2012.

Though they couldn't yet be certain if there was a link between K.C.'s disappearance and Doug Carlile's murder, James Henrikson's center-stage presence in both cases was hard to ignore. The Spokane detectives decided a road trip to North Dakota was necessary not only to meet with NDBCI agents, but to also seize an opportunity to catch James off guard and confront him in person. With the Christmas holiday looming, however, their journey would have to wait.

In the meantime, Mark Burbridge kept in close contact with the Carlile family, sharing almost every detail he uncovered. This openness wasn't typical amongst most detectives, but it was Mark's modus operandi. As hard-nosed as he was, he still went out of his way to provide solace to families in the aftermath of tragedy.

Mark's openness had its limits, however, as his willingness to provide information was always contingent on the Carlile family keeping it strictly to themselves. When Mark learned that MeLainee, the eldest Carlile daughter, had begun trickling information to a local news source, everything changed.

"MeLainee had a close friend who worked in the media, and I noticed that some of the things I had been telling the Carlile family that were not public knowledge were being shared in the news," Mark explained. "That was it. I only give one chance. After that, I stopped sharing information with the family. They weren't very happy about that."

While it was disappointing that the relationship between the Carlile family and the Spokane Police Department had frayed, Mark had made his terms clear from the start. MeLainee had deliberately acted against them, and a renegotiation wasn't going to be on the table. Despite the conflict, Mark's steadfast commitment to finding Doug's killer never wavered.

● ● ●

The description of the mysterious white van was helpful, but detectives needed more. At Mark's request, the Spokane Police Department held a press conference, asking the public to submit any possible footage their home security systems might have captured the night of the murder. That's when his first big break finally bubbled to the surface.

"Lo and behold, we received a call from the house on Christmas Tree Lane," Mark said, still excited several years later about the phone call. "It was Mr. and Mrs. Wendle, a couple in their 70s who happened to own a major car dealership in Spokane. Mr. Wendle called to let us know he had video of a van matching our description and was willing to give us the footage."

Though the video was grainy, it displayed a white van creeping slowly in front of the Wendle's home around 5:00 p.m. that Sunday evening. Mr. Wendle confirmed that neither he nor his wife had ever seen that vehicle in the neighborhood before.

Although other eyewitness accounts had described the van as simply being white, the footage showed a distinctive, two-inch-wide black stripe running horizontally along the bottom rocker panels on both sides. Another distinguishing characteristic was that the van's windows were not all uniform in shape and size. It also looked like the license plate on the rear side of the vehicle was missing or had been replaced by a blank piece of paper. A clear shot of the driver could not be seen.

"What we could see was that it was longer than a normal sized van," Mark explained. "But we had no idea the make or the model."

Detective Jeff Barrington was tasked with tracking down that information. With a still frame of the video in hand, Barrington visited nearly every dealership and mechanic shop in the Spokane area. After a week with no luck and his hopes beginning to fade, Barrington finally met with an experienced mechanic who had spent decades in the profession.

"That right there is a custom-made van," the man explained. "It's an after-market lengthening. They basically cut the van in half, then add two or three feet in the middle."

"Who do you think would need a van like this?" Barrington inquired.

"You'll be looking for carpet-layers or contractors who haul materials they need to keep dry," the mechanic said, "or are longer than a normal-sized van could fit."

Armed with this new lead, Barrington contacted the Washington Department of Licensing (WDL), and soon learned that the state used special codes for those types of vans in their registries. In response to a subpoena from the Spokane Police, the WDL provided a list of registered vans in all eastern counties of Washington. Barrington was encouraged when the list included less than two hundred vehicles. That list was whittled down even further after additional vehicle specialists were consulted, and it was determined that the make and model of the extended van was most likely a 1995 Chevrolet Sports Van.

•••

While Barrington and two additional detectives continued following leads about the van, Mark Burbridge turned his attention to technology: cell phone tower data.

"I still didn't have much to go on, so I tried a request for a cellphone 'tower dump,'" he later explained. "It isn't used very often because it is a highly arduous task. But it isn't unheard of for murder cases to be solved by using phone data. So, I issued seven total search warrants to all of the cell phone companies who utilize the roughly eight to ten cell phone towers in the area around the Rockwood neighborhood."

Mark requested data for the hours between 5:00 p.m. and 10:00 p.m. on the night of the murder. During that five-hour timeframe, anywhere between 50,000-100,000 phones could have pinged across those towers. The data report was enormous, one that would take weeks to analyze. And even with the compiled data in front of him, Mark didn't have a name, let alone a phone number, he could cross-check against. Not yet anyway.

•••

Apart from pictures of the van, the only piece of physical evidence detectives had to work with was the welder's glove found lying in a pile of wet leaves between the Carliles's backyard and the open-gated fence in their neighbor's yard. Mark clung to the hope that DNA could be retrieved from the glove. The Spokane Crime Lab notoriously processed evidence at a glacial pace, but the glove was too important for Mark to patiently wait for results.

"I had a way of getting around the red tape and delays with the crime lab," Mark said coyly. "The morning after the murder, I went over to the local coffee shop and bought a couple of gift cards for the staff. I told them I had a 63-year-old grandfather gunned down in his home and that it looked like a contract killing. I communicated, very nicely, that I needed the test results from that glove yesterday."

While he waited for the results, Mark issued several public bulletins through the local media, encouraging anyone with information to come forward. Dozens of calls poured in, but few provided any additional helpful tips. Several residents in Rockwood reported they had seen an unfamiliar man walking through the neighborhood, but the descriptions they offered were inconsistent. Some said the person was wearing dark gray clothing, while others said it was black attire. The timing of the sightings also varied greatly from early in the day to several hours after the murder.

The only potentially reliable sighting of the killer had come from surveillance cameras situated outside of the elementary school behind the Carliles's house. Administrators at Hutton Elementary provided footage revealing a figure cloaked in all black sprinting through the parking lot shortly after 7:00 p.m. that Sunday night. Eerily, the person appeared to be clutching a coat or a blanket that fluttered behind like a sinister banner in the wind.

Based on the video's time stamp and Elberta Carlile's description, Mark knew the individual captured on film had to be the killer. But the camera was situated far too high on the building to provide any facial or other physical characteristics that might help identify him.

• • •

Even though it had still only been two days since Doug's murder, the bureaucratic delays were weighing heavily on Mark. But just as his frustration was about to boil over, a call came in on the tip line that offered a ray of hope.

"Hey, I knew Doug Carlile," a male caller said. "I'll come in and talk to you."

The voice on the line belonged to someone the Spokane

Police Department knew well. A former gang member and drug dealer who had once acted as a confidential informant for state and federal authorities. He also happened to be a murderer.

His name was Robert DeLao.

CHAPTER 46

Only A Matter Of Time

On December 18, 2013, three days after Doug Carlile's murder, 38-year-old Robert DeLao bebopped into the Spokane Police Department, trying hard to create the impression that he was eager to do whatever he could to assist detectives with their investigation.

Detective Mark Burbridge was ready to pounce before the cheery former gangster even sat down. Given DeLao's sordid and lengthy criminal history, it made no sense how his and Doug's worlds would have ever collided. That in itself was a dead giveaway for Mark.

"I still can't believe that DeLao actually volunteered to come in and talk to me," he laughed later. "From the moment I heard his name, I knew he was involved. I maybe couldn't prove it right away, but I knew I'd eventually get there."

Dressed in a royal blue T-shirt, jeans, and a navy-blue baseball cap, DeLao apologized for not coming in sooner. "I saw the number on the news, and I actually would have called sooner, but my mom had a procedure this morning, and that's been my priority."

Mark had no interest in wasting time on small talk. "Robert, I want to talk to you today about Doug Carlile and James Henrikson, and everything that's been going on up there in North Dakota. And I want you to be honest with me today. Total honesty."

DeLao nodded along. "Yes, yeah, yes, okay."

Mark reminded DeLao of his previous cooperation with other law enforcement agencies—his willingness to be a snitch—which had resulted in a mere 36-month prison stint for an armed robbery instead of the 24 years he might have faced otherwise. "Help yourself out here today, okay? Why don't you start with how you know Doug?"

DeLao recounted that earlier that summer, he had been introduced to Doug through James. At the time, he had been working for Tex Hall at Maheshu Energy managing the day-to-day contractual trucking work.

"Tex told me that a job was coming up, and that we needed ten side-dumps," DeLao said.

"What's a side-dump?" Mark asked.

"Oh, yeah, okay," DeLao laughed. "Picture a semi with a trailer on the back of it and picture a big bucket that turns sideways to dump. We needed that to haul rock in and out of an [oil] site.

"I called everyone I knew saying I needed ten of them, and there was good money in this job, and the first person to call me back was James. He told me he had some friends and he was trying to help them build their company up. He said he could get me ten or more side-dumps—"

"Did you know James before that?" Mark interrupted.

"Yes, yes," DeLao said. "Yeah, I've known James for some years now."

The "friends" James was referring to were John Wark and Doug Carlile, who were at the time trying to get their trucking business, Bridgewater Energy, off the ground. Within a few days of that conversation, James and DeLao traveled back to Spokane to meet with Doug.

"I said, 'Hey, I hear you can get side-dumps, so what do you want to do?'" DeLao recalled. "But Doug's interests at the time was simply doing business with Tex Hall. That's all he wanted to do. His exact words were, 'I want to do business with Tex Hall, but everybody tells me Tex Hall doesn't pay his bills.' So, he wanted to kind of get to know me, to see if I could basically put my word that he would get paid for services done."

DeLao explained that the side-dump job fell apart when Bridgewater Energy did not obtain a TERO permit in time. Once Bridgewater had that taken care of, they were contracted by Maheshu for another job, which was hauling water to and from a fracking site. According to DeLao, Bridgewater began the work, but Hall ultimately decided he would not sign the contract.

"I think they'd hauled trucks for four or five days, and in that time earned like $38,000," DeLao told the detective. "Then Tex was like 'I don't want to use them anymore, Robert, so I'm not going to sign any contracts.' I let Doug know that, and Doug was fine."

A few weeks later, Doug called to say that Bridgewater Energy was no longer operating, and he requested that DeLao forward any remaining payment to John Wark. "From then, I never communicated with him."

Mark asked DeLao to describe his tenure with Tex Hall and Maheshu Energy. DeLao recounted that he'd worked for Hall for nearly two years, but that he'd left the job of his own accord once he realized that Hall "radiated greed," and that Hall's long-time girlfriend, Tiffiany Johnson, was an "annoying meddler."

"I was tired of people calling with lawsuits. I was tired of people calling and threatening my life because they weren't getting paid. And I was tired of Tiffiany interfering in everything, including telling me what to tell law enforcement. I couldn't take it. There's just too much drama."

DeLao revealed that when the relationship between Hall and Johnson and James Henrikson and Sarah Creveling took an ugly turn in the spring and summer, things started going downhill for everyone.

"James and Sarah and Tex and Tiff are like the Hatfields and the McCoys. They will each tell you that the other is the worst piece of crap on the planet. What they will fail to tell you is that they had an excellent relationship until ... and God, I know I'm being fucking recorded, but James started having an affair with Tex's daughter. One that continues today. They were having an affair the whole time. There's a child involved now, too. Since then it's been hell, it's been drama, and it became a miserable place to work."

Scribbling down notes as fast as he could, Mark redirected DeLao back to discussing his own personal relationship with James.

"How good of friends are you and James?"

"You know, if we went with what he says, we'd be good friends," DeLao smiled. "But, he's a pathological liar. I'm simply someone he can use as part of his plans to make money. That's the honest to God's truth right there."

Despite DeLao's portrayal of their relationship as merely transactional, he admitted that it was James who had lured him to North Dakota in the first place. Citing DeLao's well-established street credentials, and his baby mama's affiliation with a Native American tribe in Spokane, James believed DeLao would "fit in" and "speak the language" of oilfield workers and truckers who barely had a "sixth-grade education."

DeLao became wistful for a moment. "I did well. Real well. I related to the people out there. I went to the pow-wows and talked to them. I mean, I was bringing us business. At the same time—and I'm not saying I'm a badass or anything like that—but I'm not easily intimidated, so it was easy for me to organize the truckers as well."

Years later, in moments of private reflection, DeLao would realize it really was the God's honest truth that he'd been just a cog in James Henrikson's dangerous wheel—a role for which the former gangster would eventually pay dearly.

●●●

A mere 15 minutes into the interview, DeLao presented himself as comfortable and friendly, and was forthcoming with answers. But he'd already blatantly lied several times, and Mark knew it. In fact, Mark knew quite a bit more than DeLao could have anticipated. Finished with the softball questions, the detective was ready to turn up the heat.

"I talked with Tex. He told me he fired you, that you didn't leave on your own."

"No, that is not correct." DeLao was adamant. "That is not correct. I can tell you right now. I quit."

"Well, he's telling me there's over half a million dollars in fraud that went on, and they're talking with Homeland Security and the IRS and there's a big federal investigation involving you and James over all that fraud."

DeLao scoffed, but his cheery demeanor cracked.

"This is not a game," Mark warned.

"Oh, I understand, I understand," DeLao acknowledged. "And you know what? If it goes to court, I will be happy to testify in my defense, because I did quit and I did not take any money from that man."

"What do you know about James and any criminal activity?"

"Well, you know, his record—" DeLao began, before Mark cut him off.

"I don't care about his record. I care about right now."

DeLao pivoted to take the pressure off of himself. "I mean, like I said, he's a pathological liar. He got involved in the disappearance of K.C. You know anything about that?"

Mark nodded, not taking his eyes off of DeLao for a second. "Did you have anything to do with that?"

"Oh, hell no. Fuck no," DeLao insisted. "In fact, thank God, I wasn't around at that time, and that's the honest to God's truth. During that time, with the K.C. disappearance, I'm gonna tell you like this: I was in Spokane, signing in and out every single day at daycare for my son. I was a stay-at-home dad. I got out of prison in November of 2011, and I believe K.C. disappeared in February 2012. I ended up in North Dakota end of May, early June. I understand how it looks with my record, but I got alibis. Every day, I was a stay-at-home-dad."

Mark shifted gears. "Did you ever go up to Doug's house?" When DeLao denied ever doing so, Mark remembered he'd brought in a kit to get a sample of DeLao's DNA. DeLao willingly complied.

"Thanks," Mark said as he swabbed the inside of DeLao's cheeks. "I've got some evidence that was left at the scene by the shooter, and I need to be able to test people's DNA against that."

DeLao seemed unruffled by that, but Mark pressed the point anyway.

"I'm going to have a heart-to-heart with you," he said casually. "People are telling me you're the shooter."

DeLao firmly denied that he'd been the one to shoot Doug Carlile. He claimed that he had been in Watford City, North Dakota that night and had only come back to Spokane a day earlier. He told Mark to subpoena his phone records, "ping" his phone, whatever needed to be done to show that he had been nowhere near Doug's house. Not only did he deny being the shooter, but DeLao also rejected Mark's follow-up suggestion that he had driven someone there to do it.

"No, no, no, no," he repeated. "I had nothing to do with it!"

"I gotta tell you," Mark said, "I'm pretty sure that James had everything to do with it."

"You know," DeLao sighed. "Look, I know it sounds bad because I'm his friend and all this, but honestly, I don't think he did. I really don't think he did. Just let the evidence come out, and you'll see."

Mark reiterated that the ongoing federal investigations in North Dakota were a very serious matter. He reminded DeLao that when several people are entangled in a crime, eventually one of them will decide to start singing, implying that James would likely be the first to join the chorus.

"The big guy is always the one who threatens the ones below him to keep their mouths shut, but guess who usually starts talking first?" he quizzed DeLao. "So, guess who is going to start jacking their jaw when indictments start coming down?" He offered DeLao a chance to do that now, but the former Sureños gang member denied any wrongdoing.

"Did James ever ask you to hurt Doug? Did he ever call you up and say 'Hey, I need this guy taken care of?'"

DeLao shook his head. "No, no, no, no."

But he was rattled, and the detective could smell blood in the water. "I gotta tell you, you look scared to death right now."

"Well, I am!" DeLao cried out. "Look what we're talking about!"

His voice steady, Mark upped the pressure. "Let's say you didn't pull the trigger, but you were the getaway driver. Or you hooked [James] up with somebody else. We can get lawyers involved and we can get a written agreement for you. If you're the shooter, you're going to do some hard time. This will probably end up in a big giant conspiracy—two murders, millions of dollars in fraud, big federal indictments, federal death penalty shit. I mean, it's going to be ugly when this is over."

"I know, I know," DeLao repeated. "Yeah, I'm nervous, look at what you're telling me. But you'll see. You'll see. I don't care what people are telling you."

Mark asked him if he'd be willing to take a polygraph. Although DeLao acknowledged not being a big fan of polygraphs, he agreed. The detective then fished a cellphone from his pocket, scrolling through photos until landing on the still frames of the white van captured on the Wendles' security camera.

"Who owns this van?" Mark asked, holding the screen inches from DeLao's face.

DeLao hesitated, telling Mark he "honestly" did not know.

Sighing, Mark leaned forward and stared into DeLao's eyes. "My gut's telling me you know a lot more than what you're talking about today. I'm going to give you my business card. We're not done yet, but when we're done, and you get home and you start thinking about this, you better believe that I'm a far better friend to you today than James is. If you want to be able to see your kids and raise your kids, I'm the lifeline to save you. We're pulling cellphone data for about 30 people. We're pulling email data, text messages. It's going to get bad for people before I'm done. See, I think you know some things about James that you don't want to talk about."

DeLao blanched. "No, like I said, this is what I've learned with people. Don't know their business. Don't get to know them. If I meet someone, I don't pry into their lives anymore. I've already learned the hard way, it catches up to you. Am

I nervous? Fuck yeah, I'm nervous. You would be too if you were in my shoes right now. But like I said, I don't know what people are telling you right now, but you'll see. You'll see. I hate that I have my record right now. I hate it. But you'll see."

Mark's tone softened, but his words stung like a whip. "I should make something clear. I'm not after you. But if you're caught up in my truth, I will destroy you."

Leaning in even closer to DeLao, the detective added, "I think you're a part of this. At a minimum, I think James called you and said, 'I need help,' and you hooked him up with somebody. If that's what happened, and now you're like, 'Holy shit, he really did it,' you need to step forward on this and get yourself in front. Because I guarantee you, I'm coming. And those people that did the shooting? They're going to roll back on everybody. Or if we get James first, I guarantee you he's going to shit his pants and puke his guts on my table when they start talking about life and the death penalty."

But no matter how hard Mark pushed, DeLao insisted that he knew nothing about Doug Carlile's murder.

"I'm going to make sure that you know I didn't have shit to do with it," he promised.

•••

Two days later, Robert DeLao held true to his word and came to the Spokane Police Department for a polygraph. He was his usually bubbly self at first, laughing and joking with the examiner. Once all of the equipment was set up and in place, however, his demeanor morphed entirely to that of someone participating in a meditation ritual. Throughout the examination, he kept his eyes closed and concentrated on breathing deeply and steadily. His responses were measured and uttered in near whispers.

When the results of the exam came in, they showed that DeLao had passed with flying colors.

But Mark Burbridge was unfazed. "I wasn't one bit surprised he passed. I still knew he was involved. I just needed to prove it."

It was only a matter of time.

CHAPTER 47

Concerts And Confessions

The 2013 holiday season cast a dark shadow over two grieving families. For the Carliles, any chance for a festive spirit was brutally eclipsed by the fresh, raw wound of losing their beloved patriarch just weeks before. Miles away, K.C. Clarke's mother, Jill Williams, faced her second Christmas steeped in torment, the unanswered questions of her son's fate still gnawing at her broken heart.

Meanwhile, federal investigators with the IRS, U.S. Postal Service, and Homeland Security spent their holidays neck-deep in what had become a high-stakes case. The shocking murder of Doug Carlile had drastically changed the landscape of the entire investigation and added a new sense of urgency. To bolster their efforts, they soon enlisted the support of FBI Agent Eric Barker. HSI Special Agent Darrik Trudell had also finally connected with Spokane detective Mark Burbridge.

"I explained that we were investigating James Henrikson and Sarah Creveling for financial crimes, but that they also might be connected to the disappearance and possible murder of K.C. Clarke," Darrik recalled. "I described the oil boom here in North Dakota so that he understood the dynamics of what was going on."

In return, Mark disclosed that the Carlile family was convinced that James was also behind Doug's murder. He discussed his plans to travel to North Dakota with another detective, Brian Cestnik, to confront James in person.

Grateful that the ice had finally been broken between them, the two sets of investigators continued following their respective leads.

For Darrik, a call came in from the U.S. Attorney's office in Phoenix, Arizona with bombshell information. Evidently, James Henrikson's former business associate, Ryan Olness, had been spiraling since his uneventful proffer sessions weeks earlier, and was now sharing disturbing information to anyone within earshot.

While attending a country music festival with some friends, a heavily intoxicated Olness had supposedly divulged that he believed James had hired someone to kill K.C. Clarke. To bolster that belief, Olness described an unsettling incident that occurred one morning in late February 2012. James had instructed him to quickly pull together $10,000 in cash from Blackstone Trucking's coffers and bring the money to one of the trailer yards used to house oilfield workers—a task James had never requested before.

Dutifully following orders, Olness had gathered the cash and hand-delivered it to James at the yard, where he was waiting in his truck with Sarah and a man Olness didn't recognize. In hindsight, Olness now suspected that this unknown man was the hitman, and that he had unwittingly delivered the payment for K.C. Clarke's murder.

Alarmed by the information, one of Olness's friends had promptly reported it to the police. According to the report, Olness had been a wreck, sobbing uncontrollably and sharing thoughts of suicide. The weight of his potential involvement— even if unknowingly—had eaten at him for nearly two years.

When authorities followed up with Olness, he staunchly denied that he'd made any sort of "confession" at the concert. He reiterated that he knew nothing about what happened to K.C., or James's possible involvement.

Still, the level of detail in the report seemed too intricate to be fabricated. The informant who had relayed the information had nothing to gain by inventing such a salacious story.

Although investigators had long suspected James's culpability in K.C.'s presumed murder and now believed he was also likely involved in a second murder in Spokane, they hadn't yet considered the possibility that he had hired a hitman to carry out the killings.

"I didn't understand why the hell anyone would do this guy's bidding," Darrik Trudell later mused.

Olness's reported narrative also raised fresh questions as to the full extent of Sarah Creveling's involvement in her husband's crimes. Initially only suspected of her role in the financial fraud, was it possible that she also had a hand in orchestrating the murders of someone she once considered a good friend and of a 63-year-old grandfather?

CHAPTER 48

Once A Pit Bull Latches, He Doesn't Let Go

On Thursday, January 2, 2014, Spokane detectives Mark Burbridge and Brian Cestnik set out on a 789-mile trip to North Dakota in a brand-new, cherry-red Ford Taurus. The shiny vehicle came fully equipped with numerous specialized features such as hidden lights, ballistic door panels, and a powertrain calibrated for high-speed pursuits. For this particular trip in the dead of winter, however, it was missing one crucial feature: snow tires.

"I don't think we even looked at a forecast," Mark chuckled later, "so we were not at all prepared for the blizzard we drove through. I think it was like ten inches of snow. It was coming down so thick we could barely see. The wind was also blowing like crazy, and it was freezing cold with windchills of 65 below. There were semis and cars in the ditch all along the way."

While the primary objective of the trip was to catch James Henrikson off-guard with a surprise visit, the detectives also sought to connect with North Dakota officials to determine whether or not there was indeed a link between K.C. Clarke's disappearance and Doug Carlile's murder.

In addition, just before embarking on their trek, they received a tip from a businessman in Bozeman, Montana, who claimed he knew both James and Doug. The caller shared that he had interacted with James on several occasions prior to

Doug's murder and was aware of the simmering tensions between the two.

Five hours east on the interstate, they stopped in Bozeman to meet with 34-year-old Volery "Larry" Tormozov. Tormozov told the lawmen he owned a construction company based in Moses Lake, Washington, which was currently being contracted to build roads and drilling pads throughout Montana and North Dakota. He had met Doug several years prior and had offered him a job. Supposedly, this was at a time when Doug was out of work after filing for bankruptcy a second time.

"I gave him a job," Tormozov recounted, "and then I had to fire him because I found out he was stealing from me. While he was writing bids for my company, he was also writing bids for his son's company in a direct effort to undercut the bids he was writing for me."

According to Tormozov, he wasn't the only person in Washington who had been negatively impacted by some of Doug's business dealings. Pamp Maiers, another well-known and respected wealthy businessman in Moses Lake, had also been hoodwinked out of several hundred thousand dollars.

"I'm like a son to Pamp," Tormozov boasted. "Doug did business with Pamp and ended up owing him around half a million dollars, but he couldn't pay it. Pamp accepted some property in lieu of some of the debt, but Doug never paid the entire debt."

In contrast, Tormozov shared that a brief experience working with James on a previous project in Walla Walla, Washington had been positive. Curiously, he claimed that his relationship with James had no overlap with Doug, and he was surprised to learn that the two even knew each other.

"I had no idea they knew each other," Tormozov remarked. "A couple of months ago, James showed up in my office here in Montana, asking me to find someone who would be willing to finance a major oil exploration project [in North Dakota]. I knew right away he would probably want Pamp involved, but when I looked at the incorporation paperwork, I saw Doug Carlile was listed as the CEO and majority owner of Kingdom Dynamics Enterprises. I told James that under no circumstances would Pamp invest or partner in anything with Doug's involvement."

Tormozov told the detectives that upon hearing this, James appeared both shocked and dismayed. The only reason James had even considered asking Tormozov about Pamp Maiers was because Doug had lied and told him and the other KDE investors that Maiers was already interested.

"James said he was worried they were going to lose their lease because their time to come up with the additional money was running out," Tormozov said. "Two weeks prior to Doug's murder, James called and told me he had tried to get Doug out of Kingdom Dynamics by offering him a small percentage of the oil profits for life, but Doug refused. James said he didn't know what he was going to do at this point."

Tormozov's story was enlightening. For the detectives, it was a fascinating glimpse into the intricate connections that permeate the world of oil business and contracting, where alliances and betrayals seemed to unfold in the blink of an eye.

More importantly, they now had even further insight into James's state of mind leading up to Doug Carlile's murder. Significant financial incentive mixed with desperation was a dangerous cocktail.

● ● ●

The cherry-red Taurus carrying Detectives Mark Burbridge and Brian Cestnik skated into Watford City, North Dakota on ice- and snow-covered roads in the early morning hours of Friday, January 3. After grabbing a few hours of sleep in a budget motel, they were ready to confront James.

When they strolled outside, however, their fancy car was nearly buried in fresh snow. "We had to dig it out," Mark later recounted. "When we began driving, the car started vibrating, and there were loud thumping sounds coming from the tires. It felt like we were driving over rocks or something. I had no idea what was going on, but I eventually learned that's what happens when ice and snow gets compacted in the wheel wells."

Promptly at 9:00 a.m., detectives knocked on the front door of 505 17th Avenue Northeast, a sprawling brown rambler located on the outskirts of town. A petite dark-haired woman opened the door and identified herself as Robin Benson.

Mark explained that he and Brian were detectives from Spokane and were looking for either James Henrikson or Sarah Creveling. "Is James here?"

"Not right now, but both him and Sarah will be back later," Benson replied. "Would you like to come in?"

Accepting the invitation, Mark and Brian stepped into a bizarre scene. It appeared that the kitchen area had been transformed into a makeshift office space. Three laptop computers were spread out on the dining room table, surrounded by organized piles of what looked like invoices and billing paperwork.

While the owners of the house, James and Sarah, were apparently away, three people bustled about the kitchen and living area: Benson, an unknown male, and—to Mark and Brian's surprise—Robert DeLao. All of the color drained from DeLao's face when he saw the detectives from Spokane.

In DeLao's December 18 interview, he had claimed he no longer worked for Tex Hall at Maheshu Energy and did not mention that he was currently employed in North Dakota. He had also spoken as if he had distanced himself from James and all of the "drama" going on. It was beyond strange that he was casually sitting in James's kitchen just two weeks later.

Benson shared that she was formerly a bookkeeper for Maheshu Energy, but that she was now working for James at Bridgewater Energy—which was, technically, Doug Carlile's trucking business. What Benson neglected to share, however, was that she and DeLao were in a romantic relationship, unbeknownst to DeLao's girlfriend—and the mother of his children—back in Spokane.

The detectives knew word of their unannounced visit would reach James and Sarah in short order, if it hadn't already. There was some satisfaction in knowing the couple—and Robert DeLao—would likely be on edge. Mark and Brian hoped that anxiety would simmer for the next several hours. If there was anyone teetering on the brink of readiness to share information, perhaps that time would come.

"I'm going to give you my card," Mark told Benson. "Please have James or Sarah give me a call when they get back home."

•••

After conferring with law enforcement officials from the NDB-CI and Williston police department, Mark and Brian obtained the name and contact information of a local confidential informant who claimed to have knowledge of some of the "dirty work" that James and his cohorts were up to.

Later identified as Confidential Informant #1 (CI#1) in reports, the individual told the detectives that he had been a truck driver for James Henrikson for more than a year hauling water and oil. CI#1 disclosed that on numerous occasions, he had witnessed James orchestrating a scheme in which drivers would effectively double bill contractors.

"It was common practice," CI#1 explained. "I never personally participated in it, but basically how it worked was drivers would fill half of their water tank from one company's well, then fill the other half at another company's well, and charge both companies for a full load."

CI#1 also knew that James and Sarah Creveling were using aliases—Cole Johnson and Amy Peterson, respectively—and were utilizing different business names for their operations. This was a fairly new development since they had only recently been banned from doing business with oil companies on the reservation and surrounding areas.

But the informant quickly realized that false identities and shady business dealings were just scratching the surface.

"I was there on several occasions when James talked about how angry he was with Doug Carlile," he shared. "He said things like 'I'm going to kill him' and 'I'm going to kick his ass.' Back in September, he explicitly said he was going to kill Carlile and hurt his whole family. He told me he had connections to the Ukrainian mob, and that it would be easy to find someone to kill Carlile. I knew there was friction between them because of money issues, but I didn't really take it seriously at the time because James was always saying grandiose things and bragging."

Yet, CI#1's dismissiveness quickly waned when the gravity of James's intentions became apparent. Soon after the threats were made, CI#1 learned that James was already shopping for a hitman—but not for Doug Carlile. And not in Ukraine.

"He has this guy working for him, Erick Guerrero. He's supposedly been to prison for murder and has 'Mexican Mafia' tattooed on the back of his head. Guerrero told me that James was looking to find someone to kill Tex Hall. But Guerrero told me he didn't want anything to do with killing anyone."

•••

Surprisingly, Erick Guerrero answered his phone on the first ring and readily provided some basic information when questioned by Detective Mark Burbridge.

"I currently work for James Henrikson, but I'm in California on vacation right now," Guerrero stated. "I've been gone since December 17, but I'm scheduled to be back in a few days."

Mark didn't beat around the bush. "Has James Henrikson ever asked you kill anyone for him? Tex Hall? Doug Carlile?"

"No fucking way, man," Guerrero retorted.

After this exchange, Guerrero's cooperative demeanor evaporated, prompting an equally defiant Mark to attempt to poke the bear. "I've heard rumors about a Mexican Mafia tattoo on the back of your head," he said casually. "If you're not actually affiliated, that could pose a serious risk to your safety."

Guerrero scoffed. "Mind your own business," he told the detective, then ended the call.

Mark later chuckled recalling a follow-up message he received. "I got a text from Guerrero's number. It said something like, 'Don't ever call this number, bitch-ass fag.'"

Guerrero's offensive rhetoric aside, the detectives didn't give any further consideration to him being considered a suspect in Doug Carlile's murder.

• • •

Later that afternoon, the detective duo returned to James and Sarah's house, where two large black Ford pickup trucks were now sitting in the driveway—vehicles presumably belonging to the couple. Instead of approaching the front door, Mark and Brian noticed that the garage door was open.

"We walked into the garage, and there's a Bentley sitting in one of the stalls," Mark remembered. "All four of the tires were flat, and it was sitting on its belly. This is like a $60,000 car. I couldn't figure out why someone would spend that much money on a car and not take care of it."

It was Sarah herself who answered the knock this time but had nothing to say to the detectives. "James, there's people at the door for you," she called back into the house.

Her husband approached the open doorway with his signature Cheshire-like grin, clearly expecting the lawmen. Before the pair even had a chance to say a word, James reached out and slapped a hand on Mark Burbridge's shoulder. The detective's vision blurred red with rage, but he remained still, allowing the suspect's hand to linger.

"Hello detectives," James said, his tone dripping with arrogance. "I'd love to talk to you, but my attorney has advised me not to. I'm sorry you traveled all the way out here for nothing."

The next thing Mark and Brian knew, the door was slamming in their faces.

"It took everything in me to not come unglued," Mark admitted later. "I just thought, *No fucking way this guy just did that.*"

Detective Brian Cestnik would remember the incident for years to come. "I still to this day don't know how Mark maintained his composure."

For James Henrikson, this was the moment that sealed his fate. Whereas before he had simply wanted to talk to James to see if he'd trip up on his own words, Mark Burbridge was now hell-bent on taking him down, no matter what it took.

"Once a pit bull latches, he doesn't let go," one attorney later remarked of Mark's tenacious resolve.

•••

Driving out of Watford City, the detectives phoned Tex Hall to warn him that James might be plotting something against him.

"I already know," Hall said. "I carry a gun wherever I go."

CHAPTER 49

Deep Vein Thrombosis And DNA

The highways were finally clear of the remaining snow and ice, but that didn't make the journey back to Spokane any less treacherous for Detectives Mark Burbridge and Brian Cestnik. Determined to resume their investigation as soon as possible, they opted to make the 12-hour trip in one day.

As he sped down the interstate in the fire engine red Ford Taurus, Mark's mind raced, still stewing over his tense encounter with James Henrikson. In the passenger seat, Brian was increasingly distracted by a sharp, throbbing pain in his lower right leg. As the hours dragged on, the pain got worse, and his leg began to swell and became discolored.

"What the hell is going on?" Mark asked, a little freaked out.

"It's pretty sore," Brian admitted, but brushed it off. "It's probably just because I've been sitting in this car for so long."

But by the time they coasted into Spokane, the pain and swelling had gotten much worse. "He could barely walk," Mark recalled. "I tried to get him to go to the hospital as we passed through Missoula, Montana, but he refused. As we neared Spokane, Brian called a triage nurse and described his symptoms to her. She insisted he immediately go to one of the emergency rooms at a local hospital. We met Brian's wife in Spokane Valley, and she took him directly to the hospital.

It was a damn good thing she did. Doctors revealed that

Brian had developed deep vein thrombosis (DVT) in his leg, which meant a blood clot had formed in one of his veins. Interestingly, DVT could be linked to prolonged immobility, like sitting in a car for 12 hours, but it could also stem from various other factors. Regardless of the cause, the situation was extremely serious.

If he had waited much longer to seek medical help, the clot could have traveled to his lungs, possibly leading to a pulmonary embolism—an urgent and potentially fatal condition. Left untreated, the outcome could have been catastrophic.

Fortunately, he spent only one night in the hospital and had to inject himself with blood thinners for several weeks. Much to Brian's dismay, however, his superiors at the Spokane Police Department ordered him to stay home to rest and recuperate.

While the stubborn detective recovered, the investigation into Doug Carlile's murder gained momentum, transforming from a slow roll to a roaring surge within a matter of days.

• • •

Two days prior to the detectives departing for North Dakota, Anna Wilson, a forensic scientist with the Washington State Patrol Crime Lab, had shared updates on her progress. After thoroughly processing the shell casings left behind in the Carliles's kitchen, she had not found any viable DNA evidence to work with.

But the welding glove discovered in the Carliles's backyard was another story. From the inner lining of the glove, she had isolated a "major" DNA profile (identified in her reports as Individual A). While that finding was indeed promising, there was some disappointing news to follow: further testing had definitively concluded that Robert DeLao was not Individual A.

Furthermore, Wilson had entered Individual A's profile into the Washington State database, but there had been no matches. She wasn't giving up hope quite yet, however, as there was still one place left to try: the national DNA system,

CODIS (Combined DNA Index System). Wilson told the detectives not to get too excited, as it would likely be several weeks before she heard anything back. To her own surprise, it took less than ten days.

On Friday, January 10, Wilson submitted a written report for Mark Burbridge:

> *"A match was declared between the DNA typing profile identified as Individual A and the DNA profile for Timothy Eugene Suckow, DOB: 11/18/1963. The last known whereabouts (per the National Crime Information Center Criminal History Record) is the U.S. Probation Office in Spokane, WA. It is requested that a known reference sample from Timothy Suckow be submitted to the WSP Spokane Crime Laboratory to confirm this match."*

The name Timothy Suckow had not come across anyone's radar—either in North Dakota with regards to K.C. Clarke's disappearance, or in relation to Doug Carlile's murder. In fact, no one in Spokane law enforcement had ever heard of him.

"I researched Suckow's history for several hours," Mark said later, "but I didn't want to waste time having to get a search warrant to find out where and what he was doing now. I had a friend in the local branch of the FBI, Frank Herrell, and told him we might have a federal hitman case going on. The FBI can access more information pertaining to someone's employment and history, and I asked him if he could find out Suckow's current whereabouts. I called Frank on my way to work one morning, and he called me back a half hour later to tell me that Suckow was an employee at IRS Environmental."

Once again, it was information that seemed completely out of left field. IRSE was a well-established asbestos and lead removal company operating throughout the Pacific Northwest, with a location on Trent Avenue in the eastern suburb of Spokane Valley. Timothy Suckow had been employed there for nearly five years. His listed home address on Gary Laurie Court was less than a mile away from IRSE, but 12 miles away from Doug Carlile's house.

Suckow had a criminal past—quite extensive, in fact—but he had never been suspected or convicted of killing anyone, and he hadn't had any brushes with the law for several years. It was completely baffling as to why or how his DNA would have ended up on a random glove at a major murder scene, miles from where he lived.

But before that question could be answered, Mark Burbridge turned his attention back toward IRSE. Specifically, he zeroed in on the type of vehicles the company had used to remove asbestos and other harmful chemicals from dilapidated buildings for the last 30 years.

On a hunch, Mark thumbed through Sgt. Jeff Barrington's short list of 1995 Chevy Sport vans, and nearly fell out of his chair when he found that one van of that make and model was indeed registered to IRSE. In fact, it had been in IRSE's fleet for years.

• • •

Late on the evening of January 10, no fewer than 12 members of the Spokane Tactical Operations Unit and Major Crimes Unit coalesced to conduct a 48-hour surveillance mission on Timothy Suckow and the duplex he lived in, at 2724 N. Gary Laurie Court. Undercover officers were also deployed to watch IRSE, hoping to catch a glimpse of the work van with the license plate matching their report.

"Officers did confirm a van with a black stripe on the lower portion of the vehicle, and different sized windows on the side doors in the IRSE parking lot," Sgt. Barrington reported. "The plate on the van was B95800G."

A direct match. Mark was ecstatic. "I'm pretty confident at this point that Suckow is my guy, but we had to be careful. We didn't know what he was capable of."

For two full days, Suckow did nothing but go to work in the morning and return in the evening. He drove a green 1997 Chevy Tahoe and unless he was going to and from work, it seemed Suckow never left home. Those in charge of the detail had been bored to tears to say the least. But they had discovered at least one important detail: Suckow had numerous security cameras set up around the perimeter of his house.

While Mark had obtained a search warrant for Suckow's duplex and car, serving them was going to be tricky. Mark determined he had probable cause to arrest Suckow for murder, but, if the police attempted to arrest him at home, Suckow's cameras would alert him of their arrival. Perhaps even more importantly, the police had to operate under the assumption that Suckow had weapons and was willing to use them. No one wanted to be involved in either a stand-off, or worse, an ambush. To ensure that Suckow's arrest was executed with the utmost safety and precaution for everyone involved, SPD requested assistance from the SWAT team and a K-9 unit.

At 2:00 p.m. on Monday, January 13, members of the SWAT team detail assembled two blocks away from 2724 N. Gary Laurie Court and waited an agonizing seven hours before Suckow finally emerged from his house. Shortly after 9:00 p.m., Suckow's green Chevy Tahoe headed north on Gary Laurie toward E Marietta Ave; it then turned left onto North Pines Road, drove for a half-mile, and made a right turn onto Trent Avenue where IRSE was located.

Within seconds of Suckow pulling into the IRSE parking lot, his Tahoe was pinned in on all sides by a swarm of police and SWAT vehicles. Before he could grasp what was happening, officers leapt out of their cars with rifles drawn, commanding him to get out of the vehicle. When Suckow complied, exiting the Tahoe with his hands in the air, Officer Paul Buchmann and K-9 Talon swiftly moved in to secure the arrest.

"Due to the severity of the crime and the danger to the public, I decided to deploy Talon to ensure that Suckow would not flee," Buchmann wrote in his report. "Once Suckow complied without incident, I secured Talon back in my car."

Thankfully, the arrest of 50-year-old Timothy Eugene Suckow went without incident, but a few surprises awaited them inside the Chevy Tahoe. The first was a passenger, who identified himself as Lazaro Pesina. Since there was no indication that Pesina was associated with the reason for Suckow's arrest, they allowed him to leave the scene. For the time being,

Pesina had lucked out.

A secondary discovery, a folded sheet of notebook paper found in the center console, turned out to be quite valuable. At first glance, the hastily scribbled writing on the paper just looked like an ordinary to-do list. But upon closer inspection, detectives realized it was a detailed outline for something a lot more sinister.

As he sat in the backseat of an unmarked police cruiser, a handcuffed Suckow bemoaned the situation he was now in. "I've been through all this before, and I've been out of prison for nine years. I've been keeping my nose clean."

CHAPTER 50

A Checklist For Murder

While Timothy Suckow was whisked away to the Spokane Police Department, searches of his work, home, and vehicle commenced. To start, police notified the president of IRS Environmental, Maureen Fay—who in turn notified her human resources director, Robert Reed—that one of their employees had just been arrested in their parking lot. For murder, no less. They were also told that a search warrant had been issued for the property, and that their presence was urgently requested to sign off on the warrant.

An understandably rattled 43-year-old Fay and 57-year-old Reed arrived within a half hour of being summoned, ready and willing to fully cooperate with the warrant. Sgt. Joel Fertakis and Detective Corey Turman were there to greet them with a laundry list of items and information to gather.

Fay and Reed were asked to turn over registration information for the company's fleet of vehicles, speak to the possible presence of firearms at the facility, locate any supply of work gloves that the business kept, produce Timothy Suckow's employment record, and provide the employee and vehicle schedule for a stretch of time, but specifically for the night of Sunday, December 15.

"Fay provided the VIN numbers and license plates for all of IRSE's vehicles," Turman reported. "Fay also stated that to her knowledge there were no firearms at her business. Fay assisted with attempting to locate any gloves that may have been used by employees and directed us to where the gloves were stored. We were unable to locate any gloves that matched the glove left at the crime scene. But she did indicate that the welder for IRSE is Greg Burger."

IRSE's van fleet was secured in a lot behind a locked gate, but there were no cameras that monitored the premises. IRSE maintained detailed logs for where their employees and vehicles were—but only when they were assigned to a job. The van with license plate BC95800G had not been assigned to any jobs between the dates of December 9 and December 16. Furthermore, within that same time frame, Timothy Suckow had not been scheduled to use that van. Still, Robert Reed admitted that didn't necessarily mean that he hadn't.

"Tim had access to this van and occasionally keeps it over weekends," he said. "I don't know if he had it on the night of December 15, though."

Instead of cameras, IRSE employed night watchmen. Among them was Andris Ernesons, who arrived for his shift shortly after Suckow's arrest. Coincidentally, he had also been the watchman on duty the night of December 15.

When he saw the considerable police presence and noticed Maureen Fay and Robert Reed were there when they normally wouldn't be, Ernesons looked as if he might turn tail and run.

"Do you know why we're here?" Turman asked the visibly nervous Ernesons.

"I'd rather not say," Ernesons responded.

Taken aback by the odd response, Sgt. Fertakis pulled Ernesons aside. "Look, I don't think you're involved in this, but if you lie to us, or leave out any information, you could be in a lot of trouble."

Even though Ernesons said he didn't have any information to share, Fertakis and Turman weren't buying it.

"I believe it is possible that Andris was there when Suckow either came to the business to borrow the van, or to bring it back," Fertakis wrote. Time would tell if his hypothesis was correct.

As part of the search warrant for IRSE, Detective Burbridge included a provision to seize the van in question. The grainy video from Christmas Tree Lane the night of the murder showed that the van's license plates had been removed and replaced with a fake temporary tag. If Mark's hunch was correct—that this was the van in the video—there was a strong chance that whoever removed and later reattached the real plates had left fingerprints behind.

"I've seen a lot of cases like this where someone removes a license plate and then puts it back on later," Mark later discussed. "They never remember to wipe off the fingerprints on the back of the plate. So, I wanted to be able to test the whole van, but most importantly, to take those plates off and test for fingerprints.

Once the van was taken away to be impounded, and they were finished at IRSE, Sgt. Fertakis drove Suckow's green Chevy Tahoe the mile distance back to his driveway at N. Gary Laurie Court. There, Sgt. Jeff Barrington assisted Turman with the search of the vehicle.

• • •

Aside from a few stains on the gray upholstery and carpeting, the inside of the vehicle was remarkably clean and tidy. However, inside the center console was a peculiar assortment of items, including a set of binoculars, a folding pocketknife, two bags of Western Family Ice Blue Eucalyptus cough drops, a roll of black duct tape, a flashlight, a notebook, and a black ski mask.

There was also an invoice from ABC Mini Storage and a folded up single piece of notebook paper. Detectives would follow-up on the invoice, but the immediate focus zeroed in on the chicken scratched notes on the loose sheet of paper.

glove?
badge
trench coat

2 boots

led lite cap — wingman
Radios w/mics
Rig
window tinker

Greg B
wheelman (show scenic tour) (Google earth)
wingman

Check van for scheduling/magnetic sign

wipe tools down

husk pills (super supplements)

practice with pistol

With the exception of the fiber supplements — which were generally used to treat constipation — the remainder of the list was enlightening. Although it wasn't quite a smoking gun, it offered up a few clues to fill in some of the blanks in the investigation.

"It pretty much looked like a checklist for murder," Detective Mark Burbridge said.

• • •

At 11:00 p.m., another team of detectives executed a search warrant and entered the duplex at 2724 North Gary Laurie Court. Inside the residence was Timothy Suckow's wife, JoAnne Des-Jarlais, as well as her two teenage daughters, aged 17 and 13. All three females were visibly shaken. The shock of seeing a swarm of police officers and members of the SWAT team inside and surrounding their home had to have been profoundly upsetting for such young women. Yet they remained cooperative, even after being informed they would need to find somewhere else to stay while police searched their home from top to bottom.

Detective Marty Hill sat down with 46-year-old DesJarlais, who was more than willing to share information. She described her seven-year marriage to Suckow as good and stated that the couple did not have any domestic or financial problems.

"He's a great man," DesJarlais said. "He doesn't do drugs, and he doesn't drink. He doesn't go out to bars. He works all the time and when he isn't working, he's at home. He's usually up at 5:00 a.m., home by 6:00 p.m., and in bed by 9:00 p.m."

DesJarlais went on to explain that she and her husband did not have very many friends. They did not go over to other people's homes, and rarely entertained guests in their own home. On this night, however, an old friend of Suckow's, Lazaro Pesina, had come over to lend a helping hand.

"Laz used to work at IRSE, but he doesn't anymore," she stated. "He was over at the house tonight fixing up an old ratty jailhouse tattoo that Tim had on his back. Tim wanted to get rid of the old one and get a new one."

Detective Hill shifted the conversation to the purpose of the search. "The reason we are executing a search warrant tonight is because we are investigating a homicide."

DesJarlais reeled back. "Do you think Tim did it?"

"That's what we are trying to figure out," Hill said. "There was an item of evidence left at the scene that has Tim's DNA on it."

"How the hell is that possible?" DesJarlais asked.

"Do you think he could have done something like this?" Hill probed.

"No, he's a good guy and wouldn't do this," DesJarlais seemed confident.

Suckow's wife shared that he often drove an IRSE van when assigned to various jobs, and although she admitted she had seen footage of the suspected white van on a news broadcast, she had not made the connection to IRSE.

"Has your husband ever been up to North Dakota?" Hill asked.

"Once, a long time ago. He went up there for a job interview but came back and said he knew nothing about oil rigs, so the job wasn't going to work out."

"Did he drive up there?"

"No, he took the train," DesJarlais said. "I dropped him off at the station."

• • •

As soon as DesJarlais and her daughters vacated the premises, a thorough search commenced. Most areas of the duplex yielded little of evidentiary value, but upon entering Suckow's bedroom, detectives stumbled into the bizarre domain of a doomsday prepper.

Just for starters, Suckow had not one, but two different police scanners, along with a handwritten ledger that documented the specific frequencies for a number of law enforcement agencies, including the Washington State Police, Spokane Police Department, Spokane Valley Police, U.S. Marshals, Border Patrol, ATF, and DEA.

"One of the scanners was loudly broadcasting law enforcement radio traffic in live time," the search report stated.

In addition, in what was presumed to be Suckow's side of a dresser, officers found several sets of walkie-talkies, numerous survival-type knives, and a collection of DVD's referencing martial arts and firearms training. The titles on the DVDs included "Extreme Survival," "Improvised Suppressors Secrets of Firearms," and "Combat Focus Shooting and Home Defense Tips." Puzzlingly, no firearms were found at all, raising questions about why Suckow had a collection of firearms training videos if he didn't own any guns.

Also found in the dresser drawers were vials of local anesthetics, two flip phones, a black balaclava—a cloth headgear similar to a ski mask—still in its original packaging, photos of Suckow from when he was in prison, and a recent receipt from Walmart. For $43.45, Suckow had purchased a Tactical Universal Laser and Flashlight Kit, which was also still in its packaging. Next to that was another receipt for ABC Mini Storage, located at 11506 East Indiana Road, less than a five-minute drive from Suckow's duplex.

Outside, Sgt. Fertakis combed through the garage, his attention quickly drawn to a set of welding gloves. Among them was a single left-handed glove, noticeably missing its counterpart. The glove featured yellow leather on the fingers and palm and a gray cuff. Fertakis pulled out his iPhone and compared it with a photo of the glove recovered at the Car- lile crime scene. Although he would have to wait to compare the gloves side-by-side, the similarities were striking. The fact that the single glove left at the scene was right-handed further suggested that Fertakis had just stumbled upon a major break- through in the case.

• • •

An additional search warrant was issued to ABC Mini Storage, where it was discovered that Timothy Suckow had been rent- ing a storage unit, at a cost of $155 per month. After cutting off the lock, detectives walked into a space chock full of further proof that Suckow was preparing for some sort of apocalypse. Blue plastic totes were stacked from floor to ceiling, filled with canned goods, food storage containers, toilet paper, camou- flage tarps, gas masks, biohazard suits, canteens, and decon- tamination filters. Dozens more five-gallon plastic pails were filled with sugar and dry rice, and there were numerous pack- ages of bottled water.

They also discovered several items of camouflage cloth- ing, along with several gun holsters, bulletproof vests, and other tactical gear. Among the items was a case for a .45 caliber pistol, but the gun itself was nowhere to be found. However, ABC's security footage showed that Suckow had entered the storage facility on the night of December 15, at approximately 8:00 p.m., one hour after Elberta Carlile had called 911 and reported her husband had just been shot.

CHAPTER 51

This Guy Is A Monster

At 10:35 p.m. on January 13, 2014, nearly one month after the murder of Doug Carlile, a handcuffed Timothy Suckow was led into a small interrogation room at the Spokane Police Department. Following behind him was a uniformed police officer and Mark Burbridge, wearing a light blue, long-sleeved button-down shirt and black slacks. The hulking Suckow towered over both of them. He was clearly agitated, his body language speaking as if he might try to physically resist the predicament he was now in.

"I touched his arm, and I could feel him tense up," Mark later recalled. "I thought for sure he was going to try to do something. I purposely don't carry a gun in with me during interrogations, because I don't want there to be a weapon in the room for a suspect to potentially use. I told the officer that Tim is huge, he is super strong, and he will kill us if he tries to fight. I said, 'Look, I'm not fucking around here, this guy is a monster. If he starts something, you need to be prepared to shoot.'"

But instead of a confrontation that likely would have ended badly for everyone, Suckow's demeanor seemed to soften from defiance to an almost eerie sense of peace.

"Tim?" Mark began in a gentle tone.

"Yes," Suckow responded. "I'm listening."

"I'm Mark. We're gonna get you hooked to the floor. We

can take your coat for you. Then I'm going to go get you a pop or a water, or whatever you want."

"Some sleep," Suckow retorted. "That'd be nice."

While the officer worked to unlock the cuffs around his wrists, Suckow whimpered in pain. "Ow, God. I've got a fresh tattoo. It's just a little sore."

Once the arrestee's wrists were free, Mark assisted with removing his black hooded zip-up sweatshirt he was wearing, being mindful of Suckow's healing tattoo. Beneath it, Suckow sported a short-sleeved white T-shirt with a red octagon and the caption, "Stop Snitching." The irony of his chosen attire wasn't lost in the midst of the unfolding situation.

Mark cuffed Suckow's wrist to a three-foot cord secured to the floor. If he tried to break free, he wouldn't get very far.

"Pop, water, coffee?" the detective offered. "I'll get you anything you want."

"Sleep," Suckow repeated.

"Can't hurt you to sleep," Mark agreed. "It'll be a few minutes. We've got some paperwork and some stuff to do, and then I'll be in and let you know what's going on."

As soon as the detective left the room and shut the door behind him, Suckow let out a loud belch. The career criminal knew the inside of an interrogation room better than just about anyone, and his eyes scanned everything around him before affixing his gaze upon the video camera recording his every movement.

He voiced his displeasure with the cuff squeezing his wrist and being chained to the floor like an animal as if he was expecting the camera to understand his grievances. "I hate it when you guys do this."

As the minutes ticked by, Suckow tried to get comfortable in the metal chair, but the newly inked tattoo on his back made that nearly impossible. Instead, he squirmed around until finally settling on sitting sideways, one arm resting on the back of the chair, his massive hand cradling his head. Just as he began drifting off, the door squeaked open, and Mark Burbridge and Brian Cestnik strolled into the room, ready to make Suckow start talking.

• • •

Brian had been at home at the time of Suckow's arrest, still on medical leave and also on a high-dosage blood thinner to avoid any further clotting. Despite assurances that Mark and another detective could handle the Suckow interview, Brian was having none of it.

"There was no fucking way I was going to miss that interview," he later said. For the occasion, Brian donned a long-sleeved maroon button-down, khaki pants, and brown loafers.

"Let me tell you what's going on and why you're here," Mark announced as he pulled up a chair to the small table.

"That'd be nice," Suckow smirked.

Mark leaned back in his chair, folding his arms across his chest. Like the pit bull he was often described as, the detective cut right to the chase.

"Back in North Dakota, there's a large federal investigation going on targeting James Henrikson. We've got a bunch of fraud and some murders, and you are caught up in this investigation. We had a murder here in Spokane last month. I didn't come to you by accident. My killer left something up at that house and your DNA is all over it. No joke. Your van, the one you drive at work, is on video."

Suckow's eyes darkened as he stared at Mark. "You guys are scaring me now."

"You should be scared." Mark assured him. "You're looking at federal conspiracies to commit murder. Fraud. Life in prison."

"Shit!"

"Shit is right."

"I better get a lawyer," Suckow quipped.

"If you want to get a lawyer, get a lawyer, but today's your day to help yourself out."

"You guys are fucking out of your minds," Suckow said, looking over to Brian for a reaction. "I should have known it was going to be something like that eventually."

Brian shook his head in disagreement with Suckow's assessment of the accusations being lodged at him but held his tongue.

"Today's the day to help yourself," Mark reiterated.

"And do what?" Suckow asked.

"Talk about James, the murders." Mark urged. "His phone number is in your phone. That's pretty bad news."

"I know, because he was talking about a job way back when."

Mark intensified the pressure. "I'm going to read you your rights. I'd like to talk to you today, because I'm not kidding you, I have enough to book you for first-degree aggravated murder, murder-for-hire."

"Wow," Suckow was unfazed.

"I'm sure I know who is involved with you locally," Mark continued, "and we're moving forward. We're doing you first, but several more people are going to be raided tomorrow, and they're gonna be crying for help."

Mark explained that the walls were closing in and that any additional people associated with James who'd imminently face arrest would likely begin singing about K.C. Clarke's and Doug Carlile's murders in order to save themselves. Right now was the only chance for Suckow to beat them to the punch.

"I would rather pound James for the murders and let you help yourself out," Mark encouraged. "We're tearing your house apart tonight ..."

A maniacal giggle escaped from Suckow's lips. "I hope you fucking clean it too."

Suckow's attempt to appear tough and nonchalant seemed silly, as the situation was clearly no laughing matter. To hammer that home, Mark read him his rights, including his right to have an attorney.

"It would probably be smart of me," Suckow acknowledged. "That's some pretty serious accusations you're making."

"Well, that's your choice," Mark said. "But at this point, we're probably beyond accusations. You are under arrest. But you can help yourself out."

"You can take me to jail and settle this in court because you guys are out of your tree."

Mark laid one last card out on the table. "I'm not kidding you about this. I have your DNA and I can tie you directly to the guy who wanted him dead."

"I know you're not kidding. Jesus. Let's go to fucking jail and take it to court."

Suckow's goose was cooked—there was no way he was getting out of this—and his adamant refusal to help himself was no longer of concern to Mark.

"Okay. Here's what we're going to do. I have a search warrant to take a buccal swab to confirm the DNA from you. And then we're going to hang on to you while we get some more search warrants with your boss and do some searches at your work and at your home."

Suckow rolled his eyes, still unbothered. "Fine, whatever."

The detectives then left the room to gather materials for the swab. As soon as they did, Suckow again locked eyes on the camera. "Wow, you guys have lost your fucking minds."

Five minutes later, Mark and Brian were back with a DNA kit. Mark donned purple latex gloves as he explained he'd be swabbing the inside of Suckow's cheek. The detective reiterated a search was underway at Suckow's house, mentioning the discovery of a safe in his basement.

"I know you've asked for a lawyer, so you have a choice to make. You can provide us with the combination to the safe, or we can smash it to pieces to find out what's inside."

"I don't even know what's inside," Suckow laughed. "Smash it to pieces."

"Okay, no problem," Mark responded happily.

• • •

After detectives left the room, at 11:03 p.m., Suckow folded his arms on the table and laid his head over them to rest. For the next five hours, he slept.

"I've seen so many suspects fall asleep in that room," Mark later said. "It's like a load has been released from their shoulders. They knew it was coming, and they're finally able to release all of that tension. I knew when he slept like a baby that he was guilty as hell."

At 4:05 a.m. Mark and Brian walked back into the room, flanked by two uniformed officers ready to formally take Suckow into custody for the murder of Doug Carlile. After being handcuffed again, the tattooed giant was escorted away to be booked, fingerprinted, and fitted for an orange jumpsuit.

Suckow's peaceful five-hour slumber had morphed into a harsh awakening: January 13, 2014, was the last day he would ever enjoy being a free man. In one last show of defiance, he went on a 54-day hunger strike, losing over 90 pounds, nearly killing himself in the process.

"When I was arrested, I was so in shock that I stopped eating," Suckow said later. "I just didn't care to live anymore."

CHAPTER 52

Guns, Guns, And More Guns

At 2:00 p.m. on January 14, Sgt. Jeff Barrington and Detective Corey Turman pulled into the gravel driveway of 2122 East Lincoln Road, home to Timothy Suckow's co-worker Greg Burger and his wife, Beckie. If there was ever someone eager to see the police arrive unexpectedly, it was apparently Mr. Burger. Wearing a hunter green baseball cap, sweatshirt, and jeans, the 38-year-old burst from the front door of his brown rambler and ran down the driveway, waving his hands in the air. A much more subdued, petite woman with short brown hair followed behind him.

"I'm so glad to see you guys!" he said excitedly. "I've been waiting for you to show up!"

Before the detectives could even ask Burger a question, he was already leading them to a large, detached shop located behind his house. "I've been holding onto some guns for Tim Suckow," he blurted out.

Inside the shop, Burger led the detectives to a broken down 1959 silver Chevy station wagon, which he had been using to store approximately 20 of Suckow's firearms, including both rifles and handguns. Presumably, the station wagon had been a way for Burger to keep Suckow's collection separate from his own, which the Burgers admitted was quite extensive.

"My husband is an avid firearm collector," Beckie Burger

told the detectives. "Most of his are in a downstairs bedroom. But there are also some in an upstairs backroom." A later search of their home revealed that Greg stored a gun in nearly every space there was to put one.

Greg and Beckie explained that while watching the news that morning, they had been taken aback when it was reported that Timothy Suckow was arrested the night before. Prior to that, they hadn't even been aware of Doug Carlile's murder.

"We were shocked and immediately Googled the Carlile murder," Beckie said. "Greg was upset because a couple of months ago, Suckow asked him to store some firearms for him because he and his wife were having marital problems. Greg said he would. I wasn't here when Suckow brought them, but Greg told me they were out in the station wagon in the shop."

The Burgers hadn't yet called the police to share that information because Greg was busy at a dentist appointment earlier that morning. But the husband and wife now expressed their desire to help the investigation in any way possible. Barrington and Turman asked if they would be willing to consent to a search of their home, shop, and vehicles, for which both agreed. Greg also volunteered to accompany the detectives to the police department for further questioning.

Neither Greg nor Beckie had any inkling that the primary reason for the detective's visit hadn't been about any guns. Rather, it was because Greg's name had been listed on Suckow's alleged "checklist for murder" right above the words "wingman" and "wheelman." Finding out about Timothy Suckow's guns was just icing on the cake.

• • •

Detective Mark Burbridge was waiting patiently when Sgt. Barrington arrived with Greg Burger. Wearing blue jeans and a long-sleeved black Seattle Seahawks T-shirt, Mark introduced himself.

"Nice shirt," Burger laughed when he saw Mark.

Barrington, wearing blue jeans and a black windbreaker,

walked into the room, stuffing the last piece of a chocolate chip cookie into his mouth. The dark-haired, mustached detective set down a fresh cup of coffee in front of Burger with a warning. "It's a little hot, Greg."

"Wow!" Burger exclaimed after a sip. "It's like lava!"

More niceties be damned, as Mark cut right to the chase. "Greg, how in the world did you meet Tim?"

Burger explained that he had been employed with IRSE for nearly 16 years and worked with Suckow for the past six or seven of those years. Aside from their mutual interest in gun collection, however, the two didn't have much in common, and did not associate outside of work. In fact, according to Burger, Suckow was a loner and did not engage socially with any of their co-workers.

Approximately six weeks earlier, Suckow had asked Burger to store a cache of firearms for him, claiming that he was having marital problems. The request was completely out of the blue, but Burger felt compelled to help out. Plus, it was an opportunity to perhaps add some new artillery to his already massive collection. "I didn't want anyone to get hurt, so I said I would store them for him. I was maybe going to buy some from him, but I never did give him any money."

Of the guns that Suckow brought, Burger was positive that one of them was a .45 caliber 1911, which was the caliber weapon detectives by now knew had been used in the Carlile murder. Burger also admitted that Suckow had been back to his shop on more than one occasion since the night of the murder on December 15, but he could not remember exact dates, and he did not know if Suckow had removed or added any guns to the original collection—including the 1911.

"I don't babysit him when he's back there," Burger said.

When asked if he had touched any of Suckow's guns, Burger acknowledged that he had, then realized the predicament he could now be in if his fingerprints were found on a gun that might have been used in a homicide. "I've looked at everything he's … fucking God, man. Son of a bitch. I can't say for certain on the 1911, but I might have."

When detectives informed Burger that they would be

seizing and testing any .45 caliber firearms found during their search of his home and shop, he responded, "Go ahead. Take them all. This is a bad fricking deal, for what he did. I want to do whatever I can do."

Mark then shifted the conversation to the white van. Burger admitted that he had driven IRSE's van with license plate B95800G on numerous occasions, which he said was nicknamed "Sylvester." He also told the detectives that, as part of his job, he had most likely changed out the license plates on that vehicle at least once in the last 16 years. Mark immediately seized on this information and began to pummel Burger with a slew of accusations and warnings.

"Here's something you need to consider," the detective said. "The people who did this took the license plates off of that van before they went and did it. Then they put them back on when they returned it. This isn't uncommon for people to do, but where we get really lucky is, these guys don't wear gloves when they do it. Guess what they touch? The backside of the license plate. And when they put those back on, that side isn't protected from the weather. Are your prints going to be on the back of those license plates?"

"I've changed a bunch of plates out in that job," Burger shrugged.

"On Sylvester?" Barrington asked.

"If it's come up since I've been working in the shop," Burger admitted. "I've changed plates on trailers and everything else. I mean, that's part of our maintenance. If they give us new tabs or issue us new plates, I mean, I put them on there. So, maybe?"

"Greg, you're just scaring the shit out of me here," Mark said, his arms crossed over his chest. "Let me tell you how bad this is going to get. He's [Suckow] looking at forever, and the only way he's going to help himself out is if he starts talking about North Dakota and his getaway driver. I have a feeling you did go with him, Greg."

The detective moved his chair closer, placing his hand on Burger's left shoulder. "You need to trust me today. I'm your lifeline. I'm the one that's going to save you, because if you lie and walk out of this room today, the next time you see me, I'm going to have handcuffs. You're going to go away for two murders and a giant federal conspiracy, and you will never see your family again. So, today is the day. You were the driver."

Burger stayed completely calm but shook his head in disagreement. "I understand what you're saying. I one hundred and ten percent understand where you're coming from. But I did not drive that, sir."

He was bewildered when told his name was included on a "checklist" that had been found in Suckow's vehicle. Burger begged, over and over again, to be given a polygraph exam. He repeated his understanding of why he was there and why he was being questioned but remained consistent in refuting any suggestion that he had in any way aided or abetted Timothy Suckow in the murder.

Mark tried a different angle. "Did you ever hear him talk about it? Did you know it was going to happen?"

"No sir," Burger responded. "Never."

"Where were you that Sunday evening, December 15?" Barrington chimed in.

Burger was confident in his response. "Sunday? Easy. I was at home with my wife watching Sunday night football. That's what we do every Sunday."

The detectives then left Burger alone in the room for the next several minutes during which time his father called to let him know he was picking up Burger's 13-year-old son from school.

"Did you give them everything they were looking for?" his father asked.

"Oh, I told them where all his stuff is, where all my stuff is, the layout, every fricking thing I know," Burger assured him.

"Are you okay?"

Burger covered his eyes as he choked back tears. "You know, I'm fucking trying to see the good in people. I'm just disgusted."

•••

Unfortunately for detectives, none of the firearms discovered at Burger's home or in his shop were identified as the murder weapon. If the gun that killed Doug Carlile had been among the collection Suckow initially brought to Burger's house, it was no longer present. Moreover, without a detailed inventory of the collection to begin with, there was no way to determine if it had ever been.

Burger was cleared of any wrongdoing within a few hours, as no evidence was brought to light that linked him in any way to the crime. He had, in fact, been at home with his wife the night of December 15, watching the Cincinnati Bengals defeat the Pittsburgh Steelers 30-20. If Detective Mark Burbridge had ever conducted an interview with a truly innocent man, Greg Burger was it.

"When he looked me in the eye and swore up and down that he had nothing to do with it, and he's fighting back tears, I knew he was being completely sincere," Mark said later.

Questioning Burger hadn't been entirely in vain, though. The detectives now had solid proof that ex-convict Suckow had committed a felony by illegally owning firearms. No matter how long it took to piece together their homicide case, Suckow wouldn't be leaving his jail cell anytime soon. But unbeknownst to the investigators, the case was poised to unravel in ways that would make for a more thrilling movie plot than any real-life story.

It all started with a totally unexpected call from Erick Guerrero—the apparent former Mexican Mafia gang member who had previously denied any involvement with murder plots and referred to Burbridge as a "bitch ass fag" via text message in early January. By January 15, it seemed Guerrero was singing an entirely different tune.

"There's a bunch of drivers transporting James Henrikson's trucks over to Cheyenne," he told Burbridge. "One of the drivers knows a friend of mine, and called to tell him that Henrikson is asking around for someone to kill his wife. Sounds like he might also be trying to recruit some Russian guys from Chicago to do it. I'm calling you because I don't want my name involved with any of this."

Unfortunately, Guerrero refused to name the "friend" who had called him with this information, but with one person dead and a second one presumed to be, Burbridge wasn't going to waste time finding out if there would be a third. Without hesitation, the detective picked up the phone to call HSI Special Agent Darrik Trudell in North Dakota.

CHAPTER 53

Over-The-Top

The moment Spokane detectives notified Darrik Trudell of Timothy Suckow's arrest for the murder of Doug Carlile, a team was assembled consisting of himself, U.S. Postal Inspector Tom Irvin, and a host of additional state and federal law enforcement officers to execute a search warrant at the home of James Henrikson and Sarah Creveling in Watford City, North Dakota.

"We had to mobilize," Darrik later said. "We already had everything ready to go for the search warrant for the residence based on suspicion of felony firearm possession and financial fraud, but we were just waiting for the right moment to pull the plug. As soon as Spokane called to say Suckow was arrested, it was time."

On the afternoon of January 14, 2014, a convoy of police vehicles barreled down a remote, snow-covered gravel road leading to 505 17th Avenue NE. With nary a neighbor nor tree in sight, James and Sarah's brown rambler stood isolated, making it easier for the police to approach and surround the property.

As the convoy neared the driveway, a white pickup was slowly pulling out, its tires crunching on the snow and gravel as it departed. Behind the wheel was a wide-eyed Robert DeLao.

"I saw that it was DeLao driving the vehicle," Darrik said,

"but we weren't there for him."

Instead, the army of federal agents and sheriff's deputies fanned out across the driveway and yard, emerging from their vehicles dressed in tactical gear with firearms drawn, poised to confront whatever situation might await them. The whole scene may have seemed over-the-top, especially in the normally serene countryside atmosphere. Then again, every aspect of the case thus far had been over-the-top, and James Henrikson was far from a run-of-the-mill lawbreaker.

"It's standard protocol to wear tactical gear with police markings to identify ourselves as law enforcement and have our firearms when we hit a house to execute a warrant," Darrik later explained. "Plus, we were pretty confident this guy was involved in at least two murders. This definitely increased the level of risk for us."

Fittingly, the team opted to send in U.S. Postal Inspector Tom Irvin for the first contact with whoever might be inside. After all, who would be better to deliver a search warrant than someone from the postal service? Except, perhaps, one who donned a bulletproof vest and wielded a semiautomatic pistol, aimed and ready to shoot at a hostile target at a moment's notice.

But all the fanfare was for naught, as their knocks on the door went unanswered, and there were no signs that anyone was home. The search warrant authorized entry, no matter how, and a ram was used to break down the front door.

James and Sarah's 1,856-square-foot house was quickly swarmed by agents and forensic specialists, ready to scour the place with a fine-tooth comb. It didn't matter if it was a financial record, a gun, or even an innocuous dental invoice; investigators were determined to uncover even the slightest shred of proof that would provide probable cause for the arrest of James Henrikson.

It didn't take long. In the master bathroom, investigators located a huge gun safe standing wide open, displaying a plethora of firearms inside. Bingo. As a convicted felon, James Henrikson wasn't permitted to possess guns. That discovery was enough for federal agents to immediately apply for and obtain an arrest warrant for James—but only if they could find him.

Unbeknownst to the agents, James and Sarah had vamoosed from North Dakota just hours before the search had begun, heading toward new adventures in Cheyenne, Wyoming.

CHAPTER 54

A Lonely Woman

Sarah Marie Creveling was having one helluva year. It all began when her face, along with her husband's, was plastered across much of North Dakota on a flyer that detailed the various scams they had allegedly carried out together. Before the flyer, things had been going swimmingly for her and James and their company, Blackstone Trucking. They were making a fortune and had all the cars, jewelry, shoes, and clothing to show for it.

Siphoning money from their investors, Tex Hall, and Maheshu Energy, into their own coffers had been an exhilarating adventure for which neither had ever considered the possibility of getting caught. But that damned flyer had shattered that illusion like a hammer to glass.

Not long after, Sarah and James became the targets of a Facebook campaign dedicated to further exposing their extensive misdeeds, particularly their potential involvement in the mysterious disappearance—and presumed murder—of K.C. Clarke.

The public scrutiny was insufferable, but the situation deteriorated further in the fall of 2013 when Sarah—and the entire community—discovered that James was not only having an affair with the tribal chairman's stepdaughter, but that his 19-year-old mistress had also given birth to his son.

As if she weren't already humiliated enough, Sarah began receiving a series of lewd messages from men she didn't know. Shockingly, most of them included "dick pics." Eventually, Sarah discovered that someone had created a fake profile for her on Craigslist, portraying her as a "lonely woman" in search of a no-strings-attached fling because her husband was "often out of town." Not surprisingly, the profile picture of a beautiful blonde advertising a desire for casual sex attracted an inbox full of responses from men eager to show Sarah the appeal they would bring to the bedroom.

Understandably, Sarah grew concerned with the unsolicited communication, and reached out to the McKenzie County Sheriff's Office located in Watford City, where she spoke with Detective Mike Schmitz. Although they never figured out the culprit behind the bogus Craigslist profile creation, Sarah latched onto Schmitz as an ally in her corner—something she hadn't had in a long time.

Sarah also clung to her cheating husband like a piece of driftwood in a stormy sea, desperate to hold onto whatever was left of their life together. By December of 2013, she and James were actively searching for options to escape North Dakota as soon as possible. That's when even more horrific news rocked their world: Doug Carlile, a man they had been doing business with for months, had been murdered in his own home in Spokane.

Sarah would later describe her shock. "I was lying in bed, and James came in to tell me that Doug had been killed. I asked him if he was joking."

"I'm not joking," James had responded flatly. "He was shot a bunch of times."

• • •

Recognizing their time in North Dakota had indeed come to an end, on the morning of January 14, 2014, James and Sarah packed as much as they could fit into his truck and headed west toward Cheyenne, Wyoming, where James had already secured several business meetings. He had also arranged for a caravan of drivers to follow with Blackstone Trucking's fleet.

Halfway to Cheyenne, James and Sarah received a call from Robert DeLao, informing them that the feds had descended on their house in Watford City and were in the process of breaking down the door to get inside. Although the couple probably had an inkling as to why their home was being raided, Sarah called Detective Mike Schmitz to find out if he had any further insight. Her heart sank when Schmitz indicated that the situation was very dire for both her and her husband.

"I think it's probably best that you come back here," Schmitz advised.

The weight of everything finally came crashing down as Sarah faced the harsh reality that her extravagant lifestyle was over. If she was honest with herself, the 27-year-old surely also recognized that she was likely staring down serious legal consequences for some of her actions.

"I'm going back," she told James.

"Go ahead," he retorted. "There's nothing more for me there. I'm not going back."

In that moment, Sarah probably understood her short 2 ½ year marriage was also nearing its end. Though devastated by her sudden shift in fortune, she was no fool. The long, lonely 550-mile drive from Cheyenne back to North Dakota provided the perfect opportunity to contemplate how she would shift the narrative in her favor to protect herself from the fallout.

Of course, James already suspected that was exactly what his wife was planning to do. Before Sarah even exited the state of Wyoming, James was trying to recruit someone to kill her.

CHAPTER 55

He's There With Peyton

On Wednesday, January 15, 2014, Sarah Creveling drove herself to the McKenzie County Sheriff's office in Watford City, North Dakota, where HSI Special Agents Darrik Trudell and Derek Davis, along with McKenzie County Detective Mike Schmitz, were anxiously anticipating her arrival.

Darrik later described their planned approach. "Derek and I were in a conference room, waiting for Mike to bring her in. I had it all mapped out in my head. We were going to show Sarah all of the information we had, hoping she would crack. Literally three minutes before she got there, Mark Burbridge called."

"Hey, I've got reliable information that James is actively trying to find somebody to kill Sarah," Mark relayed.

It was a major setback to say the least. "Our whole game plan changed," Darrik said. "Derek and I called the U.S. Attorney's office and spoke with Gary Delorme to discuss our next steps. At this point, we believed James was responsible for the deaths of two other individuals, so we had to consider this a credible threat. We decided the best path forward was to be direct with Sarah about the information we received. We hoped she would take any protection we could provide to her, and that she would want to be honest and cooperate."

At first, Sarah didn't believe what she was hearing. "Isn't it true that you guys can lie to people in order to get them to talk to you?" she asked.

"Sure," Darrik answered honestly. "But there are still guardrails for that. I can't just come in here and make something up that's such a shock to the system, such as your husband is trying to have you killed."

As the gravity of the situation sunk in, Sarah grew increasingly upset, tears forming in her eyes before spilling down her cheeks. The agents did their best to console her.

"We told her that this was a lot to process," Darrik remembered, "and encouraged her to speak with an attorney. Because this was such an unusual circumstance, Detective Schmitz contacted a local defense attorney, explained the situation, and asked if he would be willing to talk with Sarah. Amazingly, this guy was willing to come and talk to her at no charge just to give her some guidance."

After emerging from a brief conference with the attorney, who had assured her that the threats to her life were indeed credible, Sarah seemed willing to share her story—at least the parts she wanted the investigators to know.

• • •

Sarah recalled meeting James for the first time when she was just 16 and he was 22. She had been working as a barista when the handsome older man caught her attention. With her blonde hair, wide blue eyes, and bubbly disposition, she quickly drew his as well. Although they'd flirted whenever he visited the coffee shop, their playful exchanges had never gone beyond that.

After high school, Sarah attended Washington State University, graduating in 2009 with a degree in social science. She'd then spent nearly a year away from home, first working as a tour guide in Alaska, then briefly residing in both Florida and Colorado, before returning to Washington in 2010.

While Sarah pursued her education and embraced life as a carefree young woman, James went through two divorces, served several stints in jail, and was now on probation. None of that mattered to Sarah who was still holding a torch for the convicted felon.

"I knew he was on probation for possession of marijuana, but he told me the charges weren't serious," Sarah told the investigators.

Not long after her return to Washington, the pair officially began dating. Within weeks, James convinced Sarah to move with him to Texas, where he hoped to start his own construction business. When that didn't work out, James next set his sights on the oil boom in North Dakota.

Once again, Sarah agreed to accompany him on this new adventure, and the couple arrived in North Dakota in June 2011. A few months later, James and Sarah were married. A few months after that, they were making money hand over fist with their new company, Blackstone Trucking. James and Sarah's story seemed to be that of picture-perfect success—until it wasn't.

Sarah admitted that, in her role as the de facto office manager for Blackstone, she had produced fake invoices and financial statements and sent them to investors and customers—but she said that these fraudulent activities were all done under James's direction. She further claimed that she hadn't realized these actions could be considered criminal conduct, though she acknowledged knowing they were ethically wrong.

"I knew we shouldn't be making up fake documents, but James said it was okay," she said, placing all responsibility on his shoulders.

Sarah conveniently skipped over the details of how she and James had also funneled hundreds of thousands of dollars into multiple shell accounts. Instead, she shifted the focus to how they had been the ones duped by a Spokane businessman named Doug Carlile.

● ● ●

Sarah told investigators that when James met Doug, he believed he was partnering with a very wealthy man. Doug had boasted of being worth millions, but it wasn't until much later that James discovered the truth: Doug barely had a dollar left to his name.

James, Sarah, and several others had invested hundreds of thousands of dollars in a land leasing agreement that Doug promised would yield an unrealistic 100% return within 90 days. Not only did they fail to come up with the money needed to secure the lease, but the 90 days came and went without any return on investment for anyone.

One of the investors, Renee Johnson, an accountant for Blackstone Trucking, threatened legal action if she didn't receive her $400,000 investment back along with the guaranteed 100% return. As a temporary solution, Doug Carlile convinced another Spokane businessman, Doug Helton, to buy out Johnson's $400,000 share. This placated Johnson for the moment, but she was still owed her promised return and had no intention of letting it slide.

Helton and one of his business partners invested an additional $476,800, adding their names to the growing list of people expecting to be paid back with money that didn't exist.

On top of all that, an obscene amount of money—millions and millions—was still needed if there was ever any hope of actually drilling for oil on the leased land. Ever on the quest for additional financial backing, Doug made a series of costly missteps, including being scammed by a foreign entity, losing tens of thousands of dollars of investor money in the process.

Desperate to reassure James and other investors like John Wark and Richard Curtiss that everything would work out, Doug agreed to a face-to-face meeting with the group at the Davenport Hotel in Spokane. There, Doug claimed that wealthy entrepreneur Pamp Maiers had committed to providing the necessary financial backing. Unwilling to continue taking Doug at his word, James and Sarah did some investigating.

"We looked up Pamp Maiers and called him," Sarah said. "When James asked if he had been working with Doug Carlile on financing an oil lease project, Pamp literally started laughing. He told us that Doug had ruined every business he had touched and that he would never consider working with him. James was very angry when he found out Doug had lied again."

But Doug hadn't stopped there. Soon, he was boasting that Doug Helton had offered to buy out all of the other investors just as he had done for Renee Johnson.

"I went to visit Helton myself," Sarah recalled. "I told him that Doug Carlile was telling all the other investors that Helton was going to buy us out. Helton made it clear that Doug was lying and seemed really surprised by that. Helton said all he wanted was his money back."

Following the frustrating experience in Spokane, James and Sarah traveled to Montana to visit with Larry Tormozov, a businessman from Washington who James had once worked with— and who also knew Pamp Maiers. When they mentioned their dealings with Doug Carlile, Tormozov laughed— making it the second time James and Sarah had been ridiculed for their association.

Sarah explained to the agents the reason for the desperate visit. "We knew that Larry was friends with Pamp Maiers, and James asked if he could help us get Pamp on board."

Unfortunately, Larry Tormozov had no interest in getting involved, either.

• • •

James was hardly an honest broker himself, but he'd never dealt with someone like Doug Carlile who seemed to lie and manipulate as effortlessly as he did. He was struggling to navigate this unfamiliar landscape and growing increasingly desperate to fix the situation.

"James called Doug," Sarah said, "and told him 'no more games.' He said that he was going to 'take him down, legally and financially.' He was extremely upset, but he never threatened any violence. James didn't really care about the money. The problem was more how Doug had lied, and James took it really personally."

Intentionally or not, Sarah had painted a clear portrait of her husband as a man who had everything to lose with Doug

Carlile around and everything to gain with him out of the way. She'd had a front-row seat to the escalating volatility between James and Doug.

When Doug was shot and killed by a masked intruder in his Spokane home on the night of December 15, 2013, James and Sarah were 12 hours away in North Dakota, sitting at home and watching Sunday Night Football with their friend Robert DeLao. Remarkably, the news reached James while Doug's corpse was still warm.

Sarah recounted the conversation she and James had that evening. "I was shocked and distraught that someone I knew had been killed. James was weirdly calm. I tried to ask him more questions about the shooting, and he told me that 'Doug's got a lot of enemies.' I wanted to know how [Doug's wife] Elberta was doing, but James just said, 'Doug lied.'"

Sarah explained that the Spokane Police Department had called to question James, but he stonewalled the detectives by dismissing the entire Carlile family as "compulsive liars." She reiterated James's troubling indifference to the situation, adding that he insinuated that Doug had perhaps deserved to be murdered because he "must have pissed off the wrong people."

Unbelievably, Sarah hadn't, not for a moment, considered that her husband could be one of those "wrong people" Doug had pissed off. Furthermore, even though she recalled noticing James and Robert DeLao frequently stepping away for private conversations in the days that followed Doug's murder—something she hadn't ever seen them do—Sarah never bothered to question what they were discussing.

Amid an atmosphere of tragic and strange happenings, Sarah's primary concern was herself. "I told James that I was done. I told him that I wanted nothing else to be put in my name, and that I wanted out of the trucking business. He told me to go to California, to get away for a while."

But instead of escaping to California, a month later, Sarah Creveling helped her husband pack up their belongings to flee to Cheyenne with hopes of starting a new trucking venture.

• • •

Sarah presented herself as a woman astute enough to understand complex oil leasing agreements, and successfully operate a lucrative trucking company—the fraud aspect notwithstanding—yet remained inexplicably blind to some rather rudimentary questions surrounding Doug Carlile's murder.

Whether genuine or strategic, James Henrikson's purported plan to have her killed conveniently provided the perfect smokescreen for her to evade the scrutiny she might otherwise have faced with investigators. With well-timed tears and plausible deniability, Sarah crafted a compelling portrait of naïve bewilderment.

Yet, one couldn't help but wonder: if the only thing Sarah truly knew about were a bunch of fake invoices and financial statements, would that be enough for James to want her dead?

• • •

With the imminent death threat looming over her head, authorities arranged for Sarah to be secured in an undisclosed location while they worked to find James as quickly as possible.

For the next two days, FBI Agent Eric Barker closely monitored James's phone activity under the authority of the arrest warrant that had by then been approved. James's phone had pinged intermittently from Cheyenne to Mandan, North Dakota, before finally settling in one location long enough to narrow down his vicinity. But there was just one more complication: that location was a large apartment complex with hundreds of units, making it nearly impossible to determine his precise whereabouts.

HSI Special Agent Darrik Trudell tried one last resort. "I called Sarah and asked if she had any idea who might be in that area."

Sarah knew right away, and the realization hit hard. "Yeah, Peyton has a friend who lives down there. He's there with Peyton."

"We found out later that Peyton Martin had driven to Wyoming to pick James up and bring him back to hide out in her friend's apartment in Mandan," Darrik said. "Sarah gave me the friend's name, and I was able to do a search and find out the apartment she lived in."

It seemed like it would be a simple task to find and arrest him from there, but James Henrikson wasn't about to go down that easily.

CHAPTER 56

Suicide By Cop

It was still dark outside when Darrik Trudell awoke the morning of Saturday, January 18, 2014. Anticipation and adrenaline coursed through his veins as he fumbled to quietly pull on a pair of jeans and a long-sleeved cotton T-shirt without waking his wife. Fourteen months into his investigation, the day had finally arrived to arrest the man he had been after for so long.

Local media had picked up on the story that the primary suspect in a murder investigation was on the run, and James's face had been plastered all across television screens and social media posts for three days. As a result, authorities had received reliable tips that James had been scouring Mandan, trying to squeeze cash from former business associates. As a wanted man, he knew that using his credit and debit cards would leave an electronic trail that authorities could trace. Not being able to access any of his money, James was growing desperate.

"He came in and warned me that I better come up with some money," one man reported. "He said he'd be back tomorrow. He was wearing a green, hooded sweatshirt."

That seemingly innocuous detail—his choice of attire—turned out to be one of the most valuable pieces of intel Darrik could have hoped for.

Following a quick briefing on the situation, at approximately 9:00 a.m., numerous representatives from the FBI, HSI, and Metro Area Narcotics Task Force descended on the Silver Lake apartment complexes at 4301 21st Street Southeast. Darrik, riding in a Chevy Traverse with fellow HSI Agent Randy Helderop, was passing by the front door of the apartment complex when out of the corner of his eye he spotted a man dressed in a green hoodie emerging from the building.

"All of a sudden, there's this big muscular dude that comes walking out the door in a green sweatshirt, and I'm like, 'Holy shit, Randy, that's him,'" Darrik later said. "Randy called out to everyone on the radio that we had identified him. Randy stopped the car in the middle of the parking lot, and I jumped out. As soon as I got out, all the other cars came flying up from all different sides."

Within a matter of seconds, James was surrounded with no chance of escape. "He had his back to us walking the other direction," Darrik wrote in a report. "We identified ourselves as police. I drew my gun and told him to stop walking and to show his hands."

James stopped walking but didn't turn around or show his hands as instructed. His hesitation sent a shiver down Darrik's spine, prompting the agent to repeat his command, this time with a heightened sense of urgency.

"Show me your fucking hands!" he bellowed.

Slowly, James began to turn around, revealing to the agents that both of his hands were stuffed inside the front pocket of his green sweatshirt. A smirk played on his lips as he pulled his left arm out and raised it in the air, only to abruptly shove it back into his pocket. Then he withdrew his right hand, holding a cell phone, before immediately jamming that hand back into the pocket as well.

Despite a throng of police closing in with their firearms pointed directly at him, and a cacophony of shouts—"Get on the ground!" and, "Show me your hands!"—James stood firm, like a wooden statue, his gaze fixed solely on Darrik.

Darrik later described the increasingly intense scene. "At this point, everyone else is out of their cars, their guns drawn. James had this faraway look in his eyes, and I could just tell he was thinking about something. So, he's hiding his hands and making sudden movements that could have easily gotten him killed. I knew that was exactly what he was contemplating. Suicide by cop."

It was a dangerous game that Darrik had no interest in playing. Confident that he was surrounded by people who could intervene if things went sideways in a hurry, he took a deep breath and moved in for the apprehension.

"I just said, 'Fuck it,' and I go up and grab him. He didn't fight me, but he's passively resisting. He's all 'roided up and I remember when I grabbed his arm out of his pocket, I thought, *Holy fuck this guy is strong.* So, I'm tugging on his arm and racking him on the back of the triceps to get him to go down, and he's not budging. I finally 'helped' him to the ground."

"Helped" was more like "forced," of course; nevertheless, James was no longer a threat, now flat on his stomach, his face having been accidentally planted smack into an icy puddle. "Hey, what's this all about?" he peered up with a smile, half of his face covered in a slushy mess.

"Why didn't you just show me your hands?" Darrik asked, his exasperation evident after the unnecessary physical confrontation.

"I didn't know what you wanted," James responded. "What would have happened if I hadn't taken my hands out, or if I would have just pulled them out really fast?"

"You know exactly what would have happened," Darrik answered. "Playing games like that can get people killed."

"Well, yeah, I was thinking about doing that," James admitted.

"I know," Darrik said.

Inside the apartment building, a distraught Peyton Martin watched as the dramatic scene unfolded. All the dreams of a glamorous life together on a yacht in Brazil collapsed like a house of cards with the sight of her lover being torpedoed to the ground by federal agents, placed into handcuffs and whisked away. If young Peyton fully grasped the gravity of the situation, it likely dawned on her that this was the last time she would see the father of her infant son outside of a jail cell or courtroom.

After the brief stand-off where it seemed James might prefer to die rather than surrender, he morphed into a much more cooperative suspect—sort of, anyway.

"We took him to the Burleigh County jail to interview him," Darrik noted. "The first thing he tells us is that his name is Cole Johnson. The minute we mentioned the murder of Doug Carlile, he asked if there was a deal on the table."

"Absolutely not," the agents replied.

CHAPTER 57

Everything Is An Absolute Lie

At 3:30 p.m., Cole Johnson, a.k.a. James Henrikson, was led into Room 2, a cramped space at the Burleigh Country jail that had barely enough room for two filing cabinets, a tiny round table that uncomfortably seated four, and a seven-foot-tall United States flag mounted on a gold base.

After seating a handcuffed James in a chair wedged into one corner of the room, Darrik fetched three bottles of water—a large Dasani for himself, and two smaller bottles of a generic brand for his co-pilot, HSI Special Agent Rick Hilzendager, and James.

"I'll be back in a second. Don't go anywhere. And don't spit in my water," Darrik joked.

"Which one's yours? Why do you get the good one and I get the shitty one?" James ribbed back, flashing his bright white smile.

Underneath the green sweatshirt, James was wearing his standard attire: a tight, short-sleeved royal blue shirt that accentuated his bulging biceps, light-colored jeans, and brown loafers. While they waited for Hilzendager to arrive, Darrik stood just outside the room, engaging James in lighthearted conversation to put him at ease and hopefully foster a rapport.

"How much do you bench?" Darrik inquired.

"The most ever, or right now?"

"Most ever."

"572," James answered nonchalantly.

Darrik exhaled loudly. "Jesus Christ! How much do you squat?"

"Meh," James said, "Something like 605 or 608 or something like that. Nothing real impressive, but I've never been real strong in my legs."

The two continued discussing workout and diet regimens, with James describing himself as extremely strict and disciplined when it came to taking care of his body. It was a fascinating juxtaposition—a clean-cut, handsome man sitting at a table in handcuffs, in custody for felony firearm possession and under suspicion of murder, waxing poetic over how important his health was.

Just as Darrik started settling into the casual back-and-forth, the real James—the manipulative, cocky one—emerged, momentarily catching him off-guard.

"So, tell me about Sarah," James stated, his voice taking on a sinister tone.

"Like, she's 5'10" or 5'5"?" Darrik tried to joke. "I don't know. What do you mean?"

James laughed. "You know what I mean. How is she, like seriously?"

Darrik shrugged. "I don't know."

"Ah, okay," James said, playing along. "Did you guys send her home?"

"I don't know where she's at."

James cocked his head to one side, pursing his lips. "Seriously? You guys know everything. You can't bullshit a bullshitter."

Darrik then flipped the tables. "What does she think about you having a girlfriend? That can't be good. What does your girlfriend think about you having a wife? That's gotta be a very delicate dance."

James cringed. "It is tough, that's for sure."

Just in the nick of time, Rick Hilzendager finally arrived to rescue Darrik from having to discuss Sarah's whereabouts, and to spare James from having to elaborate further on what a cheating liar he was.

Darrik and Hilzendager each took a seat around the circular table, flanking James on both sides. Hilzendager reached over with a key to free James's wrists from the gold handcuffs. As with every interview the agents conducted, they began by reading the perp his rights, asking him to provide written consent for questioning. After ten minutes of back-and-forth over what he was signing—essentially, whether he would choose to talk or not—James finally scribbled his signature in red ink, agreeing to talk to the agents.

"I don't give a shit, anyway," he said, tossing the pen back on the table.

Noticing that he hadn't yet opened the smaller bottle of water he had been given, Darrik slid his own unopened large bottle of Dasani over to James, subtly hinting that they were going to be there for quite a while longer.

Darrik began by focusing on why they were there in the first place, explaining that a search warrant had been executed at James's house for suspicion of felony possession of firearms. During that search, Darrik said, they had found ammunition, guns, and financial records that provided evidence for an arrest warrant to be issued.

"So, why did you guys search the house for financial stuff?" James asked.

"Because the information that we have is that you engaged in mail fraud and wire fraud with your businesses," Darrik answered.

"What's that?" James appeared genuinely confused. Of the many things he had gone to jail for, fraud had never been one of them.

"Well, using a wire or the mail to send information out that may not be accurate," Darrik explained. "Financial statements, profit/loss statements, and then how you structure your contracts. What name did you use?"

"What name did I use? Blackstone," James said.

"No, no. Your personal name."

"Oh, pfffff. I honestly don't recall to be honest with you."

"But it wasn't James Henrikson," Darrik countered.

The agents knew James was avoiding the answer, but they

chose to bypass the subject for the time being. The conversation had already gotten further ahead in the timeline than they intended. If they were going to fully understand everything that had transpired up until that day, they needed James to start from the very beginning.

When Darrik asked James to walk them through the reasons he had first come to North Dakota, the beefy weightlifter's arms tensed up. He leaned back in his chair, let out a loud sigh, and rubbed his hands up and down his thighs.

It was odd that James appeared uncomfortable with such a seemingly benign question, prompting Darrik to approach the subject from a different angle. "As you know, with all the stuff that's online, there's a lot that's going on out there about you. We've talked to a lot of people, but we've never talked to you. Nobody's got James Henrikson's side of the story."

"Why not?" James asked, his posture relaxing again.

Darrik reiterated that this was the first opportunity anyone had to hear directly from James. He emphasized that gathering all sides of a story was crucial to getting to the truth, and that many issues can be clarified through a straightforward conversation. Darrik's goal was to uncover the truth, not to place blame, and he needed James's input in order to do so.

First and foremost, James was asked to explain the complexities of his business, including the reasons behind establishing multiple entities, using aliases, and possessing multiple cell phones.

James was willing to share that the invention of "Cole Johnson" was a result of all the online harassment and vilification he and his wife had been subjected to in the past several months. "But is that defrauding people?" he asked.

"It depends on what it's being used for," Hilzendager answered. "So, start from the beginning and fill us in on what happened."

James repeated that the intense public scrutiny directed at him and Sarah had left him no option but to start using a different name. He pointed out that, despite the challenges, he still needed to make money and somehow try to keep his businesses operational. If using a fake name was the only way to ensure people would still work with him, then that's what he had to do.

Hilzendager tried once more to get him to discuss specifics about each of his business entities, but James deflected.

"Hey, uh, weren't we gonna talk about Sarah, too?" James asked, turning toward Darrik. "So, what's the deal with that?" Not knowing Sarah's whereabouts—or what she might have already told the agents—was eating him alive.

Darrik tried to quash this attempt to redirect their conversation. "I don't know anything about her. I want to talk about this stuff."

"I want to hear your side of it," Hilzendager added.

James wouldn't budge. "I can't help you any more than Sarah already has. She would know more … I mean, I trusted her to do all this stuff. She did a good job. So, that's why I don't understand what even led to the search warrant and all this other stuff … I'm not trying to be disrespectful, but you guys gotta ask Sarah. She knows everything that's going on."

Technically, James's claims weren't untrue. Sarah had already acknowledged that she managed the financial documentation and signed the contracts, although she had added the caveat that James directed how these tasks were to be handled. No matter how hard the agents tried, James wouldn't back down from his version of the story.

Furthermore, James wanted his questions answered. If the search warrant pertained to guns, then why were they asking him about his business contracts? How had all of this led to accusations of fraud? Who was accusing him of fraud? Where was Sarah? For the next several minutes, James and the agents danced around each other, neither side willing to give an inch.

"I'm not going to answer your questions," Darrik finally said. "You're here to answer mine. You're a sharp guy. You understand all of this stuff with the business. Nothing was in your name. We all know that. But you were the one who was out there making all the deals, getting investors. These are all just basic things, and the only person who can answer them is you."

It was still a no go for James. "I really don't want to talk to you guys about it. I know you're just doing your job, but everything I say, you're going to use against me. I mean, shit, I don't even have fucking access to guns and I'm fucking being charged with that, you know what I mean?"

"Okay," Hilzendager finally relented. "Should we start with that? What about the reports about witnesses saying that you've been out at the shooting range?"

"People say all kinds of stuff," James said, his hands intertwined in front of his mouth. "That's just what they're gonna do. I mean, look at the internet. People will say anything."

"So, did you ever go to the range?" Darrik pressed.

James continued to deflect, reverting back to his concern that everything he said would be used against him. He said he felt as though he was being blindsided. He also claimed that if the agents had simply come to his house without the pretense of a warrant, he would have gladly sat down and shared everything about his businesses with them.

Darrik scoffed. "Let's not act like if people just showed up to your house that you would talk to them. Spokane detectives showed up at your house."

"Well, that's a little bit different," James admitted. "I guess I don't even really know how to answer any of these questions."

"How about truthfully?" Hilzendager proposed. James laughed at the suggestion.

After several more minutes of talking in circles, the only thing the agents could extract from James was that Sarah held sole control over everything—from contracts and financial records to the guns and ammunition found at their house. The way he described it painted James as merely a bystander in his own life.

•••

The investigators then presented James with a formal request for consent to take custody of his two cell phones for a forensic examination. Although the phones had already been confiscated at the time of his arrest, the agents were required to inform him of the legal basis for retaining them. James had a choice—albeit a limited one: he could voluntarily consent to the seizure, or refuse, in which case the agents would seek a warrant. Regardless of his decision, investigators were going to keep his phones, and the examination would eventually proceed.

"What are you guys looking for in there?" he asked.

"We're going to look for your communications and any types of business correspondence," Hilzendager responded. Ultimately, James signed the consent form without fuss.

Perhaps as a sort of tease, Darrik had both of the phones on the table in front of him. James couldn't help but be curious if there had been any new messages that he may have missed—specifically, if Sarah had messaged him, or if anyone else had sent him information about her whereabouts. "I haven't seen or heard from my wife in … what? Three days?"

But there had been no chance for any new messages to come through. "I have them in airplane mode," Darrik said. "Trying to cut down on your data plan. I want to save you some money. See? We're from the government, and we're here to help."

Jokes aside, Hilzendager was ready to pin James down. Dressed in a cream-colored hooded sweatshirt, khaki cargo pants, and tan hiking boots, Hilzendager scooted his chair closer to James, trying to make eye contact. After over two hours in a small room together, James had been unable to look either Hilzendager or Darrik Trudell square in the eye for longer than a few seconds.

Because James refused to provide the agents with his own version of his background, Hilzendager painted a picture for him: James had come to the oilfields with a checkered past that he likely knew people would have a hard time understanding. Nevertheless, he had recognized a chance to make a fortune and figured out a way to make things happen.

Hilzendager expressed his awe at how well things had worked for James at first. Investors had quickly jumped on board, and lucrative contracts with oil companies and other contractors abounded. As long as money kept flowing, Hilzendager pointed out, nobody cared to find out more about

James's history, the embellished stories he told, or the different aliases he used. But when the cash started drying up, investors and business partners first got frustrated. Then they started digging.

Hilzendager said that he believed James had been on the brink of building something big—perhaps even an empire. But in his rush to the top, he'd cut a few corners and told too many lies. All of those things had inevitably snowballed and were now coming back to bite him.

"So, the real question comes in at the very beginning," Hilzendager added. "Were you out to rob people, or was it just a situation where you knew that if you told someone the 100% truth about your past that they wouldn't have been on board?"

Incredibly, James said he could not recall a single instance where he had lied to anyone. Furthermore, he demanded the agents show him proof that he had. "How do you know I lied to anyone? Who told you that?" he challenged.

While Hilzendager laid out how they had numerous documents and statements from witnesses that showed James had been deceitful on multiple occasions, he refused to name specific individuals. The agents were in somewhat of a bind. They were sitting across the table from a man they believed had orchestrated the murders of two people and was currently suspected of trying to do the same to his wife. Revealing names at this juncture could significantly endanger others.

But James was doing what he did best at the moment, anyway: playing games. Sitting in the tightest T-shirt the agents had ever seen, his biceps bulging out like roasted marshmallows between two graham crackers, his sole intention was to portray himself as smarter than his interviewers.

Round and round they went, the investigators pressing James to disclose whether his deceptions were driven by ambition or by intent to defraud. James, in turn, danced between challenging them to prove their claims, complaining that whatever he said would be used against him, and constantly deflecting the questions.

Although it seemed that James had the upper hand in the back-and-forth, he was merely revealing himself as the fool he truly was. No matter how much he denied, deflected, lied, and spun tales, he wasn't going to talk himself out of this situation as he had so many times before. This was the end of the line for him, whether he admitted to anything or not.

"Everything that comes out of your mouth is an absolute lie," Hilzendager challenged, "to the point that you don't even know the lies that you tell anymore."

The agents had managed to maintain their composure despite the frustratingly drawn-out game. But that patience had finally worn thin, and they warned James that they were finished tolerating the runaround. Both agents leaned in close, creating the impression they had him cornered with no way out.

For the first time, cracks appeared in James's outward display of confidence and defiance. From that point forward, whenever he attempted to deflect or spin the narrative in circles, the agents decisively cut him off.

Keeping James on his heels, Hilzendager abruptly shifted to the topic of Doug Carlile's murder. "Let's talk about Washington. Let's talk about what went wrong there. How did you get in over your head up there?"

James looked confused. "What do you mean in over my head?"

Hilzendager was blunt. "You hired somebody to have an individual killed."

James threw his head back and laughed. "No."

"How do you know Tim Suckow?" Hilzendager asked.

At the mention of Suckow's name, James's laughing stopped. His muscles tensed up and his blood ran cold. Silence hung heavy in the air for several seconds before he finally spoke. "I can't really answer any of those questions for you guys."

"Can't or won't?" Darrik posed.

"Can't," James repeated.

Darrik and Hilzendager exchanged a quick glance, ecstatic they had finally struck a nerve. Simultaneously, James swallowed back the bitter taste of the dawning realization that the investigators already knew far more than he anticipated.

He'd have to devise a new strategy.

•••

"I'm going to lay everything out on the table for you," Darrik said. "Here's where we're at. K.C. Clarke is missing, and you've been a person of interest in that case. We've got a financial case with all of this money with all of these companies. I told you that I've been investigating you for a long time. I've got a lot of puzzle pieces. Now we've got Washington, and we've got a person out there who is dead. We've got the trigger man arrested. We know that for a fact. It takes more than one person to do that. He didn't just wake up one morning and go, 'You know what? I'm going to go kill Doug Carlile.' Somebody had to put that in motion."

Gesturing with his hands, Darrik addressed one of James's initial questions about whether or not a deal would be put on the table. "I can't make those decisions, but I can make some phone calls to those who can. What I need from you today is information that I can go back with. Because right now, how this thing looks, James, is Tim's arrested and you're arrested. Those are two pieces to the puzzle. This ball is unraveling and it's not going to be held together. I don't think you want to see this thing unwind, and you're the one holding the bag on everything. This is your chance."

"You know this whole thing is going to unwind," Hilzendager jumped in, tossing wood on the growing fire. "It's coming. It's just a matter of time. As these cases progress through, everything is going to come out."

Darrik exerted more pressure. "Do yourself a favor. At least try to get yourself out from underneath some of it. Don't go down with the whole ship. Because when people start talking, guess what they're going to do when they duck for cover? They're going to point the finger at the people who are arrested. You. And guess who else? Suckow."

"Why would they point the finger?" James asked meekly.

"Because you're the one who has all this stuff out there," Darrik explained.

James was clearly still rattled with the turning of the tides, and he began mumbling his responses in a low voice. "Well, I want to see what kind of deal you guys can cut. Like, some kind of protection ... You guys don't understand what happened. You think you know, but you guys don't even have a fucking clue."

James indicated that it wasn't just him that might need protection, but that both Sarah Creveling and Peyton Martin were in danger as well—especially if any information he provided was somehow made public and was seen by the wrong eyes. It was a wild claim. Both Darrik and Hilzendager knew that Sarah was currently in protective custody due to credible intel that James was trying to find someone to kill her. The agents had to discern if there was someone else they needed to be concerned with, or if James was simply trying to manipulate the situation.

It was a conundrum, to be sure. James was finally showing signs that he might buckle if the right incentive was put in front of him. The agents weren't ready to place phone calls about making deals just yet, however. They still needed more. "If you walk away from us right now without telling us anything, where does that leave Sarah?" Hilzendager said. "At some point, there's going to have to be some give and take. Are you leaving Sarah out to dry if you just walk away?"

James brought his left hand up to his face to rub the sting of tears out of his eyes. "I wouldn't leave Sarah out to dry," he whispered. "I'm trying to protect her. Peyton too."

He also suggested that authorities might not be able to offer the level of protection required against the types of people he was dealing with.

For a moment, Darrik and Hilzendager went along with the possibility that James might not actually be the one behind everything—that perhaps there was someone more powerful, with more money who was in control.

"It's bigger than you, James," Darrik suggested.

"It always has been," he agreed.

"So, why are you taking all the responsibility?" Hilzendager asked. "By sitting there and keeping it all in, it puts everything on you. All the suspicion, all the fingers—"

Darrick completed his sentence. "You're the one taking all the arrows."

Neither agent believed James wasn't the kingpin, of course, but their bluff might chip away at James's facade. If they could create a comfortable space for James to shift blame onto a nonexistent boogeyman, perhaps he might reveal tidbits of truth. Still, they could not outright dismiss the veiled threats that James was issuing toward Sarah and Peyton.

Darrik kept at it. "I know you love Sarah. I really do think you're genuinely concerned about their safety. I don't think you're a monster, James. Let's do it this way. Are we concerned about a threat from North Dakota, or a threat from Washington state?"

"It's from California," James said.

"Is it organized crime? Is it Mexican Mafia?"

More uncomfortable seconds of silence passed before James whispered, "Organized."

The agents zeroed in on James's responsibility to safeguard his loved ones. In response, James pressed the agents for details on the protection they could offer him, Sarah, Peyton, and his infant son, Bently.

Darrik and Hilzendager explained that while authorities had many tools at their disposal, they couldn't act without more information about the specific threat. James repeated his concern that no one could guard against the people he was afraid of. For nearly two more hours, the trio exhaustively circled around these points, with neither side making any headway.

After over five hours of questioning, Darrik and Hilzendager were no closer to answers than when they started. Although the agents had hoped they were making progress, it was painfully clear that James never had any intention of providing truthful information. All along, his goal had been to deceive and extract information from the agents, primarily to goad them into revealing details about Sarah. Even his ten seconds of tears had been manufactured. Despite having indulged him longer than necessary, neither agent had given James what he wanted.

But their time with James hadn't all been for naught. Even though they didn't know it yet, their line of questioning would force James to do some hard thinking in his jail cell while awaiting his fate.

With both James Henrikson and Timothy Suckow safely tucked behind bars, each facing the pressure of their own circumstances, it was only a matter of time before one of them started talking. The only question was who would crack first.

CHAPTER 58

The Intelligence Of A Gnat

Back in Spokane, once the news of Timothy Suckow's and James Henrikson's arrests became public, more information flooded in from people who had once been too terrified to come forward. The first of them was Elton Hynson.

Like many before him, Hynson journeyed from Texas to chase the promise of fortune during North Dakota's oil boom. In 2012, he'd been hired on by Tex Hall to work at Maheshu Energy. For a time, Hynson had shared a trailer with a co-worker, Robert DeLao, and also frequently crossed paths with DeLao's friend, James Henrikson.

Any hopes he had of forging a friendship with either DeLao or Henrikson faded quickly when the young husband and father found himself reluctantly caught up in some troubling situations. For months, he kept his concerns to himself, but after seeing news reports of Doug Carlile's murder, Hynson finally mustered the courage to call the Spokane Police Department.

"DeLao had this guy who occasionally visited him," Hynson recalled. "He introduced him as Todd Bates. DeLao told me Bates was a roustabout for an oil company, but I knew that wasn't possible. I've been working in the oil fields all my life, and Bates knew absolutely nothing about the oil business."

Bates's frequent presence unnerved Hynson when the true purpose of his visits became clear. "Bates was Henrikson's muscle in North Dakota," Hynson said. "They called him in to beat up or intimidate people who were causing Henrikson problems."

At one point, Hynson said he had overheard Bates and Henrikson discussing a "job" that could "pay the same as the one in February 2012." Although he didn't have proof to back his theory, Hynson was convinced that the "job" they were referring to was the murder of K.C. Clarke.

"I became so concerned for my safety that I quit working for Maheshu and moved back to Texas."

The police in Spokane were as familiar with Todd Bates as they were Robert DeLao. Bates's criminal history was lengthy, including assault, theft, drug manufacturing, trespassing, and numerous traffic citations. It seemed that whenever Bates got behind the wheel of a car, he invariably found a way to earn himself a ticket.

It was also well-known that Bates and DeLao were friends. Bates's wife and DeLao's baby mama were besties and their families regularly spent time together. Whereas DeLao was small in stature, Bates was huge, with a bald head, thick neck, and beady eyes. If DeLao needed a muscle man to take care of business, Bates was indeed the person equipped for it.

Despite his intimidating physical presence, however, Bates was a bumbling oaf with the intelligence of a gnat. His vocabulary was limited to crude language and offensive slurs, and his favorite pastime was training pit bulls for dogfighting. The most pressing life concern for Bates—aside from his beloved dogs—was ensuring that he was never considered a "rat" amongst his drug-dealing inner circle.

Although DeLao was already on Detective Mark Burbridge's radar, Bates's name hadn't been considered until Elton Hynson's call. To add a further twist, just a few days later, Bates's own wife contacted the SPD.

• • •

On January 21, Theresa Bates, her father Thomas Weed, and her new boyfriend Daniel Serna met with Sgt. Jeff Barrington.

Theresa quickly explained that she and Todd were in the middle of a nasty divorce and child custody battle. Weed and Serna described Todd as an unstable and violent man who had often left Theresa's face and body covered in bruises, although she had never pressed charges.

Theresa shared with Barrington that throughout 2011, 2012, and 2013, Todd had made frequent trips to North Dakota, presumably to work in the oilfields with Robert DeLao and James Henrikson, whom Todd frequently referred to as "The Boss." Each trip had lasted two or three days, but there was always something notably missing when he returned.

"He said he's going up there to do some work, but he never came back with a paycheck," Theresa said.

When the news media reported that Doug Carlile's murder may have ties to the North Dakota oilfields, Theresa Bates took notice. Even more concerning was that she and her father observed that Todd's behavior had become increasingly paranoid and erratic after reports of Suckow's arrest circulated.

"Do any of you know Timothy Suckow?" Barrington asked the trio.

"No," they all said in unison.

"So, is there anything specific that makes you think Todd is connected to something here in Spokane?"

"Well, I'm kind of hoping he is involved," Theresa's father admitted. "That way maybe she can get her kids back."

If the intention was to cast a shadow onto Todd Bates in order to influence the ongoing child custody dispute with Theresa, Barrington didn't have time for it, and prepared to cut the meeting short.

"Is there anything else?" he asked, annoyed.

Theresa and her father fell silent while Daniel Serna squirmed in his chair.

"It seems like you maybe have something else on your mind?" Barrington prompted.

"He—he … he was hired to do something," Serna stammered.

Barrington's tone changed with renewed interest. "Why do you say that? How do you know that?"

"I was told," Serna responded.

"By who?" Barrington demanded to know.

Theresa looked at Serna as if she might throttle him, but then closed her eyes and sighed heavily. "Oh, gosh," she said.

"Just do it," her father urged.

"It was Robert," Theresa raised her hands in the air. "Robert is the one who set him up with all this. His boss was asking him to find somebody that would take care of the people that, um, were taking money from him. So, he called Todd, and um, had Todd come down."

"Robert called Todd?" Barrington asked for clarification.

"Yeah," Theresa said, dropping her hands back down into her lap with a loud slap.

"So, who told you this? How do you know that?"

"Todd," Theresa confirmed.

"Todd said 'hey Robert wants me to come down and take care of some guy'?" Barrington probed. "How did he say it? I mean, I don't want to put words in your mouth."

Theresa exhaled loudly, knowing that if Todd ever found out what she was doing at the moment, he'd likely kill her. "He told me that we needed money, so he said that Robert had some work for him. He said that The Boss said that if you take care of the person he is having problems with, that he would hire him out there for work."

Theresa continued, explaining that every time Todd went to "take care of the person," there was always some obstacle in the way that prevented him from carrying out the job — primarily, it was his own fear of getting caught. He didn't want to go to jail. Todd's inability to follow-through on his assignments also answered the question as to why he never brought home a paycheck from his "jobs" in North Dakota.

Furthermore, according to Theresa, each time Todd chickened out, "The Boss" became irate. In order to stay in "The Boss's" good graces, Todd had recruited another friend, "Goldie", to accompany him on at least one of the trips to North Dakota.

"He's some crackhead," Theresa said, referring to Goldie.

"Goldie, like … local Goldie?" Barrington exclaimed.

"Gold teeth?"

"Yeah," Theresa confirmed.

"We've definitely dealt with him before," the detective laughed.

Even with Goldie along for the ride, however, no one had ever been harmed. Instead, "The Boss" began sending Todd and Robert DeLao to Chicago to score some "China White" (heroin) in order to make "Roxy 80s" (oxycodone pills). One of the trips had taken a terrible turn when they had supposedly "lost" $10,000 in a drug deal gone wrong.

"Todd was scared," Theresa said. "He said that 'The Boss' told him that he and Robert were done, and Todd took that to mean that maybe someone was going to kill them."

•••

Eric T. Borders—known better to Spokane law enforcement as "Goldie"—was currently incarcerated at the minimum-security Airway Heights Corrections Center. During a visit with Sgt. Jeff Barrington, Goldie admitted to traveling to North Dakota with Todd Bates, but he could not recall if it had been in 2011 or 2012. The 43-year-old also acknowledged that the purpose of the trip had been to "take care of someone."

"Bates offered me $5,000 to take care of someone," Goldie said. "I took that to mean he wanted me to kill someone."

Goldie said that the pair had stayed in a trailer for a few days, but that a "Hispanic male" eventually told them the job had been called off. "After that, we just returned to Spokane."

He didn't know the name of the man, and he hadn't made any further trips to North Dakota—because, well, he'd been a little preoccupied sitting in jail on other unrelated offenses.

•••

Eight days later on January 29, Detective Brian Cestnik received a call from the Spokane County Sheriff's Office with news that an informant had come forward with another major revelation about the Doug Carlile murder. The person wished to remain anonymous and was eventually known as Confidential Informant #5.

"This person advised that they were afraid to be seen talking with me at their residence," Cestnik documented, "and they did not wish to have their name used. They know at least one of the people involved in this homicide case, and they are afraid of him. They agreed to meet me in an unmarked patrol vehicle in a parking lot."

During this covert meeting, CI #5 openly admitted to Cestnik that he had been involved in many crimes—both past and present. He knew coming forward could possibly shine a spotlight on his own activities, but the information he had to share was too damning to keep quiet. More importantly, though, the informant was terrified—not only with the information he knew, but also because of what might happen to him if anyone found out he was sitting in a police car ratting out a friend.

"I've done a lot of things," CI#5 said, "but I don't want anything to do with murder."

"Okay. What do you have to tell me?" Cestnik prompted.

CI#5 recounted a recent night spent with his longtime friends, Robby Wahrer and Ryan Cheers, the three of them throwing a few back and casually shooting the breeze. With Doug Carlile's murder making waves in the news, the topic inevitably came up in conversation. Nothing could prepare the informant for the jolt he felt when Wahrer casually confessed his involvement in the crime.

"Robby told us he was the one who was driving the white van that the police are looking for," CI#5 blurted out. "He said he drove a man to South Hill, and that he thought the man was only supposed to break Carlile's kneecaps, not kill him. Robby said he was parked at the end of a long driveway, and that he waited a long time. He couldn't figure out what was taking so long."

"Who was the man in the van with him?" Cestnik asked.

"He never said," CI#5 responded, "and we didn't ask. We didn't ask him any questions at all. We just listened."

When asked if he knew Wahrer's cell phone number, the

confidential informant provided the one he had. Unfortunately, however, he had no idea where to find Wahrer.

"He bounces from couch to couch and doesn't stay in any one place for long."

The confidential informant was right—Wahrer was a chameleon, elusive and hard to track. Fortunately, his phone wasn't. Alas, Detective Mark Burbridge's massive cell phone tower data dump from weeks earlier finally came in handy. Once Mark knew what to look for, Wahrer's cell phone number leaped off the pages—placing him directly in the vicinity of Doug Carlile's home at the time of the murder.

• • •

Another week passed before the Spokane County Crime Lab delivered more good news: latent fingerprints lifted from the license plates on the 1995 Chevrolet Sports Van, nicknamed "Sylvester," at IRS Environmental came back with a positive match.

Mark's hunch—the one he had shared with Greg Burger—had been spot on. The person who removed and replaced the plates the night of the murder had likely wiped down the front side but had overlooked the reverse. As Mark had suspected, the culprit had left prints behind. According to the lab, those prints belonged to 38-year-old Lazaro Pesina, the same man who had been in the vehicle with Timothy Suckow the night he was arrested.

Much like everyone else on Mark's list, Pesina had a lengthy criminal history. The detective soon learned that Pesina had worked with Suckow at IRSE for a time, but that had been several years prior. There was no plausible reason for his prints to still be on one of their license plates after all that time. An additional development came when it was learned that Robert DeLao had also been previously employed at IRSE.

According to other employees, the trio of ex-cons—Suckow, Pesina and DeLao—had formed a close-knit group, excluding nearly everyone else from their circle. Although Pesina and DeLao's time at IRSE hadn't lasted long, their friendship with Suckow hadn't ever ended.

From the moment DeLao volunteered to talk with police just days after Doug Carlile's murder—before anyone had a clear picture of the situation—Detective Mark Burbridge had been convinced of his involvement.

Since then, the suspect list had greatly expanded to include James Henrikson, followed by Timothy Suckow, then Lazaro Pesina, Robby Wahrer, and Todd Bates. Among them, Robert DeLao stood out as the clear common denominator.

•••

With Henrikson and Suckow already behind bars, Mark was eager to have additional warrants drafted and approved for the remaining four. Instead, he encountered a significant roadblock: the lead prosecutor at the Spokane County Major Crimes Attorney's Office demanded that Mark stop adding names to the list.

"Keep it small," the attorney urged.

Although the prosecutor had a reputation for shying away from tough cases, his refusal to proceed with this one felt like a slap in the face.

"This guy was so lazy," Mark later described his frustration. "I couldn't believe it. I've got two murders, and a minimum of six or seven arrests. I didn't care what he said, I was going after all these motherfuckers. So, I asked my boss, Lt. Mark Griffiths, if I could approach the U.S. Attorney's Office with the case. He said yes, so I went to Aine Ahmed. He had prosecuted several of my narcotics cases before, and I trusted him."

•••

While the U.S. Attorney's Office in Spokane mulled over the case, Mark upped the pressure on Robert DeLao.

"We made an unannounced visit to DeLao's house," Mark recalled. "He lets us in, and we sit down in his living room. In the corner of the room is this five- or six-year-old little boy, quietly playing with his toys. We're talking, but DeLao isn't giving us anything. So, I finally looked him dead in the eye, pointed to his son, and said, 'That kid is going to be 40 years old by the time you see him again if you don't get a good lawyer and negotiate a good deal for yourself.' He just stared at me, but I knew that got to him."

• • •

It didn't take long for U.S. Attorney Aine Ahmed to express his interest in the case. The very next day, Mark Burbridge received a call from a lawyer representing Robert DeLao. The warning Mark had given had clearly made an impact.

"I'm representing Robert DeLao," the lawyer said. "We might be interested in discussing a deal. Who's the prosecutor on the case?"

"Aine Ahmed," Mark said.

"Oh, fuck," the lawyer responded.

CHAPTER 59

But For The Grace Of God There Go I

At 44 years of age, Assistant United States Attorney Aine Ahmed had already experienced more than what some might in an entire lifetime. Born in 1969 in Sialkot, Pakistan, he was just two when his father emigrated their small family to Chicago to fulfill his dream of becoming a college professor.

After completing a PhD in sociology in 1977, the Ahmed patriarch secured a professorial position at North Carolina A&T University in Greensboro, North Carolina, where he would spend the entirety of his 40-year teaching career. Raised in the South, Aine and his siblings—an older sister and younger brother—developed distinct southern drawls that transcended their Pakistani heritage.

After high school, Aine enrolled at Wake Forest University (WFU) in Winston-Salem, just 30 miles west of Greensboro, where he was one of only three Muslim students in his freshman class. He was only able to afford the private school's tuition by taking out significant student loans and juggling part-time jobs alongside his daily class schedule. He attended as many summer school classes as possible, since they were cheaper than those offered during the fall and spring semesters.

Nearing graduation, on a whim, Aine applied for a researcher position with the CIA. Much to his surprise, he was soon called in for an initial interview at the headquarters in

Fairfax, Virginia. Realizing his parents might not approve of that line of work—and believing it unlikely he'd be offered the job—he kept the interview a secret.

"I remember going, and there were a lot of people waiting to be interviewed, most of them in military uniforms," Aine recalled. "The guy who interviewed me sat behind a cheap metal government desk and just stared at me. Finally, he asked if I had any relatives in Pakistan and if anyone would recognize me. It caught me off guard and I wasn't optimistic after the interview."

Despite those odd questions, he received an offer letter to join the Clandestine Division of the CIA—but only if he survived an obstacle course of additional interviews and procedures. After enduring eight months of polygraph exams, written tests, physical tests, psychological profiling, and doctor examinations—including one particularly uncomfortable visit with a proctologist—Aine grew frustrated and pulled the plug on his CIA career before it even began. His mother also eventually stumbled upon some of the secret correspondence Aine had been hiding, and in no uncertain terms, both she and Aine's father forbade their 21-year-old son from joining the agency.

"My father told me this wasn't going to be some sort of James Bond shit," Aine said later. "But I still kid my parents that I could have been Bond and probably retired by now."

With the CIA now out of the picture, Aine plowed forward with his education, earning a master's degree in public affairs at the University of North Carolina at Greensboro. Aiming to follow in his father's academic footsteps, he was soon accepted into a PhD program at George Washington University.

"I had decided to become a professor like my dad," Aine said, "but while I was considering which PhD program I could get into, my dad actually told me that I should think of an alternative profession because I would not make much money being a professor. That's how I decided to attend law school."

Even though it had never been part of his life plan, the 23-year-old finally left North Carolina to attend law school at the West Virginia University in Morgantown. What he didn't know then was that this serendipitous turn of events would be precisely what was needed to discover his true calling.

• • •

Several years passed before Aine had the opportunity to become a federal prosecutor. In the interim, he'd been a state court prosecutor in both North Carolina and Georgia and a Judge Advocate General with the Army at a base in San Francisco.

"While I was in San Francisco, I had been dreaming about becoming a federal prosecutor," Aine recalled later. "I'd applied and interviewed, but it went terribly. I'd given up, but then I got a call that there was an opening in Spokane. To be honest, I didn't even know where that was, and my wife did not want to go there. But she knew it had become a dream of mine, and we were worried that I'd never be given a chance again."

Aine was something of a unicorn in blue-collar Spokane, his Pakistani appearance and deep southern drawl garnering surprised looks both in the courtroom and the larger community. With cropped salt-and-pepper hair, piercing hazel eyes, dimples as deep as the ocean, a square-cut chin and a wide smile, the prosecutor exuded charm and wit. But he also had a habit that often landed him in hot water: a penchant for colorful language for which he seldom offered apologies.

"I once received a reprimand from the executive office for calling an employee 'indignant' during a meeting," Aine remembered. "I told my boss at the time that if I knew calling someone 'indignant' would get me in trouble, I would have called him a motherfucker instead."

At his core, Aine was driven by a deep passion for seeking the truth and ensuring that justice prevailed. Unlike most federal prosecutors, who rarely spend significant time in the courtroom, Aine thrived in the arena of trial, where his acumen and presence truly distinguished him.

He'd handled more than 600 federal cases, tried over 80

of them to verdict, and experienced numerous other instances of defendants pleading guilty in the midst of trial sometimes even right after his opening statement. Winning was never expected but he was proud to say he'd only lost three times throughout his career. Still, not every aspect of victory was worthy of celebration.

"The hardest part of a case for me is sentencing," he acknowledged. "I always think, *But for the grace of God there go I.*"

The expression, often attributed to English Reformer John Bradford in 1553, reflects the acknowledgment that witnessing another man's misfortune should serve as a reminder of one's own susceptibility to a similar fate.

•••

Were it not for Aine Ahmed's determination, the James Henrikson case would have never seen the inside of a federal courtroom. By 2014, he was serving as the Criminal Chief of the Eastern District United States Attorney's Office in Spokane—a well-earned position he had held for nearly three years. When Detective Mark Burbridge presented him with a complex case that posed significant challenges for even the most seasoned criminal prosecutors, Aine stood out as the only one willing to at least give it consideration. He did so largely out of respect for the detective.

"When the case began, I didn't even know that Mr. Carlile had been killed or about K.C. Clarke's disappearance in North Dakota. But I had worked with Mark Burbridge before and I knew him to be very competent and had great respect for him. He was flustered that the Spokane DA's office wasn't taking the Carlile murder very seriously. He also knew that I wasn't a prosecutor who demanded a case be packaged and presented in a bow before I took it. I wasn't sure it could be considered a federal case, but I agreed to look into it."

Aine soon discovered that not only did prosecutors in Spokane want to distance themselves from what had become a sprawling case, but that both state and federal prosecutors in North Dakota were more than happy to pass it off. Their hesitancy stemmed from resource constraints and the complexities of the case. Aine faced the same hurdles and more, but opted to address them head-on.

One of them was his own boss. "Why are we taking on a murder case that isn't necessarily extraordinary?" he asked of his most experienced trial attorney.

"I told him I thought it was bigger than that," Aine recalled. "Everything kind of blew up for me when I found out about James Henrikson's corporation, Blackstone. We knew they were committing fraud, but it seemed like that was Blackstone's primary mission: to commit fraud against basically everyone. It's not standard to charge a stand-alone murder case in federal court. You have to connect it to something like a RICO (Racketeer Influenced and Corrupt Organizations) or drug case. I felt I had a pretty strong case for RICO. I just needed to get the green light from Main Justice in D.C."

Inside the Department of Justice in D.C. is a unit dedicated solely to RICO cases. Together with FBI Agent Eric Barker, Aine spent hours preparing a comprehensive proposal. Unfortunately, when they presented the information, the head of the RICO unit and his deputy kiboshed the proposal outright.

"The guys we talked to weren't super helpful" Aine said later of his disappointment, "and didn't give me any alternative options, so I had to come up with something else. I spent about 20 hours flipping through the pages of a federal manual until I finally came up with a possibility: murder-for-hire."

Though the law supported the case, Aine had never prosecuted one like it, nor did he know anyone else who had. But that wasn't going to stop him from at least attempting to find out where to start. As such, he spent an entire day sifting through the popular legal research database known as Westlaw.

"There were literally only three other federal cases like it that had been prosecuted in the past ten years," he said later. "Two of the prosecution teams wouldn't return my calls, but the most recent case was out of New Orleans, Louisiana. It was a male and female team, and they called me back a week or two later. They were so responsive, very helpful, and gave me everything I needed."

Fortunately, prosecuting the case this way didn't require any formal approval from the brass at the DOJ. However, instead of stepping away, the powers that be decided to deploy an Ivy League greenhorn to assist. Aine had little confidence in the young lawyers dispatched from D.C., his experience showing them to be inept transients, many of them nepo babies to boot who stuck around just long enough to eventually land themselves cushy jobs at prominent law firms.

"In the meantime, they usually fucked up all their cases and blamed everyone else," Aine later remarked.

At first, Aine dismissed the new addition as just another routine intrusion from D.C. But it didn't take long to find out there was more at play. True to form, Aine handled the situation in a way only he could.

"This guy comes in, he's sitting in meetings, he's interrupting people, he's rubbing everyone the wrong way. I just kind of ignored it, until one day he told me he planned to take over my case. I remember saying, in a straight manner, 'You can suck my dick before that happens.' I don't even know why I said it, but he promptly reported me to his higher-ups."

While the incident wasn't one of Aine's proudest moments, it succeeded in getting the DOJ to back off and let him pursue the case on his own terms. But it was still only the beginning of what was going to be a long road ahead. With any luck, someone already on the list of suspects would decide to save themselves, start talking, untangle the remaining mystery of motives and alliances, and finally point the finger where it truly belonged.

CHAPTER 60

I Still Wish I Wuda Died

It was Timothy Eugene Suckow who blinked first. After spending nearly 60 days in jail, deliberately trying to starve himself to death, the pressure from his wife, JoAnne DesJarlais, and his attorneys finally caught up with him.

The day after Suckow was arrested in January, DesJarlais wrote a heart-wrenching post on her Facebook page: *I can't breath (sic) choking back the taste of complete desolation. I am shattered. WE are Completely. Fucking. Shattered. It will never ever ever be okay again.*

The man she had loved and trusted had betrayed and humiliated her in the most unfathomable way—by being accused of gunning down a 63-year-old grandfather in cold blood. Once Suckow was behind bars, the situation had only worsened. Federal prosecutors had since taken over the case, which now extended to inquiries about a second murder in North Dakota.

U.S. Attorney Aine Ahmed didn't hide his intentions with Suckow's state-appointed attorneys, Jill Nagle and Tom Krysminski. "I told them that the death penalty was an option and that I planned to recommend it," he later shared.

Suckow had refused to meet with his lawyers for several weeks. Running out of options and time, Nagle and Krysminski leveraged DesJarlais as the key to breaking through to her husband. The strategy paid off, but Suckow later resented all of them for "tricking" him.

"My lawyers were sweating me about the feds wanting to talk about K.C. [Clarke]," Suckow later wrote. "I stalled and just kept starving myself quietly. Then, one day my wife came to visit. I almost didn't agree to see her. All she did was cry and paw at the glass, telling me to do something. I relented. Just as I left the visit, my lawyers were in the next visiting booth. I'm sure they heard everything. I sat with them and agreed to talk with the feds. If the lawyers weren't next door, I wuda just continued my starvation. The way I felt, I didn't have but maybe a week at the most left. To this day, I still wish I wuda died."

A few days later, Suckow's lawyers notified the U.S. Attorney's Office that their client was ready to talk. Not only would he confess to Doug Carlile's murder, but he would also reveal the truth about K.C. Clarke's fate. In return, they sought a deal that would spare their client from either the death penalty or life imprisonment without any chance of parole.

In response, Aine Ahmed drafted a proffer agreement, outlining the terms under which such a deal could be considered. At the top of the list was the requirement that everything Suckow told them had to be verifiably true. Additionally, he had to agree to testify in court against James Henrikson and anyone else facing trial. But the most crucial provision was that Suckow would have to lead authorities to the location of K.C.'s remains.

If Suckow met these conditions, the federal government was prepared to consider a reduced sentence of 30 years. Three decades behind bars wasn't ideal for the 50-year-old, but it gave him at least a faint hope that he wouldn't leave prison in a pine box.

• • •

At 9:45 a.m. on Friday, April 25, 2014, seven people gathered around a square table in a cramped conference room at the Spokane Police Department, including Timothy Suckow, Spokane detectives Mark Burbridge and Brian Cestnik, U.S. Attorney Aine Ahmed, FBI Agent Eric Barker, and Public Defenders

Jill Nagle and Tom Krysminski.

Dialing in remotely were HSI Special Agent Darrik Trudell and U.S. Postal Inspector Tom Irvin. For the detectives in the room, this meeting had been four months in the making, but for Darrik and Irvin, it had been 17.

The atmosphere was nothing short of tense, verging on eerie. All eyes were focused on Suckow, who was dressed in dark red jail attire. He sat with his cuffed hands resting in his lap beneath the table, rocking back and forth and whimpering softly. Dramatic weight loss had left his skin an unhealthy shade of gray, and his sunken in eyes were shadowed by deep, dark circles.

Aine opened the meeting with a detailed explanation of the proceedings and a reiteration of the proffer terms and sentencing recommendations contingent on Suckow's cooperation. As Aine spoke, Suckow continued rocking while frequently wiping away tears and blowing his nose with tissues that had been provided to him by Detective Mark Burbridge. When Aine mentioned that the federal government would be seeking a 30-year prison term, Suckow gasped, and his face contorted with anguish.

"Why does it got to be 30 years? I'm already 50 years old. I have already done 20 years of my life because of this fucking illness ..."

"Mr. Suckow, let me just say this," Aine responded. "There is evidence to indicate that you have killed at least two people."

"I understand what you're saying," Suckow murmured. "I just don't understand why nobody is listening."

Tom Krysminski interjected. "So, we are clear today, I believe approximately a week ago, Mr. Suckow started taking some anti-depressants."

"It's for bipolar disorder," Suckow added. "I was diagnosed a week before I was sentenced to 15 years in federal prison back in 1991. No one would listen then."

Aine was genuinely sympathetic. "Okay, well then I am here to listen, Mr. Suckow. I make no assurances to you, but I am here to listen."

"I know," Suckow wailed. "It's just hurts, that's all. It just hurts."

"Then get it off your conscience by talking to us," Aine urged.

Suckow broke down further. "I didn't mean to do any of this stuff, and I don't know why I did it!"

For the next five excruciating hours, Suckow's demeanor fluctuated between torrents of emotion to a near-catatonic state. His responses were barely discernable, whether spoken between heaving sobs or in whispers. Nevertheless, he never balked at telling the truth, no matter how terrible it was.

• • •

Detective Mark Burbridge, wearing brown slacks and a navy-blue polo shirt, posed the first question. "Tim, how did you meet Mr. Henrikson?"

Suckow recalled that in February 2012, his friend Robert "Mugsy" DeLao had recruited him for a rather dubious job opportunity. "DeLao called me one day and told me his boss in North Dakota wanted someone beat up or something."

At the time, Suckow had been laid off from his job at IRS Environmental and was desperate for money, willing to do almost anything. He had booked an Amtrak train ticket to Williston, North Dakota, where "the boss"—James Henrikson—was waiting to pick him up. While the two new acquaintances chatted over a late-night burger, James revealed that his desire to have someone beaten up had now changed to needing that person killed.

"He was talking about Steve Kelly," Suckow stated. "I guess they had some kind of falling out."

He had tried to talk James out of such a crazy idea and encouraged him to hash it out with Kelly mano a mano. By the next morning, James seemed to have had a change of heart and no longer wanted Kelly dead. Suckow was relieved the situation had deescalated, but this also meant he wouldn't be making any money. Before he could voice his concern over a wasted trip, James assured him there was still work available.

"He came into my cabin that morning and was kind of angry at one of the guys that had been working for him," Suckow conveyed. "He asked me if I wanted to go to work, and I said, 'Sure.' On our way to his shop, he started telling me about K.C. That's when he asked me if I'd kill him."

Suckow told the attorneys and the detectives he had felt blindsided, but he was even more stunned when James revealed he had already envisioned exactly how K.C.'s murder would happen. Conveniently, K.C. was scheduled to visit the office that day to turn in his company gas card to Sarah Creveling. Seeing this visit as an opportunity, James planned to lure K.C. into the shop area with something he knew the 29-year-old couldn't resist—a shiny new bike.

"[James] brought me into the shop and there was a motorcycle in the corner," Suckow remembered. "He was telling me that he would bring K.C. back here, and that I should put a chokehold on him. Even though I was a big guy, I didn't feel very comfortable about doing that. I'm not a fighter. I'm not very confident about my strength. And then he told me that [K.C.] carries a gun, and I said I wasn't going to choke him out if he carries a gun. [James] said, 'Maybe you can hit him with something.' I looked around the shop and all I could see was a floor jack and the handle that comes off."

Suckow then paused for a moment and shook his head in disbelief as the awful memories of that day surged back into his consciousness like a tidal wave. "I still didn't believe it was real. I'm really not violent," he whined in agony.

Mark Burbridge encouraged him to go on. "Sometimes you just get in situations, Tim, and I understand that. I can tell this is very emotional for you and I'm sorry for that."

Suckow's shoulders trembled, and his voice shook, as he struggled to articulate what happened next. "[James] introduced me to K.C., and I shook his hand. Then James turned him around to take him over by the motorcycle. I didn't even think. I just grabbed the handle, and I walked up behind him, and I hit him in the back of the head. He stumbled and fell. He tried to get up and I hit him about three or four more times. He stopped moving. I could tell the last ... the last hit wasn't so solid."

"You say you hit him three or four more times," Mark interjected. "Where were you striking him at?

"In the head," Suckow confirmed. "I stopped and blood started coming out of his head and James, uh, James said we needed to stop the blood. I put the handle down and I turned around and ran over by the bathroom and dumped the garbage out and ran back, and I put the bag over his head. I tied it and then dragged him away from the puddle that was on the floor. I ended up dragging him into the bathroom and closing the door."

"How did you know he was dead?" Detective Brian Cestnik inquired.

"Umm," Suckow whimpered. "When I hit him the last time the hit wasn't so solid. It was like I hit a watermelon. It just kind of gave way and I assumed I crushed his skull."

Suckow recounted how he had gathered anything he could find—rags, towels, bleach, motor oil—to begin cleaning up the bloody mess. James, meanwhile, was busy making sure that no one came into the shop. He'd enlisted the help of two of his workers, Justin Beeson and George Dennis, to guard the door and not let anyone in.

In the midst of Suckow's efforts to erase the evidence, a panicked James soon informed him that K.C.'s friend, Rick Arey, was coming to the shop to look for him. James told him they needed to get rid of K.C.'s truck—and quickly. With a dead man still lying in the shop's bathroom and plenty of mess left to clean up, Suckow felt uneasy about leaving, but James assured him both the bathroom and the shop would be secured and guarded by Justin Beeson while they were gone. Suckow drove K.C.'s truck, with James and George Dennis following behind. The convoy traveled 48 miles to Watford City, where they abandoned the truck on a random side street as a temporary holding spot.

By the time they returned to the shop, it was late afternoon, and the calls from people concerned about K.C.'s whereabouts had stopped. Suckow spent the next few hours finishing the clean-up, but his next priority was disposing of K.C.'s body.

"I told [James] we had to get him outta here," Suckow recalled. "He goes, 'Yeah, I know.' Well, right there beside the door was a cardboard box that had had a toilet in it. So, I told him to give me a hand, and we put K.C. in the box and then we pushed it over by the door. Then we went outside and talked to George about backing his truck up to the door. We opened up the garage door and George backed in. James had to help me lift the box from the bottom into the bed of the truck. I also threw a shovel in the back."

Once the large garage door to the shop was opened for the first time that day, several workers approached the building to speak with James. As they stood there, not a single one of them had the slightest clue they were inches away from a freshly murdered corpse stuffed inside a toilet box. Two years after the fact, Suckow still marveled at the aloofness of the dozens of people roaming the yard that day, completely unaware of the heinous crime that had unfolded right under their noses.

The entire plan to kill K.C. had been sloppy with both Suckow and James flying by the seat of their pants as they navigated their next moves. Yet they'd so far managed to pull it off without raising any questions or attracting unwanted attention.

Incredibly, killing K.C. and cleaning up the shop had been the easy part. Finding a suitable location to dispose of his body would be a whole different ballgame.

CHAPTER 61

Sloshing

The North Unit of Theodore Roosevelt National Park in North Dakota—more commonly referred to as "The Badlands"—is located less than 30 minutes from Watford City on U.S. Highway 85. Spanning over 24,000 acres, the park's terrain is a magnificent tapestry of cliffs, buttes, and colorful rock formations. Vast swaths of prairie grasslands are roamed by some of the area's most remarkable wildlife, including bison, elk, eagles, and hawks. Visitors can enjoy hundreds of miles of hiking and horse trails, beautiful open skies, scenic viewpoints, and rustic camping sites.

What the breathtaking landscape was never intended to be, however, was a crypt for murdered young men. Nevertheless, it was where Timothy Suckow and James Henrikson decided to unceremoniously lay K.C. Clarke to rest.

Hours after the 29-year-old had been bludgeoned to death, had his mangled head wrapped in a dirty garbage bag, his blood and brain matter covered up with motor oil and bleach, his body crammed in a cardboard box, and his makeshift coffin hoisted into the bed of a truck, his corpse was driven by James, Suckow, and George Dennis to a secluded ravine hidden among thick brush and twisted trees in the shadow of the Badland's rugged cliffs.

Suckow described how they discovered what seemed to be the perfect spot. "We pulled off on a turnout so to speak, and there was a barbed-wire gate with a sign on it, something about the Badlands. Then James got out, took the gate off, and George drove through. We probably drove maybe a half-mile, three-quarters of a mile, something like that—it wasn't very far. It was out of sight of the road, and we stopped at one of the ravines. James and I got out, walked down into the ravine, and then he asked, 'Where do you think?' I found a spot by a tree, and I said, 'Right here is good enough,' and I started digging."

"What was George doing?" Mark Burbridge asked.

"George just sat in the truck," Suckow replied. "He was a trucker and he was tired, so he said he was just going to stay in the truck and sleep. We asked him to be a lookout in case any cars came by."

While Suckow dug, James stood by and watched. "James didn't help at all. I dug about all the way up to my chest. It was probably a three-and-a-half by two-and-a-half-foot-wide hole. I remember standing in the hole, and James asked how much this was going to cost him. I said $20,000."

"Twenty thousand?!" James had exclaimed, choking at the steep price tag.

Suckow had been unfazed by James's objection. "I told him, 'It's first-degree murder, man. It's the death penalty.' He was standing behind me while I'm down in this hole, and I asked him, 'Don't shoot me in the back of the head, okay?' He really should have."

When he felt confident that he'd dug a whole wide and deep enough, he returned to the idling truck to fetch K.C. "I tipped the box on its side so I could grab K.C. He was getting stiff by then. I cradled him and carried him down to the ravine spot. I remember hearing the blood sloshing around in the bag. And I got him down there to the hole. I took his clothes off, and I took the bag off his head, and put his clothes in the bag and I put him in the hole, facing down. Then I started putting the dirt back on him. When we were done I took the extra dirt and flung it all over the place. I laid a stick across the grave, and we left ..."

Suckow trailed off and a heavy stillness settled over the room. There was no way around it—this story was as depraved and nausea-inducing as any the highly experienced investigators and attorneys had ever heard. A collective shudder ran through them.

"I'm so sorry," Suckow whispered to the group. "I'm a really horrible person."

"I don't think you're a horrible person, Tim," Mark Burbridge said softly. "I think you made some choices that you wish you hadn't made and you're trying to do the right thing now. I think that's good."

Suckow's upper body convulsed in sobs. "Yeah, but I ruined so many lives. That's what bothers me."

"You have the rest of your life to try to fix that," Mark added.

"I don't have the rest of my life!" Suckow complained. "The rest of my life is all gone … The last couple of years I have wanted to commit suicide so many times."

The detective acknowledged that Suckow's life was going to be different but emphasized that didn't necessarily mean it was over. He reminded the weeping and remorseful hitman that many people were depending on him for answers and closure—especially K.C. Clarke's mother, Jill Williams, who still had yet to receive definitive confirmation that her son was dead.

● ● ●

After K.C.'s body was buried in the ground, George Dennis drove them back to the cabins in Watford City, where Suckow shed his dirtied and bloodied clothes and boots before taking a long, hot shower. By then, it was nearing 12:00 a.m., but there was more work left to do. They still had a bag full of K.C.'s clothes that needed to disappear, and Suckow wanted to get rid of his own clothing and boots.

Returning the conversation to the burial for a brief moment, Suckow recalled, "I asked for some help in carrying K.C.'s body, and James said he wouldn't, so I had to carry him myself. I am a big guy, but I was out of shape, so it took me a minute. I fell on my ass, too. That's how I got blood on me because when I fell, [K.C.] landed on me. I wanted to burn it all. George picked out a spot. I couldn't even tell you how we got there but there were a bunch of oil rigs around. He and James sat in the truck while I burned everything."

After that, they realized they still needed to find a permanent home for K.C.'s truck. Suckow couldn't recall exactly how it was decided to transport the vehicle to Williston, but once again, he drove K.C.'s vehicle while James and George Dennis followed behind for the 50-mile trip. The truck was ultimately abandoned near the corner of 4th and Broadway, a random decision that proved quite fortuitous to investigators.

Suckow detailed how he had deliberately left the keys in the ignition and the doors unlocked, hoping it would be stolen and sold for parts.

Instead, the truck sat untouched for four months until a curious Joe Uzdavinis had gone through the glove compartment and discovered it belonged to a missing man. That discovery alone had been the catalyst for authorities to begin seriously considering that K.C. Clarke's sudden disappearance hadn't been voluntary.

Before exiting the vehicle, Suckow said he used underwear he found in the cab of the truck and wiped down everything he had touched. He also removed K.C.'s phone and wallet from the center console. As they drove back to Watford City, he dismantled the phone, tossing its pieces out the window along the highway.

At last, at around 2:00 a.m., the men arrived back to camp, exhausted from their labors. Suckow walked into his cabin and realized that he'd missed several calls from his worried wife, JoAnne DesJarlais. He called her back and told her that he'd been busy working and was going to bed because he had a train to catch back to Spokane in nine hours.

Despite Suckow and James Henrikson's belief that they had successfully cleaned up the shop, buried K.C.'s body, and abandoned his vehicle, they had overlooked one critical detail that would ultimately become a significant factor in their undoing: cell towers. By the time they decided it would be a good idea to power down their phones, they were already halfway to K.C.'s burial plot. Worse still, K.C.'s phone—full of juice and a strong signal—had been in the center console of his vehicle the entire time. Suckow hadn't realized this mistake until he heard it ringing during his drive to Williston in the wee hours of the night. No doubt, the calls were from K.C.'s concerned friends and family.

All three phones, along with George Dennis's, had pinged off the same tower for several hours that morning—just before and during the murder—then traveled together from Mandaree to Watford City, where K.C.'s truck was first abandoned. From there, Suckow's and James's phones pinged all the way back to the shop, and later, halfway down U.S. 85 before they finally thought to shut them off and ditch them somewhere along the side of the road. Fortunately, it only took a few minutes to go back and search around in the dark to find them later.

When Suckow located and shut off K.C.'s phone, an entire day's worth of activity had already been captured by the cell towers. Starting with K.C. leaving his home in New Town that morning, the phone had pinged all the way to the shop in Mandaree, where it stayed for several hours while he was being killed. It then traveled to Watford City, remaining in one spot throughout the afternoon and most of the evening, before finally pinging along the way to Williston near midnight. After that, it never connected with another tower again.

Eventually, authorities would have hundreds of pages of cell tower data to piece together exactly what had happened that day. Even without Suckow's confession, that information alone was damning.

● ● ●

The morning after the murder, James dutifully arrived at the cabin to drive his hired hitman to the train station in Williston. Although he was accompanied by his wife, Sarah Creveling, he had neglected to bring the money he owed Suckow.

Suckow recalled that James had made a phone call to one of his employees with instructions to get money together and deliver it to him at the cabins. Not long after, a man Suckow didn't recognize arrived with a manila envelope that contained $10,000 in cash—only half of what James owed.

James promised he would have the second half very soon. He also assured Suckow that if he continued doing "jobs" like the one he'd just completed, there would be plenty of legitimate opportunities waiting for him in the oilfields—including a seat on a fictitious board of directors with a guaranteed income of more than $200,000 a year. Suckow, who readily admitted he wasn't the sharpest tool in the shed, had bought James's snake oil sales pitch hook, line, and sinker.

A few weeks later, he and his wife JoAnne drove from Spokane to North Dakota to collect the remaining $10,000. During their brief visit, the couple also planned to explore the possibility of making a permanent move to the oilfields.

"I was thinking [James] was going to take care of me no matter what," Suckow remarked. "My wife wanted to go with me because she's never been anywhere past Billings. I didn't see any harm in it. But I brought a shovel because I was going to move K.C. I didn't trust George [Dennis]. James told me not to sweat it."

After a day of sightseeing and looking at housing options—only to discover that the cost of rent was astronomical—JoAnne quickly determined that she did not want to move to North Dakota.

"I was kind of in agreement," Suckow said. "Yeah, there's a lot of money to be made, but it's bleak out there. I also wanted to put distance between me and K.C. I just didn't want my face being around."

But there was still one last piece of unfinished business he wanted to address before leaving North Dakota— making absolutely certain his fingerprints hadn't been left behind in K.C. Clarke's truck. To his great fortune, the vehicle was still sitting at the corner of 4th and Broadway in Williston. According to Suckow, his trusting wife remained blissfully unaware as he entered and rummaged through the truck.

"I told the wife, 'I'll be right back.' I had some cotton gloves on me and I had a can of WD-40. I sprayed the WD on my gloves and rubbed my hands together while I walked up to the truck. Nobody was looking. I opened the door and got in. I wiped everything I thought I had touched just to make sure. I looked behind the seat and I saw a case and I pulled it out and it was the gun. I thought, *Well fuck it, I'll just take it.* So, I took it, stuffed it in my pants and put my coat over it. Got back in my rig. The wife wasn't paying attention, so I pulled the case out and stuffed it behind the seat, threw the gloves in there, took off, and went back to Watford City."

The next day, James hand-delivered the remaining $10,000 he owed in a small box, the crisp bills rolled up and secured by a rubber band. After collecting the money, Suckow and his wife hit the road for the long drive back to Spokane.

• • •

Before Timothy Suckow could finish spending his $20,000 windfall, James had another "job" lined up for him. Thankfully, this time it didn't involve killing anyone. Robert "Mugsy" DeLao had also reentered the scene, again serving as James's personal messenger.

"It was one or two months later or so," Suckow said. "By then, Mugsy was over in North Dakota so if any messages needed to be transferred, it was Mugsy telling me. I can't remember if it was a text or phone call, but I got invited to come back over there to take care of the [Steve] Kelly thing. I didn't go there armed, so I didn't go over there to kill him. I remember Mugsy saying James wanted to muddy up his [Kelly's] name."

Suckow explained how he had driven to North Dakota on a Friday evening and shared a bunk with DeLao that night. As usual, James appeared early the next morning with marching orders for his minions.

"James told us he wanted some graffiti done," Suckow recalled. "They told me Kelly had raped his wife and he was a child molester. I think they said it to get me riled up. So, he wanted us to write, 'Kelly raped his wife' and, 'Kelly is a child molester' all over his business. I had some money on me, so

Mugsy and I went to the Walmart in New Town and fiddle-farted around and bought some spray paint."

That night, the pair drove to Steve Kelly's business, Trustland Oilfield Services, and proceeded to deface and vandalize as much of the building and property as they could, spray-painting vile accusations and words about Kelly—none of which were remotely true. They also opened valves on several tankers, spilling thousands of gallons of oil onto the ground.

James hoped the false accusations crudely scrawled in spray paint would catch a lot of attention and ultimately lead to the Kellys being ostracized and their business destroyed. But while repairing the reckless vandalism had been costly for Steve and Sandy Kelly, not a single set of eyeballs had actually seen it.

Suckow snorted, a flicker of amusement crossing his face. "The next day, Mugsy and I went back and we were all proud of ourselves. But from the road, you couldn't even see what we had done. James was pissed that no one could see what was painted on the buildings. So, that was a failure."

For that job, James had only paid him a measly $500—hardly enough to even cover the gas for his 1,600-mile roundtrip drive.

• • •

In late summer of 2012, DeLao unexpectedly appeared on Suckow's doorstep in Spokane, bringing worrisome news: authorities in North Dakota were probing the mysterious disappearance of K.C. Clarke. James Henrikson had been summoned to answer questions from NDBCI Agent Steve Gutknecht. Minutes after that meeting ended, James called DeLao in a state of panic.

"I guess whoever talked to James knew K.C.'s gun was missing," Suckow told the group. "So, Mugsy was there to ask me if I had the gun, and I told him I did. He said we had to get rid of it. So, I took him out to the garage, and I put the gun in a vice, and I cut the barrel in half and smashed a couple of pieces."

After dismantling the gun, Suckow drove to IRS Environmental and tossed the pieces into an asbestos waste dumpster. Meanwhile, back in North Dakota, an anxious James awaited confirmation of the gun's disposal. DeLao had snapped photos of Suckow destroying the weapon and assured James that its remnants had been dumped where no one would ever find them.

• • •

Though Suckow never had to travel to North Dakota for another "job," it wasn't the last time he would agree to do James Henrikson's dirty work. After spending several hours discussing the grim details of his actions regarding K.C. Clarke and Steve Kelly, he still hadn't touched on the subject of Doug Carlile.

CHAPTER 62

Piñatas

When the police probe into K.C. Clarke's disappearance failed to yield results in the summer of 2012, James Henrikson felt emboldened, confident he'd gotten away with orchestrating his best friend's murder. Timothy Suckow, on the other hand, spent the next 13 months torturing himself over what he'd done.

Yet, when DeLao—once again acting as James's intermediary—approached Suckow in the fall of 2013 with a new assignment, he was all ears. This time, it was closer to home in Spokane.

"Mugsy asked if I was interested in a job that's local," Suckow recalled. "I asked what it entailed, and he said it was to beat a guy up. I said alright and asked for the name and address. But I told him not to text me. He told me was going to set up a bogus email account and I said I would do the same."

A few days later, DeLao and Suckow exchanged their fake email account names via text message. "His was like *bigfatblackgirls.com* or something stupid like that. Mine was *kittykittykitty17*, and my password was *frogs are green*."

In one of the first emails DeLao sent in late September, he attached a photo of a picturesque mansion, along with an address: 2505 South Garfield Road. He also included the name of the intended target: Doug Carlile.

"Mugsy was referring to treating Carlile as a piñata, meaning just to beat him up," Suckow said. "Somewhere along the line, he changed it to killing him."

According to DeLao, James wanted Doug dead over a business deal gone wrong. But for Suckow, the reason was of little importance—it was money he was most concerned with. DeLao relayed that the amount James was willing to pay for the job was the same as he had paid for K.C. Clarke's murder—$20,000. Suckow described how DeLao spent the next several weeks sweetening the deal by telling him that Doug had mountains of cash and jewels squirreled away in the house on Garfield.

Although he assured DeLao that he was on board, the truth was that Suckow no longer had the stomach for killing. He had no qualms about robbing someone, though, and he soon began secretly devising a parallel plan for a home invasion. In his mind, all he needed to do was force his way into Doug's house, incapacitate whoever was inside, then raid the place for the money and jewels. If he was successful, he'd be able to tell James Henrikson and Robert DeLao to take their paltry $20,000 and shove it.

The first task on his to-do list was acquiring an extensive collection of tactical and SWAT gear. It was Suckow's belief that people were much more inclined to follow commands, such as "put your hands up" or "get on the ground" if the directives were coming from someone who looked like a police officer. But even if he was able to get Doug Carlile—and anyone else in the house—to comply, he still doubted he could pull off the heist alone. His next step, then, was to recruit a team.

"Laz Pesina, he's an old guy I worked with," Suckow explained. "He had gotten laid off from a job in Arizona or Utah or wherever it was, and I told him that I had a job for him up in Spokane. He didn't have a way to come up here, so I bought him a plane ticket. This was probably right around Halloween … Robby [Wahrer] then came into the picture. He's a good kid. He would rather be robbing drug dealers, but there's only so many drug dealers you can rob. So, Robby comes over and is bugging me if I had something going on, and I told him about this job."

With their motley crew now assembled, they had surveilled the Carliles's house and scoped out the surrounding area several times, but they were still missing one crucial element to make their plan foolproof: an untraceable vehicle. When neither Pesina nor Wahrer could secure a suitable option, Suckow resorted to using one of the vans from his employer, IRS Environmental. All it needed was a few cosmetic changes.

"The IRS van was a last-minute thing," Suckow added. "I went to Hobby Lobby, and I bought white masking tape to go over the lettering on the van. I bought some black construction paper for the windows."

Despite these purchases, the trio hadn't bothered to prepare the van ahead of time. Instead, on the night of December 15, 2013, they drove to a park near the Carliles's residence, where Suckow instructed Wahrer to remove the plates from the van, place the construction paper inside the windows, and cover up the IRSE logo with the white tape.

While Wahrer did his best to disguise the van, Suckow and Laz Pesina were busy in the back of the vehicle suiting up in a ridiculous ensemble of trench coats, helmets, balaclavas, bulletproof vests, and walkie-talkies. Suckow had brought along an AR-15 rifle that he claimed was only going to be used to scare Doug Carlile. However, he had also packed a .45 caliber pistol with a fully loaded magazine.

Suckow recalled how he and Pesina had lurked in the shadows of the neighborhood, mapping out an escape route leading away from the Carliles's back door. Meanwhile, Wahrer slowly maneuvered the white van around the neighborhood, occasionally pulling up to the curb in front of a house to wait for instructions over his walkie-talkie.

One of those instructions—sternly issued by Suckow—was for everyone to turn off their phones. However, Wahrer, bored while waiting for the masked home invaders to finish their business, decided to turn his phone back on to watch cartoons. That poorly timed decision, later corroborated by cell phone tower data, was what sealed his eventual fate.

●●●

Through a fresh round of tears and sobs, Suckow revealed that a number of factors could—and should—have prevented Doug Carlile's death that night, the most important of which, he insisted, was that he truly "didn't want to kill Doug."

Additionally, the home invasion Suckow envisioned as a sophisticated operation quickly unraveled into a series of absurd blunders. While one crew member sat parked in the van at the end of the escape route on Rockwood Blvd., giggling at videos on his phone, the other two crept through backyards in tactical gear, quickly realizing how burdensome their equipment was. Before long, they abandoned both their trench coats and helmets.

Suckow had brought along a single welding glove, intending to use it if he needed to break a window to avoid cutting his hand. But as he fumbled with his gear in the dark, he dropped the glove without even noticing. He'd also somehow lost the .45.

"I had a little light on the bottom of my walkie-talkie," he recalled. "I was poking around with the light trying to find this fricking pistol, and it was right out in the middle of the neighbor's yard." Amazingly, no one had noticed a strange man, dressed all in black, scrabbling through the wet grass and leaves frantically looking for a loaded gun.

When they were done floundering around, Suckow and Pesina finally approached the Carliles' back door, only to realize that no one was home. This gave the duo time to make one more adjustment. Suckow decided that the AR-15 he was carrying was too cumbersome. If he had to act quickly when the Carliles returned, the rifle would likely hinder his movements. On top of that, he had inadvertently brought the wrong ammunition for it.

"I figured out the shells I had didn't fit the shotgun," he said. "I didn't want to fumble around with a long gun, so I gave it to Laz and told him to bring it back to the van."

Although it wasn't explicitly said, Pesina knew that Suckow wasn't expecting him to return. Now on his own, Suckow crouched down in one of the far corners of the Carliles's backyard and waited. "I told myself that if they weren't home in two minutes, I was fricking out of there. Not more than 30 seconds later, I see headlights hitting the back fence as they pulled in."

• • •

"It wasn't my intent to shoot," Suckow whimpered. "I was just going to scare them and get them to the ground."

He recalled that it was Elberta Carlile who got out of the car first. As she made her way to the back door, Suckow impulsively ran up behind her. Somehow, she hadn't even noticed him. When he heard noises coming from Doug tinkering with the gate further down the driveway, the assassin in SWAT gear retreated into the darkness to wait for his prey.

"I watched Mrs. Carlile go in," he remembered. "She walked through the kitchen and went through a hallway to her right before he even came up. Right when I thought [Doug] was getting close to the door, I came out of my spot and came up right behind him. He tried to close the door with a backhand, just like we all do. I kicked the door, and it startled him. He turned around and I had the pistol pointed at him. I told him to back up and get in the house. He was reluctant, and with my left hand I just pushed him in the chest a little bit. He took a couple steps back and as we broke the threshold of the kitchen he had his arms up and he turned his head."

Suckow remembered that Doug had softly cried out for help from his wife. "Elberta, get your gun."

Out of the corner of his eye, Suckow caught a glimpse of Elberta slowly descending the staircase in the hallway, a look of fear etched on her face. Their gazes locked for a fleeting moment before she gripped the railing to frantically drag herself back up the stairs. Noticing the gunman was distracted, Doug made a sudden gesture that would ultimately cost him his life.

"Mr. Carlile moved his hands and I panicked," Suckow blubbered. "I fired—and it seemed like the fourth shot, and he didn't move. I don't know why I unloaded it. I can hear the casings bouncing off the floor. I turned to leave before he even hit the floor. I remember seeing him fall. It was like, I played *Call of Duty* a lot and on that game, you have a pistol and if you have a target that's far away you have to shoot at it a lot. It was kind of like the game in a way. I think that's why I unloaded because I had no practice. And then I ran. I ran fast. I picked up the trench coat and wrapped the pistol in it and ran back to the van."

● ● ●

Having allowed Suckow to navigate through his story with minimal interruption, the detectives in the room had some questions.

"When you went back to the van, what happened?" Mark Burbridge asked.

"I got in the van, and I told Robby to drive," Suckow answered. "I remember telling them that I couldn't believe I shot him, and that if he had just laid down, it would have been alright."

"Where did you go?"

Suckow said that they had driven a little ways out of the neighborhood and stopped so that they could remove the construction paper and tape from the windows and outside panel of the van. They had also changed out of the tactical gear they'd been wearing. After dropping Wahrer off at his car, Suckow and Pesina returned the van to IRSE and unloaded all of their belongings, including the guns, into Suckow's Tahoe. Pesina reattached the real license plates on the van, unknowingly leaving his fingerprints behind.

"I didn't mean to kill him," Suckow whined to the investigators. "I really didn't mean to kill him."

Mark, now exhausted from patiently sitting through hours of Suckow's emotionally tortured confessions, pressed on. "Where'd you guys go then, Tim?"

"I went to Mirabeau Park, and I went over to the rocks by the [Spokane] river. I took the gun apart and threw the pieces into the river." A search was later conducted of the river, but no traces of the gun used to kill Doug Carlile were ever found.

Aine Ahmed stepped in then, asking Suckow to confirm that it was James Henrikson who had, in fact, hired him to kill Doug. That was true, Suckow said, but he still maintained that he hadn't ever intended to follow through with it. Regardless of his claims, he had shot Doug to death. Suckow had even sent a text message to Robert DeLao afterward: *Tell the boss to watch the news.*

Once the deed was done, Suckow started asking about the money that was promised to him—$20,000 to be exact. The plan was to split it three ways with Robby Wahrer and Lazaro Pesina, and Suckow's accomplices were impatiently waiting for their cuts.

"They were fucking sweating me, man," he remembered. "I mean, Robby was really sweating me. I had to cut him off."

Ultimately, none of them ever received a single red cent.

"I was arrested the day before DeLao was supposed to bring me the money," Suckow said forlornly.

● ● ●

When the marathon session with Suckow finally came to a close, everyone breathed a collective sigh of relief, but there would be no time to rest. Although many questions had been answered, a great deal of work still lay ahead. Chief among their priorities in the coming days would be to locate K.C. Clarke's remains. At the moment, the only person who could help with that was Suckow himself—that is, if he could manage to get his emotional state under control.

● ● ●

Years later, Aine Ahmed, Mark Burbridge, and Darrik Trudell would still reflect on that day. Timothy Suckow had admitted to murdering two men he had never even met, in the most savage and merciless of ways. As he sat in the room confessing to his crimes, even Suckow had no explanation for why he had done it. And that, perhaps, was the most chilling part of all.

The aftermath was far-reaching, leaving no one untouched. Watching a man collapse under the weight of his own guilt and self-flagellation was unsettling, but it offered no solace. It served only as a stark reminder of the horror that could never be undone.

CHAPTER 63

His First Instinct Was To Kill Them

Thirty-nine-year-old Robert Andrew DeLao caved next. Of the three things he excelled at most, being a snitch and saving his own hide ranked number one. A close second was a knack for associating with criminal enterprises and repeatedly finding himself in trouble with the law. The third? Never learning a damn thing.

DeLao had spent a significant portion of his adolescence and adult life as a rough-and-tumble gangbanger. While he was willing to participate in just about any form of lawless shenanigans, his main specialty was running drugs for whichever kingpin he served at the time. This rogue lifestyle had kept him bouncing between juvenile detention centers, county jails, and federal prisons for the better part of his nearly four decades on earth.

He would later describe himself with dramatic flourish: "A charismatic, fallen angel, running around with Lucifer for the sake of adventure, creating a grand comedy of errors."

Although DeLao liked to portray himself as a hardened criminal with heart, Detective Mark Burbridge had a slightly more nuanced perspective. "You could meet him in a bar and spend all night laughing at his jokes," he mused. "But he'd have no problem slitting your throat in the parking lot and stealing your wallet."

DeLao had, in fact, slit someone's throat before—a member of a rival gang—though he claimed it was self-defense. "I was at a party when someone came from behind me and sunk a knife in my back," he later wrote. "He was accompanied by two others, both had knives. In the process of defending myself, I lost control and took the life of the one who first stabbed me."

Although he'd spent only a few years in prison for the act, he carried a permanent reminder inked on his back: a tattoo of himself urinating on the grave of the man he had killed. "I marked that on myself with the thought of showing the victim's gang (who I knew I'd see in prison) that I had no remorse…" he admitted.

From the moment DeLao walked into the Spokane Police Department three days after Doug Carlile's murder—insisting on his innocence and passing a lie detector test—Mark was convinced the brown-eyed miscreant was involved. It turned out the detective's instincts were right on the money. With others starting to sing like canaries, DeLao saw the writing on the wall and was determined not to be left out in the cold. True to form, he got in line to save himself and throw a few others directly under the bus while he was at it.

With assistance from his lawyer, Andrea George, and in cooperation with U.S. Attorney Aine Ahmed, an agreement was reached between the U.S. Attorney's offices in the Eastern District of Washington and North Dakota, as well as the Spokane County Prosecutor's Office, to provide DeLao the opportunity to fully and truthfully cooperate with law enforcement. If he complied with the terms—namely, telling the truth—he could potentially mitigate the charges against him as well as the punishment he would face.

DeLao knew he was going back to prison—there was no way around it. But he also knew from experience that cooperating with the feds could provide him a decent chance of turning it into a round-trip ticket back to the free world one day.

However, coaxing the unvarnished truth from Robert DeLao proved to be a formidable task, requiring several wide-ranging interviews with attorneys and investigators to peel away the layers of his confessions. The tale that ultimately emerged resembled a dark comedy, with a cast of characters who were as bumbling as they were dangerous. It might have even sold as a bestselling novel—if only the conclusion hadn't been so real and deadly.

•••

DeLao's story began in Spokane in November 2011, when things seemed like they were finally looking up for him. He had just been paroled after serving time for armed robbery and had promised himself and everyone else—including his longtime partner and the mother of his children, Barbara Gongyin—that he was finally "reformed."

Grateful for the chance to reintegrate with his family, he was determined to keep it that way. While attempting to play the role of stay-at-home and out-of-mischief dad, he began researching news about the recent oil boom in North Dakota. It sounded like there could be great opportunity if he could just get his foot in the door somewhere. He was elated when he heard through the grapevine that one of his old chums, James Henrikson, was already running his own business there.

From a cultural and socioeconomic standpoint, the two men couldn't have been more different. DeLao had spent his formative years in poverty, surrounded by domestic violence and substance abuse. Trouble—especially in the form of violent street gangs—was always lurking just outside his front door. In stark contrast, James's white, upper-middle class upbringing had insulated him from some of those harsh realities. He had to, and did, actively search for them.

Predictably, they both eventually settled into a similar criminal trajectory. In fact, jail is where the felonious duo officially became acquainted sometime around 2006. The notoriously ruthless gangster remembered feeling awestruck the moment he first saw James, whom he would later describe as an "effeminate pretty boy who hadn't yet come out of the closet."

"We actually both had a membership at Gold's Gym at

one point and I had watched him working out," DeLao told the lawmen, "but I never said anything to him until we were both in jail in Benton County [Washington]. So, I told him that I had seen him working out in the gym and asked him what kind of steroids he was using. He was real honest about that."

They had bonded over their love of fitness and weight training and DeLao thought he'd made a pal for life. However, when he was sent to prison and James shuffled through his own series of stints in jail over the next few years, the pair lost touch. Nevertheless, DeLao felt certain his good friend would give him a shot in the oilfields.

"I actually found his wife, Stacey, on the internet," DeLao said. "I told her that James seemed like someone who was chasing success, and that I wanted to work with him. She gave me his number and said, 'Be careful, he's kind of a liar.' She told me he had run off with some 21-year-old girl. I shrugged it off, like, 'Oh, well.'"

Much to the ruffian's chagrin, James ignored his calls at first. When he finally did answer, he claimed not to remember DeLao. It wasn't unsurprising, given they hadn't seen one another or spoken in almost six years, but the snub still stung.

"I gave him a rundown of who I was, and he was like, 'Oh yeah, yeah, yeah.' I asked him about what he was doing in the oilfields and told him that I needed a job. He told me that he was building his business but that he couldn't get me a place to stay. He said he would call when he had something available."

Undeterred, DeLao pestered James over the ensuing weeks. "I wanted to work with him bad, and I texted him constantly. I mean, I used all of my charm, all of my wit, to get this guy to like me. I kept hearing that people were making $5,000 a week, and I figured if I could get up there, I'd have it made."

Maybe he would have eventually given up, but the tables suddenly turned, and it was James who needed something. His foggy memory had conveniently refreshed, and he now fondly remembered DeLao as someone "everyone liked" and who "knew a lot of people." With that in mind, James was confident DeLao was the perfect guy to help him with a pressing issue.

"He called me up and said he was having some problems with somebody," DeLao remembered. "He asked if I knew anyone who could scare somebody. Because I always thought James carried himself a little feminine, and I heard that things were kind of rough in the oilfields, I thought maybe a truck driver was picking on him. He gave me the impression that he was in trouble, and that someone was threatening him."

Desperate to score James's approval, DeLao was eager to assist, but hesitant to take on the task of "scaring" someone himself. Instead, he reached out to a former co-worker, Lazaro Pesina, who in turn suggested their mutual friend, Timothy Suckow, for the job. It was a small world after all.

DeLao said it hadn't taken much for Suckow to get on board, especially after James dangled a few thousand bucks for the work. Suckow went to North Dakota sometime in February 2012, but DeLao professed ignorance about what went down during that trip.

"Suckow asked to meet with me after he got back," he explained. "I asked him how it went, and he just told me that he had done more than what he signed up for. He said he made $20,000, and that he had to go back up there to finish what he started. At the time, I still wasn't fully aware of the situation up there."

DeLao's initial assertions that he was uninvolved past a certain point and unaware of what happened were blatant lies. In time, he eventually acknowledged the awful truth: James had asked him to find someone willing to kill.

But DeLao swore he hadn't known that the intended target was switched at the last minute from Steve Kelly to K.C. Clarke. He also later admitted to helping Suckow get rid of K.C.'s gun, but he remained adamant that he had no idea where the young man's body was buried.

Those particulars aside, the key point for detectives was that he had organized a murder. What stung even more for DeLao was having to admit that he'd done it for free. Tragically, his resolve to stay "reformed" had lasted less than two months, and things only got worse from there.

•••

Throughout 2012 and 2013, DeLao became both James's right-hand man and his punching bag. When he was finally invited to visit North Dakota, he still clung to the hope of landing one of the lucrative oilfield jobs he'd dreamed about. After what he'd already done for James, surely he was owed at least that.

But James had other plans. First came the drug-running. James was hell-bent on starting his own pill manufacturing business and had purchased a pill press machine. Given DeLao's previous gang connections and experience in that world, James tasked him with procuring a massive amount—two kilograms, to be exact—of China White heroin.

"[James] said if I could get him China White, he had everything else covered," DeLao recounted. "Ryan Olness and Jed McClure were his partners. They had to find a machine that could produce 90 pills a minute. He said they had enough clients who would purchase 40,000 pills at a time, on a weekly basis … One kilo of China White can easily produce 20,000 pills. On the streets, they go from $85-120 a pop. So, we were talking like ten million dollars a week, literally. I was mind blown. I told him I would do it if he gave me a half-million-dollar interest free loan. I knew what I could do with that. That's how I wanted to walk away from this."

Even though DeLao's math was slightly off, it was indeed a hefty chunk of money they were looking at—if successful. Regrettably, DeLao's old connections in California, Texas, Washington, and Illinois weren't as reliable as they once had been—primarily because he had ratted out quite a few of his former comrades, and now carried the stigma of being a snitch. As the old adage goes, "Snitches get stitches," and the former Sureño was certain there was likely a bounty on his head for being a traitor.

Efforts to tap into alternative sources also fell flat, and they'd even botched purchasing the right binding agent to make the pills. They hadn't even been able to figure out how to work the pill machine itself. And when every attempt to get what James wanted failed, he punished those who disappointed him.

According to DeLao, this was a familiar pattern. James would demand he carry out a task; DeLao, or someone else, would fail. James would then berate, scold and "fire" him. In fact, the first time DeLao had been "fired" was a mere ten days after arriving in North Dakota. Rather than hold onto an ounce of his dignity, he would beg to get back into James's good graces. After a sufficient amount of groveling, James would eventually need something and let him back in. Lather, rinse, repeat.

A falling out between James, Jed McClure, and Ryan Olness put the final nail in the coffin of the "$10,000,000" pill operation. While McClure and Olness cut and ran, DeLao couldn't bring himself to do the same. The fact was that the once tough-as-nails gangster was terrified of the man he viewed as "effeminate."

Reflecting on James's temperament, DeLao remarked, in his thick Hispanic accent, "When people upset James, his first instinct was to kill them. I took him seriously, because I knew what he'd already done."

Bitter and angry that his heroin business had fizzled, James's back-up plans continued to escalate in risk and severity. Among them, fraud was the most prevalent. For James, no possibility was off the table if it meant he could scam others out of money. Not even something as simple as hauling water.

DeLao detailed just one of James's many fraudulent schemes, in which Blackstone Trucking's tankers were subcontracted to transport water from an oil company's fracking site. "We'd tell the company that it was a three-hour job. But we'd fill up the tanker and then go dump the water ten minutes away, but still charge the company for three hours of work. Man, it was just so stupid."

• • •

After several months of floundering while doing James's bidding, DeLao was hired by Tex Hall to work at Maheshu Energy. By all accounts, Hall was impressed with the short, charismatic Mexican and continued to reward him with increasing responsibilities and opportunities. Of course, the former tribal chairman had no idea that his trusted employee was secretly conspiring with James and Sarah Creveling to embezzle money from him.

"[James] started directing me to steal unauthorized checks from Tex," DeLao admitted.

He revealed that Sarah had also enlisted the help of the two administrative assistants who worked in the office at Blackstone Trucking, Mallarie Milano and Ashley Goodfellow. According to DeLao, the trio forged documents and exploited Hall while he lay helpless in the hospital.

In yet another audacious play, James and Sarah established Geneva Investments, a façade that allowed them to siphon money directly from Hall's accounts. With everyone contributing in one way or another, hundreds of thousands of dollars vanished from Hall's grasp.

The deception continued smoothly until Hall was released from the hospital and began asking questions. Soon, he found out that James was having an affair with his stepdaughter, Peyton Martin. When it was revealed that she was carrying James's child, all hell broke loose.

DeLao explained that Hall had not only abruptly severed Maheshu Energy's relationship with Blackstone Trucking, but he also ensured that James Henrikson and Sarah Creveling would never operate in the oilfields on the reservation again. True to form, James met that obstacle with murderous ambition, but Hall wasn't the only one in the crosshairs. He also wanted hits on Hall's longtime partner, Tiffiany Johnson, and their nephew, Lathan.

DeLao admitted that he had willingly played an integral role in yet another murder-for-hire plot. He and James had attempted to enlist Erick Guerrero, a driver for Blackstone and a self-proclaimed former member of the notorious Mexican Mafia.

"James wondered if he would get everything if Hall and Johnson were dead," DeLao said. "I was working in earnest with Guerrero to kill Hall, and he kept asking me why James wanted 'this Indian' killed so bad."

The arrangement came to a screeching halt when Guerrero got cold feet. Upon reflection, he realized he had no interest in being involved in a murder, especially with a couple of muttonheads like DeLao and James. Guerrero eventually shared this same information with investigators, who then warned Tex Hall and Tiffiany Johnson that their lives might be in danger. DeLao and James found out that Guerrero had coughed up the goods to the feds, but who had tipped them off with that intel?

"After the split, Peyton was always James's 'inside guy,'" DeLao shared. "Peyton would tell James everything. She was there when the feds had Tex and Tiffiany on speakerphone and told them that James was trying to hire Guerrero to put a hit out on Tex. James showed me the email Peyton sent him about it. Anything that happened in Tex's house, Peyton would report to James, and James was always one step ahead of Tex on everything."

DeLao stopped short of implicating Peyton Martin any further but noted that the young woman hadn't cut ties with the father of her baby, even after she learned he was plotting to kill her mother and stepfather. Perhaps James's promises of a luxurious life together in Brazil were still blinding her to the reality that was slapping her across the face.

CHAPTER 64

Crossing James Henrikson Was A No-No

Tex Hall, Tiffiany Johnson, and a nephew named Lathan hadn't been the only ones to wind up on James Henrikson's "kill list." Not by a long shot. Before them, there had been Steve Kelly, K.C. Clarke, Jamieson (Jay) Wright, Jedediah McClure, Ryan Olness, and Jill Williams.

Each time James uttered the words, "I want (insert name) maimed or dead," Robert DeLao was front-and-center, serving as the hitman recruiter. Timothy Suckow had been a successful hire in February 2012, but he'd opted out of any future assignments after handling the K.C. Clarke situation. Tapping Erick Guerrero again was also obviously out of the question.

DeLao instead had to scrape the bottom of the barrel to fish out Todd Bates, a friend from Spokane he had known for years. At first, Bates came on board with the promise of making millions of dollars as part of James's pill-manufacturing business. But when he was asked to procure China White heroin, Bates's efforts were just as unsuccessful as DeLao's had been.

After that setback, James wondered if Bates could be useful in other areas. "I asked him what he had in mind," DeLao recalled. "There was this guy who was operating Blackstone Crude. Jay was his name, but I can't for the life of me remember his last name. Anyway, there was some sort of conflict and what he wanted was for Jay to be assaulted."

Forty-six-year-old Jay Wright was a former Customs Inspector who left the profession after ten years in search of a more lucrative career, eventually landing in North Dakota during the oil boom. James and Sarah hired him to manage operations for Blackstone Crude—the company the husband and wife had established to divert work and money from Blackstone Trucking and its investors—but it never felt like the right fit. Wright had been networking on the sly and found a partner to launch their own venture, Power Crude Trucking.

Perhaps everyone but Jay Wright knew by then that crossing James Henrikson was a serious no-no. Then again, everyone but James was aware that job-hopping in the oilfields was commonplace; employers dealt with it regularly and there was never a shortage of people waiting in line to fill a vacancy. It seemed James was the only one who spent years seething and plotting to murder the employees who opted to go elsewhere.

When the ruthless boss caught wind of Wright's plans, he threatened legal action. Unfazed, Wright laughed in his face, his flippant mockery pushing James over the edge. Through DeLao, James offered Todd Bates a choice: $4,000 to $5,000 to assault Wright severely enough to land him in the hospital, or $10,000 to $20,000 to kill him.

DeLao recounted for investigators that Bates had traveled to North Dakota three times to carry out his assignment, bringing along a reinforcement each trip. The first was Eric T. "Goldie" Borders, the second, Irvin "Smurf" Fentroy, and the third, Sean "KK" Thompson. Outwardly, these were all big, beefy guys who looked tough and intimidating. In reality, not one of them could organize a trip to the corner store, let alone handle the job they were sent to do.

To pull off their devious plan, they had to figure out a way to get Jay Wright alone, ensuring there would be no witnesses. That involved attempting to lure him to a secluded spot with some enticing bait. The snag? Wright wasn't stupid. He had zero interest in playing cockamamie games and flatly refused to cooperate.

"Nothing worked out." DeLao shrugged. "Just nothing."

All three of Bates's trips to North Dakota ended in failure, but James always offered a consolation prize—when nothing else worked in their favor, he simply sent the crew over to further vandalize Steve Kelly's property and business.

DeLao revealed that James was also desperate to have K.C. Clarke's mother, Jill Williams, killed. "James wanted Todd and Goldie to conduct a home invasion at Clarke's mother's home to kill her and her boyfriend and retrieve the password for the findmissinggimpdaddy Facebook page. He also wanted me to find a computer hacker to get into the webpage and wipe it out." Thankfully, neither of those plans had materialized.

The team attempted to get a bit more sophisticated when James ordered a hit on his former business partner, Jedidiah McClure. "James was very passionate about having Mr. McClure killed, but he never told me why," DeLao recalled.

This time, James sent DeLao and Bates to Chicago, armed with thousands of dollars to pay a local kingpin known as "The Wiz" to carry out the murder. The Wiz took the money, promised to handle the job, and then promptly ghosted them—ignoring their calls and giddily bragging to everyone he knew that it was the easiest $10,000 he'd ever made. After that, Bates officially retired from the hitman business, his record a big, fat donut.

James wasn't ready to throw in the towel, however. There were still names on his list. His other former business partner, Ryan Olness, had bolted North Dakota back to his home turf in Arizona, making it a lot trickier to organize a hit on him without any local connections. Now that Bates was out, DeLao tried one last time to reengage Timothy Suckow.

By then it was the fall of 2013, and it seemed Suckow had shaken off most of the guilt that had haunted him since bludgeoning K.C. Clarke to death in 2012. That, and he was also strapped for cash. While he wasn't keen on a long-distance operation, he was open to handling something closer to home in Spokane. As luck would have it, James had added yet another person to the kill list: Doug Carlile.

•••

DeLao recalled that James's desire to have Doug murdered felt much more sinister than all the others; he had obsessed over it for weeks, talking about little else. But when pressed by detectives to reveal the motive behind James's fixation, the only reason DeLao could offer was money.

Maybe it was because everyone assumed Doug was loaded—he lived in a mansion, he and his wife drove expensive vehicles, and, of course, Doug had told everyone he was worth millions. Whatever the case, the approach to planning his murder was far more deliberate and calculated than any of the previous plots.

DeLao described how he and Suckow had created fake email accounts and used burner phones to communicate with one another for weeks, referring to Doug as "The Troll" in their exchanges. In one message, Suckow asked, "Do you just want The Troll wiped off the map?" James's response, relayed through DeLao, was a resounding "yes." The sooner, the better.

Their clever use of code words to evade detection included phrases like "piñata party" to suggest roughing Doug up, "trick or treat" for the planned surprise home invasion, "nailers" and "roofing tools" for guns, and "when the ink dries" to describe the spilling of Doug's blood.

According to DeLao's retelling, on the night of December 15, 2013, Suckow lay in wait while the Carliles attended a Christmas celebration at their church. Upon their return, Suckow ambushed Doug, shot him dead, then fled like the coward he was. In his wake, he left the one piece of evidence that would ultimately take them all down: the lone welding glove.

That same evening, in North Dakota, DeLao, Robin Benson, and a group of friends gathered at James and Sarah's house to watch the Kansas City Chiefs demolish the Oakland (now Las Vegas) Raiders 56-31 on Sunday Night Football. While the others were engrossed in the game, DeLao and James kept checking their phones, anxiously awaiting confirmation that the "ink had dried." That came later, with a cryptic text from Suckow, reading ,"Tell the boss to watch the news."

After finding out that Suckow had left behind a witness—Elberta Carlile—James became enraged. "James pulled me outside to the garage that night," DeLao recounted. "He asked me why Suckow did not kill Carlile's wife. He said he shouldn't have to pay him."

As fate would have it, he needn't have been concerned about that. Detectives had quickly pieced together the puzzle, and Suckow was arrested before the exchange of money could ever happen. The only thing they had to worry about now was the hefty price each would pay behind bars.

• • •

Though Robert DeLao hadn't wielded the floor jack that had crushed K.C. Clarke's skull or fired the .45-caliber gun that plunged bullets into Doug Carlile's chest, he certainly had blood on his hands. Whereas Timothy Suckow had sobbed and pleaded for forgiveness during his own interviews, DeLao remained unflappable, a fascinating study in composure.

If there was even a flicker of contrition or remorse for his actions, he kept it tightly hidden. His primary concern had always been himself, and it seemed the only regret he had ever felt was when he got caught. Not even the betrayal of the only person in his life who had dared to offer him a fair shake at success—Tex Hall—was enough for DeLao to utter the simplest of words: *I am sorry.*

CHAPTER 65

Are You Ordering Me To Do This?

The confessions of Timothy Suckow and Robert DeLao had served more than one purpose. First and foremost, they confirmed that K.C. Clarke was indeed dead. Next, they solidified the theory that James Henrikson was the mastermind behind the murders of both K.C. and Doug Carlile. It wasn't just that Suckow's and DeLao's stories aligned—and notably, they hadn't had the chance to coordinate their statements—it was also that they admitted their own culpability, with investigators holding ample evidence to corroborate those admissions. Moreover, the confessions had opened Pandora's Box, implicating a host of others.

What they had not yet done was lead the authorities to K.C.'s remains, a key condition of the proffer agreements both Suckow and DeLao had accepted. For U.S. Attorney Aine Ahmed, the absence of a body was a potentially major obstacle to his case.

"I was very worried we would not be successful without K.C. Clarke's body," Aine later acknowledged. "I was deeply vested in finding him … It was a must."

Though DeLao insisted he had no knowledge of the burial location, Suckow believed he would be able to find it, despite the passage of two years since he had been there. He and Detective Mark Burbridge spent a significant amount of time huddled around the detective's laptop, poring over Google

Earth maps to pinpoint the spot—zooming in on every outcrop and ravine in the unforgiving landscape of the rugged Badlands, hoping for a spark of recognition.

Perhaps because there had been nothing better to do than stare out the window as they transported K.C.'s body in a cardboard box in the back of George Dennis's truck, Suckow had paid close attention to the roads, signs, and landmarks along the way. He was certain they had driven about 20 miles south of Watford City on Highway 200/85 toward Theodore Roosevelt National Park, then turned down a dirt road across the highway from a scenic overlook. Making an educated guess on Google Maps, he pointed to what he believed could be that same road, marked as Roadway 842.

Suckow remembered there had been a barbed wire fence blocking the entrance with a metal sign that read, "DO NOT ENTER." According to him, James had moved the fence aside to allow Dennis to pull the truck through, then put it back in place.

"We drove another 100 or 125 yards from the main road," he recounted. "We came up to a ravine, and I said I thought it would be a good spot ... I remember walking through a row of trees, a row of high shrubs, then another row of shrubs to get to the crevice of the ravine. It had a tree there."

The area was completely hidden from the highway, Suckow noted. He had chosen a grassy spot about 12 to 15 feet away from the tree and began digging, tossing fresh dirt onto a blue tarp they had brought along.

It was near the end of February in normally frigid-cold North Dakota, and yet remarkably, the ground was neither covered in snow nor frozen. "It was really good digging," he said before adding, "That sounds sick."

Investigators were hopeful that Suckow's detailed description of the location was accurate, but confirmation would require springing him from the Spokane County Jail to identify the site firsthand.

"Can we fly?" he asked Mark. "You know, man, that is a long fucking drive."

• • •

Not because Suckow had requested it, but because it was deemed too dangerous to take him on a 12-hour road trip or a commercial flight, Detective Mark Burbridge brokered the use of the Washington National Guard's C-26 Metroliner, stationed at the Fairchild Air Force Base in Spokane. The C-26, a 20-passenger plane, was outfitted with specialized surveillance tools including radar and infrared cameras designed to track vehicles and capture clear, high-resolution images from great heights. Mark knew the plane well from his days as a detective in the narcotics division.

He later marveled about the aircraft. "This was a plane assigned for drug interdiction. We used it for some of our biggest stings. It can fly at 10,000 feet and you can't even see it. It has a surveillance pod that can laser in on something as small as a license plate and follow it everywhere."

Despite the extraordinary ability of the plane's equipment, it wasn't designed to detect human remains buried underground. But it was quick and efficient. And, if everyone was being honest, it felt pretty cool flying in it.

Piloted by Guardsman from the 141st Air Refueling Wing, the plane arrived at a private executive terminal at Spokane International Airport to pick up Mark, Brian Cestnik, Suckow, and his lawyers, Tom Krysminski and Jill Nagle. Less than two hours later, they landed at a small regional airport in Williston, where marked SUVs from the McKenzie County Sheriff's Department and HSI Agent Darrik Trudell were waiting to transport the group to the location that Suckow had pinpointed on Google Maps—a roughly 45-minute drive.

Handcuffed and clad in a blazing red jail jumpsuit, Suckow led a caravan of investigators and lawyers on an eerie tour of the Badlands, starting on a desolate stretch of highway that eventually wound toward a dusty, narrow dirt road, blocked by a barbed wire fence and a rusted DO NOT ENTER sign.

The group exited their vehicles and followed Suckow through tall prairie grass, past rows of shrubs, and down into a ravine where a lone tree stood, the surroundings exactly as he'd remembered.

Standing in the shadows of barren branches, with the wind rustling through the grass and dark clouds looming overhead, the place felt serene and untouched, as if nothing sinister could possibly have happened there. If K.C. was indeed buried somewhere in the earth beneath them, there was only one way to find out: start digging.

The challenge lay in the strict restrictions against disturbing federal land, rendering any attempted excavation a complicated process. Busting through layers of bureaucratic red tape for approval would have taken months—time no one was willing to spare. The resounding consensus amongst investigators was simple: they'd let the paperwork catch up to the shovel—especially if they could get the U.S. Attorney on board.

Aine Ahmed fondly recalled the conversation with Darrik Trudell. "Darrik called me beforehand and told me what he wanted to do. He said getting permission would take forever, so I told him it was better to ask for forgiveness if we got caught. Whenever we were on shaky ground, he'd call me up and ask, 'Are you ordering me to do this?' and I'd respond, 'Yes.'"

The cheeky exchange underscored an unspoken understanding between them: if things went sideways, Aine would gladly shoulder the blame.

"We were determined to do whatever it took," Darrik later said of the resolve to find K.C. "We spent a few days out there just digging holes with shovels. Then Mike Schmitz with the McKenzie County Sheriff's Department found a backhoe and brought that out there."

Toward the end of the backhoe excavation process, a park ranger came out to reprimand the crew, which also included NDBCI Agent Steve Gutknecht.

"You're out of control!" the Ranger screeched at the group of dirt-and-sweat-drenched investigators. "You've ripped up five acres!"

"Fuck off!" was Gutknecht's blunt response.

Recognizing he was far outnumbered and outranked, the

ranger wisely reconsidered his stance and quickly retreated. But the contempt directed at him stemmed less from his attempted interference and more from the mounting disappointment as efforts to find K.C. turned up zilch. Three full days of digging and five acres of national land had been effectively bulldozed, yielding not even so much as a bone fragment. They'd even brought in highly trained cadaver dogs to assist.

Aine later shared his frustration. "We had that whole area run through by the most preeminent cadaver dogs in the United States. These dogs had once located a body 12 feet underground, under a paved road. They ran the dogs for three days and could not find him. Nothing."

Timothy Suckow never wavered in his assertion of where he had buried K.C. He was just as surprised as anyone when nothing was found, leaving detectives grappling with haunting questions. Was Suckow simply mistaken? It was possible, though unlikely, given his detailed recollection of the landscape and landmarks. Being untruthful didn't seem logical, either—why admit to killing a man only to lie about where the body was buried? This left one final, more disturbing thought: had someone moved K.C.'s body between February 2012 and the spring of 2014?

CHAPTER 66

I Turned White

Much had been said about George Dennis and Justin Beeson to this point, but detectives had yet to speak with them directly. On May 5, 2014, HSI and NDBCI Special Agents Darrik Trudell and Steve Gutknecht, along with U.S. Postal Service Inspector Tom Irvin, tracked the pair down at an oilfield location west of Watford City.

Sitting in a tanker truck with Beeson at the wheel and Dennis in the passenger seat, they could have attempted a high-speed getaway. But they'd both known this day was coming and besides, there was nowhere to run. So, they watched, fear and resignation etched on their faces, as the three lawmen approached.

After the investigators introduced themselves and explained the purpose of their visit, they separated the two young men for questioning—Irvin climbed into the truck with Beeson while Dennis followed Darrik and Gutknecht to their car. Tucked in the backseat of a government-issued vehicle with two very serious and imposing agents was enough to turn George Dennis into a puddle.

"I'm scared for my life and the safety of my family," he cried.

"Our investigation hasn't uncovered any current viable threats to anyone," Darrik assured him. "But if there was, we would take precautionary steps to ensure the safety of both you and your family."

"You can also call 911 if you believe you're in any danger," Gutknecht added.

Fear aside, Dennis was ready to talk. For two years, the burden of guilt had gnawed at him, breeding paranoia and depression, nearly destroying him. Even if it meant paying a hefty price for his actions, the catharsis of finally speaking out was worth it.

"The first time I met Timothy Suckow was the day K.C. Clarke was murdered," he began. "James brought [Suckow] out and introduced him as the cleaner for the shop. There were approximately 30 other guys standing around in the yard when they got there."

Dennis said he couldn't recall exactly when K.C. arrived at the shop that day, but he remembered seeing K.C.'s familiar truck parked near the building. He also hadn't seen when James, Suckow and K.C. apparently entered the shop together. However, later that morning, James approached him outside in the yard, looking frantic.

"James told me to stand in front of the door to the shop, and not let anyone in," Dennis recalled. It was a strange request, he thought, but he nevertheless obliged the boss. "Then Suckow came out of the shop, and his pants were covered in shit."

"What do you mean by 'shit?'" Gutknecht inquired.

"Blood," Dennis replied. "I turned white. I was so shaken up. One of the other drivers, Keith, saw me and ran over to ask what was wrong. I couldn't even talk."

The next thing he knew, he was being ordered to back his own truck up to the shop's garage door so James and Suckow could load it with more unmistakable signs that something sinister had happened. "They lifted a big cardboard box and a blue tarp into the bed of my truck," Dennis told the agents. "They also put two or three garbage bags and a shovel in there. James got into the passenger seat, and Suckow sat in back. They told me to drive, and they both threatened to kill me if I said anything."

Once again, Dennis said he had followed orders, driving

on Highway 200/85 out of Watford City until James directed him to turn off onto a dirt road across from a scenic overlook. There, Dennis recalled, James got out of the truck to remove a rusty DO NOT ENTER sign blocking the gravel path that led further into the dark, desolate Badlands.

Hearing Dennis echo Timothy Suckow's account stunned the agents, prompting Darrik Trudell to propose immediately taking a road trip. "Are you willing to take us there right now?"

"Drive," urged Dennis.

One of two things could happen: If Dennis led them to a different location than Suckow had, it could warrant a fresh search. On the other hand, if they arrived at the same spot, it would likely confirm their gravest concern—that someone had moved the body, further diminishing the chances of ever finding it. Either way, the time to find out was now.

Darrik documented the brief journey in his reports. "We drove south of Watford City, over the bridge on Highway 200/85, then Dennis told me to turn onto a dirt road across from a scenic overlook location. There was a barbed wire fence that needed to be taken down. On a map, this road identified as Roadway 842. The exact road Suckow took us to."

They traveled a short distance on 842 until Dennis directed Darrik to stop. "I'm positive this is the location," he said, pointing. "I remember that tree."

Unfortunately, he had not seen the exact area that Suckow chose to bury K.C. "I never got out of the pickup. They threatened me to not do anything stupid. I watched them carrying K.C.'s body down the hill and then I lost sight of them. I think they were gone for approximately two hours." The young oilfield worker had fallen asleep during that time, his slumber drowning out the inner voice begging him to leave, to drive away as quickly as possible.

"George, did you know what James and Timothy did inside that shop?" Gutknecht asked.

"I knew they killed K.C.," Dennis nodded. "I also knew that it was his body inside the cardboard box." Still, he insisted he hadn't known they were going to do it and had only pieced it together afterward once it became obvious.

Darrik turned Dennis's attention to the subject of where Suckow had burned his bloody clothes and the clothes that he had stripped from K.C.'s corpse. "We received information that it was you who chose the burn site. Is that true?"

"Yes," Dennis once again acknowledged. "I was familiar with it because I had driven truck there for work."

"Where is it at?" Darrik asked.

"It's west of Willison, off Highway 2."

"What happened when you got there that night?"

"When we arrived, Suckow got out and burned two or three bags full of stuff. James and I stayed in the truck and watched."

The agents then drove Dennis to the McKenzie County Sheriff's Office, where he gave a recorded statement to support everything he had just admitted to. When asked if he would also provide a written statement, he whined.

"Can I please do that at a later time? I'm exhausted."

Understandably so, the investigators thought. They drove him back to where his truck was, still parked in the oilfield near Watford City. Inspector Tom Irvin even brought him a hamburger for dinner.

• • •

Justin Beeson was initially less forthcoming than George Dennis, but he eventually came around. While Dennis claimed he figured out on his own that K.C. had been murdered after it happened, Beeson admitted he was aware of the plan ahead of time.

"James told me he was going to kill K.C.," he said. "It was after we had the company meeting that K.C. was going on vacation. But he didn't tell me when it was going to happen."

However, Beeson knew as soon as it did. "James came out of the shop and said, 'It's done.' Then he had me go around the yard and collect keys to the shop." Presumably, to keep everyone out while Suckow cleaned up the mess. Like George Dennis, Beeson had followed orders from the boss. But gathering keys and keeping his mouth shut were the only things James asked of him.

Beeson's role in the aftermath was arguably much smaller than Dennis's, but of the two, he was the one who could have stopped K.C.'s murder from happening, if only he had reported James's murderous plans to the authorities. Sadly, out of fear of retaliation toward himself and his family, he had chosen not to.

Likewise, had Dennis left James Henrikson and Timothy Suckow stranded in the middle of nowhere, driven straight to the nearest police station, and told them exactly what was happening, at the very least it would have spared K.C. Clarke's mother two years of agonizing uncertainty over her son's fate. Even more significantly, if James and Suckow had been apprehended that night or soon after, it would have prevented Doug Carlile's tragic murder 22 months later.

The charge was minor: A misprision of a felony—not for participating in the crime, but for knowing about it and deliberately failing to report it to authorities. It carried a penalty of up to three years in prison, yet neither George Dennis nor Justin Beeson spent any time behind bars. They were just two scared kids, doing what they were told, terrified of the consequences of disobeying a killer. Enduring the guilt and silence for over two years, it seemed, had been punishment enough.

CHAPTER 67

Building A Case

By the summer of 2014, James Henrikson had spent nearly eight months in a North Dakota jail cell. After legal discussions between state and federal prosecutors, it was agreed that he would not face any charges in that state. Similarly, prosecutors in Spokane declined to bring charges against James or any co-conspirators involved. This left the entire case in the hands of Aine Ahmed and the U.S. Attorney's Office in the Eastern District of Washington. Soon, "The Boss" would be behind bars in an even smaller cell at the Spokane County Jail.

Meanwhile, state and federal investigators worked around the clock, collaborating to build an airtight case against James and his criminal enterprise. Preparing a prosecution of this magnitude was no simple task. More than a dozen individuals had been part of his orbit, their offenses ranging from minor infractions to murder. Sooner or later, justice would come knocking for them all.

Despite tireless efforts from Spokane Detectives Mark Burbridge and Brian Cestnik, HSI Special Agent Darrik Trudell, FBI Agent Eric Barker, and many others, it still took 18 months of meticulous work. Together, they synthesized countless pieces of evidence and conducted dozens of interviews. Much of the work also involved analyzing thousands of pages of phone records, digital data, and financial transactions, each piece requiring careful examination to connect the dots. The result was a case file spanning more than 30,000 pages.

•••

An extensive search was finally conducted at Tex Hall's shop in Mandaree. Although a significant amount of time had passed since K.C. Clarke had been bludgeoned to death that fateful morning in February 2012, investigators were cautiously optimistic that some trace of his DNA might still be detected in the porous concrete floor.

It was another longshot met with disappointment. "There was a machine brought up to Hall's shop to find any DNA, but nothing was found," Aine Ahmed later said.

The tenacious prosecutor eventually came to terms with the fact that he would have to present his case without a body or DNA evidence. There was no question that K.C. had been murdered—and that it had happened inside that shop—but as much as everyone hated to admit it, the desperate search for what remained of him had to end at some point. Their only option was to keep moving forward.

•••

There were still two people left to answer for their role in Doug Carlile's murder. In September 2014, a team of FBI agents, led by Eric Barker, arrested Lazaro Pesina in Walla Walla, Washington. Pesina had been evading the authorities for months, careful not to stay in one place for too long, knowing all along it was only a matter of time before they caught up with him.

Pesina chose to remain silent, but there was no escaping the evidence against him. His fingerprints were on the license plate of the van used the night Doug was killed. That evidence, reinforced by Timothy Suckow's detailed confession, left him with no way out.

Getaway driver Robbie Wahrer was apprehended in Spokane. Word spread quickly that it was Suckow who had ratted him out. Wahrer's trusted comrades—a few of whom were also conveniently incarcerated at the Spokane County Jail on other charges—began a pressure campaign to force Suckow into recanting the statements he had made regarding Wahrer's involvement. Their efforts nearly succeeded.

Intimidated by the not-so-subtle "do this or else" messaging that seeped through the jail walls like smoke, Suckow had eventually penned a statement to absolve Wahrer of any wrongdoing. The letter then made its way to Wahrer's lawyer, who quickly forwarded it to Suckow's new court-appointed defense counsel, Roger Peven.

In response, Peven conferred with his client, who said he'd written the statement under duress, a concession to those threatening him. Suckow reiterated that Wahrer had been the getaway driver the night Doug was killed—a fact also corroborated by cell phone records.

Peven then passed the information along to FBI Agent Eric Barker. Once the situation was in federal hands, the jailhouse pressure on Suckow quickly subsided. Witness tampering is a serious offense—a charge even Wahrer's staunchest allies wanted no part of. In the end, Wahrer followed the path of those before him, admitting his involvement and praying for a reasonable outcome.

• • •

Todd Bates was next. At 41, he wasn't exactly known for his intellectual prowess. He had bungled every task James Henrikson and Robert DeLao had thrown his way, never even making a penny for his efforts. Now faced with a likely stint in the slammer, he agreed to cooperate with the investigation. But that also meant becoming the very thing he hated most—a snitch. It was a bitter price, but one he had no choice but to pay.

The predicament the 300-pound Bates was now in had all started with just one phone call. "[DeLao] called and said someone messed up, and that he needed some help," he recounted. "He asked if I could come to North Dakota and talk about it."

Having been friends with DeLao for 15 years, he wasn't

about to turn down the request. However, he wasn't keen on making a solo trip, so he brought along Eric T. Borders. Known as "Goldie" to both law enforcement and the seedier corners of Spokane, Borders was a heavy drug user, who was happy to accept crack cocaine as payment for his assistance.

When they arrived in North Dakota, Bates said the first thing DeLao did was hand them a baseball bat. "He told me that someone owed James Henrikson a lot of money, and that the guy was subcontracting trucks rather than sending the business to Henrikson. They wanted this guy hurt badly."

Bates claimed he couldn't recall the name of the guy who had wronged James, but when investigators suggested it might have been Jay Wright, he agreed that sounded right. Though DeLao had previously told detectives that Wright was to be killed, Bates maintained that he had only ever been asked to assault him. Frankly, he said, even that had made him uneasy.

Still, he was willing to give it at least a perfunctory effort. Bat in hand, Bates and Goldie hid outside Wright's cabin in the early morning hours, poised to ambush the unsuspecting man the moment he stepped outside. Fortunately, it was winter, and a fresh blanket of snow on the ground provided Bates with the perfect excuse to back out.

"I was supposed to assault the target as soon as he came out of his house to get into his vehicle," he recalled. "But I couldn't do it because the snow on the ground was really crunchy and there was too much light."

James and DeLao reprimanded them for their failure, sending Bates and Goldie back to Spokane with their tails between their legs. They weren't about to let Bates off the hook, though. According to Bates, DeLao had relentlessly pestered him, resorting to emotional blackmail to compel him to return and finish the job for James. Knowing DeLao for as long as he had, Bates had never seen his friend kowtow to anyone, and the strange dynamic between him and James was unsettling.

"He was in love with Henrikson," Bates snorted. "He considered him to be Superman."

Nevertheless, he complied with DeLao's pleas, making

additional trips to North Dakota with a different companion in tow each time. "I brought Smurf, and then KK," he explained. "I knew that James wanted the target beaten up badly. But in the end, I just couldn't beat a man with a bat for no reason. I was fired as a hitman after my failures in North Dakota."

Bates then retold the story of how he and DeLao had later traveled to Chicago to procure China White heroin, and to find a hitman to take out Jed McClure. It was there that the notorious gangster "The Wiz" had taken their money and run, leaving them to look like the fools they truly were. After that embarrassing debacle, DeLao warned Bates that they would both likely end up on James's kill list.

"I told my mother that my wife and kids might be in danger," the failed hitman revealed. But nothing had ever happened to him or his family.

Having shared all that he could remember, Bates's story then took a bizarre turn when he began discussing what was happening inside the Spokane County Jail. By this time, James, DeLao, Suckow, Laz Pesina, Robbie Wahrer, and Bates were all being held there. The jail, an 11-story facility designed to house up to 700 inmates, was hardly a small space. Yet, inmates somehow found ways to communicate with one another.

In Bates's case, he was getting hammered from all directions. On one hand, James and Pesina urged him to say that Tex Hall and DeLao had set James up. If he went along with that request, James promised he would be "set for life." On the flip side, DeLao told him to outright lie and deny. The cacophony of mixed messages sent the dimwitted Bates into a tailspin, convinced they were all conspiring to set him up to take the fall for everything.

In perhaps the smartest move he ever made, he decided to shut out the chaos around him, and—to the best of his recollection—told the truth. Now, he would wait to learn his fate.

● ● ●

Erik Guerrero, the alleged former Mexican Mafia gang member who had once hung up on Detective Mark Burbridge in a brazen display of defiance, was now eager to clear his name of any wrongdoing. Having played a pivotal role in tipping off authorities about James's plot to have Sarah killed, Guerrero still had more to reveal.

He had begun working as a truck driver for James in October 2013. Given Guerrero's history and prior gang affiliation, it didn't take long for James to broach a darker subject—after only a few weeks on the job, he asked Guerrero if he or someone he knew was capable of carrying out not just one but several murders.

"He asked me if I knew anyone who could kill Robert DeLao, Sarah Creveling, Tex Hall, and one other person whom I can't recall," Guerrero told the detectives. "He offered to pay $100,000 for each killing."

Stunned and repulsed by the request, Guerrero told James that neither he nor anyone he knew would be willing to carry out such a task. Perhaps equally taken aback by the sharp rebuke, James never asked again.

Guerrero told the detectives that he and James had ended their relationship on poor terms, and that James still owed him $5,600 in unpaid wages—money he would never see.

•••

While sophisticated analysts with the FBI pored over hundreds of pages of cell phone records and data files subpoenaed from multiple carriers, Darrik Trudell and Eric Barker took on the lion's share of examining the physical phones collected as part of their investigation. But there was one phone in particular that neither agent wanted to touch: Doug Carlile's. Perhaps it was intuition, but there was an unspoken sense that something in Doug's phone would tug at even their steely resolve.

Following a brief stalemate, Darrik stepped up. "Fine, I'll do it."

Darrik's investigation had centered primarily on the murder of K.C. Clarke, and his involvement with the Carlile family had been minimal. What he knew of Doug as a person was limited, mostly confined to the bare facts of the case. That still didn't lessen the emotional impact he felt after reviewing a touching text exchange between Doug and one of his grandchildren.

Even years later, Darrik struggled to talk about that moment without tearing up. "I'm reading through these messages and it's one of Doug's grandsons, excited about how well his life is going. Doug just kept telling him how proud he was, and how much he loved him. Doug might have had his faults as a businessman, but he didn't as a grandpa. I didn't feel right reading his personal conversations with his family—they were special memories from a grandfather who loved his family very much. So, that was it. I slid the phone back across the table and told Eric, 'Sorry, I can't. You're going to have to do this.' And I got up and walked out of the room."

Eric Barker understood.

• • •

Perhaps one of the biggest breakthroughs the detectives achieved was getting Sarah Marie Creveling to finally admit that K.C. Clarke had dropped off his gas card to her the morning of February 22, 2012. She was still adamant, however, that she had no inkling he had been murdered less than 100 feet away from her merely minutes later. Until now, no one had emerged to challenge her version of events or accuse her of being involved.

But that was about to change.

CHAPTER 68

What Sarah Knew

Ryan Olness was not a happy camper. By 2015, he had been living in Arizona for nearly three years, supposedly in constant fear that James Henrikson would send someone to kill him. It didn't help that Olness's name was now appearing in multiple online and printed news articles, linking him to the case, making him feel like an even bigger target. He blamed the authorities for "leaking" his name.

He had spoken with investigators a few times before, insisting he knew nothing. But since then, detectives had gathered a lot more information and figured out he had been lying, and they were pissed. There was now a clear, not-so-subtle suggestion from federal prosecutors: it was time to start telling the truth or face serious charges.

A "free talk" scheduled in Phoenix with Olness, his attorney, Gene Stratford, U.S. Attorney Keith Vercauteren, DEA Special Agent Bill Neal, Eric Barker, and Darrik Trudell turned out to be anything but "free." Getting straight answers from the blonde, buck-toothed young man was like trying to extract blood from a stone.

For the first 30 minutes, Olness whined about his life being in danger. "I'm concerned because two people have already died. I mean, I'm looking over my shoulder everywhere I walk now. It's nerve racking."

"It's unnecessary for you to be looking over your shoulder

at this point," Barker assured him.

"I mean, is it?" Olness asked in disbelief. He complained about the specific quote attributed to him in the news, one in which he had mentioned joining James at a gun range. Olness worried his statement was the catalyst for James's arrest.

Barker again tried to quell his concerns. "The reason he wanted to kill you was something totally separate than anything you said and to be honest with you, the charge on firearms is the least of James Henrikson's worries right now."

"I know, but that's what you guys have him on to get more evidence on something else," Olness squeaked. "It doesn't matter what he is, he's crazy, he's just not there. I don't mind helping you guys, I just don't want my name leaked all over."

Darrik Trudell eventually interjected, telling Olness that they were not there to coddle him. Rather, they were there to give him one last chance to save himself. Specifically, in relation to Olness conspiring with James to distribute heroin—a charge that could carry up to a ten-year prison sentence. If he started talking, there was a good chance he could avoid that.

"The last time we came down here," Darrik said, "you weren't honest with us."

"I wasn't honest?" Olness asked defensively. "I told you everything."

"No, you didn't," Darrik said firmly. He stated they were willing to give Olness the benefit of the doubt, attributing his earlier dishonesty to fear—after all, James had still been a free man at the time, and Olness clearly felt his life was at risk. But now that James was behind bars and no longer a threat to anyone, it was time for Olness to come clean, starting with admitting the real reason that James wanted him dead.

"I hear you," Olness responded. "That's why I'm here."

Although it seemed like he understood the assignment, Olness came out of the gate with more lies. When he wasn't dancing around the truth, he was derailing the conversation with bellyaching diatribes about how he was living in constant fear. "Poor, pitiful Ryan Olness" was the narrative he desperately tried to sell. It was a pathetic display—one that left everyone in the room, including his own attorney, shaking their heads in disbelief.

Soon, Darrik had enough. "I'm done trying to pull things out of you."

Beyond frustrated, he, Eric Barker, and U.S. Attorney Keith Vercauteren took a short break to step outside and call Aine Ahmed.

"Hey, this guy just keeps lying," they told him. "What do you want us to do?"

"Give him one more chance," Aine said. "If he still won't give anything up, then shut it down and tell him he's going to prison for a very long time."

When the group returned with that stern warning, and his lawyer issued one of his own, Olness finally seemed to grasp the seriousness of the situation. Having recently married, he realized spending the next ten years with his new bride was far more appealing than prison.

• • •

Though it wasn't easy, and still took half a day, Olness finally confessed the real reason James wanted him dead: he knew James had hired Timothy Suckow to kill K.C. Clarke—but wasn't aware of any of it until after the fact. Olness revealed that he had been at the shop the morning K.C. arrived to turn in his gas card. While he hadn't spoken with K.C. directly, he had noticed him and James conversing near K.C.'s truck.

He hadn't seen them enter the shop together and had been too preoccupied with his own business to sense anything suspicious. But later in the day, James approached him in the yard and revealed something truly horrifying.

"What did James tell you?" Darrik had to ask three times before Olness finally mustered the courage to answer.

"He told me he hired Suckow to beat him up, and he hit him in the head, and he broke his neck or something. He said, 'K.C.'s dead,' or something like that. I said, 'Are you fucking serious?' and he told me not to say anything to anyone … I was immediately a nervous wreck … All I know is that I don't want to fucking die from James shooting me in the back of the head."

Darrik sighed. "We get that."

Olness then surprised the detectives by revealing he had gone into the shop. "I went in there, and it was lights out and I grabbed some tools, and the guy was in there."

Mostly a silent observer until now, U.S. Attorney Keith Vercauteren sat up in his chair, excited over this revelation. "Which guy?"

"The Suckow guy," Olness responded. "Never met this guy in my life … he was sweeping and like 15 minutes later, that's when James said he beat up K.C."

The agents pressed Olness to describe anything he might have seen aside from Suckow "sweeping." But no matter how hard they pushed, Olness stuck to his script, repeating the same statements until they became a hollow mantra: "I didn't want to be involved. I didn't want to know anything. I didn't want to be told anything. I didn't want to see anything. I didn't want to talk about anything. I was scared for my life."

His demeanor was almost childlike, as if squeezing his eyes shut would make the monster go away. Whether he had truly blocked out the memory of something awful or was simply determined to avoid reality was anyone's guess. Whatever the case, the detectives gave up and the conversation moved on.

Olness said the next thing he knew, the garage door to the shop was open and he saw James and Suckow loading items into George Dennis's truck. Though he admitted seeing the blue tarp he flatly denied noticing the large cardboard box that held K.C.'s corpse. At this point, such a denial seemed absurd but it was what the lawmen had come to expect.

Olness remembered feeling so distraught that he needed to leave work early and drive straight home—a place he shared, interestingly, with James and Sarah. He had been temporarily renting a room from them at the time. He had stayed put in that room most of the evening contemplating his next move. Should he pack up and skip town? Should he lock himself in his room until he felt safe enough to come out?

Until he could come up with a better plan, Olness said

he kept a knife under his pillow in case he needed to defend himself. Perhaps it was understandable that he felt scared. However, what didn't make sense was why, instead of going straight to the police, he chose to return to the house he shared with the very person he now knew was a cold-blooded killer. Olness couldn't provide a satisfactory explanation.

To a one, the detectives were growing increasingly desensitized to the repeated excuse: "I was scared he would kill me." They'd heard it from multiple people, and it no longer seemed like a valid reason for the binary choice of either participating in James's devious plans or turning a blind eye. It was perplexing how James had exerted such iron-fisted control over so many.

• • •

Olness still had more to reveal. He admitted to becoming overly intoxicated at the Country Thunder music festival in April of 2012 and blurting out everything he knew to his best friend at the time, Jason Fox.

"You know what?" he shrugged, "I did tell Jason. I told him James did a horrible thing … That he hired someone to kill [K.C.], and it's eating me alive. I started crying to him. I was emotional and drinking and I didn't know what to do."

Olness also divulged that he was with James the night of his terrible motorcycle accident, which happened just a few weeks after K.C. was murdered. Leading up to the crash, Olness had somehow procured a small quantity of Phenazepam from China—a benzodiazepine drug used to treat disorders such as schizophrenia and anxiety. He, James, and Sarah had taken turns "tasting" the drug to test its purity and potency. It hadn't turned out well for any of them.

"James wrecked his motorcycle. I blacked out for like a week … I almost died. Sarah crashed her truck. And then I went and frigging flushed it all."

While it was great that Olness was finally admitting to what he had denied a year earlier about his drunken confessions, the information was long past being useful to investigators. They of course now already knew James had hired Suckow. But then, out of nowhere, Olness dropped a bombshell.

Reverting back to the day K.C. was killed, Olness mentioned how, later that evening, James still hadn't returned home. Having somewhat calmed down, he snuck out of his locked bedroom and stepped onto the patio to clear his mind in the brisk night air. He hadn't known Sarah was home and was unsettled when she joined him outside. He sensed she was about to bring up K.C. and wanted no part of the conversation.

"Oh my God, I'm freaking out!" she exclaimed. "I can't believe he's dead!"

"Me too," Olness had agreed. But as Sarah seemed poised to say more, he stood up and walked inside.

"I didn't want to talk about it," he told the agents.

Stunned at the revelation, Eric Barker stammered, "She for certain knew that K.C. was killed that day?"

For the first time, Olness answered without hesitation or elaboration. "Yes. She knows."

In fact, he said, Sarah had known about everything. The drugs. K.C.'s murder. The fraud. As far as he knew, there was nothing James did that Sarah wasn't privy to. "I mean, she was married to the guy."

That damning conversation between him and Sarah wasn't the end of it. The next morning, James asked Olness for a $10,000 loan to pay Suckow for his services. Olness claimed he had the cash in his safe and delivered it in a manila envelope to James, who was waiting in his truck with Sarah in the passenger seat and Suckow in the back.

Evidently no longer "freaked out," Sarah sat calmly in the same vehicle as James's hired assassin, apparently aware he had killed her friend, K.C., less than 24 hours before. She didn't so much as flinch when Olness handed her husband the money nor did she question it when James passed the envelope back to Suckow. In fact, according to Olness she was the one who later reimbursed him for the $10,000.

"I asked her a couple of times and she blew me off for like a day or two," he remembered. "The third time I asked her, she gave it to me in two different checks from two different accounts." He could not recall if the two checks had been six and four, or seven and three.

"Did she know exactly what it was about?" Darrik asked.

"Yes, of course she did," Olness confirmed.

Then, as if a switch had flipped in his brain, Olness's memory started to glitch. Perhaps it hadn't been the night of K.C.'s murder that Sarah disclosed she was "freaked out." Maybe that had happened a week or two later. He said both James and Sarah talked about being nervous over possibly having to submit to lie detector tests, but once again, he couldn't pinpoint when they had said that. He claimed any time either James or Sarah broached the subject, he interrupted them, saying, "I don't want to know." The reason he couldn't remember exact times or dates, he said, was that he had been too overwhelmed with fear.

Olness said that by April 2012, he had fled back to Arizona, where he spent a drunken few days crying on the shoulder of his best friend. He never stepped foot in North Dakota again. But that hadn't stopped James from harassing him with an unrelenting daily barrage of text messages and phone calls.

"It was seriously like he sent me a message every 30 minutes."

If James's goal had been to keep Olness paranoid so he'd keep his mouth shut, it had worked like a charm.

• • •

Though the information Olness supplied about Sarah incriminating herself seemed valuable, the team of lawmen knew they had little chance of proving it to be true. No prosecutor worth their salt would ever rely on Olness's statements. He'd lied so much that even the most incompetent defense attorney could shred his credibility in seconds.

Furthermore, Olness was the only person in the entire investigation who pointed to Sarah's involvement. James had thrown his wife directly under the bus with regards to their financial dealings, but he had never insinuated anything beyond that. For their part, both DeLao and Suckow felt confident she hadn't known anything about the murders.

Unless someone else came forward to corroborate Olness's account or presented a credible story of their own, pinning a serious crime on Sarah would be next to impossible.

No one ever did.

Amazingly, even Ryan Olness was able to skate without so much as a misdemeanor charge. If rumors are to be believed, however, he still roams the streets somewhere in Arizona, constantly looking over his shoulder, convinced a trigger-happy henchman of James Henrikson will be aiming at his head.

CHAPTER 69

James And The Giant Rope

Last in the long line of those granted the opportunity to come clean and negotiate a reasonable punishment was James Terry Henrikson. On the table for his consideration: a 40-year sentence at a maximum-security federal penitentiary. If he lived that long, he'd emerge in his mid-70s, a shadow of the man who once flaunted a chiseled physique, fast cars, designer clothes, beautiful women, and extravagant wealth.

His third wife, Sarah, and his former lover, Peyton Martin—both much younger than him—would by then be well into their golden years, their lives far removed from the turmoil and deceit they once embraced. Though James had fathered two children, he would leave behind no meaningful legacy.

It was even possible that his children would never be told the name of their true biological father, ensuring he became nothing more than a forgotten chapter in the family history books.

But perhaps in those four decades, James would find the time to confront the monster he had become and maybe even feel some shred of remorse for the destruction he'd caused. No one would hold their breath for that.

Faced with the possible alternative of life behind bars with no chance of parole, James accepted the deal and entered a guilty plea in federal court. Hoping for the death penalty against the person who orchestrated the slaying of their beloved patriarch, Doug Carlile's family was incredulous he might be offered anything less.

U.S. Attorney Aine Ahmed didn't like letting people down, but there was little he could do. "I had to tell them that the death penalty in a federal court isn't common. They weren't very happy with that."

There was just one last detail to iron out: the location of K.C.'s remains. Detectives had long suspected James, or someone else, had moved the body sometime after Suckow first buried it. Rather than cooperate, James reverted to what he did best: lying and manipulating. He started out blaming the Mexican drug cartels and ended somewhere between aliens and the apocalypse. But nowhere in his meandering tall tales did he tell the authorities what they needed to know most.

Aine wasn't ashamed to admit he had even begged. "I was willing to offer him just about anything for an answer. I pleaded with him to let us know where K.C.'s body was. He did not wince. He did not blink. I knew right then that motherfucker moved the body."

When James realized no one believed him, and that there wasn't anyone left who cared to hear what else he had to say, he asked, "What happens to me now?"

"You go to jail for the next 40 years," Aine responded, and walked out of the room.

But James had other ideas for how he would be spending those 40 years, and none of them included being behind bars.

•••

After being housed in cell 5E33 on the ninth floor of the Spokane County Jail in 2014, James spent the next year plotting his escape, à la Andy Dufresne in *The Shawshank Redemption.* But instead of a poster of Raquel Welch and a rock hammer, James's tools were a broom handle and hoarded bed sheets from the laundry.

Early the morning of Wednesday, August 20, 2015, jail personnel arrived for work, only to look up from the parking lot to see one of the windows on the ninth floor had been busted out. A long metal rod, dislodged from the window frame, had hurtled through the air and somehow pierced through the roof of a KIA sedan in the parking lot below. The odds of it striking at such an angle and with such precision were infinitesimally small, but had it hit a person instead, the outcome could have been deadly.

Dangling from the open window above was a 108-foot long, 1.5-inch wide, one-inch-thick braided rope, which James had meticulously crafted using hundreds of jail-issued white sheets. He had tightly knotted one end around the bedpost of the cell's bunk as an anchor while the other reached the ground below. But before attempting a nine-story descent—assuming the rope was strong enough to support him, he was able to hold on all the way down, and the anchor didn't come loose—James first had to figure out how to squeeze through the narrow window opening.

Detective Mark Burbridge later laughed at the prisoner's desperate plight. "He wasn't going to be able to go anywhere. Those windows are sized specifically so that a human adult head cannot fit through."

Instead of making a harrowing escape, the only thing James could do was feel the cool morning breeze on his face and breathe in the fresh summer air, a stark reminder of the freedom that remained just out of reach.

It wasn't yet 6:00 a.m., but agents from the local FBI field office, along with members of the U.S. Marshals Service, were called in. A security breach this serious—whether successful or not—warranted an investigation.

First and foremost, James hadn't acted alone. His cellmate, Bud Brown, had been fully complicit in the escape plan. Over the course of months, they had covertly collected materials including sheets, blankets, and a broom. They had torn open one of their mattress covers and hidden their work-in-progress sheet rope inside. The blankets were intended to make pants—something they would need once they got out. The broom's head had been detached from the handle, leaving both pieces useful for breaking the window. Most of their work had been done in the dead of night, while the rest of the cell block slept.

Two key factors worked in their favor the night they decided to put their plan into action: a television set in the common area of their wing, and a lenient female guard who didn't mind if inmates stayed up all night watching the TV from the small window in their cell doors.

For her part, the guard provided FBI agents insight into what had transpired. "I conducted rounds approximately every 30 minutes. I walk up to every cell and check on the inmates for signs of life. Each time I did my headcount, either James or Bud were standing in front of the cell window, watching television, which essentially blocked my view of the inside of their cell."

From their vantage point, James and Bud could also see where the guard sat and knew exactly when she started her rounds on the other side of the wing. That part of the floor was far enough away that the guard wouldn't hear any disruptive noises or loud banging coming from their cell. That's when the cellmates made their move—knocking out the window facing outside and lowering their rope.

"I didn't hear anything out of the ordinary," the guard admitted.

But some of the other inmates did. In follow-up interviews, several mentioned hearing odd sounds, but that wasn't an uncommon occurrence in a jail. None of them had been worried or bothered, and simply went back to sleep.

The guard had returned to her station after her last break of the night at 4:30 a.m., completely unaware that two of the inmates under her watch had attempted to escape. Not even a minute later, her radio chirped with an urgent message incoming from another guard in a different area of the jail.

"He told me to check the cells near 5 east 33," she explained. "When I got there, James was again blocking my view into the cell, and I ordered him to move."

When James reluctantly shuffled aside, the guard first noticed Bud, sitting in a chair, flashing a wide grin back at her. She gasped when she saw the broken-out window and the rope tied to the bedpost. By then, other officers were on the floor to assist and placed both James and Bud in handcuffs.

Though she had been in her job for nearly five years, the guard was mortified at her own oversight. "I realized that they must have been purposely blocking my view into the cell by pretending to watch television."

The would-be fugitives were ordered to strip down to their shorts so the FBI agents could snap photos. Covered in tattoos, Bud smirked at the camera, unfazed. James, on the other hand, looked completely crushed, his pride shattered into as many pieces as the window he'd smashed. The grotesque scars from his motorcycle accident still marred his face and shoulders. His right eyebrow had never grown back. Though still lean, the effects of his steroid use had faded, leaving him far from the hulking muscle man he once was.

A subsequent search of their cell revealed that James had been collecting spiritual guidance literature and had received several cards and letters from his mother and sister, encouraging him to find God, expressing confidence he could be redeemed. He had also received a few letters from a heartbroken Peyton Martin. In time, the now single mother would come to realize her paramour was never coming back to her.

● ● ●

Despite the failed escape attempt, James wasn't ready to throw in the towel. Instead, he hatched a different scheme. This time, he offered another inmate, Justin Shanks, $500,000 to destroy the van that transported him to and from court hearings—and to kill the two U.S. Marshals responsible for his escort.

Shanks disclosed James's plans to federal agents. "He wanted two getaway cars and someone standing by on a corner or bridge … He asked for live ammunition, grenades, and suggested splashing the windshield with oil and lighting the transport vehicle on fire. He was going to hit the side of the van to let them know which one he was in. Two guys were supposed to get him out of the burning van and throw him in the getaway car."

The absurdity of it all was too much, but James still had one more card to play.

In November 2015, he stood before a judge, seeking to withdraw his guilty plea. Believing he could charm his way to an acquittal, he insisted on taking his chances with a jury. His request was granted.

PART IV

CHAPTER 70

James Was The Real Victim

By the time James Henrikson's trial finally began on Friday, January 29, 2016, K.C. Clarke had been dead for nearly four years, Doug Carlile for three. Even though the significant passage of time had diminished both public interest and media attention, James's defense team petitioned for a change of venue, asserting that their client could not receive a fair trial in Spokane.

The presiding judge, the Honorable Salvador Mendoza, Jr., concurred, and the trial was relocated 140 miles away to the U.S. District Courthouse in Richland, Washington. The distance made it difficult for the victim's family members to attend much of the trial, leaving the courtroom sparsely populated as the final chapters of the marathon tale unfolded.

After a week-long jury selection process, the lawyers on both sides readied for battle. At the prosecution table were U.S. Attorney Aine Ahmed, his co-chair Scott Jones, FBI Agent Eric Barker, and HSI Special Agent Darrik Trudell.

Jones had only recently joined the Eastern District of Washington U.S. Attorney's Office, transferring from the office in San Diego. Perhaps because he was new, he had been the only one willing to step in to assist with the case. Whip-smart, he spoke with a distinctive baritone that captivated the courtroom. His calm, measured approach was a perfect counterbalance to Aine's intensity.

For his part, Aine was a study in focus and determination. He exuded a fierce energy and confidence that commanded attention whenever he spoke. Several detectives and federal agents lauded him as the most thorough prosecutor they had ever worked with. A true legal virtuoso, his deep understanding of the law shone through in every word, and his quick thinking and sharp instincts made him a formidable opponent in any courtroom.

Though wickedly funny, the Pakistani with a Southern drawl rarely laughed. The truth was that he felt anxious at the start of every trial. "I'm always nervous the first few days. By the time I get to the third or fourth witness, I start to feel more comfortable."

He never forgot to tuck his silver 3D Armored Cavalry Regiment lighter—a cherished memento from his Army days—into the pocket of his suit pants. "I carry it with me at all times during a trial, always in my right pocket. It calms my nerves and it's my good luck."

If anyone in the gallery listened closely enough, they'd catch the distinct, metallic click of the Zippo opening and closing as Aine stood at the lectern or paced the floor.

But there was one aspect of a trial that always intimidated him, lighter or no lighter: the opening statement. It was his kryptonite.

"Look," he later explained, "I come from a family of highly intelligent people, but we swear a lot. I'm always afraid I'm going to drop an F-bomb in my opening remarks, and risk offending someone on the jury."

Thankfully, Scott Jones was more than willing to handle that part.

• • •

Seated at the defense table with James were two of Washington's most revered defense attorneys: Mark Vovos and Todd Maybrown. At 74, Vovos exuded the same spunk and quirkiness that had marked his nearly 40 years of practicing law. Known for his signature silk bowties, wire rimmed glasses, and a full head of disheveled gray hair, Vovos had a talent for using his endearing charm and self-deprecating humor to win over jurors.

"Vovos will play stupid," Aine later joked. "He's definitely not."

Maybrown, a few decades younger than Vovos, was far more serious with his approach. His expertise in capital murder cases had earned him tremendous respect and made him a highly regarded figure in legal circles.

Aine later had this to say about him: "If I'm ever in trouble and need a defense attorney, I'm calling Todd Maybrown. James had the cream of the crop."

It was true. Because James's case qualified for consideration of the death penalty, he was automatically appointed two of the state's top capital punishment litigators. Although the government ultimately chose not to pursue that route, Vovos and Maybrown remained on the case, their combined fees—paid by taxpayers—totaling nearly $800,000.

Judge Mendoza was respected for his fairness and prudence. Even when the trial unexpectedly stretched into its sixth week, Mendoza allowed the proceedings to unfold at their own pace, never rushing either side. He was determined to ensure that no technicality could later undermine the integrity of the process. The judge expected things to go smoothly, and they did—for the most part, anyway.

• • •

Scott Jones began his opening remarks by playing the gut-wrenching recording of the 911 call Elberta Carlile made the night her husband was gunned down in their home. He told the jury they would be hearing directly from the man who had killed both Doug and K.C. Clarke, and from the person who'd helped organize the murders. He acknowledged that they wouldn't like the things that Timothy Suckow and Robert DeLao had done but reminded the panel that they still needed to listen and consider their testimony with open minds.

"Now, ladies and gentleman," he said, "many of the government's witnesses in this case are not outstanding citizens. Tim Suckow shot Doug Carlile in cold blood in front of his wife. He literally beat K.C. Clarke's brains out with a metal bar. Robert DeLao has a tattoo on his back of him urinating on the headstone of the last man he killed."

Upwards of 50 additional witnesses, he revealed, would corroborate Suckow and DeLao's accounts. Each of whom, he said, would point directly at the defendant, James Henrikson, as the mastermind behind everything.

In his opening, Vovos began with a bizarre discussion about mudslinging, methane, fracking, and water. While he might have been trying to cleverly tie the oil business into his message, the attempt fell flat and confusion spread across the juror's faces. He even mixed-up James's love child for one being born to Sarah and was a decade off in pegging the year of Doug Carlile's murder.

Vovos ticked off Suckow's and DeLao's various past transgressions—facts no one intended to dispute—before boldly claiming that they were the true culprits. They were the greedy ones who aspired to dominate in the oilfields, not his client. James, he contended, had simply been in their way.

The bespectacled lawyer described his client as a very successful, albeit sometimes aggressive, businessman who was making hundreds of thousands of dollars. He suggested that James had been focused on building an empire, not looking for trouble. In fact, Vovos argued, James was merely a scapegoat—a sacrificial lamb for those seeking forgiveness for their own grave sins.

"James Henrikson never told or ordered Mr. DeLao or Mr. Suckow to kill anybody," he assured the jury. The attorney further stated that his client was not involved in the financial fraud or drug smuggling. Those misdeeds, he insisted, rested squarely on the shoulders of others.

The truth, Vovos promised to prove, was that James Henrikson wasn't the villain. He was the victim.

CHAPTER 71

The Trial—Part I

Timothy Suckow was the prosecution's first witness, but ensuring he was prepared to testify hadn't been easy. Wracked with guilt over what he'd done and grappling with the reality of his ruined life, Suckow had retreated into a dark despair. He again contemplated the idea of ending it all, hoping that another hunger strike or a refusal to take his medication might hasten the process.

Aine Ahmed later recalled the frustrating situation. "Two nights before the trial, our star witness is lying on the floor of his jail cell in the fetal position sucking his thumb. We had to make sure he took his meds so he would be able to testify."

Fortunately, when the time came, Suckow was ready to take the stand and much to the prosecution's relief delivered compelling testimony that spanned nearly three full days with Aine at the helm meticulously guiding him through every aspect of the case.

Though he became emotional when describing the horrific murders of K.C. Clarke and Doug Carlile, Suckow largely maintained his composure. Despite the heinous nature of his actions, he admitted responsibility, and the remorse he displayed struck the jury as sincere.

When it was the defense's turn, Mark Vovos tried his best to poke holes in Suckow's story. His strategy hinged on pressuring Suckow to slip up and admit that it was he and Robert DeLao who orchestrated everything, effectively removing James from the entire equation.

The flaw in Vovos's argument, however, was that the prosecution possessed hundreds of pages of text message and email records revealing that the content of nearly every message from DeLao to Suckow had originated with James. More importantly, in those messages it was clearly James who was giving the orders.

Scott Jones later explained the back-and-forth communication loop during an interview with *Dateline*. "You could see exactly how it went. James sent a message to DeLao, then DeLao relayed it to Suckow. Then it went back—from Suckow to DeLao, and DeLao to James."

Vovos then tried to discredit Suckow by focusing on his past criminal behavior, including a conviction for robbery, and his history with mental illness. At the very least, Vovos hoped to provoke Suckow into downplaying his past or denying his ongoing mental health issues.

But Suckow did neither. In fact, his struggle with mental illness and the perceived lack of care in the penal system were topics that he quite enjoyed discussing. Aine sat back and let this go on for a while, but when Vovos introduced Suckow's medical records from 1982, he requested a sidebar with the judge.

"Mr. Suckow admitted to bashing somebody's head in on the stand," the feisty prosecutor said bluntly. "Something that happened 35 years ago in terms of mental illness is irrelevant to this case."

By the end of Suckow's lengthy direct, cross, and re-direct examinations, the prosecution had effectively outlined four dominant conclusions: he had murdered two men in cold-blood, James Henrikson had both ordered and paid him to do it, he was going to prison for a minimum of three decades for what he had done, and he was now very remorseful for his actions.

Robert DeLao was next on the stand. Aine's first focus was confronting DeLao's extensive criminal history, including the fact that he had once killed a man—though he claimed it had been in self-defense. With that cleared up and out of the way, the prosecutor delved into the more pertinent details of the case.

Everything that DeLao had previously admitted to in his proffer agreement—serving as the intermediary between Suckow and James to orchestrate the murders of K.C. and Doug, recruiting Todd Bates, attempting to secure drugs for James as part of efforts to enter the pill-making business, defrauding Tex Hall—was now brought to light, each detail laid bare for the jury to hear.

Todd Maybrown's cross-examination was a valiant effort to challenge the former gangster's credibility. Once again, the defense reached into the dustbin of history—this time 2007—to produce court transcripts of DeLao lying with regards to a robbery.

DeLao didn't crack. "You're right," he said. "I did lie then. I apologize." Beyond that, he had already freely admitted his role in a host of far more serious crimes and was also going to be spending at least the next two decades of his life in prison. What he'd lied about 11 years ago felt irrelevant.

● ● ●

Several more witnesses, including George Dennis and Steve Kelly, testified to James's cruel and vengeful nature, stating that he had no qualms about harming or killing anyone who crossed him.

Tex Hall was finally given the opportunity to talk about how James and Sarah had stolen hundreds of thousands of dollars from him. It was also a chance for him to clear his own name. Many people still harbored suspicions that Hall had somehow been involved in James's murderous plots, but the absolute truth was that he hadn't.

"We investigated that angle inside and out," the detectives later said, "and there was no evidence that linked him to any of it. He was completely innocent."

Peyton Martin described for the court how her love affair with James had started out with grand romantic gestures and promises and ended with her being a single mother and her baby daddy behind bars. The reason James wanted to move to Brazil, she said, was because the country did not have an extradition agreement with the United States. No one challenged her with the fact that the two countries actually do have such an agreement. In addition, neither the prosecution nor defense questioned her on any knowledge she might have had about her lover's murderous plots.

CHAPTER 72

The Trial—Part II

On the tenth day of trial, Sarah Creveling—now officially James Henrikson's third ex-wife—walked into the courtroom with her head hung low. Although a half-hearted attempt had been made to ensure that James's wife and mistress steered clear of one another, Sarah and Peyton inadvertently crossed paths in the hallways of the courthouse and reportedly exchanged hostile barbs. Truth be told though, no one really cared—even if their clash had escalated.

"I didn't like Sarah," Aine later admitted. "She really rubbed me the wrong way. I thought Scott would do a much better job of questioning her."

Scott Jones agreed.

Sarah revealed to the jury that she was being charged with money laundering and mail fraud in the state of North Dakota. She, too, was possibly looking at jail time for those crimes, but the federal government had granted her testimonial immunity for this trial.

"What is your understanding of what that means?" Jones asked her.

"That my statements today won't be used against me," she answered.

Jones then guided Sarah through a series of questions regarding the genesis of her relationship with James. She had only been 16 when she first met the handsome bad boy. Eight years later, she would become his wife and soon after, find herself fully entrenched in every financial scheme the pair could concoct.

When the newlyweds first arrived in North Dakota, she said, they'd been making money hand over fist; sometimes hundreds of thousands of dollars a month. But it had never been enough. The witness admitted to the court that the initial dust up with Steve Kelly in late 2011 over a lucrative contract had set the stage for a gradual unraveling of their trucking business—and, perhaps, her husband's sanity. James, Sarah revealed, had been furious with Kelly and was incapable of letting it go.

"He started to get a little frantic because we were going to lose all the contracts; we weren't going to get any money," she said.

Jones moved on to discussing the next major conflict the couple had to navigate: Jed McClure. When asked what happened with McClure, Sarah had to admit that their original primary investor grew increasingly concerned when his monthly revenue stream dried up. Because, of course, James and Sarah were siphoning it to their shell companies.

"Um," she stammered, "Jed was concerned with the books and where the money was going."

"Where did he think it was going?"

"To other companies," Sarah said quietly.

The prosecutor then asked the court to display the "Beware" flyer that McClure and Lissa Yellowbird had distributed across much of western North Dakota.

"What is this document, Ms. Creveling?" Jones asked.

Sarah winced at the sight of the flyer; the very thing that had arguably been the catalyst for destroying her reputation. "Um, it's a poster that I believe Jed created and had mailed out to every bank, post office, grocery store, any sort of company, plus homes. He went through the phone book and mailed one to every single person."

"Would it be fair to say that the document contains some pretty embarrassing allegations?"

"Yes," Sarah agreed.

"Did the fraud alerts make it harder for you to do business in that community?"

Sarah once again answered with an affirmative.

When Jones pivoted to discussing Tex Hall, Todd Maybrown objected to any line of questioning that had to do with the money James and Sarah had stolen from the former tribal chairman. Jones had to tread carefully, as any attempt to ask Sarah to reflect on something James had "told" her versus what she had "observed" crossed a strict line in the sand for marital privilege, and Maybrown didn't hesitate to object or request frequent sidebars.

At one point, while the lawyers stood around the judge's bench for the umpteenth time, Jones asked, "Is everybody else ready to ban sidebars?"

"I thought I did that already," the judge responded, equally exasperated.

The one thing the defense did not object to the prosecution asking—and Sarah answering—was that Hall's main reason for terminating the relationship between Maheshu Energy and Blackstone Trucking was because of James's affair with Peyton Martin.

Next came questions about K.C. Clarke.

"Were you present at a company meeting before K.C. was murdered?" Jones asked Sarah.

Maybrown immediately sprung from his chair. "Your honor, I object to the characterization."

Mendoza agreed. "Sustained."

Jones rephrased. "Were you present at a company meeting before K.C. disappeared?"

Sarah said that she was there and testified that the meeting had been James's idea. "It started off just open table for people to talk about their concerns and anything that needed to be updated, and then we talked about K.C. needing a vacation."

When Jones asked if a meeting like that had ever taken place before, or if anyone else who worked for Blackstone had ever been told they "needed" a vacation, Sarah said no. She also acknowledged that it had been her who called K.C. on February 21 to request he come to the office the next day to turn in his company credit card.

According to her testimony, Sarah had specifically asked him to come "mid-morning" on February 22—which K.C. had done. However, Sarah claimed she had not seen K.C. after he turned in his card. For that matter, she said, she didn't see her husband between the time they had breakfast together that morning, and when he finally came home that night.

"Do you remember what time the night of February 22 that the defendant came home?" Jones asked.

"I don't know the exact time, but it was extremely late," Sarah answered.

At this point in her testimony, Sarah's memory became fuzzy. She told the court that she remembered driving to Williston with her husband the next day, on February 23, but she did not recall Timothy Suckow riding in the truck with them, or Ryan Olness hand delivering $10,000 in cash to James.

But she was able to remember at least one thing with remarkable clarity. Prompted by Jones, Sarah discussed following the Facebook page created by K.C.'s mother, Jill Williams. It was through posts on the page that she learned a rumor that K.C.'s body had been found. Sarah explained that she had told James, and his reaction had startled her.

"It looked like he'd seen a ghost," she said. "He went completely white and started asking me questions as to—"

Jones gave her a stern look to stop before she divulged anything James might have said. The prosecutor did not want yet another sidebar. He asked Sarah about any other conversations that she may have had in regard to K.C.'s disappearance. Sarah testified that she had spoken with Rick Arey and Gloria Paulino—the mother of K.C.'s ex-girlfriend, Josephine.

"I thought he was missing, but Rick told me he was found," Sarah said. "And then Paulino called me and said absolutely not, and that's when I thought: okay, he really is missing."

Yet neither she nor James had ever called the authorities to alert them to the fact that one of their most valued employees—and friend—had mysteriously disappeared. If it hadn't been for the Facebook page devoted to finding answers about what had happened, there was a good chance K.C. Clarke would have disappeared from both James and Sarah's memories altogether.

Scott Jones once again changed directions and began asking Sarah a series of questions related to the numerous trips she and James took, oftentimes with Robert DeLao in tow. Sarah had to admit that none of the trips to Chicago, Portland, Seattle, or Los Angeles had anything to do with their Blackstone Trucking business. DeLao had already testified the purpose of those trips was to procure heroin for their pill-manufacturing business.

But Sarah had no idea about any of that, she said. Most often, she was dealing with some ailment that kept her in a hotel room while James and DeLao gallivanted around the city, evidently never telling Sarah what they were up to.

Jones moved on to the oil leasing agreement between James, Doug Carlile, John Wark, Richard Curtiss, and a host of other investors, including Renee Johnson and Doug Helton. The prosecutor prompted Sarah to describe her impressive understanding of complicated contracts and business dealings, as well as provide a detailed rundown of the nearly two million dollars that had been invested in the doomed endeavor.

She illustrated how the relationship between James and Doug had quickly deteriorated, helping the jury understand that their mutual frustration and distrust eventually reached a boiling point. Sarah said that James had been utterly humiliated and irate when Pamp Maiers and Larry Tormozov laughed in his face for getting involved with Doug Carlile. Worst of all, the thought of losing out on millions of dollars sent James into a tailspin. Every word Sarah spoke wove a vivid picture of her husband's descent into anger and despair.

With this line of questioning, the prosecution had brilliantly set the stage to dismantle the defense's strategy. As Mark Vovos explained in his opening statement, the defense planned to argue that James had wanted only to build a successful business for himself and claimed that it was Robert

DeLao and Timothy Suckow who were the greedy ones standing in his way—and, therefore, the ones truly and solely responsible for the murders of both Doug and K.C. Clarke.

But as Scott Jones got Sarah to explain for the court, neither DeLao nor Suckow were involved in the oil leasing agreement, or the ensuing disputes among those who were. If DeLao and Suckow had been trying to sabotage James to enrich themselves, it hadn't been through this deal—and therefore, not with Doug Carlile.

Sarah's testimony had accomplished exactly what Aine Ahmed and Scott Jones intended: it clearly demonstrated for the jury that the only person who had any reason to want Doug dead was James Henrikson.

Try as they might—and they did—Vovos and Maybrown could not put that toothpaste back in the tube.

CHAPTER 73

The Trial—Part III

The witnesses called so far had done significant damage to the defense's hopes of painting James in a favorable light. Attempts to discredit their testimonies had failed, and the defense had yet to create any reasonable doubt as to the extent of their client's involvement. The reality was that James had operated like a mob boss punishing those who stepped out of line—sometimes with lethal consequences.

Every person who took the stand provided examples of his manipulation, control, and devious nature. The conclusion was inescapable: James Henrikson was a thoroughly reprehensible human being. Perhaps even evil. Recognizing that their strategy was crumbling, the defense attorneys resorted to their last remaining tactics: distract and delay.

"Mark Vovos was always making noises," Aine Ahmed recalled. "Breathing hard, muttering to himself, clearing his throat. He's known for it."

But Scott Jones grew tired of it. During a break, he asked the judge to instruct the defense to knock it off. Vovos nearly fell out of his chair, mortified that he'd been called out. A few minutes later, he confronted Jones in the men's restroom.

"You could have just told me," he said.

"It's slimy, Mark," Jones retorted. "It's frigging slimy."

Later, Aine couldn't help but laugh at the situation. "I had no idea Scott was going to do that, but Vovos lost it. There was a crowd looking on, and they just about got into a fight."

Back inside the courtroom, Judge Mendoza had also heard about the incident. "I understand Mr. Jones and Mr. Vovos almost got into fisticuffs in the bathroom?" He fought to stifle a smirk as he urged the attorneys to maintain professionalism.

No longer able to get away with grunting and groaning at the defense table, Vovos and Maybrown became objection-happy, frustrating both the prosecution and the judge with constant interruptions and sidebars. They filed dozens of motions, forcing the prosecution team to work through the night on responses and still appear in court early the next morning.

"People don't understand the time and effort it takes to put a case like this together," Aine later lamented. "Then to have to respond to these nonsense motions. We were sometimes up until two or three in the morning working on it. I had young kids at the time. It can be destructive to a family."

Vovos and Maybrown weren't concerned with that. They kept pushing, relentlessly grilling detectives and federal agents who had poured their hearts and souls into the investigation, attempting to tarnish their credibility and reputations. At one point, they even questioned Mark Burbridge's integrity, incensing the seasoned detective.

"They were trying to make a big deal out of some text exchanges between Burbridge and DeLao," Aine later explained. "Mark was really upset. I had to talk him down, but he got on the stand and made them look stupid."

"No one had ever questioned my integrity before," Mark later said. "I was so fucking angry."

But who could blame the defense attorneys for their efforts? They had nothing else to work with. Their client was guilty, and everyone including them knew it.

When the prosecution finally rested its case, there had been no bombshells or surprises—only a focused, almost surgical presentation. Not a stone was left unturned.

When it was their turn, Vovos and Maybrown called just one new witness: Ryan Olness's former best friend, Jason Fox. "Olness said that a hired hitman from Chicago or New York flew to North Dakota and landed a single blow on [K.C.]

Clarke," Fox testified. "Olness cleaned the machine shop where K.C. was killed."

Under cross-examination, Fox admitted to Scott Jones that he had been high on marijuana and cocaine, and had been drinking, when Olness supposedly shared these details. But it wasn't exactly clear what Fox's testimony aimed to achieve, anyway. It didn't exonerate James; instead, it tried to pin the murder and clean-up on someone other than Timothy Suckow—who had already admitted to both.

•••

The only surprise of the trial was that Henrikson chose not to testify in his own defense. Perhaps his lawyers recognized that putting him on the stand would only make matters worse. Then again, maybe James had resigned himself to the fact that this was the end of the road—he wasn't going to smooth talk his way out of this one.

After lengthy closing arguments from both the prosecution and defense, Judge Mendoza read the instructions for the jury and sent them to deliberate.

They would not be gone for long.

CHAPTER 74

The Verdict

As expected, the jury returned unanimous guilty verdicts on all 11 counts, including murder-for-hire, conspiracy to commit murder-for-hire, and conspiracy to distribute heroin.

Aine Ahmed addressed the court at James's sentencing hearing in May 2016. "Just by sheer happenstance, Mr. Henrikson is not a serial killer. Several other people would be dead if people had followed through with his murder plots. He's got a black heart. At the very least, he should receive two consecutive life sentences plus 20 years."

Although the widowed Elberta Carlile had chosen not to attend the trial, she was determined not to miss the sentencing hearing—or the opportunity to deliver a victim impact statement. She began by offering praise to everyone who had worked to bring James to justice, then pivoted to the devastating impact Doug's murder had on her family.

"Our loss is great," she said through tears. "My children don't have their father to go to anymore. I don't choose to focus on loss because it is very painful. I am going to live. I am going to rise from these ashes."

When James refused to look at her, she said, "James Henrikson does not have a heart. I do not believe that he has ever known real love." It was possible she was right.

Elberta asked the judge to make sure that James would never be set free. She expressed fear that he would most certainly destroy more lives. After Elberta finished, her daughter MeLainee, and son Shane, echoed their mother's sentiments and pleaded with the court to give James the maximum sentence it could.

"He has no business walking the earth," Shane said. "Lock him up and throw away the key."

Seeing the pain etched across the Carlile family's faces, and hearing the devastation in their voices, defense counsel Mark Vovos stood to address the court. "I have heard from people in this case and it's hard not to be moved. We're attorneys, but we are also human beings." Nevertheless, he asked that the judge not impose a mandatory life sentence for his client.

• • •

Having chosen not to testify at his trial, James prepared a statement for his sentencing hearing. What followed was a disturbing ramble, filled with references to abortion, marijuana, scripture, and poetry.

"I believe this should have been a death penalty case from the beginning," he surprisingly admitted. Then, he bizarrely compared the death penalty to abortion. "They want to kill innocent children and save the criminals … America is instilling in people it's okay to kill children. This is actually murder-for-hire."

He droned on for nearly an hour, causing unease among everyone in the gallery. Even the judge and James's own lawyers shifted uncomfortably in their seats.

"I thought James was crazy before," Scott Jones later said, "but after that, I knew he was completely insane."

Nowhere in his remarks did he include an acknowledgement of his crimes. Nor did he offer any sense of remorse or regret. True to form, it was all about James.

"This case is not about abortion, marijuana, drinking, or jail," Judge Mendoza admonished. "It's about you deciding to take the lives of people for greed. Your comments continue to show the court a complete lack of remorse."

Ultimately, the judge sentenced James to life in prison plus 30 years. In other words, he had granted the requests of both the federal government and the Carlile family. James will never again see the light of day as a free man.

●●●

Though K.C. Clarke's mother, Jill Williams, did not attend either the trial or the sentencing, there was at least a small sense of closure in knowing that those responsible for her son's death were brought to justice. Still, nothing can ever fill the empty void left by the fact that K.C.'s remains have never been recovered.

CHAPTER 75

The Rest

On May 20, 2016, Judge Mendoza sentenced Timothy Suckow, Robert DeLao, Lazaro Pesina, and Robby Wahrer. With the exception of DeLao, all received the sentences recommended by the U.S. Attorney's Office as outlined in their plea agreements. Todd Bates was sentenced separately in a state court.

Robby Wahrer, the getaway driver the night of Doug Carlile's murder, was given a ten-year sentence. Wahrer apologized to the court and said he had since cut ties with Suckow. Released early, he was arrested again in 2023 for possessing 260 grams of illegal drugs and 3,500 fentanyl pills, landing him back in jail.

Lazaro Pesina, the man who had changed out the license plates of the van but was fortunately not in the vicinity when Suckow ambushed Doug, received a 12-year sentence for his role in the crime. He was released on parole in February 2024, having served only eight years. True to form, Pesina never stays in one place for long.

For one count of conspiracy to commit murder and one count of conspiracy to distribute heroin, Todd Bates was sentenced to 100 months—roughly eight years—in prison. Having served his time, he is now back in Spokane, still concerned over ever being thought of as a "snitch."

The federal government had recommended a sentence of 14 to 17 years for Robert DeLao, but Judge Mendoza rejected

it. While he acknowledged and appreciated DeLao's cooperation with this case, the problem was that DeLao had done that
many times before. Each time he had been an informant, he'd
received a lenient sentence for his own crimes, only to get out
of prison and become involved in even more serious offenses.
The judge said he wanted to impose a 30-year sentence but ad-
journed the proceedings to consider it further. A few months
later, Mendoza landed somewhere in the middle and handed
down a 22-year punishment.

DeLao, now 50, is in the eighth year of his sentence at
the federal penitentiary in Tucson, Arizona. He is training to
become an electrician and enjoys receiving emails and letters
from female admirers. By the time he has finished serving his
sentence, he will be 64 and hopefully too old to participate in
any further criminal activity. He has never apologized for his
role in the deaths of K.C. Clarke and Doug Carlile.

Timothy Suckow was sentenced to the 30 years Aine
Ahmed had promised him. Elberta Carlile was once again
present at the hearing, and this time, she would finally hear
what she had been waiting so long for.

Suckow looked directly into the grieving widow's eyes
and said, "I am so sorry."

"I believe you." Elberta nodded. "And I forgive you."

Suckow, now 61, is housed at a medium security federal
prison located in Fairton, New Jersey. With 22 years left to
serve on his sentence, he will be 83 by the time he is eligible for
release—though he doesn't believe he will live that long.

He is currently receiving the much-needed mental health
care that he had wanted for so long. Suckow has embraced
his faith, turned to God for forgiveness, and still clings to the
hope that the end of the world is near. When that happens, he
claims, all the inmates will be freed from the confines of their
prison cells.

In North Dakota, Sarah Marie Creveling pleaded guilty
to one count of conspiracy to commit mail fraud and was sentenced to three years of supervised probation and ordered to
pay $342,500 in restitution. She was also barred from conduct-
ing business in the oilfields. What hadn't been mentioned,

however, was her connection to the deaths of K.C. and Doug. For Jill Williams, it was a slap in the face.

"She shows no remorse or sorrow except for herself," Williams said in a statement. "She has never offered any condolences or apology to K.C.'s family."

The only interview Sarah ever granted was with Keith Morrison on NBC's *Dateline*. In it, she skillfully played the role of victim, dabbing at manufactured tears as she spoke of the hardships she had to endure in the dangerous oilfields. The irony was unmistakable: the real danger was from her and her husband.

Sarah, portraying herself as the naïve, misunderstood blonde, somehow "missed" everything—except her own selfishness, fraud, and deceit. The truth, however, is that many believe she should have paid a much higher price for her actions. Instead of prison or any real accountability, she has embraced the role of a tragic figure—one for whom sympathy is in very short supply.

James Terry Henrikson, now 45, is serving his life sentence at the high-security U.S. penitentiary in Atwater, California. He has never spoken of his case with anyone or attempted to appeal his conviction. Had he not withdrawn his guilty plea, he would be eligible for release at the age of 77. Instead, he will only leave the concrete walls and steel bars of his existence in a pine box.

At one point, James was well on his way to having it all. A real shot at redemption stood right in front of him. His criminal past could have been put in the rearview mirror as he made a name for himself in the oilfields. Had he conducted his business with honesty and integrity, he would have likely become a millionaire several times over. But it was never enough.

Greed, control, manipulation, and violence were the chains that bound him to a life of destruction, and he will die penniless and alone having spent the majority of his life in a prison jumpsuit.

EPILOGUE

After I completed my first book, *Wilder Intentions: Love, Lies and Murder in North Dakota*, I immediately began searching for the subject of my second project. I stumbled upon the story of James Henrikson after watching a 2016 *Dateline* episode titled *A Dangerous Man*. Excited for another intriguing case with ties to North Dakota, I put out a feeler on my Facebook page, hoping to connect with someone close to the situation.

Within minutes of my post, an old acquaintance from high school, Dean Frantsvog, sent me a private message, letting me know that his good friend, Darrik Trudell, had played a major role in the investigation. According to Dean, Darrik was very interested in speaking with me.

The first phone call with Darrik was extremely informative. He then put me in touch with Mark Burbridge and Aine Ahmed. The three of them seemed eager to share their stories—especially since another book had already been written, one they felt hadn't been completely accurate in portraying them or their roles.

To be fair, the book wasn't written solely for the purpose of discussing the James Henrikson case, nor was it intended as a spotlight on their work as investigators. Nevertheless, I listened and understood their concerns—if they wanted their stories told, and were willing to trust me, I wanted to tell them. But that's where the cooperation for this new project came to an abrupt halt. As it turned out, the only people willing to speak with me were Darrik, Mark, and Aine. No one from the

Carlile family wanted to share their stories, and Jill Williams was only willing to speak with me if I agreed to co-author the book with her.

How could I blame them, really? They had suffered tremendous losses, and it had been over eight years. Their healing had finally begun. Why would they be interested in drudging all of that hurt back up again with a total stranger?

While I did have luck connecting with Timothy Suckow and Robert DeLao, Suckow mainly wanted to talk about his early struggles with mental illness, his newfound faith, and his continued belief in the end of times. DeLao's only interest was flirting with me.

Darrik had given me Sarah Creveling's phone number, and though it seemed at first she perhaps wanted to talk, eventually she stopped responding, and I stopped trying. Despite the several letters I sent to him in prison, James never responded.

Attempts to procure case files from the Spokane Police Department were met with reluctance and hostility. They, too, had long since moved past this case, and had little interest in devoting time and effort into pulling together files from 2013. They'd updated their systems, and some of it wasn't even yet in electronic form. If I wanted the files, I was told, it would cost me thousands of dollars. I was willing to pay some, but that amount seemed punitive, so it became a stalemate. Agencies in North Dakota weren't super friendly, either. I eventually did get the information I needed from Spokane, but it was 18 months later and required a strong nudge from Mark Burbridge.

Then the pandemic hit, and the schools in Arizona shut down, which meant my time at home needed to be devoted to monitoring my kids while they attended school via remote learning.

Every single sign was pointing me toward tossing this project in the trash bin before I even got started. If it hadn't been for Darrik, Mark, and Aine, I absolutely would have. When months went by without them hearing from me, and when those months turned into years of little progress, none of them ever gave up on me. I honestly have no idea why, because I would have walked away from me many times over.

In the summer of 2021, I visited Mark and Brian Cestnik in Spokane. Mark and his wife, Sue, hosted a BBQ at their cozy home tucked in the woods, where I got to know them and the Cestnik family. All of them were beyond welcoming and kind. Mark was also my tour guide for the two days I was there.

We drove through the Rockwood neighborhood where Doug and Elberta Carlile had once lived. Elberta had never returned to that house after Doug was killed, and in the eight years since it happened, everything had changed. New owners had remodeled both the interior and exterior of the mansion. It was a beautiful transformation, but still an eerie sight. Mark and I retraced the escape route Suckow had taken that fateful night. Standing on the edge of the gravel trail gave me shivers.

He then took me to the main SPD building and the separate location a few blocks away where he had spent the vast majority of his career as a detective. He had retired in 2020 after 32 years of service and hadn't returned since. As we walked through the hallways of both locations, I marveled at the amount of people who remembered Mark and were excited to see him. Many of them, including the public relations director, wondered why he had never come to collect his retirement plaque. According to her, several attempts had been made to reach him, but he'd apparently ignored them all.

It was that day that I learned that Mark was someone who didn't let many people into his orbit. A few remarked how he never allowed anyone to hug him. When he finally looked at the beautiful plaque made in his honor, he quickly tried to hide his chest swelling with pride. He'll deny that, but I was there.

We lunched at Arby's, where I listened intently as Mark shared a glimpse of his difficult childhood. I learned that right before he was about to enter into an interrogation room with Robert DeLao many years before, he had received devastating news that his mother had passed away after her brief battle with cancer.

Later that afternoon, we visited the makeshift memorial Mark had kept in the woods near his home for so many years. He told me the story of two-year-old Victoria Ramon and became emotional when describing how deeply her death still impacted him. Why he trusted me to share that, I'll never know. But I am beyond grateful that he did.

These days, Mark spends his time working on projects around his house, babysitting his grandchildren, golfing, and watching his beloved Seattle Seahawks.

• • •

I took multiple trips to North Dakota, meeting with Darrik Trudell on several occasions. Tall, fidgety, and the proud father of four—each named after former Republican presidents—the first thing I learned about Darrik is that he frequently shields himself with self-deprecating humor. While he is extremely uncomfortable acknowledging his own good work, he'll never hesitate to go above and beyond in complimenting others. I had to tell him more than twice to stop diminishing his accomplishments.

Because in reality, he is a force to be reckoned with. His large office is a source of constant chaos. He has three phones—a work cell, a personal cell for his kids to Facetime him while he is at work so he can walk them through the house when they get home from school and show that no monsters are hiding in the closets or under the beds, and a desk phone, which I didn't realize people still had. All three of them are usually ringing at the same time. I still haven't figured out how he knows which is which. Along with the ringing, a large TV mounted on the wall blares the Fox News Channel all day long. While all of this is going on, Darrik is somehow able to focus his attention on two huge computer monitors, tapping out responses to emails in seconds. You wouldn't think it, but he is remarkably organized and detail oriented. He is funny, but very serious about his work.

There's a worn, leather couch in one corner of the room. That's where I usually sat, taking all of this in. In between the phone calls and emails, Darrik would share some of the most fascinating information about the James Henrikson case. He'd point to the wall behind me, where he had assembled a massive collage of photos, newspaper clippings, and more, which served as a map of how he had worked to solve the mystery of K.C. Clarke's disappearance.

Though he was proud of the display, he told me, in no uncertain terms, that I wasn't allowed to take a photo of this. When he ran down the hall to help someone with a question, leaving me alone on the couch with Fox News and phones ringing in my ears, I could have easily fished out my cell and snapped a few photos of the wall. But I didn't.

Government work, I now know, is sometimes a tricky business. Business that isn't always available for public consumption. When I asked Darrik questions, or wondered if there was a document or file I could have, he frequently had to check with someone else to make sure it was okay. Narrator: The author did not, in fact, ever get the files.

But there was plenty he could tell me. I will never forget the day he told me about scrolling through Doug Carlile's phone for evidence, when he stumbled across a message exchange between Doug and one of his grandchildren. Even years later, the former football star gets emotional when he recalls that moment. It was the first time the full weight of the Carlile family's devastating loss had truly hit him.

Today, Darrik is still an agent with Homeland Security Investigations. He is also back on the gridiron, coaching his son's youth football team.

•••

I can honestly say I've never met anyone quite like Aine Ahmed. Well, actually, I haven't met him. Not in person, anyway. But I've spoken with him over Zoom, spent hours on the phone, and exchanged dozens of emails.

Aine is a man who hides nothing. Whatever he's thinking spills out of his mouth in a nonstop stream of words—most often riddled with F-bombs and other profanity. If you want to keep up, you'd better be a lightning-fast typist or a master of shorthand. Forget about trying to get a word in edgewise. But here's the thing: I had no problem with any of that.

I could listen to Aine talk all day—F-bombs and all. He is an endless source of knowledge, with an incredible backstory, and so many colorful experiences and anecdotes to share. He is refreshingly honest, and he's wickedly funny—without even realizing it. Most importantly, he knew the James Henrikson case like the back of his hand and provided me with a level of insight that I never would have gotten from case files, news articles, or crime shows.

I found out that being a U.S. Attorney is a taxing and thankless job. After spending two long years building a rock-solid case, enduring a grueling six-week trial that kept him away from his wife and kids, securing a conviction and a life sentence for James Henrikson, as well as a combined 82 years for the other five defendants, Aine didn't even receive so much as a "good job" from any of his colleagues or superiors.

Eventually, he left behind his role as a prosecutor and crossed to the other side of the aisle, running his own private practice as a defense attorney in Indiana. Becoming his own boss had always been his dream, and he's found a real sense of satisfaction in the work he does. Plus, the pay doesn't hurt.

• • •

I can say that without them, this book would have never been finished. They responded to every single call, email, and text message—and there were a LOT—and answered every question I had. They took time out of their busy lives to meet with me when I came to town. Each time I talked to them, they revealed a new tidbit or detail that I couldn't leave out. The sheer breadth of this case still astounds me, and their vivid recollection and storytelling is what made this so compelling.

To Mark, Darrik, and Aine: Thank you for the honor and privilege of telling your stories.

ACKNOWLEDGEMENTS

I'll start by saying that writing a book isn't necessarily difficult, but it's far from easy. Writing a book about this case, however, was downright brutal. There were multiple timelines, dozens of people involved, hundreds of articles to research, thousands of pages of case files and court records to read, documentaries to watch, and several hours-long taped interviews to dissect and analyze. That was just to get started.

At one point, I thought I was almost done—then I stumbled upon a flash drive Aine Ahmed had given me two years earlier, which I had completely forgotten about and for which neither of us could remember the password. After some searching, I found a note with the password—and voila! Ten thousand more pages of information to read and sort through. That meant another five months of work. But it also resulted in the chapter about the harrowing prison escape attempt, which, to me, was well worth it.

Understanding the history of oil and the oil business was completely out of my wheelhouse. I'm not entirely certain I understand it even now after studying it for weeks. The dozens of pages of contractual agreements between all the parties were like reading a foreign language—and in some cases, they literally were.

The vast amount of information in this case could have filled a thousand-page book. At some point, I had to figure out how to distill it all into a manageable—and hopefully engaging—format. To be frank, there were many times I didn't think I could do it, and I got so overwhelmed that I just stopped trying.

Over the course of roughly three years, so many people would ask, "How's your book coming along?" or "When's that book going to be done?" I'd cringe, then fib, and say, "Soon." The absolute worst was receiving emails from my publisher with the subject line reading, "Checking In." Out of my own frustration and embarrassment, the question would inevitably rise in my mind: "When will these people finally give up on me?"

Miraculously, no one ever did.

First and foremost, all glory to God, the one who has never given up on me the most, who has forgiven me, blessed me, and guided me on a path I could have never dreamed possible.

I am forever grateful to Black Lyon Publishing, especially the beautiful and magnificent Kerry McQuisten, for believing in me the first time, and sticking with me for a second. Perhaps someday there might even be a third—if you (and I) can wait that long.

To my amazing besties, Denise Kellen and Tena Best, thank you for always being in my corner, cheering me on. My love and admiration for you both runs deep, and our friendship these past two decades has meant more to me than you will ever know.

Rob and Kim Semingson, Tammie Moore, and Carrie Herity—I am truly honored to call you friends. Your encouragement and celebration at every step of this journey has meant the world to me. I am so thankful for all the laughter and joy you bring into my life.

I've always believed that the older we get, the harder it is to make new friends. Christy Dodson and Monica Martinez, you've proven my philosophy to be a bunch of baloney. You've become the friends I never knew I needed and now couldn't imagine my life without. I look forward to many more years of watching our boys play baseball, and maybe someday, Monica will share her Skittles, and Christy and I will have enough blankets and bug spray.

Much gratitude goes to the WOW (Women's Outing Weekend) posse—Lynn, Ronda, Nancy, Denise, Teri, Robin,

Kris, Joni, Dawn x2, Sarah, Fay, Lori, Lacey, Penny, Karen, Holly, Diana, Dorothy, Steph, Sheryl, Ginger, and Deana—each of them dynamic women who have been champions for one another for over three decades. From pull tabs to ice fishing tournaments, and every adventure in between, someday there will be a book written about the love, laughter, and shenanigans that have been shared together—with or without photo evidence.

I have "known" Sharon Funkhouser for almost 11 years via Facebook but have never actually met her in person. To me, she is one of those rare people you just know is good, kind-hearted, and genuine. She is an avid book reader, and a literacy advocate for PaperPie—an organization with a mission devoted to "transform lives, one story, one book, one family, one child at a time." She regularly posts reviews of the numerous books she reads each month and, although I don't think it was her intention, those posts have become highly engaging discussions about titles and authors from all different genres. I've purchased a book based on her recommendations more than once. On a whim, I reached out and asked if she would be willing to read a few excerpts from this book and provide her opinion. Sharon wasn't familiar with the story, and isn't an avid true crime reader, but I knew she'd be honest and tell me if it was terrible. To my relief, she liked it, and even asked me to read more. It made me feel that I was on the right track. Sharon, you are a gem. Thank you so much.

Along those same lines, Steven B. Epstein will forever have a special place in my heart for never being afraid to tell me like it is. He has perfected a very gentle, eloquent, and diplomatic way of telling me something I've written sucks. Ninety-nine-point nine percent of the time, he is completely right. I am choosing to withhold the remaining .01 percent for the very few times I disagreed with his suggestions—even though I most often relented and realized he was right. The truth is, he was never obligated to read anything or provide me any feedback at all. Nor was he obligated to check in with me every few weeks to see how I was doing. Words cannot express my gratitude for the fact that he did both. His encouragement kept me going all the times I wanted to quit. Thank you a million times, my dear friend. Someday, I hope to return the favor. I highly recommend checking out all four of Steve's brilliantly written true crime novels: *Murder on Birchleaf Drive, Evil at Lake Seminole* (my personal fave!), *Extreme Punishment,* and *Deadly Heist.*

To my friends and family throughout North Dakota, your continued support, encouragement, and enthusiasm for the work I'm doing has been a tremendous gift. North Dakota will always be the place I call home, and the people there are some of the best you'll ever meet. From the bottom of my heart, thank you all so much.

Thank you to my parents—my dad, who wisely knew not to ask how things were going, and my mom, who never stopped asking. Thank you for taking me out for queso and enchiladas and to the casino to clear my mind, and for always being my source of support and guidance. I'll never be too old to listen, argue, and then listen some more.

To my children, Bennett and Emma: I hope one day you'll look back and feel proud of me. When you're older and think about the nights Mommy spent in the red room, typing away on that ancient laptop, you'll understand that everything I did was for you.

Last, but certainly not least, to my husband, David: you are the calm to my crazy, the voice of reason to my overanalyzing. You have a way of simplifying things when I insist on making them more complicated. It may take me a while, but I eventually get there. Thank you for always understanding me and letting me be myself. You are the place I know my heart will always be safe. I love you.

PHOTO GALLERY

Public Domain Photo.

Elberta and Doug Carlile lived a life filled with big dreams and business plans.

Photo courtesy of C.J. Wynn.

The home of Brett and Jamie Roberts, across the street from the Carlile residence. Jamie was upset to see a strange white van parked in front of her house the night of December 15, 2013. Her husband, Brett, came home twice from work to make sure everything was okay.

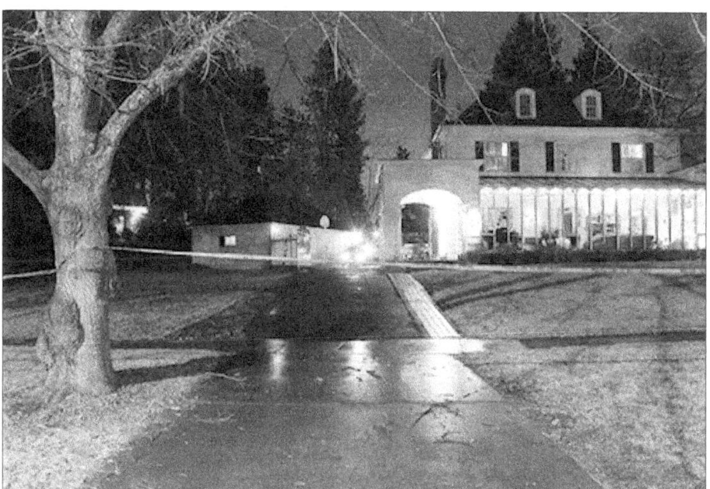

Photo courtesy of the Spokane Police Department.

The Carlile home on the night of the murder. Police officers swarmed Garfield Avenue and immediately cordoned off the home with police tape.

Photo courtesy of the Spokane Police Department.

The Carliles were broke, unable to remodel or fix major issues throughout their 5,200sq. ft. mansion, including wallpaper and paint peeling from the walls.

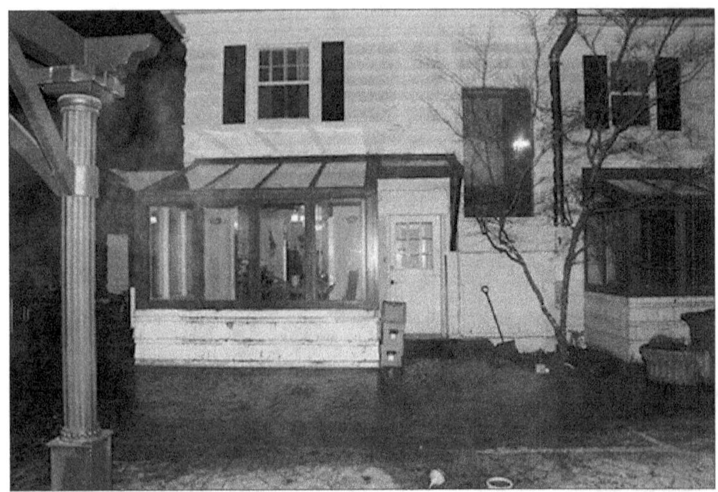

Photo courtesy of the Spokane Police Department.

A view of the backdoor and breakfast nook. Elberta used a spare key hidden on the top ledge of the backdoor. Once she was inside and upstairs, Doug was ambushed from behind as he entered the house.

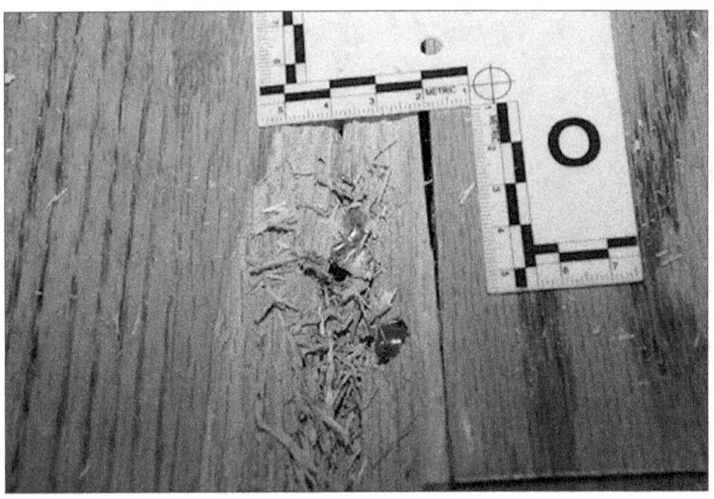

Photo courtesy of the Spokane Police Department.

A spent bullet that exited Doug's body lodged into the Carliles's dining room table.

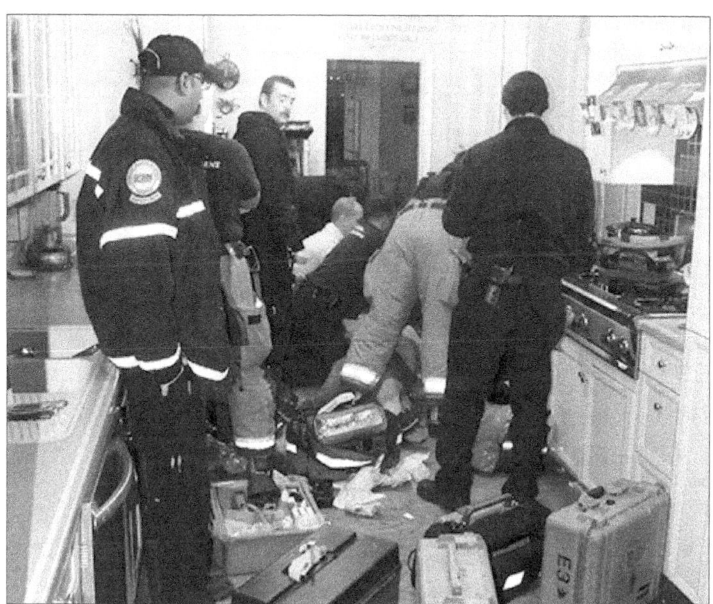

Photo courtesy of the Spokane Police Department.

First responders gather around while paramedics worked to save Doug's life. In the frenzy, medical equipment was left strewn across the kitchen floor, and shell casings were inadvertently moved from their original positions.

Photo courtesy of the Spokane Police Department.

When Doug Carlile was tragically shot in his kitchen, EMTs could not save him despite their best efforts.

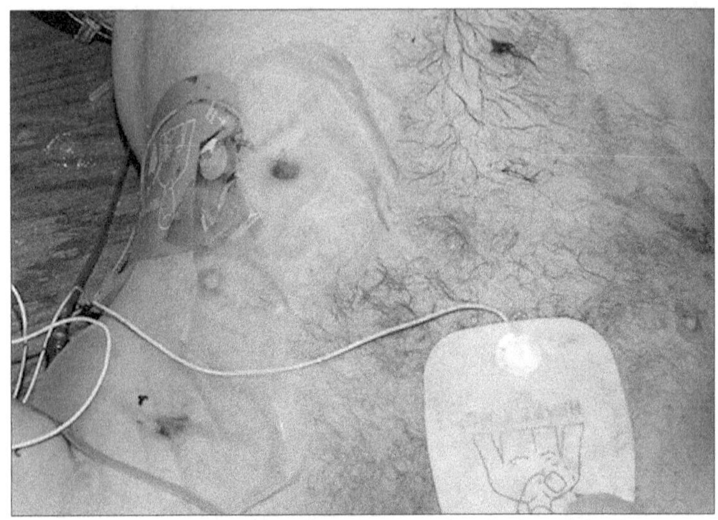

Photo courtesy of the Spokane Police Department.
Doug Carlile's upper torso was riddled with bullet holes.

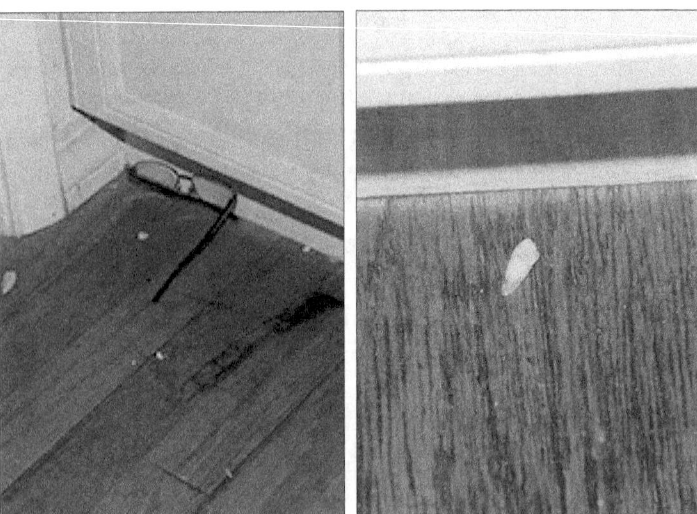

Photos courtesy of the Spokane Police Department.
Above Left: Doug's glasses flew off of his face and landed near a baseboard in the kitchen. Right: One of Doug's teeth dislodged from the root after the impact of being shot in the mouth.

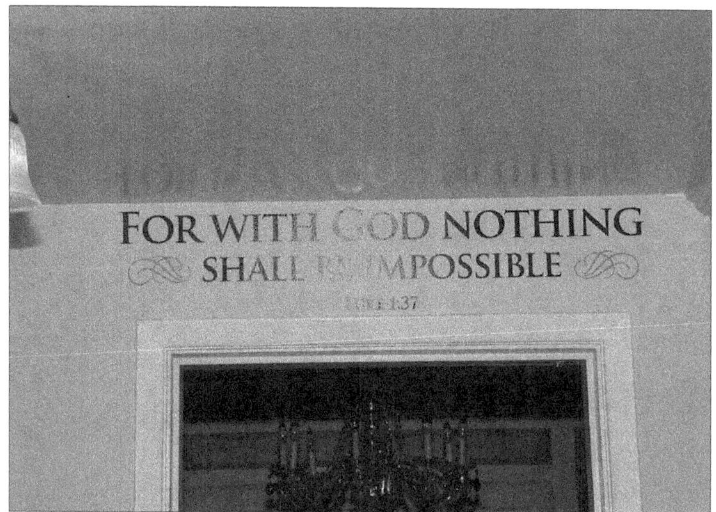

Photo courtesy of the Spokane Police Department.

Doug and Elberta were very religious, and displayed several Bible verses throughout their home.

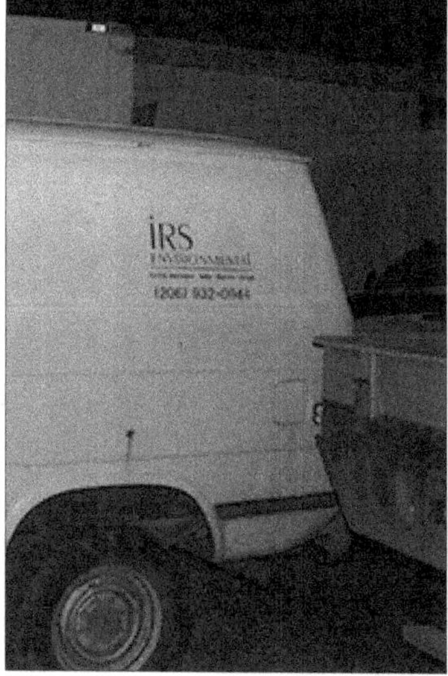

Photos courtesy of the Spokane Police Department.

A mysterious white van drove through the Rockwood neighborhood on Sunday, December 15, 2013. Leveraging video footage and records from the state of Washington, detectives were able to narrow down the make and model as a 1995 Chevrolet Sport Utility Van. Once Timothy Suckow was identified as a suspect in Doug Carlile's murder, detectives discovered his employer had this van in their work fleet. Lazaro Pesina's fingerprints were later found on the backside of the license plate.

The pathway through the Carliles's yard.

Officers could make out a fresh footprint left behind in a muddy puddle in the Carliles's backyard.

Photo courtesy of the Spokane Police Department.

A single, dry welding glove was found not far from the muddy footprint. The glove was the key to unraveling a convoluted mystery.

Photo courtesy of the Spokane Police Department.

The gate in the neighbor's yard was left wide open.

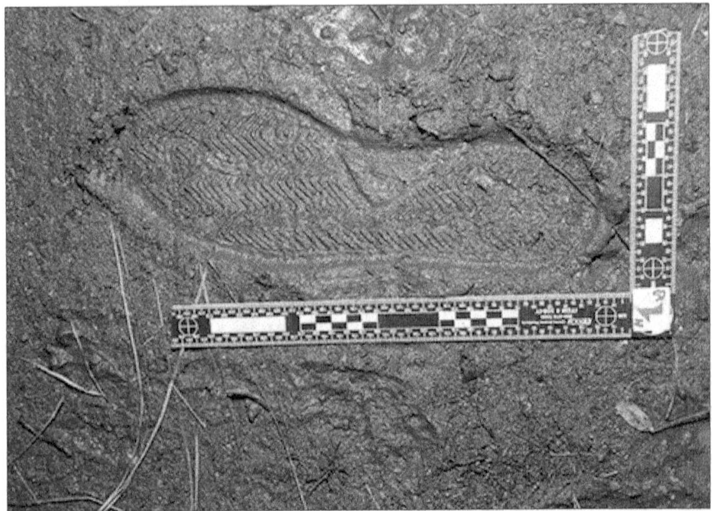

Photo courtesy of the Spokane Police Department.
Officers found footprints on the muddy trail leading to Rockwood Blvd, where they believed the killer had then gotten into a vehicle and fled the neighborhood.

Photo courtesy of the Spokane Police Department.
K-9 Leo led officers to a gravel pathway that could only be seen using flashlights. Another indicator that the killer had planned out his escape route.

Photo courtesy of the Spokane Police Department.

In the light of day, officers marked the footprints on the trail with orange placards.

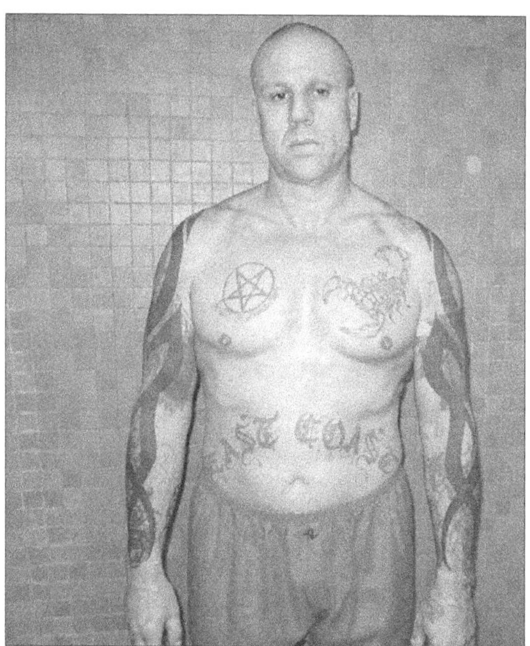

Photo courtesy of the Spokane Police Department.

Timothy Suckow was arrested one month after Doug Carlile's murder.

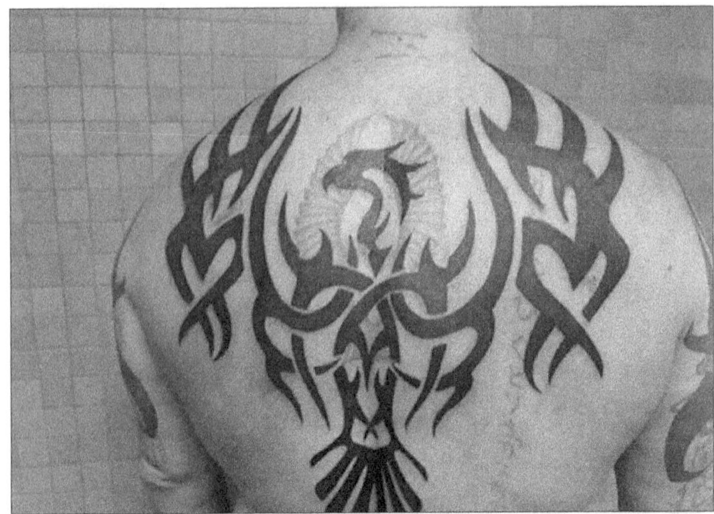

Photo courtesy of the Spokane Police Department.
A tattoo of a Phoenix spanned across Suckow's upper back. Its symbolic meaning one of rebirth and transformation and rising from the ashes seemed ironic given he was going to be spending the next 30 years in prison.

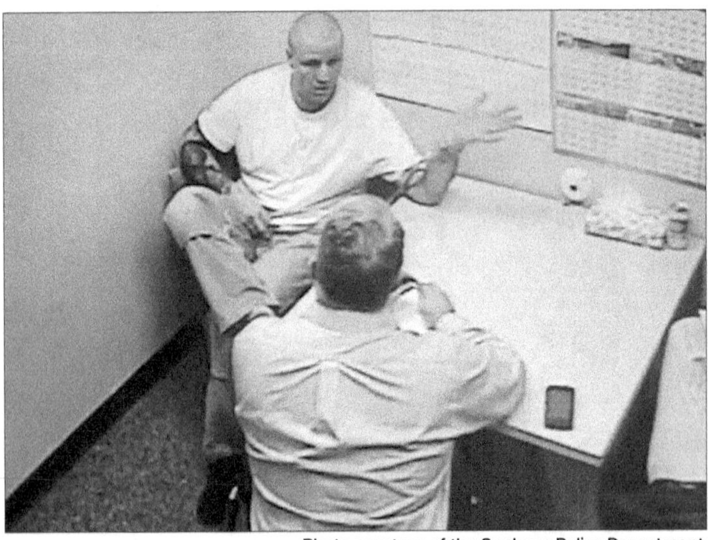

Photo courtesy of the Spokane Police Department.
After his arrest in January 2014, Timothy Suckow told Det. Burbridge he was "out of his tree" for thinking he had killed Doug Carlile.

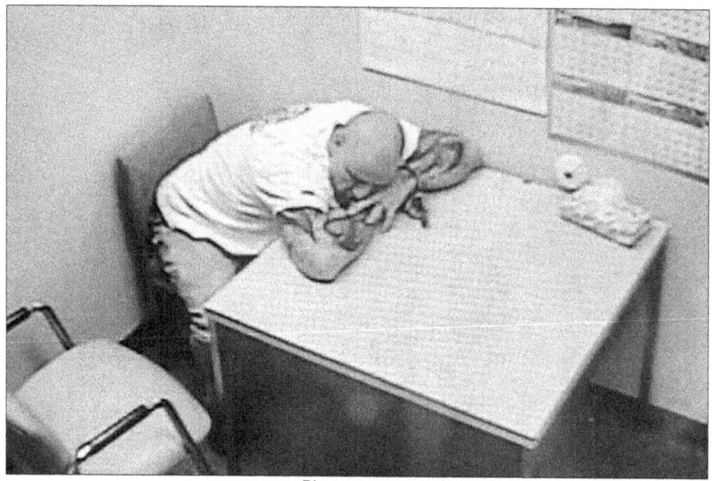

Photo courtesy of the Spokane Police Department.
After invoking his right to counsel, Timothy Suckow laid his head on the table in the interrogation room and fell into a deep sleep for several hours while search warrants were being executed at his place of employment, his home, and his vehicle. Detective Burbridge later said this was a sure sign that Suckow was guilty.

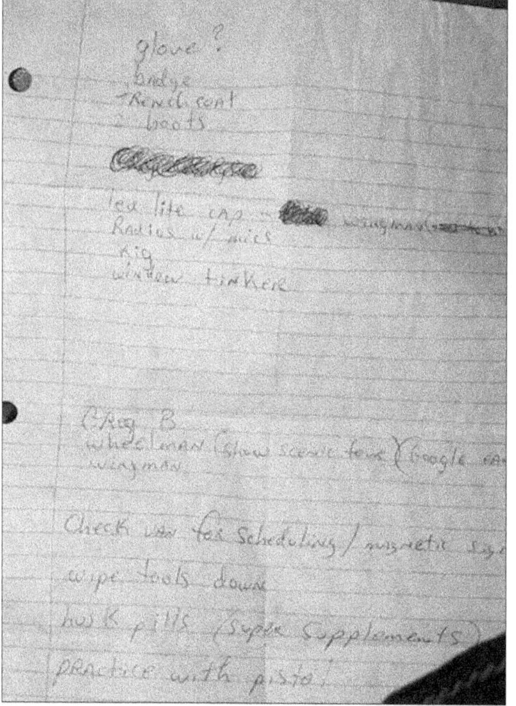

Photo courtesy of the Spokane Police Department.
A checklist for murder found inside Timothy Suckow's Chevy Tahoe.

Photos courtesy of the Spokane Police Department.
Left: Robert DeLao, laughing and relaxed right before his polygraph exam is about to begin. He then closed his eyes and controlled his breathing during his polygraph. He passed with flying colors, even though he had been responsible for hiring Timothy Suckow to kill both Doug Carlile and K.C. Clarke. Right: Earlier mugshot.

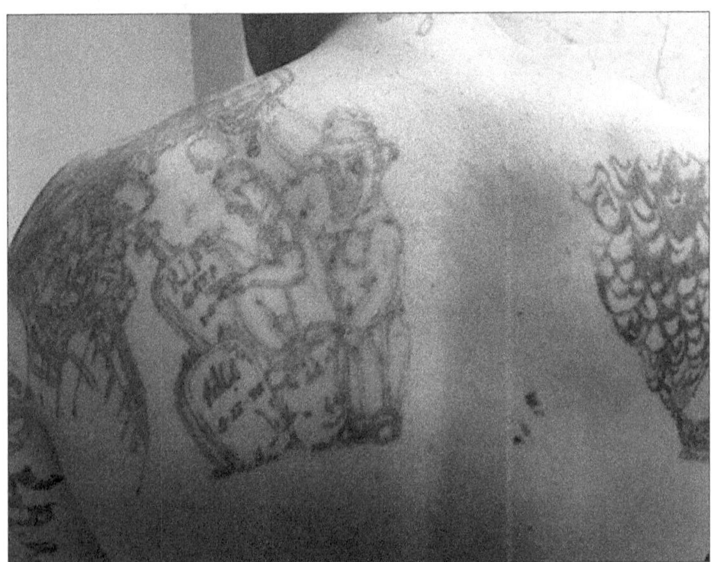

Photo courtesy of the Spokane Police Department.
Robert DeLao's tattoo of him urinating on the grave of a rival gang member he killed, although DeLao claimed it was done in self-defense.

Public Domain Photos. Meanwhile in North Dakota, Kristopher "K.C." Clarke was still missing, his family desperately seeking help from the public to locate him.

JAMES T. HENRICKSEN   SARAH M. CREVELING

CON-ARTISTS AND THIEVES

Alias: Henrikson, Henderson, Hennikson
Date of Birth: MARCH 21, 1979 Race: WHITE
Sex: MALE Height: 5'10 Weight: 180-200 LBS
Eyes: BROWN Hair: SHORT BROWN
Scars or Tattoos: MISSING RIGHT EYEBROW WITH
MAJOR BURNS ON ARMS AND CHEST.

Sarah M. Crevelin
Date of Birth: JULY Race: WHITE Sex: FEMALE
Height: 5'5 Weight: 110-120 LBS Eyes: BLUE
Hair: SHOULDER LENGTH BLONDE
Scars or Tattoos: NONE

They own Blackstone LLC, Blackstone Trucking, Blackstone Crude, Blackstone Electric, Blackstone Building Group, Blackstone Construction and Blackwell. They work on the Fort Berthold Reservation.

James may wear a baseball cap to cover the burn scars over his eye and on his forehead.

Arrest: RAPE 1/SEXUAL ABUSE 1, June 29, 2000	Arrest: AGGRAVATED THEFT/1ST DEGREE, June 22, 2001
Arrest: ELUDE POLICE ATTEMPT - Vehicle, 2001	Arrest: THEFT, June 22, 2001
Arrest: BURGLERY 2, October 3, 2001	Arrest: FRAUD-OBTAIN SIGNATURE, November 8, 2001
Arrest: TAMPER W/PHYSICAL EVIDENCE, November 8, 2001	Arrest: ASSAULT IV, C#0264391
Arrest: DELIVER MARIJUANA, June 12, 2009	Arrest: MANUFACTURE MARIJUANA, June 12, 2009
Arrest: ASSAULT-2, c# 845018	Arrest: THEFT-1, June 12, 2009
Arrest: ASSAULT II ATTEMPT, C# 0264391	Arrest: THEFT I ATTEMPT, C# 0264391

CAUTION

James is very charismatic and charming. He may claim to have money in order to build confidence with vendors or companies to steal from them. He owes thousands to vendors and investors. James has a history of filing for bankruptcy and running off with people's money.

James and Sarah may also have been involved in the disappearance of former Blackstone employee Kristopher D. Clarke (K.C.), but have refused to cooperate with the BCI. Consider them dangerous!

If you are owed money by James, Sarah or any of their companies, or for more information, please visit www.BlackstoneFraud.blogspot.com

Public Domain Photo.

The Beware Flyer that Lissa Yellowbird and Jedediah McClure distributed across much of the western part of North Dakota.

Photo courtesy of the Deschutes County Sheriff's Office.
Mugshot from James Henrikson's earlier criminal days in Oregon.

Public Domain Photos.

James Henrikson and Sarah Creveling. With their flashing white teeth and tanned skin, they were known as the Ken and Barbie of the oilfields.

Photo courtesy of the NDBCI.

James Henrikson is questioned by NDBCI Agent Steve Gutknecht about the disappearance of K.C. Clarke. James was still healing from the injuries sustained in a near-fatal motorcycle accident weeks after Clarke was murdered. Fluids from a skin graft done on his leg seeped through his signature tight jeans.

Photo courtesy of the NDBCI.

During his hours-long free talk, Timothy Suckow sobbed uncontrollably and expressed deep remorse for killing both K.C. Clarke and Doug Carlile. Pictured, left to right: Det. Mark Burbridge, attorney Jill Nagle, Timothy Suckow, attorney Tom Krysminski, Det. Brian Cestnik.

Photo courtesy of the Burleigh County Detention Center in North Dakota. James's mug shot after his arrest in North Dakota in 2014. His right eyebrow still had not grown back after being severely burned in a motorcycle accident in 2012.

Photo courtesy of the NDBCI.

Sarah Creveling met with NDBCI Agent Steve Gutknecht, telling the investigator that K.C. Clarke had become depressed and withdrawn in the weeks before his disappearance, which prompted she and her husband to require K.C. take a mandatory two-week vacation. She first denied K.C. coming to the shop to hand over his company gas card to her the day he went missing but later admitted that he had.

Photo courtesy of the NDBCI.

Joseph Uzdavinis put on a suit to meet with Williston detective Ryan Zimmerman. Zimmerman chastised Uzdavinis for making Sarah Creveling cry, and flippantly regarded the valuable information the young sleuth had collected in just a few short days.

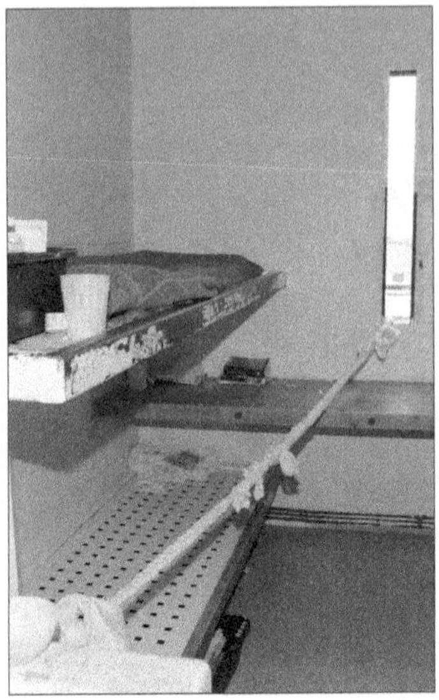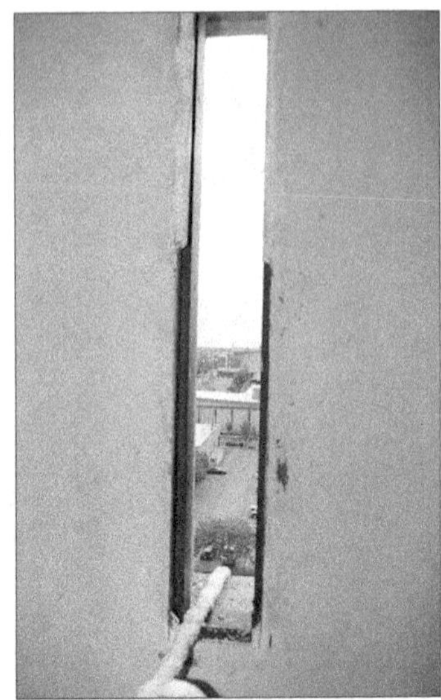

Photo courtesy of the Spokane Police Department.

Left: A view from inside James Henrikson's cell, showing the rope tethered to the bed frame, stretching out the window. The frame of the window was specifically designed to prevent a human adult head from fitting through. The rope was tethered to his bunk bed. Right: A view from inside James Henrikson's cell, showing the rope tethered to the bed frame stretching out the window.

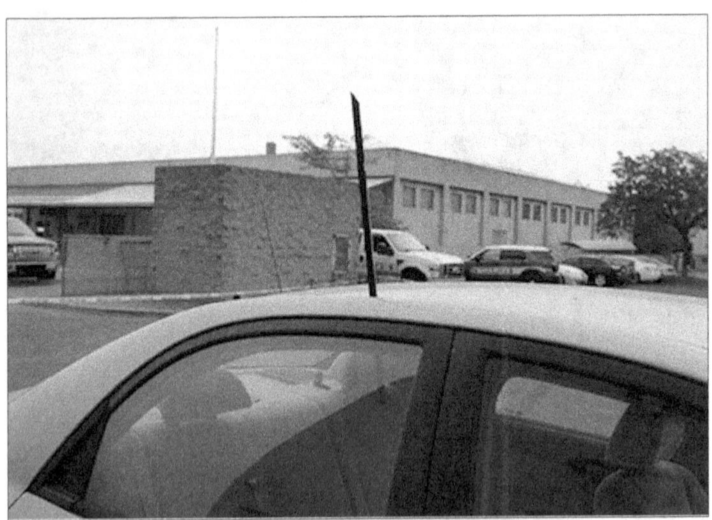

Photo courtesy of the Spokane Police Department.

A long metal rod from the broken-out window somehow pierced the roof of a KIA sedan in the parking lot.

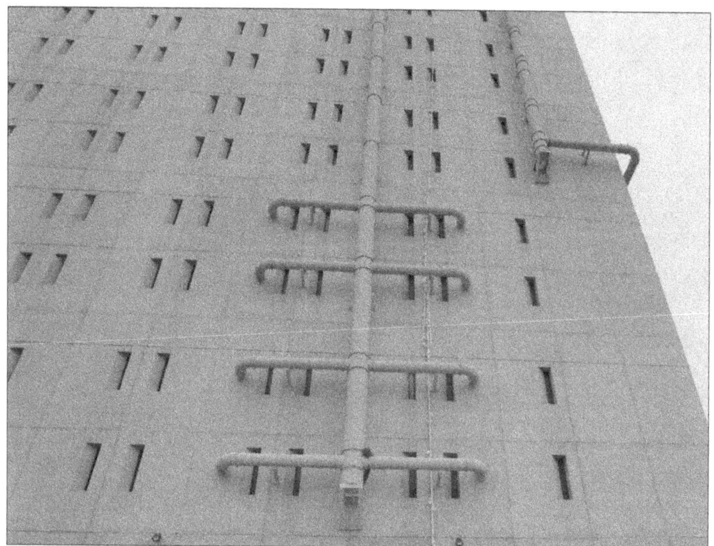

Photo courtesy of the Spokane Police Department.
Spokane County Jail staff arrived early the morning of August 20, 2015, to find a 108-ft rope made of sheets hanging from a ninth-floor window.

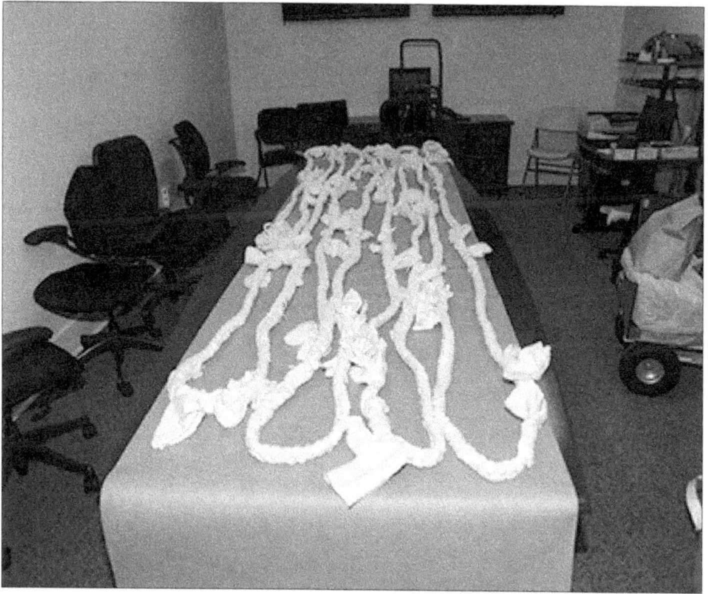

Photo courtesy of the Spokane Police Department.
The intricate design of the sheet rope.

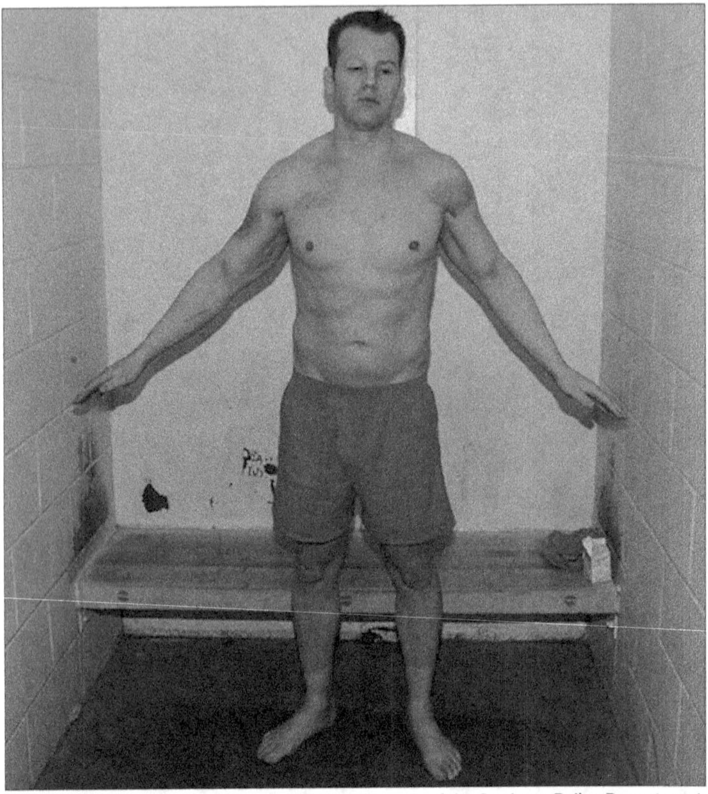

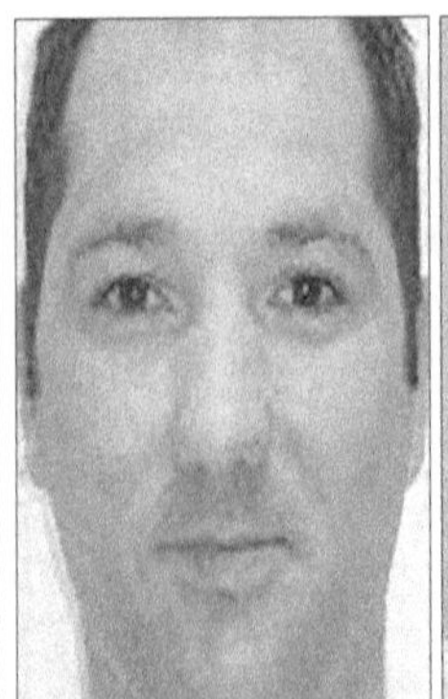

Photo courtesy of the Spokane Police Department.

After being caught trying to escape, James looks despondent. The scars from his near-fatal motorcycle accident a few weeks after K.C. Clarke's murder are still present on his shoulders, chest, and face. After a year in jail with no access to testosterone injections, he had lost most of his muscle mass.

Photos courtesy of the Spokane Police Department.

Mugshots for Lazaro Pesina, Robby Wahrer, and Todd Bates as released to the media.

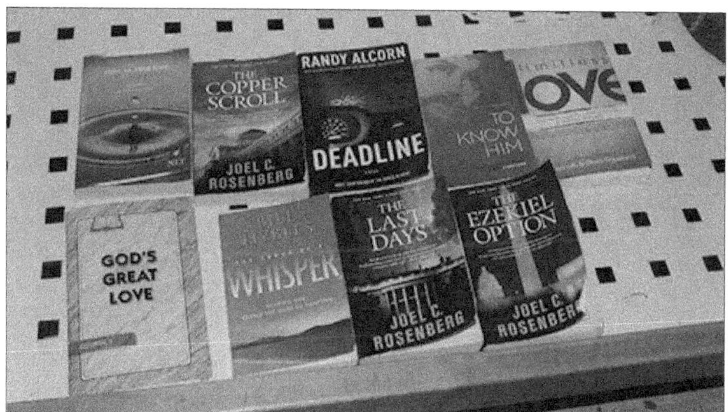

Photo courtesy of the Spokane Police Department.

James's interesting collection of spiritual literature sent to him by family in an effort to save his soul.

Photo courtesy of Mark Burbridge.

Timothy Suckow led detectives through a fruitless search of the Badlands in North Dakota for K.C. Clarke's body.

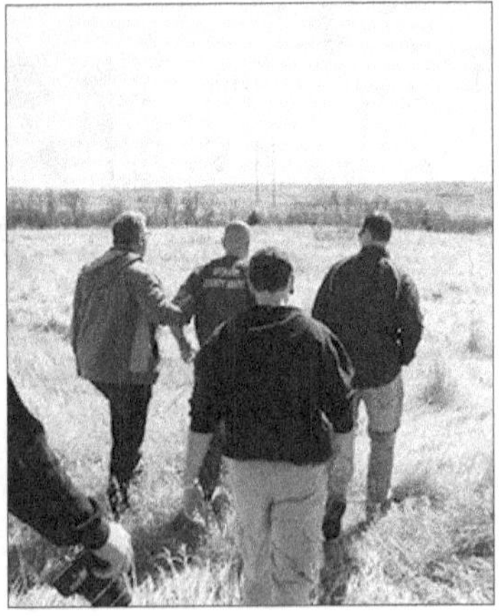

Photo courtesy of the Spokane Police Department.
Left: Timothy Suckow and Det. Burbridge. Right: Det. Burbridge (left) leads Suckow on the search for K.C. Clarke's body while Darrik Trudell (right) walks along.

Photo courtesy of Mark Burbridge.
Det. Mark Burbridge pictured working security at a marathon race, embraced by his oldest granddaughter.

Photo courtesy of Aine Ahmed.

L to R: FBI Agent Eric Barker, Detective Brian Cestnik, U.S. Attorney Aine Ahmed, Detective Mark Burbridge, and HSI Special Agent Darrik Trudell. James Henrikson's trial lasted a grueling six weeks, underscored by courtroom drama and antics from the defense team. All five men put everything they had into making sure justice was served.

Photo courtesy of Aine Ahmed.

Left to right, FBI Agent Eric Barker, U.S. Attorney Scott Jones, U.S. Attorney Aine Ahmed, Homeland Security Special Agent Darrik Trudell.